The UFO DOSSIER

100 Years of Government Secrets, Conspiracies, and Cover-Ups

About the Author

Kevin D. Randle retired from the military in 2009 as a lieutenant colonel. He flew combat missions in Vietnam as a helicopter pilot and recently received the Bronze Star Medal for his service in Iraq. In 1974 he got his first credit as a freelance writer with an article about UFO landing traces. He has investigated such cases all over the United States, including the famous Roswell crash of 1947. Randle has written more than two dozen books on the topic, is a frequent guest on radio and television, and is one of the participants in Discovery Canada's newest UFO program. He continues to research the topic but at a most leisurely pace than before. He lives with his wife in Iowa.

ALSO FROM VISIBLE INK PRESS

The UFO DOSSIER

100 Years of Government Secrets, Conspiracies, and Cover-Ups

KEVIN D. RANDLE

VISIBLE
INK
PRESS

Detroit

The UFO DOSSIER
100 Years of Government Secrets, Conspiracies, and Cover Ups

Visible Ink Press®
43311 Joy Rd., #414
Canton, MI 48187-2075

Visible Ink Press is a registered trademark of Visible Ink Press LLC.

Most Visible Ink Press books are available at special quantity discounts when purchased in bulk by corporations, organizations, or groups. Customized printings, special imprints, messages, and excerpts can be produced to meet your needs. For more information, contact Special Markets Director, Visible Ink Press, www.visibleink.com, or 734-667-3211.

Managing Editor: Kevin S. Hile
Art Director: Mary Claire Krzewinski
Typesetting: Marco DiVita
Proofreaders: Sharon Gunton and Shoshana Hurwitz
Indexer: Larry Baker

Cover images: Transosonde launch (U.S. Navy); all other images are courtesy of Shutterstock.

Library of Congress Cataloging-in-Publication Data

Randle, Kevin D., 1949-
  The UFO dossier : 100 years for government secrets, conspiracies and cover-ups / Kevin D. Randle.
    pages cm
  ISBN 978-1-57859-564-8 (paperback)
1. Unidentified flying objects—Sightings and encounters—United States. 2. Government information—United States. 3. Conspiracies—United States. I. Title.
TL789.4.R365 2015
001.9420973—dc23   2015017853

Printed in the United States of America

10 9 8 7 6 5 4 3 2 1

CONTENTS

UFOs in the
Twenty-first Century [319]

PHOTO SOURCES

Ardfern (Wikicommons): p. 242.

Ra Boe (Wikicommons): p. 59.

Butch (Wikicommons): p. 138.

CIA: p. 209.

Jerome Clark: p. 46.

Dutch National Archives: p. 70.

Barbara Eckholdt: p. 345.

John Fowler: p. 354.

Bernard Gagnon: p. 296 (modified by Kevin Hile).

German Federal Archives: p. 254.

Mario Gonzalez: p. 295.

Billy Hathorn: p. 180.

K50 Dude (Wikicommons): p. 192.

Stefan Kranz: p. 292.

Simon Leatherdale: p. 165.

Edal Anton Lefterov: p. 260.

Mary Evans Picture Library: pp. 51, 86, 126, 187, 226, 238, 249, 302, 315, 348, 362.

David Merrett: p. 167.

NASA: pp. 23, 346

National Investigations Committee on Aerial Phenomena: p. 109.

Nijuuf (Wikicommons): p. 333.

Jacques Poulet: p. 33.

Kevin Randle: pp. 5, 6, 7, 10, 38, 66, 68, 82, 87, 89, 91, 94, 98, 101, 105, 106, 111, 113, 131, 147, 150, 154, 159, 161, 171, 178, 182, 208, 211, 212, 216, 232, 320, 325, 326, 328.

RuthAS (Wikicommons): p. 271.

Robert Schaeffer: p. 44.

Sgerbic (Wikicommons): p. 56.

Shahram Sharifi: p. 288.

Mikhail (Vokabre) Shcherbakov: p. 122.

Shutterstock: pp. 43, 55, 64, 72, 83, 85, 134, 144, 156, 189, 193, 195, 196, 198, 200, 202, 221, 222, 244, 268, 269, 273, 280, 300, 311, 313, 331, 341, 357, 370.

Kurt Stüber: p. 309.

U.S. Air Force: pp. 3, 31, 67, 108, 228, 235, 236, 267, 277, 356.

U.S. Coast Guard: p. 117.

U.S. Forest Service: p. 372.

U.S. Geological Survey: pp. 29, 281.

U.S. National Archives and Records Administration: pp. 25, 32.

U.S. Navy: pp. 27, 127, 233.

S. Veyrié p. 255.

Charly Whisky: p. 250.

Alan D. Wilson: p. 375.

Public domain: pp. 19, 22, 35, 40, p. 75, 184, 252, 334.

INTRODUCTION

In the creation of this book it was necessary to revisit some of the cases that I have explored in detail in other books. For those who have read those books and find some of the information redundant, it simply can't be helped. For those who are new to the field or who have not read those earlier works, some explanation for context is necessary. I have attempted to hold that redundancy to a minimum, explaining enough that the novice or newcomer to my work will understand the context of these cases.

I have also attempted to look at UFOs as a worldwide phenomenon and place it in that context. Too often we here in the United States are unaware of what is happening in other countries. That is a function of our reporting rather than a lack of interest by those living in Europe, Asia, Africa, South America, and Australia. There are some lengthy sections based on the research conducted by those in other parts of the world.

I have included here some of the "classic" cases that I now believe to be resolved. My thought was to take those cases out of the mix so that we might concentrate on those cases that deserve additional attention. In the years since some of the cases were reported, newer and better information has surfaced. I believe that a viable solution for a case should be reported, especially for those cases that have been used time and again by others. This is not to say those other researchers have failed or were misrepresenting the information, only that later and better information is available.

Finally, at the end, there is a long list of sightings from the last several years. These lists could have been much longer and the space simply did not exist to use as many of the cases as I would like. My selection criterion here was completely arbitrary and not always consistent. I tried to select interesting cases that included enough basic information that someone with a desire to do further research would have a place to begin. Unfortunately, sometimes all the necessary information wasn't present. To make matters worse, there are probably cases included that can be resolved as mundane, meaning that conventional solutions can be found for them. My goal was to provide information for those who wanted it so that we could remove the cases from the list that can be explained, or to learn more about those that cannot.

This, like all books on the topic, can be seen as a work in progress. I'm sure that at some point a case that I see as evidence of alien visitation might be resolved as something ordinary and explained if I had better information. On the other hand, there are some cases in which the latest information is buried deep in some archive and I've been unable to retrieve it before my deadline. As they say, "There is always something else to be done."

Kevin D. Randle

A Short History
of the UFO Projects

On September 23, 1947, U.S. Air Force Lieutenant General Nathan F. Twining, in response to an inquiry about the "Flying Disks," wrote, "The phenomenon reported is something real and not visionary or fictitious."[i] To the surprise of nearly everyone in the Air Force chain of command at that time, Twining also wrote that he wanted the creation of a project to study the flying disks, he wanted it assigned a high classification and code word, and he wanted to share the information developed with various other military commands and intelligence functions.[ii] This resulted in the creation of Project Sign under the control of the Air Force, which was officially launched in January 1948.[iii]

Although this study seemed to be the first to investigate strange aerial phenomena, it was not. During the Second World War, aircrews, among others, in all theaters of the war, reported strange lights chasing them, and in some cases reported solid objects that buzzed them.[iv] Although it was shown after the war that the Foo Fighters, as they were known, were not secret German or Japanese weapons, the appearance of them during the war was considered serious by Allied intelligence. When the war ended, interest in the Foo Fighters also ended. (See "The World of Official UFO Studies" for more detail on the Foo Fighters.)

In 1946, Scandinavia was the scene of the Ghost Rockets. These, too, were unidentified objects. Although reported throughout the summer, photographed on several occasions and reported to have crashed on others, no logical solution for them has been advanced. Some believed the Ghost Rockets to be Soviet experiments, but the collapse of the Soviet Union proved that they had not been responsible for the flights.

During the summer of 1946, military attachés in Sweden reported on the Ghost Rocket sightings. The Swedish government ordered an investigation, but most of that dwindled away when the government ordered the news media to halt reporting of the Ghost Rockets, and the sightings stopped[v].

In December 1946, however, Colonel Howard McCoy, who had been one of the American officers involved in the investigation of both the Foo Fighters and the Ghost Rockets, was ordered to set up an unofficial investigation into these various unidentified aerial manifestations. This began in a single, locked office at Wright Field (later Wright-Patterson Air Force Base) outside of Dayton, Ohio.

This investigation was also interested in reports of strange craft seen over the United States in the spring of 1947. McCoy and Colonel Albert Deyarmond collected all the data they could on the Ghost Rockets and the sightings in the U.S., including an important one from April 1947.[vi] On April 1, 1947, a series of sightings began near Richmond, Virginia that involved the U.S. Weather Bureau. This would later become Incident No. 79 in the U.S. government files, in this case, the Project Grudge final report. It should be noted that the case had disappeared from the Project Blue Book files before they were released to the public. (See Chapter 7 for more detail on these early sightings.)

This series of reports, made by Walter Minczewski, is not mentioned in the Project Blue Book Index, which lists only a couple of reports made prior to the Kenneth Arnold sighting. All were reported after the press coverage of the Arnold sighting, so there is currently no way to document the actual date of the sighting, except for Minczewski's reports.[vii]

When Kenneth Arnold made his sighting on June 24, 1947, near Mt. Rainier, Washington, the tone of the unofficial investigation changed.[viii] What had been an unofficial interest housed at Wright Field expanded into a more official investigation with intelligence officers from around the country involved. The FBI, in July 1947, was asked for assistance, and then Director J. Edgar Hoover thought it was a good idea as long as the FBI was kept fully informed.[ix]

Little of what McCoy found was turned over to the investigators for Project Sign, not that it mattered. The summer of 1947 provided more than enough data for investigations. Captain Edward Ruppelt, who took over the official UFO investigation in 1951, would write that the Pentagon was in a panic, with high-ranking government officials demanding answers.[x]

Ruppelt also made the claim that the intelligence community involved in the research prepared what is known as an estimate of the situation. According to Ruppelt, in what has become one of the most plagiarized sentences in UFO literature, "The situation was the UFOs; the estimate was that they were interplanetary!"[xi]

The estimate was passed up the chain of command to the Air Force Chief of Staff, Hoyt S. Vandenberg, who, according to Ruppelt, "batted it back down." Vandenberg didn't believe that the evidence offered proved the case for interplanetary visitation.[xii] Later the report was ordered to be declassified and burned.[xiii]

Air Force Chief of Staff Hoyt S. Vandenberg

The additional fallout was that nearly everyone who had a hand in creating the estimate, who had suggested that UFOs were alien spacecraft, found themselves ousted from Project Sign. Those who remained, and those who were brought in, got the message. The Chief of Staff did not want to hear that UFOs were alien spacecraft, and those who suggested otherwise found their careers crippled. For example, Alfred Loedding, whose work evaluations that had been excellent before the estimate, began to deteriorate according to those analyses, and he finally resigned in the early 1950s.[xiv]

With that, Project Sign began to evolve into Project Grudge, which did little in the way of investigation.[xv] No one cared about UFOs, and no one was spending time on the project. At a meeting to discuss a series of sightings over Fort Monmouth, New Jersey, a general officer asked Lieutenant Jerry Cummings what was happening with the UFO investigation. With a candor rare when a junior officer talks to the general, Cummings told him that it wasn't much.[xvi]

With that, there was a new emphasis on the UFO investigation, and it was about that time that Ruppelt was brought in to lead the project. Not long after that, the name was changed to Project Blue Book, and for a short time there was a serious attempt to investigate cases reported to them.

In July 1952, UFOs were reported over Washington, D.C., on two consecutive Saturday nights. There were both visual sightings and those detected on radar. In one case, the UFOs were reported on radars at three locations. Intercepts by jet fighters were attempted and in one case, that became quite "hairy." This resulted in the largest press conference held by the Air Force since the close of the Second World War.[xvii] When it was over, the conclusion that the UFOs had been caused by temperature inversion had been given. In the years to follow, that became the official explanation.[xviii]

An outgrowth of the summer saucers was a CIA-sponsored panel chaired by Dr. H. P. Robertson, who had also had a hand in the Foo Fighters investigation. In five days they reviewed the UFO information, seemed to have

An outgrowth of the summer saucers was a CIA-sponsored panel chaired by Dr. H. P. Robertson, who had also had a hand in the Foo Fighters investigation.

access to everything that was being held by various military and governmental offices, and, in the end, suggested that national security agencies take immediate steps "to strip Unidentified Flying Objects of the special status they have been given and the aura of mystery they have unfortunately acquired."[xix]

Another aspect of the Panel report was to create a "educational program" that suggested, "The training aim would result in proper recognition of unusually illuminated objects (e.g., balloons, aircraft reflections) as well as natural phenomena (meteors, fireballs, mirages, noctilucent). Both visual and radar recognition are concerned. There would be many levels in such education.... This training should result in a marked reduction in reports by misidentified cases...."

The report continued, "The 'debunking' aim would result in reduction in public interest in 'flying saucers,' which today evokes a strong psychological reaction. This education could be accomplished by mass media such as television, motion pictures, and popular articles.... As in the case of conjuring tricks, there is much less stimulation if the 'secret' is known. Such a program should tend to reduce the current gullibility of the public...."[xx]

It was also in 1953 that the Air Force released AFR (Air Force Regulation) 200–2, which provided for a UFO officer at most Air Force bases and guidance on how to handle those reports. The important part of the regulation was the directive that when solutions were available, those were to be released immediately, but when there was no solution, there would be no public release. Those sightings would be classified.[xxi]

Given all that, and that Ruppelt had been reassigned from Project Blue Book, the nature of the investigation changed. He returned briefly, only to see that the staff had been cut drastically and the tone at Air Technical Intelligence Center (ATIC) had changed. In March 1954, Captain Charles Hardin became the director of Blue Book, and his attitude was driven by his distaste for UFOs and his desire to be a stockbroker. He was only interested in the day he could retire.[xxii]

In April 1956 Captain George T. Gregory replaced Hardin, but Gregory thought even less of the UFO phenomena than did Hardin. To add to this attitude, in February 1958, a revised AFR 200–2 was issued with the order that "Air Force activities must reduce the percentage of unidentified to the minimum."[xxiii]

In 1959, there was a push to transfer Project Blue Book from ATIC into the Secretary of the Air Force, Office of Information (SAFOI). This would be a reduction in the prestige of the UFO investigation. Rather than be an intelligence function in the Air Technical Intelligence Center, it would now be viewed as nothing more than public relations.[xxiv]

This attitude would continue. Lt. Col. Robert Friend, who was another of the men to lead Blue Book, wrote to his headquarters in 1962 that the project should be handed over to some civilian agency that would word its final report in such a way as to allow the Air Force to drop the study. At about the same time, Edward Trapnell, an assistant to the Secretary of the Air Force, when talking to Dr. Robert Calkins of the Brookings Institute said the same thing. Find a civilian agency to study the problem and then have them conclude it the way the Air Force wanted it. Trapnell also suggested that this civilian committee say some positive things about the way the Air Force had handled the investigation.[xxv]

A major stumbling block was a new wave of sightings that began in April 1964 and lasted for nearly three years. First up was a report from Socorro, New Mexico, that received national attention, including mentions on various network evening news programs, as well as national front-page newspaper coverage.

Lonnie Zamora, a police officer in Socorro, was chasing a speeder in the early evening, when he heard a loud roar and saw a flash of light. Believing that a dynamite shed had exploded, he broke off the chase, altering his course to take him by the shed.[xxvi]

Zamora was driving near a gully when, over 400 yards away, at the bottom of the gully, he spotted a bright white object. At first he thought it was an overturned car, but as he neared it, he could see two "people." Zamora stopped short and got out of his car. He couldn't see the individuals in the gully very well but thought they were shorter than normal adults.

Studying the scene, Zamora realized that the object wasn't an overturned vehicle, but something else entirely. As he started forward, the figures apparently saw him. Everyone turned to run, the figures back into the UFO, and Zamora toward his patrol car.

Seconds later, in a roaring of flame, the UFO lifted off and disappeared. Zamora called his superior, Sergeant Sam Chavez. Although Chavez was not involved in the sighting and saw neither the craft nor the aliens, he did see the markings left behind. One bush was burning, and some clumps of grass were burned. Four holes, apparently from landing gear, were pressed into the soft earth.

During the next several days, the official Air Force investigation was started. Air Force

Lonnie Zamora

Dr. J. Allen Hynek

officers examined the landing site, interviewed the witnesses, and took photographs. Air Force consultant, Dr. J. Allen Hynek, made a one-day investigation. Hynek was impressed with the sincerity displayed by Zamora, the physical evidence in the form of landing gear markings, and said that he found no evidence that Zamora was capable of creating such an elaborate hoax.

A few months later, Hynek returned for another short investigation. He visited Zamora, Chavez, and the editor of the Socorro newspaper. In his final report, Hynek wrote, "The more articulate Sergeant Chavez still firmly believes Zamora's story … although I made a distinct attempt to find a chink in Zamora's armor, I simply couldn't find anyone, with the possible exception of a Mr. Philips, who has a house fairly near the site of the original sighting, who did anything but completely uphold Zamora's character."

Hynek's full report continues for eight pages but does not once suggest how the sighting could have been faked or why it would have been. He mentioned that Felix Philips lived close to the landing site but did not hear anything strange, even with the windows and French doors of his house open. Hynek wrote that he was not concerned with this seeming discrepancy because "the wind was blowing down the gully," and the Philips house is in the opposite direction. "This, of course, can make a tremendous difference in the ability to hear."

The final conclusion by Hynek was that he could not identify what had landed in Socorro. He didn't like Philip's claim of a hoax because "there are just too many bits of evidence that militate against this hypothesis."[xxvii]

Philip Klass, who entered the UFO community sometime after the Socorro sighting, made his own investigation. He wrote in *UFOs Explained*, "My investigation led me to disagree sharply with Hynek's statement that the Socorro case was 'one of the soundest, best substantiated reports.' Contrary to Hynek's observation, I found many 'contradictions or omissions.'"

Klass, interviewing the same witnesses interviewed by Hynek and others to whom Hynek never spoke, led him in a different direction. He talked to several "scientist-professors" at the New Mexico Institute of Mining and Technology in Socorro. Klass was surprised that, with a single exception, none of the scientists were interested in the Socorro UFO event. He wrote, "If the story was true, the most exciting scientific event of all time—a visit from an extraterrestrial spacecraft—had occurred almost within sight of the institute. How could these scientists be so uninterested?"

Because, he shifts gears, one of the scientists told him to "nose around a bit." Klass asked for more information and was told that Socorro had no industry other than the Institute. Tourists passed through on the main highways (one of which is now Interstate 25 leading from Albuquerque to El Paso, Texas), but they never stopped except to buy gas and to eat.

Klass quoted from the local newspaper that he read that night, "One of the best ways a community can boost its economy is to attract new industry. *Today, the fastest, most effective way to attract new industry is by first attracting tourists.* The reason is that industrialists, in selecting plant locations, are seeking for their employees the same kind of 'community atmosphere' that appeals to tourists."[xxviii] (Emphasis added by Klass.) He had found his answer.

A year after the Socorro landing, on April 24, 1965, an article in the *El Paso Times* written by Jake Booher, Jr., reported that the town officials were

A photo taken of what Zamora felt was an imprint of landing gear that the UFO had left behind.

quick to realize the significance of the UFO landing. Although Booher report-ed that Zamora wanted to forget the sighting, the town's 7,000 residents didn't. They were going to turn the landing site into the tourist attraction that would also attract industry.

Klass wrote, "The place where the UFO reportedly landed was especial-ly convenient—almost midway between the two highways that bring tourists through Socorro—so it was relatively easy and inexpensive for city officials to provide an improved road that connected the site to the two highways."

> "... Despite Phil Klass, I found no indications suggesting that this was a tourist-attracting ploy by the local Chamber of Commerce...."

In the next paragraph, Klass exposed the real story. The land next to the landing site was worthless. But, if the site was developed as a tourist attraction, then the worthless land would suddenly become valuable. It could become the site of hot dog stands, souvenir shops, and maybe even a motel or two. This property, according to Klass, "... by a curious coincidence ... was owned by Mayor Bursum, Officer Zamora's boss."[xxix]

The Socorro sighting, according to Klass, was the result of the mayor attempting to create a tourist attraction. Of course, the tourist attractions were never developed, and the cars still flash by Socorro unless someone is hungry or they need gas. If someone stops, it is to find directions to the Very Large Array, a radio telescope on the Plains of San Agustin some 50 miles to the west, along Highway 60.

According to Volume 41, No. 8, November 1, 1994, of Jim Moseley's *Saucer Smear*, Charles Moore, a professor at Socorro's New Mexico Institute of Mining and Technology wrote, "At Jim McDonald's request, I investigated the residue of the Socorro sighting in 1967 or 1968.... Despite Phil Klass, I found no indications suggesting that this was a tourist-attracting ploy by the local Chamber of Com-merce, *nor was it a prank by the New Mexico Tech students*"[xxx] (emphasis added).

The problem with Klass' analysis, one that has been repeated by others, was that it was untrue. Apparently no one, including Klass, bothered to check with the local assessor's office to find out who actually owned the land. According to a story published in the *El Defensor Chieftain* in 2008, the land in question had been part of the estate of Delia Harris in 1964, and in 1968 the land was brought by the Richardson family, and they apparently still own it. They mayor had never owned it.[xxxi]

At the end of 1965, with UFO sightings gaining national attention, the Air Force decided to review the UFO question using the Scientific Advisory Board known to a few as the O'Brien Committee.[xxxii] This was a one-day assess-ment of the problems of Project Blue Book held in February 1966. Here, again, the idea was floated to find a university to investigate UFOs, studying, in depth, a hundred sightings per year. The work would be as public as possible, and there would be regular briefings to Congress.[xxxiii]

But the final inspiration for the Condon Committee were the sightings in Michigan that began in 1966. Interest grew on March 20 when, at about 8:30 in the evening, Frank Mannor heard his dogs barking and ran outside. In the swamp to the east, he saw a flashing light and with his son, Ronald, ran toward it. They saw an elliptical object with a brown or tan quilted surface hovering in a patch of mist. It glowed a bright red and as they tried to get closer, they lost sight of it. Neither of them saw it take off.[xxxiv]

Mannor's wife, Leona, called the police, including Bob Wagner, who happened to be Mannor's father-in-law. The object was described in a police report as "flat on the bottom and cone shaped toward the top, however being low in height. Two small lights appeared at the outer edges of the object, glowing with a blue-green light, intensifying into a brilliant red."[xxxv]

It is also clear that one of the deputies, Stanley McFadden, also saw the object, or rather "the lights and heard the sound made by the object. He did not view the object as long nor as close as Frank Mannor, but is in agreement with him on what he observed."[xxxvi]

Mannor said, "It wasn't like the pictures of a flying saucer, and it had a coral-like surface. I've never seen anything like it."[xxxvii]

The following night, March 21, the UFOs shifted to Hillsdale, Michigan and a college campus. Nearly 100 people, including the local Civil Defense Director, who was also an undertaker and an assistant dean, saw the red, blue, and white lights as they hovered above a nearby swamp. One witness said that there was an object behind the lights. The state police were called, but they saw nothing at all.[xxxviii]

Hynek spent a couple of days in Michigan interviewing people about the case. In a press conference held on March 26, 1966, Hynek suggested that some of the sightings, but by no means all of them, were the result of marsh gas, more commonly called swamp gas. Almost no one heard Hynek's qualification. Newspapers around the country announced that the sightings were nothing more than swamp gas.[xxxix]

The response to Hynek's swamp gas theory was immediate. No one believed it. The explanation sounded too much like a guess that had little foundation. It seemed to be an explanation offered just to explain, without any thought given to the facts, though Hynek had qualified it. Hynek was now seen as the "chief debunker" paid by the Air Force who had been hiding the information ever since the first UFO wave back in 1947. It doesn't matter if any of this is true because it was what was believed by the general public. The Air Force was not believed when they offered any explanation about UFOs.[xl]

Hynek was so savaged by the press that documents from the Project Blue Book files suggested that explanations no longer be offered by him. They suggested that the Office of Information issue the statements as a way of insulating Hynek from the now-expected public criticism.[xli]

Public pressure was mounting. For three years in a row, a series of UFO sightings had grabbed national headlines. The explanations offered were found by the press to lack credibility. Gerald Ford, a congressman from Michigan, was demanding congressional hearings about UFOs.[xlii]

The outgrowth of this pressure by the public and Congress was the Condon Committee, organized at the University of Colorado and funded by more than half a million dollars of Air Force money.[xliii] Several universities had been approached, but they had all turned down the research grant. The University of Colorado had been way down the list of possible sites.[xliv]

The scientific director of the project, the man who received the Air Force grant, was Dr. Edward U. Condon, who was a professor of physics and astrophysics and a Fellow of the Joint Institute for Laboratory Astrophysics at the University of Colorado. Condon, prior to the Air Force assignment, had a distinguished career as a scientist. He was a former director of the National Bureau of Standards and was a member of the National Academy of Sciences. In 1941, he was named to the committee which established the atomic bomb program. He was a scientific advisor to a special Senate atomic energy committee for naval atomic bomb tests in 1946. Twenty years later, Condon was at the University of Colorado.[xlv] As a career scientist, Condon had the sort of prestige the Air Force wanted.

Edward Condon was a distinguished nuclear physicist and member of the Manhattan Project who led the 1968 Condon Committee. The resulting report, funded by the U.S. Air Force, concluded that UFOs could all be explained as ordinary phenomena.

As noted by the documentation that appeared after the declassification of the Project Blue Book files, the formation of the Condon Committee was part of an already existing plan. Find a university to study the problem (flying saucers) and then conclude it the way the Air Force wanted it concluded (which was that there was no threat to national security and the Air Force had done a good job). It is obvious that the first universities approached did not agree to the conditions placed on them by the Air Force contracts.[xlvi] It is clear that the Air Force was beginning its attempt to get out of the UFO investigation business.

Hector Quintanilla, then the chief of Project Blue Book, Hynek, and the Secretary of the Air Force at the time, Harold Brown, were called in front of the House Armed Services Committee. During that investigation, the recommendations made just a year earlier for a public, civilian committee to investigate UFOs was was mentioned several times. The House Armed Services Committee thought it was a good idea and suggested that it be implemented as quickly as possible. Brown told the Air Force Chief of Staff that the research was to be conducted and to find a university that would undertake the work.

According to Dr. Michael Swords, a longtime-respected UFO researcher, the search for a university fell to Lieutenant Colonel Robert Hippler of the Air Force's Directorate of Science and Technology, part of the HQ, USAF in Washington, D.C. Hippler put together a high-level group to find the proper university, and the bait was the several-hundred-thousand-dollar grant.[xlvii]

On January 16, 1967, before the real work began, Hippler wrote to Condon. The letter was received by Condon on January 23, and it laid out what the Air Force wanted from the study.

Hippler wrote:

This is an informal letter expressing some thoughts on our round-table discussion on the UFO program and does not constitute the formal letter requested by John Coleman.

There are two items which leave me a little uneasy. The first is the Wertheimer Hypothesis, and its corollary that one cannot "prove" the negative on extraterrestrial visitations. The second is an apparently obscure understanding of what the Air Force wants. Since I will discuss this second item, you will see why this is an informal letter expressing my own opinion–and hence is not binding on you.

On the first item, I wish to present a slightly different approach. When we first took over the UFO program, the first order of business, even before approaching AFOSR [Air Force Office of Scientific Research], was to assure ourselves that the situation was as straightforward as logic indicated it should be. In other words, we too looked to see if by some chance the intelligence people have information other than what exists in Blue Book files. There were no surprises. While there exist some things which may forever remain unknowable in the universe, certainly an extraterrestrial visitation must fall in the "knowable" category. An alien would not come light years merely to pick up surreptitiously some rocks, or melt holes in reservoir ice (a la Edwards). He would have long since gone through the geologic bit and would be fairly knowledgeable of the makeup of stars and planets. You have stated that President Truman was unaware of the Manhattan Project until he became president. In that same time

> "An alien would not come light years merely to pick up surreptitiously some rocks, or melt holes in reservoir ice...."

period, physicists not connected with the project were aware of the possibilities and knew that something was going on.

No one knows of a visitation. It should therefore follow there has been no visitation to date. As you are aware, if UFOs are an Air Force "sacred cow," the other services in the usual competitive spirit would not be constrained by this "sacred cow." Nor is the "fear of panic" holding anyone's tongue. No one is reticent about the horror of an ICBM [intercontinental ballistic missile] attack. Words such as "end of civilization" have been used many times.

This brings us to the second item. When you have looked into some sightings, examined some Blue Book records, and become acquainted with the true state of affairs, you must consider the cost of the Air Force program on UFOs and determine if the taxpayer should support this for the next decade. It will be at least that long before another independent study can be mounted to see if the Air Force can get out from under this program. If the contract is up before you have laid the proper groundwork for a proper recommendation, an extension of the contract would be less costly than another decade of operating Project Blue Book.[xlviii]

Robert Low, of the Condon Committee, provided the response. In several sections, he merely wrote, "Yes, you're right," but he did address some of the issues in question. On January 27, 1967, he wrote:

Maybe we will find that extraterrestrial visitations have occurred, but there's no way to demonstrate that they haven't. This is a logical problem that can't be skirted, and I'm sure, if we were to miss the point, the National Academy would set us straight…. We don't know what technology exists on other planets. I think one can assert, however, that for a spaceship to get to the earth from a planet outside the solar system, it would be necessary to employ a technology more advanced than we enjoy. Since we have no knowledge of that technology, speculation on it brings one right into science fiction, and once one has crossed that boundary the sky is the limit. He can argue anything, and the rules of scientific evidence and methodology have been abandoned. So there is no point in stepping across the boundary except to engage in idle speculation! Such speculation isn't useful in helping to close in on an answer to the problem of whether there have been extraterrestrial visitors or not. And probability won't help.

You mention that the fear of panic is not holding anyone's tongue. That's an extremely good point; I had not thought of it. On the second page, you indicate what you believe the Air Force wants of us, and I am very glad to have your opinion. In fact, you have answered quite directly the question that I have asked—you may remember that I came back to it a couple of times at our meeting on Thursday evening, January 12.[xlix]

Low then signed off, after suggesting that he and Condon would be in Washington, D.C., and they could "perhaps" get together.

But the leader of the investigation was Condon, so what two of the underlings agreed to might not have carried much weight. Just three days after that letter was received, Condon delivered a lecture to scientists in Corning, New York, telling them, "It is my inclination right now to recommend that the government get out of this business. My attitude right now is that there is nothing in it. But I am not supposed to reach a conclusion for another year."[l]

This was the environment into which the other scientists entered. The civilian UFO organizations NICAP (National Investigations Committee on Aerial Phenomena) and APRO (Aerial Phenomena Research Organization) agreed to assist, believing that what they wanted had finally come to pass. The Air Force was going to open up their secret files, and a civilian university would review the data in a fair and objective scientific fashion.

That wasn't the only controversy about the study. Jacques Vallée, writing about the Condon Committee in *Dimensions*, said, "As early as 1967, members of the Condon Committee were privately approaching their scientific colleagues on other campuses, asking them how they would react if the committee's final report to the Air Force were to recommend closing down Project Blue Book." This tends to confirm that the real mission of Condon was not to study the phenomenon but to study ways to end Air Force involvement in it.[li]

Condon, it seems, at the beginning of the study, in late 1966 through the summer of 1967, agreed to accept the grant and was having fun with the UFO phenomenon. He attended UFO conventions and was seen with the most outrageous of the devotees, according to Dr. Swords. The crazier, the better. But in the summer of 1967, late June or early July, his attitude began to change. For some reason, Condon began to fear UFOs. The theme of his discussions with others after June 1967, according to Swords, was that UFOs could be harmful to children.[lii]

There was something wrong with interest in UFOs. Even in the summary to the report, he wrote, "Therefore we strongly recommend that teachers refrain from giving students credit for schoolwork based on their reading of the presently available UFO books and magazine articles. Teachers who find their students strongly motivated in this direction should attempt to channel their interests in the direction of the serious study of astronomy and meteorology and in the critical analysis of arguments for fantastic propositions that are being supported by appeals to fallacious reasoning or false data."[liii]

This is a theme that he comes back to frequently. Condon told colleagues that the Betty and Barney Hill case pointed out the problem with a belief in UFOs. Condon believed that "all this kooky" stuff was the product of some sort of mental instability and not just boys having fun. Because of that, he saw UFOs as dangerous.[liv]

In 1969, the Condon Committee released their findings. As had all of those who had passed before them, the Condon Committee found that UFOs posed no threat to the security of the United States. Condon in Section I, Recommendations and Conclusions, wrote, "The history of the past 21 years has repeatedly led Air Force officers to the conclusion that none of the things seen, or thought to have been seen, which pass by the name UFO reports, constituted any hazard or threat to national security."

After suggesting that such a finding was "out of our province" to study, and if they did find any such evidence, they would pass it on to the Air Force, Condon wrote, "We know of no reason to question the finding of the Air Force that the whole class of UFO reports so far considered does not pose a defense problem."

Included in the Recommendations was the idea that "it is our impression that the defense function could be performed within the framework established for intelligence and surveillance operations without the continuance of a special unit such as Project Blue Book, but this is a question for defense specialists rather than research scientists."

That seems to have taken care of most of the requirements. Condon had confirmed that national security wasn't an issue, had said some positive things about Air Force handling of the UFO phenomenon, and had recommended the end of Project Blue Book. He had done his job.

Finally, Condon wrote, "It has been contended that the subject has been shrouded in official secrecy. We conclude otherwise. We have no evidence of secrecy concerning UFO reports. What has been miscalled secrecy has been no more than an intelligent policy of delay in releasing data so that the public does not become confused by premature publication of incomplete studies or reports."[lv]

With that, the Air Force announced that they were concluding their investigation into UFOs. This scientific study had shown that there was no reason to continue. The trouble, beyond the infighting and the obvious collusion between the Air Force and the Condon Committee, was that the conclusions did not fit the data, cases of importance were ignored, and the Air Force policy of accepting solutions based on limited information continued. The data in the Condon Committee report did not lead to the conclusions it reached. There was more information that something was going on than there was that it was nothing to be researched.

This, then, was the climate of the UFO field at the end of just over two decades of acknowledged work and more than that of hidden or special studies. Even with all this "scientific" research, the general public continued with their fascination with UFOs. They were as interested as ever, and they were only just beginning to learn of UFO reports that would have met any rigor of scientific standards if the truth was told.

Asteroids, Meteors, and UFOs

It could be said that almost from the beginning of recorded history, when we knew much less about the sky above us, we saw strange things that fooled and confounded us. There are written records of flaming swords and glowing shields seen as armies formed to fight one another. There are tales of strange apparitions that frighten everyone from the peasants in their fields to the kings in their castles.[lvi]

If we apply today's knowledge with yesterday's observations, then sometimes we understand that what was seen was not something extraterrestrial visiting Earth but something natural. The flaming swords were probably bolides—bright meteors not seen on a regular basis—rather than alien craft. We now know that rocks do fall from the sky, and there are those who make a living by finding and selling meteorites.

As our knowledge increased, such things were no longer frightening and while now commonplace are seen as exciting. They make the headlines and help us understand the development of our civilization. Dublin, Texas, on June 13, 1891, is the perfect example. According to the *Dublin Progress*, an article on page four reported, "A Meteor Explodes in the City."

The newspaper said that there were many witnesses to the meteor that exploded near a cotton mill, and that those nearby heard the detonation. The newspaper quoted one of the witnesses as saying the meteor was no more than three hundred feet in the air, but such estimates are usually wrong. In this case, the witness, who was not identified, said that he had returned the next day and found a place where the vegetation was burned. There were a number of "peculiar stones and pieces of metal, all of a leaden color…" found in the area.

The newspaper noted that no scientific investigation had been completed. They also said that when the reporter requested to see the fragments, the man

> The newspaper said that there were many witnesses to the meteor that exploded near a cotton mill, and that those nearby heard the detonation.

seemed to become so excited that he failed to understand the request.[lvii] Or, in the words of the 21st century, he had been caught spinning a tale when asked for just a look at the material.

That there was a meteor fall is not in dispute. That it exploded some three hundred feet in the air is probably a misinterpretation of the distance, or in mundane words, a simple mistake. That someone picked up the fragments not far from the town is probably a fabrication. But that doesn't mean that other meteors, or asteroids, or alien craft, haven't entered the Earth's atmosphere and been destroyed by natural forces. In a few cases, the nature of the explosion is in dispute. Such is the case from Tunguska, Siberia.

June 30, 1908: Tunguska, Siberia

Early on the morning of June 30, 1908, those living in the sparsely populated area of Siberia were awaked by an explosion of such power that it shook them from their beds. Those outside were knocked from their feet, and seismographs half a world away registered the detonation. There might have been as many as 1,000 witnesses who saw something in the sky and who saw it leave a trail before it blew up. The blast knocked down trees over a huge area of thousands of square miles and blew the roofs off houses.[lviii]

According to some reports, the skies in the nights that followed were lit by a bright greenish-red glow, and people as far away as Paris claimed they could read their newspapers at midnight because of the light. The event, whatever it was, had been documented, and scientists knew that it had happened at 7:14 in the morning.

Given the remote nature of the area, there was no scientific expedition into Siberia at the time. World War One and the Russian Revolution got in the way. It wasn't until 1927 that Leonid A. Kulik and a group from the Soviet Academy of Sciences mounted an expedition to find the meteorite.

This first of the scientific expeditions into the region also gathered some of the first eyewitness testimony. Unlike UFO reports, there was no dispute about the event. It had been recorded on various instruments in 1908, so the testimony was accepted as real. According to S. Semenov, as recorded by Kulik:

> At breakfast time I was sitting by the house at Vanavara Trading Post facing north.... I suddenly saw that directly to the north, over Onkoul's Tunguska Road, the sky split in two and fire appeared high and wide over the forest. The split in the sky grew larger, and the entire northern side was covered with fire. At that moment I became so hot that I couldn't bear it, as if my shirt was on fire; from the northern

side, where the fire was, came strong heat. I wanted to tear off my shirt and throw it down, but then the sky shut closed, and a strong thump sounded, and I was thrown a few meters. I lost my senses for a moment, but then my wife ran out and led me to the house. After that such noise came, as if rocks were falling or cannons were firing, the earth shook, and when I was on the ground, I pressed my head down, fearing rocks would smash it. When the sky opened up, hot wind raced between the houses, like from cannons, which left traces in the ground like pathways, and it damaged some crops. Later we saw that many windows were shattered, and in the barn a part of the iron lock snapped.

Other testimony was gathered from the witnesses, though sometimes decades after the event. The testimony of Chuchan was recorded in 1926:

Leonid Kulik was a Russian mineralogist who is now noted for his study of meteorites.

We had a hut by the river with my brother Chekaren. We were sleeping. Suddenly we both woke up at the same time. Somebody shoved us. We heard whistling and felt strong wind. Chekaren said, "Can you hear all those birds flying overhead?" We were both in the hut, couldn't see what was going on outside. Suddenly, I got shoved again, this time so hard I fell into the fire. I got scared. Chekaren got scared too. We started crying out for father, mother, brother, but no one answered. There was noise beyond the hut, we could hear trees falling down. Chekaren and I got out of our sleeping bags and wanted to run out, but then the thunder struck. This was the first thunder. The Earth began to move and rock, wind hit our hut and knocked it over. My body was pushed down by sticks, but my head was in the clear. Then I saw a wonder: trees were falling, the branches were on fire, it became mighty bright, how can I say this, as if there was a second sun, my eyes were hurting, I even closed them. It was like what the Russians call lightning. And immediately there was a loud thunderclap. This was the second thunder. The morning was sunny, there were no clouds, our Sun was shining brightly as usual, and suddenly there came a second one!

Chekaren and I had some difficulty getting out from under the remains of our hut. Then we saw that above, but in a different place, there was another flash, and loud thunder came. This was the third thunder strike. Wind came again, knocked us off our feet, struck against the fallen trees.

We looked at the fallen trees, watched the treetops get snapped off, watched the fires. Suddenly Chekaren yelled, "Look up!" and pointed with his hand. I looked there and saw another flash, and it made another thunder. But the noise was less than before. This was the fourth strike, like normal thunder.

Now I remember well there was also one more thunder strike, but it was small, and somewhere far away, where the Sun goes to sleep.

It was discovered that within twenty-five to thirty miles of the estimated point of impact, the trees in unprotected areas had been flattened. Those that had been protected by hills had not been as badly damaged and those that seemed to be under the center of the detonation, or at what might be thought of as the epicenter, were still standing but had been stripped of their branches. The sides of the trees that had been facing the blast area were blackened, but on the other side, the damage was significantly reduced.

> Kulik and his colleagues believed that what had fallen had hit the ground at a tremendous speed and with such force that it was vaporized in the impact.

They also encountered other sorts of damage. Some of the trees seemed to have been snapped in two and the tops thrown a distance from the trunks. At the center of the devastation, in the area where the trees still stood, there was a marshy depression that might have been the result of the impact, and that area was riddled with what might have been additional craters that were ten to twenty feet in diameter. Given that it reminded the scientists of meteoric craters, they probed them looking for the meteorite, but they found nothing. They later determined that the holes were a natural formation and had nothing to do with the meteorite impact.

Kulik and his colleagues believed that what had fallen had hit the ground at a tremendous speed and with such force that it was vaporized in the impact. This sent up clouds of dust and debris to such altitudes that the winds aloft carried it around the world, which explained some of the phenomena reported in the days and weeks that followed the impact. Their conclusion was that this was a meteorite and that the terrain and marshy ground had obliterated any crater that might have formed.

Dr. Fred Whipple suggested that rather than a meteorite, what had hit was a small comet. His belief was that comets were little more than dirty snowballs, meaning they were ice with rocks in them, and this explained the event. The icy comet did not have the tough internal structure that a stony meteorite had, so it broke up, or actually blew up, when it encountered the resistance of the atmosphere.

But meteors and comets weren't the only explanations being offered. In 1946, a science fiction writer and a former colonel in the Red Army, Alexander Kazantsev, said that what had exploded was an interplanetary craft. This was a theme that he repeated in a number of his books, both fiction and nonfiction. The idea was incorporated into the 1960 East German science fiction film *First Spaceship on Venus*, though it was not based on a Kazantsev novel.

In 1961, the Soviets launched two expeditions into the Tunguska region. Both were led by geologists. Kyrill Forensky concluded that what had hit was a small comet rather than a large meteorite. He believed that a blast had taken place several miles up. Members of the other expedition, led by Alexei Zolotov, thought the cause was a nuclear explosion. Part of that is based on the visual evidence left, meaning that the damage done to the forests looked like the aftereffects of the atomic bombs that had been dropped during the Second World War.

Analysis by academicians at the Potsdam Geophysical Institute estimated that the explosion had taken place about three miles above the ground. They based this on the barograph readings from 1908 and the destruction reported to have been observed.

Given what was known back in the middle of the last century, it was believed that the kinetic energy potentials were not sufficient to explain the destruction observed. They concluded, based on this analysis, that meteors or comets could not have been the cause.

In 1976, John Baxter and Thomas Atkins, both of whom had researched the Tunguska explosion, concluded that a spacecraft had exploded. They wrote in their book *The Fire Came By*, "In 1960 Albert Parry, an expert on Russian technology, commented: 'Looking for incontrovertible proof that the messenger from the sky of 1908 was a spaceship and not a mere chunk of stone and metal is fast becoming a favorite sport for many adventurous souls in Soviet Russia.'"

They end the book with a fictional account of what had happened that morning, telling of a spacecraft that was "Propelled by nuclear fire…." It had come from the "depths of interstellar space at a velocity close to the speed of light, then decelerated before orbiting into our planetary system."

They continued, talking of the stresses of entry into the atmosphere, how the craft would glow as bright as a bolide and that there would be the roar of the object overhead. But the spacecraft's heat shield disintegrates, "steaming an incandescent trail of molten particles."

Then, in what is complete speculation, they suggest that the fuel cells of the craft had melted and that the nuclear material "reaches a density that is

This photo of knocked-down trees in Tunguska was taken by the Leonid A. Kulik expedition in May 1929.

supercritical, and in an instant a chain reaction is triggered." The craft and the creatures inside it are vaporized in "a blinding flash of light."

That, according to Baxter and Atkins, is what exploded on that morning in June. While there is some evidence to support the idea that what detonated was not natural, there is no evidence to support these speculations about what transpired on an alien spacecraft before it exploded.

Dr. James A. van Allen had taken an interest in the Tunguska explosion and in the late 1970s added his opinion to that of others. He said that the Russian meteor expert E. L. Krinov had compiled a massive amount of scientific evidence that included dozens of eyewitness reports, microbarograph records, and seismograph records from around the world. There was a great acoustical blast in the atmosphere and then a series of loud explosions heard by witnesses miles away that was described like artillery fire and, of course, the cloud of dust that lingered in the atmosphere for days and spread around the world. What impressed van Allen was the massive amount of objective data.

Having reviewed all that evidence, van Allen said, "Krinov's conclusion is the one that I accept and that I think is generally respected and generally accepted … by scientific workers, and that is that this was very likely a cometary impact. No large pieces of physical matter have been recovered that are extraterrestrial in origin, but there have been a substantial amount of small magnetites and silicate globules found in the soil in the center part of the impact."

This debris, if it could be labeled as such, was consistent with the material that was found in other recorded meteorite falls. In this case, the meteor exploded in the atmosphere so that there wasn't a large piece to be found.

Van Allen, in fact, said that a comet would account for all the reported facts such as the shock wave, the brilliant flash of light, and the detonations reported by so many.

The interesting thing was that van Allen said that a nuclear engine is basically running at near critical when it is working normally. He thought it would be quite difficult to get such an engine, at least as it was understood on Earth at the time, to explode. And while there were heightened levels of various radioactive compounds found in Tunguska, van Allen said that snowfalls in Iowa City, Iowa, in the 1960s

Dr. James A. Van Allen, best known for his magnetospheric research (the Van Allen Belts are named after him), also took an interest in the Tunguska event.

also had heightened levels of various radioactive isotopes given the number of atmospheric atomic tests that were being conducted.

In the end, van Allen accepted the more mundane explanation simply because, as he said, "If you're in the middle of Wyoming and hear hoofbeats, you don't expect zebra." Of course, he conceded that they might be zebra, but before you reached that conclusion, you had to eliminate the mundane.

But then, in 1989 came a report from a Soviet scientist that suggested that evidence of two objects had been found. According to an article by J. Antonio Huneeus, published in the *New-York Tribune* on November 30, 1989, "The most interesting new fact about Tunguska was that a new detailed study of older eyewitness accounts revealed that *two* [emphasis in the original] objects were seen over the area at different times on the same day."

According to the story, they had studied all the witnesses' reports they could find, talked to the relatives of those witnesses, and re-interviewed all those who were still alive. They noted:

[S]ome people said they had seen the object in the morning, approximately 8:00 A.M. local time, and it exploded, but according to some other witnesses as reliable as the previous witnesses, they saw the second object—not so bright—in the afternoon. I should stress that both testimonies of witnesses are equally reliable…. [The afternoon] object was flying from east to west, and the body which exploded earlier in the morning was flying from east [to] north…. [The second object didn't crash] but flew away…. [One] can get the impression that the second object was looking for the first one.

But some four years later, according to a *Washington Post* article published on January 25, 1993, there was a new solution. Scientists at the University of Wisconsin at Eau Claire said that the best explanation was that it was a stony asteroid about two hundred feet in diameter that exploded before it hit the ground. They theorized that lightweight rocks such as comets or carbon-rich asteroids would disintegrate at a higher altitude than the object that caused the Tunguska blast.

> In 2009, a Russian scientist, Yuri Lavbin, said that a UFO had destroyed the asteroid to save the Earth from devastation.

In cases like this, there is never a final answer. In 2009, a Russian scientist, Yuri Lavbin, said that a UFO had destroyed the asteroid to save the Earth from devastation. Lavbin has been described as the president of the Tunguska Spatial Phenomenon Foundation and has been researching the explosion for seventeen years.

He said that he had found strange quartz crystals at the site of the explosion. These crystals had holes drilled through them and diagrams or illustrations etched on them. Lavbin said that they had found ferrum silicate which, according to what he said, can only be formed in space.

He said that he, and his team, made up of other scientists with an interest in the explosion, had found two strange, black stones that were regular cubes measuring five feet on a side. He claimed that they were made of an alloy similar to that used in rockets, but in the early part of the 20th century, the technology didn't exist on Earth. He did say that analysis of these cubes had not been started.

Nick Pope, who worked the United Kingdom's UFO desk in the 1990s, told the wire services, "Previous theories suggest it was caused by an impact from a comet, a mini black hole or a piece of antimatter. This new theory is the strangest yet. We need an analysis of the quartz slabs to be able to prove this one way or another."

While it would be fun to believe that whatever happened over Tunguska, whether a single spacecraft exploding or some sort of suicidal mission by aliens to protect Earth, it seems that the weight of the scientific evidence suggests a meteoric impart. It's those damned zebra in Wyoming that keep getting in the way.

February 25, 1942: Battle of Los Angeles

In the evening of February 23, 1942, a Japanese submarine surfaced about a mile and a half off the coast of California near Ellwood, which is eight miles from Santa Barbara, California. For 20 minutes, the sub crew fired at the gasoline storage tanks near the shore and then retreated. There was no real harm done, other than to the psychology of the citizens, still reeling from the surprise attack on Pearl Harbor just a couple of months earlier.

As a warning, President Franklin Roosevelt was telling a national radio audience that no part of the United States should consider itself safe. Two years later, the Japanese would launch 9,000 of their Fugo Balloons in an attempt to set the forests of the Northwest on fire. Although the damage was limited, six people were killed when they found the remains of one of the balloons. It exploded when they tugged on part of the balloon wreckage.

But in 1942, war nerves were running high, the Pacific Fleet was in ruins, and the Pacific Ocean was becoming part of the Japanese Empire. People didn't know what was going to happen and the war news from the Pacific, and from Europe, was going from bad to worse. It was in this environment that the Battle of Los Angeles was "fought."

This abandoned Japanese submarine was discovered after the Pearl Harbor attack. A similar one was spotted off the coast of California during World War II, making Americans anxious about possible attacks on the U.S. mainland.

At 7:18 P.M. on February 24, strange blinking lights and flares were seen near Los Angeles defense plants. The military went on alert, expecting the worst. But nothing more happened, and the alert was cancelled at 10:23. Although no one actually mentions much about this aspect of the case, this seems to be an example of the Foo Fighters' work. The descriptions match, more or less, with some offered by flight crews in all theaters of the war. But it wasn't until 1944 that any investigation into the Foo Fighters would begin.

At 2:15 A.M. on February 25, radar picked up something approaching 120 miles west of Los Angeles. A blackout was ordered at 2:21 A.M., and within four minutes ground observers were reporting an enormous, luminous object. Searchlights seemed to catch something at the point where the light beams converged, and it was photographed. Nearly 1,500 rounds of anti-aircraft artillery and .50-caliber machine ammunition were fired with no results, other than falling shrapnel and spent bullets.

In an article in *Fate* in July 1947, Paul Collins reported on what one of the witnesses had said. According to that story:

> The eerie lights were *behaving* strangely. They seemed to be navigating mostly on a level plane at that moment—that is, not rising up from the ground in an arc or trajectory or in a straight line and then following back to earth, but appearing from nowhere and then zigzagging from side to side. Some disappeared, not diminishing in brilliance or fading away gradually but just vanishing *instantaneously* into the night. Others remained pretty much on the same level and we could only guess their elevation to be around 10,000 feet, but some of them dived earthward only to rise again, mix and play tag with about 30 to 40 others moving so fast that they couldn't be counted accurately.

There were other witnesses who talked about other, luminous objects in the sky that night. Jerome Clark, in his massive *UFO Encyclopedia, Second Edition*, quoted from an air-raid warden who remembered a "formation of six to nine luminous, white dots in triangular formation … visible in the northwest. The formation moved painfully slowly."

He also mentioned that another young man, also an air-raid warden, who said he'd seen a brightly glowing, spherical red object. "It traveled horizontally a short distance, very slowly, and then made an abrupt 90-degree [turn], rising abruptly. Again it stopped and remained motionless." After a few minutes, it disappeared into the distance.

The firing broke out at 3:16 A.M. and continued for 58 minutes. According to newspaper reports, three people were killed as unexploded shells and bullets rained down. Three others died from heart attacks, which were attributed to panic. By 7:21 A.M. nothing else was seen, and if there had been an object or objects, they were all gone.

Now the speculation began. Some believed there had been Japanese aircraft over L.A., but no evidence of that was ever found, even after the war when records could be searched. An artillery officer claimed the objects were hydrogen-filled nickel balloons that had been launched as some sort of radar test that wind had pushed over L.A., but again, there was no evidence for this.

On February 26, the Secretary of the Navy, Frank Knox, said that all the excitement was simply a false alarm. The next day, the Secretary of the Army, Henry Stimson, said that there was no doubt that some fifteen planes may have been involved flying at various speeds and at various altitudes. Stimson could not identify the airplanes, but it would seem that had they been American, either Knox or Stimson would have known about it and could have confirmed it.

Secretary of the Navy Frank Knox (pictured here) tried to ease panic about what people speculated was a Japanese aircraft flying over California during World War II.

As mentioned, this is a classic UFO sighting that was confirmed by radar, or maybe more accurately, started by the radar report. Witnesses at various locations reported seeing objects in the sky, and there seemed to be photographic evidence to support that. A picture was published in the newspaper that seemed to show the searchlights focused on a point that suggested an object. That would make this one of the best of the UFO cases given the multiple chains of evidence, but in 1942, no one was talking about UFOs, flying saucers, or alien spacecraft. They were all concentrating on enemies that were earthbound.

In 1983, the Office of Air Force History produced an analysis of the evidence that pointed to meteorological balloons as the cause of the initial alarm. That document, *The Army Air Forces in World War II*, … recapped the history of what became the Battle of Los Angeles and added a few conclusions about it:

> During the course of a fireside report to the nation delivered by President Roosevelt on 23 February, 1942, a Japanese submarine rose out of the sea off Ellwood, a hamlet on the California coast north of Santa Barbara, and pumped thirteen shells into tidewater refinery installations. The shots seemed designed to punctuate the President's statement that "the broad oceans which have been heralded in the past as our protection from attack have become endless bat-

tlefields on which we are constantly being challenged by our ene-mies." Yet the attack which was supposed to carry the enemy's defi-ance, and which did succeed in stealing headlines from the Presi-dent's address, was a feeble gesture rather than a damaging blow. The raider surfaced at 1905 [7:05 P.M. Pacific Time], just five minutes after the President started his speech. For about twenty minutes the submarine kept a position 2,500 yards offshore to deliver the shots from its 5-inch guns. The shells did minor damage to piers and oil wells, but missed the gasoline plant, which appears to have been the aiming point; the military effects of the raid were therefore nil. The first news of the attack led to the dispatch of pursuit planes to the area, and subsequently three bombers joined the attempt to destroy the raider, but without success. The reluctance of AAF [Army Air Force] commanders to assign larger forces to the task resulted from their belief that such a raid as this would be employed by the enemy to divert attention from a major air task force which would hurl its planes against a really significant target. Loyal Japanese-Americans who had predicted that a demonstration would be made in connec-tion with the President's speech also prophesied that Los Angeles would be attacked the next night. The Army, too, was convinced that some new action impended, and took all possible precautions. Newspapers were permitted to announce that a strict state of readi-ness against renewed attacks had been imposed, and there followed the confused action known as "the Battle of Los Angeles."

During the night of 24/25 February 1942, unidentified objects caused a succession of alerts in southern California. On the 24th, a warning issued by naval intelligence indicated that an attack could be expect-ed within the next ten hours. That evening a large number of flares and blinking lights were reported from the vicinity of defense plants. An alert called at 1918 [7:18 P.M., Pacific Time] was lifted at 2223, and the tension temporarily relaxed. But early in the morning of the 25th, renewed activity began. Radars picked up an unidentified target 120 miles west of Los Angeles. Antiaircraft batteries were alerted at 0215 and were put on Green Alert—ready to fire—a few minutes later. The AAF kept its pursuit planes on the ground, preferring to await indications of the scale and direction of any attack before com-mitting its limited fighter force. Radars tracked the approaching tar-get to within a few miles of the coast, and at 0221 the regional con-troller ordered a blackout. Thereafter the information center was flooded with reports of "enemy planes," even though the mysterious object tracked in from sea seems to have vanished. At 0243, planes were reported near Long Beach, and a few minutes later a coast artillery colonel spotted "about 25 planes at 12,000 feet" over Los Angeles. At 0306 a balloon carrying a red flare was seen over Santa Monica and four batteries of antiaircraft artillery opened fire, whereupon "the air over Los Angeles erupted like a volcano." From this point on reports were hopelessly at variance.

Probably much of the confusion came from the fact that antiaircraft shell bursts, caught by the searchlights, were themselves mistaken for enemy planes. In any case, the next three hours produced some of the most imaginative reporting of the war: "swarms" of planes (or, sometimes, balloons) of all possible sizes, numbering from one to several hundred, traveling at altitudes which ranged from a few thousand feet to more than 20,000, and flying at speeds which were said

Ruins of California airfields that were once used during World War II still exist. The state—and entire West Coast—was under high alert. Might UFOs have been mistaken for Japanese aircraft?

to have varied from "very slow" to over 200 miles per hour, were observed to parade across the skies. These mysterious forces dropped no bombs and, despite the fact that 1,440 rounds of antiaircraft ammunition were directed against them, suffered no losses. There were reports, to be sure, that four enemy planes had been shot down, and one was supposed to have landed in flames at a Hollywood intersection. Residents in a 40-mile arc along the coast watched from hills or rooftops as the play of guns and searchlights provided the first real drama of the war for citizens of the mainland. The dawn, which ended the shooting and the fantasy, also proved that the only damage which resulted to the city was such as had been caused by the excitement (there was at least one death from heart failure), by traffic accidents in the blacked-out streets, or by shell fragments from the artillery barrage.

Attempts to arrive at an explanation of the incident quickly became as involved and mysterious as the "battle" itself. The Navy immediately insisted that there was no evidence of the presence of enemy planes, and [Secretary of the Navy] Frank Knox announced at a press conference on 25 February that the raid was just a false alarm. At the same conference he admitted that attacks were always possible and indicated that vital industries located along the coast ought to be moved inland. The Army had a hard time making up its mind on the cause of the alert. A report to Washington, made by the Western Defense Command shortly after the raid had ended, indicated that the credibility of reports of an attack had begun to be shaken before the blackout was lifted. This message predicted that developments would prove "that most previous reports had been greatly exaggerated." The Fourth Air Force had indicated its belief that there were no planes over Los Angeles. But the Army did not publish these initial conclusions. Instead, it waited a day, until after a thorough examination of witnesses had been finished. On the basis of these hearings, local commanders altered their verdict and indicated a belief that from one to five unidentified airplanes had been over Los Angeles. Secretary Stimson announced this conclusion as the War Department version of the incident, and he advanced two theories to account for the mysterious craft: either they were commercial planes operated by an enemy from secret fields in California or Mexico, or they were light planes launched from Japanese submarines. In either case, the enemy's purpose must have been to locate antiaircraft defenses in the area or to deliver a blow at civilian morale.

The divergence of views between the War and Navy departments, and the unsatisfying conjectures advanced by the Army to explain the affair, touched off a vigorous public discussion. *The Los Angeles Times*, in a first-page editorial on 26 February, announced that "the considerable public excitement and confusion" caused by the alert, as well as its "spectacular official accompaniments," demanded a careful explanation. Fears were expressed lest a few phony raids undermine the confidence of civilian volunteers in the aircraft warning service. In the United States Congress, Representative Leland Ford wanted to know whether the incident was "a practice raid, or a raid to throw a scare into 2,000,000 people, or a mistaken identity raid, or a raid to take away Southern California's war industries." Wendell Willkie, speaking in Los Angeles on 26 February, assured Californians on the basis of his experiences in England that when a real air raid began, "you won't have to argue about it—you'll just know." He conceded that military authorities had been correct in calling a precautionary alert but deplored the lack of agreement between the Army and Navy. A strong editorial in the *Washington Post* on 27 February called the handling of the Los Angeles episode a "recipe for jitters" and censured the military authorities for what it called "stubborn silence" in the face of widespread uncertainty. The editorial suggested that the Army's theory that

> "The Fourth Air Force had indicated its belief that there were no planes over Los Angeles. But the Army did not publish these initial conclusions."

commercial planes might have caused the alert "explains everything except where the planes came from, whither they were going, and why no American planes were sent in pursuit of them." *The New York Times* on 28 February expressed a belief that the more the incident was studied, the more incredible it became: "If the batteries were firing on nothing at all, as Secretary Knox implies, it is a sign of expensive incompetence and jitters. If the batteries were firing on real planes, some of them as low as 9,000 feet, as Secretary Stimson declares, why were they completely ineffective? Why did no American planes go up to engage them, or even to identify them?.... What would have happened if this had been a real air raid?"

U.S. Army Air Force craft such as this P-38 constantly flew over California during the war, so one might wonder why no airplanes were sent to engage or identify the unknown craft witnesses reported.

These questions were appropriate, but for the War Department to have answered them in full frankness would have involved an even more complete revelation of the weakness of our air defenses.

At the end of the war, the Japanese stated that they did not send planes over the area at the time of this alert, although submarine-launched aircraft were subsequently used over Seattle. A careful study of the evidence suggests that meteorological balloons—known to have been released over Los Angeles—may well have caused the initial alarm. This theory is supported by the fact that antiaircraft artillery units were officially criticized for having wasted ammunition on targets which moved too slowly to have been airplanes. After the firing started, careful observation was difficult because of drifting smoke from shell bursts. The acting commander of the antiaircraft artillery brigade in the area testified that he had first been convinced that he had seen 15 planes in the air, but had quickly decided that he was seeing smoke. Competent correspondents like Ernie Pyle and Bill Henry witnessed the shooting and wrote that they were never able to make out an airplane. It is hard to see, in any event, what enemy purpose would have been served by an attack in which no bombs were dropped, unless perhaps, as Mr. Stimson suggested, the purpose had been reconnaissance.

In keeping with a tradition that would begin in earnest in 1947, the Air Force, on its re-examination of the evidence, concluded that there was an object or objects over Los Angeles, but those objects were weather balloons. Since the

World War II air raid wardens such as these men were trained to identify aircraft even at a great distance. So why were their reports ignored by the Air Force?

battle had taken place before there was talk of UFOs and a long history of sightings, no one thought in terms of something other than a craft built on Earth.

It is also clear from the press release that the Air Force, in keeping with its history of rejecting eyewitness testimony when it didn't fit the conclusions they had reached, did just that. Those air-raid wardens who saw multiple objects, and provided descriptions of them that don't match weather balloons, were ignored.

There are two problems here. First is the photograph taken in 1942. It seems to show an object at the point where the searchlight beams meet, as if focused on a single object. Here is evidence that something other than a weather balloon was present. Or was it?

According to Ed Stockly, a *Los Angeles Times* writer, "As reported by *Los Angeles Times* bloggers Scott Harrison and Larry Harnisch, the version of the photograph that ran in the paper in 1942 had been retouched in ways that would not be acceptable today. They skyline was darkened with ink; paint (similar to correction fluid) was used to brighten searchlight beams and to turn lens flare dots into anti-aircraft bursts. The part of the image identified by UFO experts as an alien spacecraft was shaped by drops of paint on print."

Stockly reported that the original, unretouched negative was available in the UCLA Archives and that Simon Elliott of the Department of Special Collections at UCLA's Charles E. Young Research Library would provide it to any researcher who would have requested the negative. The implication seems to be that UFO researchers had not bothered with this rather basic bit of investigation.

Dr. Bruce Maccabee, an optical physicist, has examined the original negative as retrieved by Scott Harrison. Working from the information as provided on the negative as opposed to the picture as printed in the newspaper, he was able to make some calculations. Although he provided the information at his website at http://brumac.8k.com/BATTLEOFLA/BOLA1.html, his explanation can be confusing for those not versed in his specialty. He concluded, "Based on the above calculations, and realizing that a much better estimate could be made if we had more accurate information on the spotlights, camera, etc., I would hazard a guess that the width of the illuminated 'object' is on the order of 80 feet or more in size. Without more solid information to go on, this has to be no more than a WAG (wild ... rear-end ... guess) (but I bet it's close to right!)."

The other problem that Stockly had was that *Fact or Faked: The Paranormal Files*, a television investigative show, did some research into the Battle of Los Angeles. He worried about the way they investigated the sighting. The team included a former FBI agent, Ben Hansen, who Stockly confirmed had some employment with the FBI, Bill Murphy, who is the resident scientist, Jael De Pardo, who identified as a journalist, a photographer expert, Chi-Lan Lieu, the tech expert Devin Marble, and a stuntman, Austin Porter. The plan was to use searchlights that were technically the same as those used in 1942 to see if the lights could create an optical artifact where all the beams met. They also had a weather balloon or two, not to mention some heavy artillery, or more accurately, a .50-caliber machine gun and a 40 mm grenade launcher, to use in their experiments.

Optical physicist Dr. Bruce Maccabee, who once worked for the U.S. Navy and is also a ufologist, examined the 1942 photo and guessed the flying object to be about eighty feet in width.

While all that made for some entertaining television, the scientific value of this could be questioned. There was one point, after they showed that the lights, when the met in the air, didn't stop, but the beams continued on into space, while in the photograph they seemed to be partially blocked, that suggested something was in the way. Their experiment suggested that the smoke from the exploding anti-aircraft artillery wouldn't have been dense enough to block the beams as shown in the photograph, and it seemed to indicate that the object was not an artifact of the searchlight or the photographic processes.

But the interesting point in the experiment was to test the resistance of a weather balloon to the heavy machine-gun fire. The .50 caliber is effective to about 11,000 feet, but that is actually against aircraft as opposed to a neoprene weather balloon. When the team from the TV show opened fire, the balloon was hit and it deflated immediately, falling out of the sky in mere seconds. Had there been a weather balloon in the sky above Los Angeles in 1942, it shouldn't have lasted very long under the sustained and sometimes heavy anti-aircraft fire.

Given the number of rounds fired, and given the caliber of the weapons used, it would seem that they would have hit and destroyed a weather balloon quickly. They would have seen it fall. If they couldn't hit it, and remember, this was before much of the U.S. Army had combat experience, they were still fairly poor shots. Just by sheer chance they should have knocked it down, and yet the Air Force in 1993 claimed that all this came about because of a weather balloon. Weather balloons had been their standard answer for decades when they had nothing else to say.

July 24, 1948: Chiles–Whitted Cigar

As research into UFO sightings continue, there are times when old cases should be re-examined using modern techniques and modern information. Such is the case that some originally found quite puzzling when others believed that a meteor, or more accurately, a bolide, was responsible for the sighting. In fact, with this case, the original explanation was "meteor."

According to the Project Blue Book files, Eastern Airlines pilots Clarence S. Chiles and John B. Whitted were flying their DC-3 at 5,000 feet on a bright, nearly cloudless and star-filled night. They were twenty miles southwest of Montgomery, Alabama, when they spotted what they at first thought was a jet aircraft slightly above them, to the right, and coming at them. Within seconds it flashed by, and both pilots got a look at the torpedo-shaped object that had a double row of square windows and what seemed to be a glowing exhaust extending beyond the rear of the craft.

Chiles, who had seen it first, said to Whitted, "Look, here comes a new Army jet job."

Chiles and Whitted were piloting a DC-3 like this one when they saw the UFO. Chiles later observed that the cigar-shaped craft had a fuselage about three times the size of their airplane.

The object approached in a slight dive, deflected to the left, and passed the aircraft on the right. It was almost level to their flight path. After passing them, it seemed to pull up and disappear into a cloud.

Questioned within hours of the sighting by Air Force investigators, both men said that they believed the object was about a hundred feet long. Whitted told the investigators, "The fuselage appeared to be about three times the circumference of a B-29 fuselage. The windows were very large and seemed square. They were white with light, which seemed to be caused by some type of combustion. I estimate we watched the object for at least five seconds. We heard no noise *nor did we feel any turbulence from the object* [emphasis added]. It seemed to be at about 5,500 feet."

Chiles, in a statement dated August 3, 1948, wrote, "It was clear there were no wings present, that it was powered by some jet or other type of power shooting flame from the rear some fifty feet.... Underneath the ship there was a blue glow of light."

None of the passengers saw anything except Clarence L. McKelvie. Chiles wrote, "After talking to the only passenger awake at the time, he saw only the trail of fire as it passed and pulled into the clouds."

WCON radio in Atlanta, Georgia, interviewed Chiles and Whitted within hours of the sighting. They were also interviewed by William Key, a newspaper reporter. At some point during the interview, someone suggested they had been startled by a meteor, but both men rejected the idea. They had seen many meteors during their night flights and were well aware of what they looked like and how they performed.

In a newspaper article written sometime after the sighting, Albert Riley quoted the pilots as saying, "Its prop-wash or jet-wash rocked our little DC-3."

In another newspaper report contained in the Project Blue Book files, Chiles is again quoted as having said there was some prop- or jet-wash. "[B]oth reported they could feel the UFO's backwash rock their aircraft."

Curiously, they used the term "UFO," except that term wasn't in use in 1948. This was a term that was coined, more or less, by Edward Ruppelt who, in the early 1950s, took over Project Grudge, which eventually evolved into Project Blue Book. To help create an aura of professionalism in the investigation, Ruppelt changed flying saucer to unidentified flying object, abbreviated as UFO. They still talked of flying saucers, but it was used in the pejorative sense, suggesting the witness was less than credible and the sighting was more of an illusion than anything real.

Ignoring all this, a search of the file shows that in 1948, they did search for an answer to Chiles and Whitted's report and did go to extraordinary lengths to find evidence. They gathered information from every airline which could possibly have had an aircraft in a position to have seen the object. They also queried all branches of the military, searching for any other pilots who might have seen the object at the same time as Chiles and Whitted but who had failed to report it.

They did find that there were other witnesses who had some "strange" encounters that night. Incident Number One, according to the Blue Book files, took place between 0140 and 0150 [1:40 to 1:50 A.M.] from the ground at Robins Air Force Base in Georgia. Walter Massey, then a twenty-seven-year-old ground maintenance crewman, said that he saw a cigar-shaped object fly over. Massey was interviewed on August 10, 1948, by Lieutenant Colonel Cropper, the Acting District Commander, Sixth District Office of Special Investigation (AFOSI).

> "... as it got overhead, it was a fairly clear outline and appeared to be a cylindrical-shaped object with a long stream of fire coming out of the tail end."

Massey, according to the report, "was standing fire guard on a C-47 [coincidentally, the military version of the DC-3], directly across from Operations, and I had to take down the takeoff time, which was between 0140 and 0150." This gave him a good idea of the exact time of his sighting.

Massey said, "It [the object] was coming out of the north. I was facing the north and actually didn't see it until it was overhead, but it came out of the north and was in my view for about 20 seconds. The last I saw of the object, it was taking a southwest course.... The first thing I saw was a stream of fire, and I was undecided as to what it could be, but as it got overhead, it was a fairly clear outline and appeared to be a cylindrical-shaped object with a long stream of fire coming out of the tail end. I am sure it would not be a jet since I have observed P-84s in flight at night on two occasions."

Massey thought that the object was about 3,000 feet high but said that at night he couldn't be sure. He also said that he thought, at first, it was a "shooting star or meteor, but a shooting star falls perpendicular. This object was on a straight and level plane."

Of course, it needs to be mentioned that meteors often seem to be flying straight and level, and sometimes can even seem to be climbing. It has to do with the location of the witness, the angle at which the meteor entered the atmosphere, and if there are clouds that hide part of the meteor's flight. Some bolides have been known to skip on the atmosphere, bouncing out again after grazing the upper limits. These would actually climb out of the atmosphere.

Cropper asked Massey, "Did it give you the impression that there were windows or holes, and did the decks appear to be divided into sections?"

Massey said, "I am not sure. It would be hard to tell if there were windows, and a divided deck could not be recognized from the ground."

That was a good answer on Massey's part because it showed that he wasn't taking cues from Cropper. It was also a very leading question from Cropper as he attempted to find out what Massey had seen. To clarify the situation, Cropper asked, "Did you read the newspaper account of the two civilian pilots who saw this strange object about the same time, and did the paper's description seem to refer to the object you saw?"

Massey said that he had read the write-up about the rate of speed. He added, "I don't see how they could tell if it had square windows or round windows, but the description seemed to fit my impression.... It looked like it was about the size of a B-29.... It was too large for a jet. It seemed to be a dark color and constructed of an unknown metallic type."

Massey then said, "During the Battle of the Bulge, a sergeant and myself were on guard duty and saw something that resembled this object in question. We later found that we had witnessed the launching of a German V-2 rocket. It carried a stream of fire that more or less resembled this object. This object looked like rocket propulsion rather than jet propulsion, but the speed was much greater."

Because of all the similarities of the cases, the Project Blue Book file links this report to that of Chiles and Whitted and suggests that all the witnesses in both locations mentioned the "cigar or cylindrical" shape. Investigators were

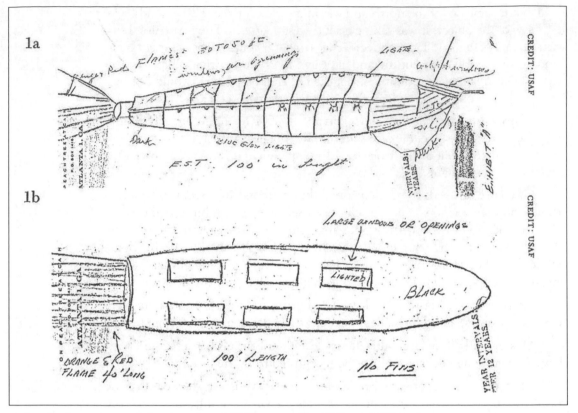

A drawing by a witness of the cigar-shaped UFO reported by Chiles and Whitted.

puzzled by the speed. If the object was flying at the 700 miles an hour that Chiles believed, it should have covered the 200 miles faster than it apparently had. But if the link is solid, meaning it was the same object, then, of course, an explanation suggesting a meteor is eliminated by the timing of the two sightings.

About fifteen minutes before Chiles and Whitted had their sighting, there was a report from Blackstone, Virginia. According to the Blue Book files, "Object Number 2 was observed by Feldary, Mansfield, and Kingsley at 0230 hours [2:30 A.M.] 24 July, 1948, while airborne between Blackstone, Virginia, and Greensboro, North Carolina. This sighting is considered separately [from Chiles and Whitted] since the descriptions of speed as 'meteoric' or 'terrific,' the manner of travel described as an arc or horizontal, and the fact that it 'faded like a meteor' seem to indicate that the object was not the one observed in Incident 1 [Chiles–Whitted]."

Other sightings contained in the folder created by the investigators for Project Blue Book are from events that took place two nights later. They were included because the descriptions of the objects seem to match, generally, those made by Chiles and Whitted. But as mentioned in the file, these seem to also be of meteors and might not be relevant to the Chiles–Whitted sighting.

Dr. J. Allen Hynek, the Air Force science consultant, was asked to review the case. He said that he could find no "astronomical explanation" if the case was accepted at face value, meaning that the Massey sighting and the Chiles–Whitted cases were linked. He wrote, "[The] sheer improbability of the facts as stated … makes it necessary to see whether any other explanation, even though far-fetched, can be considered."

Eventually the Air Force offered an explanation. Hynek, in his attempts to explain the case, suggested that Massey might have been mistaken. Maybe he saw the object at the same time as Chiles and Whitted. It would seem more likely that the pilots were mistaken about the time, given the situation on the ground, but Hynek was attempting to keep the link. If they all saw the same object, then "the object must have been an extraordinary meteor." The glowing ion trail might have produced the "subjective impression of a ship with lit windows." Hynek thought that psychological research would be needed to answer the question of whether such an impression would result from the stimuli of a bright meteor seen close.

> On March 3, 1968, over parts of Tennessee, Indiana, and Ohio, thousands watched as a strange object flew over.

While that psychological experiment was not performed, a real-world situation might answer the question. On March 3, 1968, over parts of Tennessee, Indiana, and Ohio, thousands watched as a strange object flew over. In Tennessee, three people, including the mayor of a large city, were talking when one of them saw something in the distance and pointed it out to the others. As the object approached, they saw an orange-colored flame firing from the rear. All thought the object was a fat cigar, "the size of one of our largest airplane fuselages.…"

The woman sent a letter to the Air Force in which she described square-shaped windows that appeared to be brightly lit. She thought the fuselage had been constructed of flat metal which was riveted together. She provided a drawing for the Air Force investigators.

At about the same time, a group of six near Shoals, Indiana, saw a huge, cigar-shaped craft with a flaming tail and many brightly lit windows flash overhead. The people thought the object was at treetop level. One of them reported the sighting to the Air Force and suggested that it wasn't a meteor because "meteors don't have windows and don't turn corners."

Others also saw the object. In Ohio, a school teacher "with four academic degrees including a Ph.D." was out walking her dog when she saw three objects fly overhead. These craft looked like inverted saucers, and she thought they were about 1,500 feet about the ground.

The *Zond IV* spacecraft, shown here, was re-entering the earth's atmosphere at the same time as the UFO sightings in Tennessee, Ohio, and Indiana. Could this have been the mysterious cigar-shaped craft?

An industrial executive who lived in Dayton, Ohio, was returning from Cincinnati when he saw three bright objects in what he thought of as a triangular formation. As they flew, they seemed to make a "distinct curve" in their flight path. Because of their speed, and a lack of noise, the executive believed that the three objects were under intelligent control.

The timing of the sightings in Tennessee, Ohio, and Indiana matches the re-entry of the Soviet booster of the *Zond IV* spacecraft. It is possible that the re-entry of the *Zond IV* was responsible for the series of sightings, including those of a cigar-shaped craft, that is quite similar to that reported by Chiles and Whitted some two decades earlier.

While it is true that some of the witnesses in 1968 reported three objects and others reported a single object, their descriptions do match closely the observations made by Chiles and Whitted. It is also true that all the witnesses reported what they had seen; it doesn't mean that they hadn't seen the same thing. As the *Zond IV* broke up, those in one location might have seen one object while others saw three. It is the same thing that is seen in meteor falls. Some of them are seen to break up so that in part of their flight there is one object and later, seconds later really, there are more pieces seeming to fly in formation.

The real connection is the similarity in the drawings made by Chiles and Whitted and those made by witnesses in the 1968 case. If those witnesses did see the *Zond IV* re-entry, then it would be suggestive of the psychological aberration that would induce the belief that there were bright windows on a streak of light. Or, as can be seen on any number of meteor falls recorded by digital cameras, as the meteors break up, there is a stream of brightly lit particles following a large, bright light in the front. It could give the impression of a lit cockpit and a row of brightly lit windows on a cigar-shaped craft.

Given what is known today, it seems that a logical explanation for the Chiles–Whitted sighting is that they saw not just a meteor, but a bolide, an extremely bright and rare meteor. If Massey saw the same object but had his timing off, or Chiles and Whitted had had theirs off, then it wasn't a meteor. If they saw the same object, then it is unlikely that it was a meteor or bolide. And if they didn't see the same thing, then Chiles and Whitted may well have seen a bolide.

October 18, 1973:
The Coyne UFO Sighting

Meteors have become, in recent years, the "go-to" answer for many puzzling UFO sightings. Philip Klass seems to have used meteors to explain several cases, even when there is a real doubt that a meteor could have been the cause. When the UFO was seen to maneuver, hover, and then accelerate, meteors don't seem to be a viable answer. Such is the case of Army Reserve Captain Lawrence Coyne and his flight crew as they were returning to their home station in Cleveland, Ohio, flying in a Huey helicopter.

Initially it was Sergeant John Healey, seated in the left rear, who spotted an object or a red light off the left side of the aircraft at about 2300 hours (11:00 P.M.) He thought it was brighter than the red navigation lights on an aircraft, and he could see none of the other aircraft lights required by the Federal Aviation Administration This light disappeared behind the helicopter, and Healy thought nothing more about it.

A few moments later at 2302 hours, Specialist Five (Spec 5, E-5) Robert Yanacsek, seated in the right rear, saw a red light on the eastern horizon. He, at first, thought it was a red warning light on a radio tower, but the light wasn't blinking and it seemed to be pacing the aircraft. He watched for a minute or two, that timing being critical to understanding the case. Finally the light seemed to turn so that it was coming toward the helicopter and when it did, he mentioned it to the pilot, Captain Lawrence Coyne. Coyne glanced out the right window and saw the light. He suggested that Yanacsek keep an eye on it, though there didn't seem to be any real danger from it.

After about half a minute, Yanacsek thought that the light was coming at them and Coyne agreed. Coyne then took the controls of the aircraft and believing the object might be on a collision course, he pushed down the collective (or technically, the collective pitch, that is, a lever on the left side of the seat of the pilot or copilot), which changes the pitch of the rotor blades so that the aircraft will gain or lose altitude. He also called Mansfield Approach Control to ask about other aircraft in the area, including F-100 fighters that were based there.

The problem here is that he couldn't raise Mansfield. He had been in communication a few minutes earlier, but this time there was no response. He then ordered his copilot First Lieutenant Arrigo Jezzi to try again. They simply could not raise approach control, but Coyne knew the radio had been working.

Healey now left his seat and moved forward, crouching between the seats occupied by Coyne and Jezzi. The light was getting brighter, or as Healey would later say, brighter than the landing lights of a commercial jet.

The red light was closing on them quickly and dangerously. Coyne again pushed down on the collective to increase his rate of descent, eventually pushing it all the way to the stop. Believing that he was not descending fast enough, he pushed the cyclic (think of the yoke on an airplane here) forward so that he would be descending even faster.

At this point Coyne looked up and said the light, which he could now see was an object, was covering the front of the windshield. Coyne said that there was a red light at the front of the object, a green light that seemed to reflect off the rear of the object, and a green light, like a searchlight, coming from the rear. The overall shape seemed to be that of a cigar or cylinder, and under the tail was a pyramid-shaped structure from which a green beam came. The overall object was not glowing, but Coyne, and his crew, could see the general shape against the bright, starry background.

According to Jennie Zeidman, who published the results of her investigation through the Center for UFO Studies in 1979, Yanacsek said:

> The object may have hovered over us for 10 to 12 seconds. It seemed like a long time. It seemed like it was there for so damn long. It was just stopped, for maybe 10 to 12 seconds, and I mean stopped. It wasn't cruising, it was stopped. It didn't waver, it didn't put on the brakes, it didn't gyrate—it was just like in a cartoon. It was coming at us, and then, in the next frame, it was there, just like that. No noise, no flaps. It reminded me very much of a submarine. I really didn't think we would collide, because the object was obviously completely in control of the situation.

The object hovered there for those long seconds and then took off toward the northwest. They could see the light at the rear of the aircraft was bright white. Coyne glanced at the altimeter and realized they were at 3,500 feet. Coyne said the collective was still full down, and he couldn't explain the ascent. With what he was doing, the helicopter should have been descending rapidly. Coyne then pulled up on the collective (which, of course, was the opposite of what he should have done to stop an ascent, but then, the collective was full down, so he couldn't have pushed it any lower) and at 3,800 feet, they felt a bump and the climb ceased.

Coyne said that there was a red light at the front of the object, a green light that seemed to reflect off the rear of the object, and a green light, like a searchlight, coming from the rear.

With the climb stopped and Coyne now in control again, he began a descent back to the cruising altitude. At the same time, they could now make radio contact with the various flight-following agencies.

Philip Klass, when he heard about the case, decided to take a look at it. He was on a television show about UFOs with Healey, and he recorded another show that aired the next

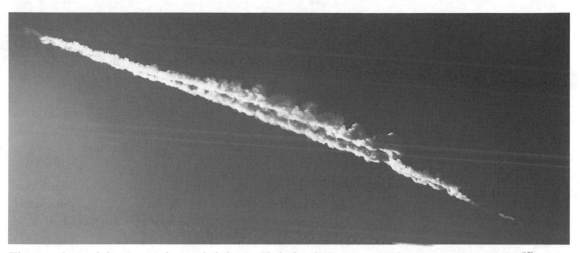

This is a photo of the meteor that exploded over Chelyabinsk, Russia, on February 15, 2013. Philip Klass initially suspected the 1973 Coyne report to be a sighting of a similar meteor.

night that featured Coyne as the guest. Klass, in his book *UFOs Explained*, wrote, "As I studied the transcript of my tape recording [of Coyne on *The Dick Cavett Show*], my attention began to focus on the possibility that the UFO might have been a bright meteor-fireball."

He then spent a great deal of time reporting on his search for a record of a meteor at the time and place in question but failed. True, not every meteor is reported and logged, but this one would have been spectacular enough that someone else should have seen it. No one did, and no reports were filed. But even with that lack of evidence Klass hung on to the meteor explanation and cited examples of many people being fooled by fireballs, miscalculating the distance to them, their altitude, their shape, and the length of time they are visible, and some other UFO cases that were explained by fireballs (such as the possible solution for the Chiles–Whitted case above).

Klass mentioned nothing of Healey's sighting of the red light that was seen out the left side of the aircraft and that it slid to the rear. If it was the same object, then that approach from the other side moments later clearly proves that it wasn't a meteor and Klass' explanation fails at that point.

Klass mentioned that the cockpit was bathed in green light as the object passed overhead and reported that there were two Plexiglas panels set above the pilots' heads and that these were tinted green. They were called, cleverly by the flight crews, the greenhouses, but they were directly over the pilots and were not part of the windshield. Klass seemed to have confused these green-tinted areas for something on the windshield, much as cars used to have a green tint at the top of the windshield. The crew was not looking through the greenhouses, and the light was not coming through them. Besides, the crew described other colored lights on the object which they were watching through the clear, Plexiglas windshield.

Klass admitted that the climb was the "real puzzler." He discussed it with Dave Brown, an "experienced pilot with some hours in a helicopter" (which tells nothing about his experience in a helicopter, and it doesn't say if those hours are as a pilot or a passenger and if there are very many of them). Brown suggested that perhaps the pilot or copilot might have unconsciously pulled back on the collective and/or cyclic-pitch control(s) as he leaned back in his seat to view the luminous object overhead.

The copilot, Lieutenant Arrigo Jezzi, would never have done that. Coyne and Jezzi had both gone through the same flight training. Had Jezzi felt the aircraft was in danger and he needed to take over the controls, he would have put his hands on them and said, "I've got it."

Coyne would have relinquished control, taking his hands off, and said, "You've got it."

This was done so that the pilots wouldn't be fighting each other for control. In similar circumstances, meaning if one of them in the cockpit saw something the other didn't that might endanger the aircraft, this is what was done, and that includes combat assaults under fire, which can easily be as stressful as seeing a UFO. Every Army-trained helicopter pilot followed the ritual even at times like that, so it is clear that Jezzi didn't take over control and didn't touch the controls.

Could leaning back in the seat, trying to see the UFO above, have caused Coyne to pull up on the collective (as opposed to pulling back, as Klass suggested)? Not really, given the way the controls are configured. Could he have pulled back on the cyclic in such a circumstance? Maybe, but there would have been other consequences to that action, including a slowing of the airspeed and a change in the orientation of the view in the cockpit, which would have suggested that something had happened. Or, in other words, that would have been noticed. Besides, given the circumstances, it is more likely that Coyne would have pushed the cyclic forward as he attempted to see the object, which would have increased the rate of descent.

Philip Klass was a renowned skeptic of UFOs, explaining away the Coyne report as a meteor, for example.

Klass continued his speculation about all of this, based on the information he had collected, some of which he failed to report, and he concluded that "we should all be grateful for the instinctive, if unconscious, reactions of pilot Coyne or copilot Jezzi in pulling their helicopter out of its steep descent barely four hundred feet about the ground."

So Klass had solved the case by creating a meteor where none was reported, ignoring the flight of the light when it didn't conform to his ideas, misunderstanding the configuration of the cockpit controls that didn't fit his belief, and his failing to understand the flight procedures of Army-trained helicopter pilots. His analysis is badly flawed and his speculations are not driven by facts and can be rejected because of that.

He did mention the report from someone on the ground who might have seen the UFO, but he never found him, and for that reason Klass concluded that witness did not exist. There are two other witnesses who saw the UFO from the ground and they have provided statements about what they saw corroborating, after a fashion, the sighting by Coyne and his crew.

According to what Jerome Clark wrote in his massive *UFO Encyclopedia*, 2nd edition:

> Three years later, investigators found that other witnesses had seen the strange encounter. [Although the names are known to researchers, they asked to remain anonymous.] Around 11:05 P.M. on October 18, 1973, a woman and four adolescent children, driving east on a deserted rural road and approaching a bridge which spans the Charles Mill Reservoir east-southeast of Mansfield, saw two lights in the sky. The one in front was bright red, the other, behind it, a dim green, flying as a unit and coming from the east at a one-or-two o'clock position in the sky. They first thought it was probably a Cessna aircraft. Then to their right (south to southwest), they saw the lights of a helicopter at a low altitude. As the helicopter lights and the red and green lights converged, the mother pulled the car over, and two of the children, Charlie and Karen, jumped out while the others rolled down windows and gazed upward.
>
> They could now see that the red light was attached to an object resembling a blimp with a dome. Apparently the size of a school bus, it "went over the top of the other one [the helicopter] and then stopped." According to the woman....
>
> Charlie recalled, "When we got out of the car, it was right *there*, sitting *there*.... It was longways [sic]. Then the green light flared up. When we got out of the car, everything was green. I saw that thing and the helicopter." Another child said, "Everything turned green. It lit up everything green. There was a whole bunch of noise [from

the helicopter]. I saw the green light for 10 seconds. Not very high. I think the green came from above the helicopter. It kind of looked like rays coming down.

Jennie Zeidman, who conducted an extensive investigation of the case, interviewed a mother and son, Jeanne and John Elias, who also had an experience that is related to the case. She said that she remembered the date because it was her younger son's birthday, and they'd had a party for him.

Again, according to Clark, Jeanne Elias heard a helicopter flying over, but they were in the path of the Mansfield Airport, so they had aircraft flying over frequently. The helicopter, according to what she told Zeidman, was so low she thought that it was going to crash.

While that isn't much in the way of corroboration, there is a second part to the report. The son, John, called to his mother to ask if she had seen the green light. When she said that she hadn't, he said that his whole room had lit up green. He hadn't gotten out of bed to check on it, but had said that it was a bright green.

There is another aspect to Zeidman's investigation that is important. She had spent a great deal of time talking to the flight crew together and separately. She said that through her analysis of the testimony, the sighting, from Yanacsek's seeing the red light in the distance to the object's disappearance over the western horizon, lasted some 270 to 300 seconds or about four and a half to five minutes.

Jerome Clark reported on the Coyne incident in his book the *UFO Encyclopedia*.

Even with that, Klass, in two of his books, one magazine article, and many letters, suggested that the solution to the case was a meteor. He continued to argue that Jezzi or Coyne had instinctively pulled up on the collective to arrest the rapid descent, but he had no evidence to back up his claims. He was arguing from an almost indefensible position without an understanding of Army helicopter operations. That didn't stop him from claiming that a meteor was responsible for the sighting.

In the end, this is a case that screams to be labeled as "unidentified," because there is no valid explanation for it. Klass was simply wrong in his analysis, and his speculations should be ignored because of his manipulation of the evidence and his lack of understanding of the flight characteristics of the helicopter. There is no easy solution here, and sometimes that is about all that can be said about a case.

Analysis

It might be said that from the beginning of recorded history, there have been reports of bright lights moving through the sky. It can also be said that these early reports were probably of meteors or other natural phenomena, since the ancient people didn't understand the world around them. The Tunguska case is rare in human history. It was a sizable object, it exploded in the air, and it caused widespread devastation. It is also an event that was widely reported with eyewitnesses and on the ground instrumentation. There is no question that something happened. What caused it is the area of speculation.

Although the scientific evidence seems to suggest that the Tunguska event was a meteor, probably an asteroid, and there was the most recent fall over Russia that isn't as spectacular but did cause injuries and widespread damage to underscore the theory. There is just enough that is strange about the event to suggest that it might have been something else. The evidence, examined by a variety of researchers, scientists and journalists, provides each with a legitimate point of view. While scientists are confident in their explanation, there is enough that isn't easily explained to raise questions.

The Battle of Los Angeles has no easy answers. The Air Force is satisfied that it was caused by war nerves and a weather balloon, but then, the Air Force is always claiming that weather balloons are responsible for UFO sightings. The evidence, on the photograph, from the primitive radar in use at the time and from the eyewitnesses, suggests that something real was over Los Angeles. Skeptics claim that the photograph shows an artifact created by the convergence of the searchlight beams and touch-up by the photo editors, and there is nothing solid there, not even the weather balloon the Air Force claims.

The number and kind of rounds fired suggest that had there been a weather balloon, it would have been destroyed easily and rapidly. A single round from the anti-aircraft artillery or the .50-caliber machine guns would have caused instant deflation. There is no evidence that such is the case.

Skeptics and the Air Force believe they have solved the case, but their solutions are based on speculation and a refusal to look at other evidence. To them, there was nothing in the sky that night, regardless of what the witnesses say, what the radar tracked, or what the photograph showed. There is no acceptable solution here.

Such is not the case with the Chiles–Whitted sighting. J. Allen Hynek, in his original analysis, thought it might be explained by a meteor, but that solution was rejected. Those in the UFO research community held it up as a solid case based on the observations of two experienced airline pilots. Even the Air Force, in the beginning, were at a loss to explain the case, and it was used as supporting evidence in various Air Force reports, documents, and analyses.

An increase in the understanding of meteors, especially fireballs, suggests that this is exactly what they saw. The re-entry of the *Zond IV* spacecraft, with some witnesses seeing the same thing as Chiles and Whitted, showed that a fireball could be perceived as a cigar-shaped craft with square windows. There is a very good chance that what Chiles and Whitted saw was a bolide.

The situation with the Coyne case is just the opposite. While skeptic Philip Klass attempted to shoehorn the meteor explanation into the case without the benefit of evidence, it is clear that a meteor is not the solution. The evidence by the four experienced helicopter crew men, the timing of the events, and the physical effects argue against a meteor. Add to that the radio failure at the close approach of the UFO, a fairly well-known side effect in many UFO cases, and there is an added dimension.

> The re-entry of the *Zond IV* spacecraft, with some witnesses seeing the same thing as Chiles and Whitted, showed that a fireball could be perceived as a cigar-shaped craft with square windows.

Then there are the witnesses on the ground. Klass dismissed those who weren't identified in the UFO literature, and a case can be made for that exclusion, since their names are known to few. Klass didn't have the opportunity to interview them, so for him, they didn't exist. But there are others, whose names were known, who observed some of the events, and they tend to corroborate what Coyne and his crew said.

In the end, there are some cases that are ambiguous. Tunguska was probably an asteroid, but there are some strange components to it. The Battle of Los Angeles is even more ambiguous, with the current Air Force answer not standing up to dispassionate scrutiny. The Chiles–Whitted case is probably solved as a bolide, and the Coyne case is the very definition of an "unidentified."

Of all the cases examined in this chapter, the Coyne case is the best. The witnesses were well trained, they had an opportunity for a detailed observation, and there were other witnesses to the event. There simply is no terrestrial explanation for this case.

The Photographic Evidence

It has been said, repeatedly, that there is no evidence that UFOs are craft from other worlds. Testimony about the performance of the objects might be suggestive, but that is open to interpretation of the witness. Something more is needed, and one of those things is photographs that show more than a blob of light or a fuzzy mass that could be nearly anything. There are some photographs that provide better evidence, and the size and shape of the object in those photographs does suggest something extraterrestrial.

Such is the case of the two photographs taken near McMinnville, Oregon, on May 11, 1950. Given the photographs and what they show, there are but two explanations for them. They either show an alien craft, or they are a hoax. It seems unlikely that they are of some kind of rare natural phenomenon photographed under strange conditions or some sort of optical illusion.

May 11, 1950:
McMinnville, Oregon

Evelyn Trent, according to what she would say later, was outside the house about 7:30 P.M. having just fed the rabbits. As she walked back to the house, she saw a slow-moving, disc-shaped object that had a metallic look to it. She yelled to her husband, who came out, saw the object, and then thought of their camera.

Paul Trent took two pictures of the UFO. This was 1950, and the film in camera had to be advanced manually. He took a second picture of the object, which he thought was some twenty or thirty feet in diameter and that was now gaining speed, heading to the west.

> Trent, according to the story, was leery of allowing the pictures to be published because he thought they had photographed some sort of secret military project.

Evelyn said that she noticed her in-laws were on their back porch. She yelled at them, but they didn't hear her. She rushed inside and used the telephone. Her mother-in-law apparently heard the telephone and went inside to answer. Her father-in-law did glimpse the UFO, but he apparently was never interviewed about what he had seen.

In what would later become a controversial decision, Trent didn't have the film processed immediately. According to him, there were two exposures remaining, and they didn't want to waste the film. Trent eventually mentioned the sighting to Frank Wortmann, a banker who displayed the pictures in the window. Bill Powell, a local reporter, saw the pictures and interviewed the Trents. He convinced them to let him borrow the negatives. Trent, according to the story, was leery of allowing the pictures to be published because he thought they had photographed some sort of secret military project.

It wasn't until June 8, after the Trents finished the roll of film and had it developed and after the banker put the pictures in the window, that the story appeared. Not long after the pictures, including blow-ups of them, were printed in the *McMinnville Telephone Register*, other reporters began calling for additional information.

Two days later, on June 10, the International News Service (INS) transmitted the story and the pictures around the world. *Life* then borrowed the pictures and published them in their June 26 (1950) issue. With all that publicity, the Trents were flown to New York City to appear on a national TV show, *We the People*.

With all of that finished, the Trents were visited by Air Force investigators, apparently in civilian clothes. Powell said, according to Bruce Maccabee, that two weeks or a month after the June story, or some two months after the sighting, an Air Force agent in civilian clothes visited him in the office. The officer apparently flashed credentials, demanding the negatives. These were surrendered and never returned, according to Powell, even after he had sent registered letters and telegrams asking for them.

There is very little in the Project Blue Book files about the case. The Master Index lists it, but there is no evaluation offered. That space is blank. After the date, it is marked as "Info," which means that there is no investigative file, but it is included because they have information on it. Normally this would be newspaper articles, but in this case, the information is letters from citizens asking questions about the case.

The answer to one of these, written by Lieutenant Colonel John P. Spaulding, who was the Chief, Civil Branch, Community Relations Division, Office of Information, noted that:

The Air Force has no information on photographs of an unidentified flying object taken by Mr. & Mrs. [redacted but quite obviously Paul Trent] of McMinnville, Oregon.

In this regard, it should be noted that all photographs submitted in conjunction with UFO reports have been a misinterpretation of natural or conventional objects. The object in these photographs have a positive identification.

Overlooking the fact that he said they had no information on the photographs, he offered a solution for them anyway. If they had no information, how would he know that the object, singular, in the McMinnville photographs had been identified?

Assuming that there was no Air Force investigation at any level, then the first official investigation of the photographs came when the University of Colorado agreed to study UFOs for the Air Force. Dr. William Hartmann was assigned as the principal photo analyst and was given the task of reviewing the case.

Hartmann interviewed the Trents and reported in the final report what they had told him. According to his written statement, appearing in the Con-

One of the two photos taken by Paul Trent in 1950 of the UFO over McMinnville, Oregon.

don Committee report, "Witness [Evelyn Trent] was feeding rabbits in the backyard, S [south] of the house and E [east] of the garage, when the object was first sighted … apparently toward the NE [northeast]. Witness II [Paul Trent] in the house at this moment, as three of the accounts … refer to Witness I [Evelyn Trent] calling to him and running into the house to fetch him from the kitchen, although one account … states that they had 'been in the back yard,' and 'both … saw it at the same time.'"

Philip Klass found this point to be very interesting. He wrote, "The Portland newspaper story revealed some significant discrepancies in the Trents' account of the incident based on a tape-recorded interview with them on station KMCM, compared to their original version given to the McMinnville newspaper. Where originally Mrs. Trent had said that both she and her husband had been outside and had spotted the UFO at the same time, now Mrs. Trent said that she had been outside *alone* (emphasis in the original) when the object was first seen. She said she hollered for her husband, who was inside the house, and when he failed to reply, she had run inside to get him and the camera."

> The discrepancy here might not be with what Evelyn Trent actually said but with the interpretation of what she said by a secondhand witness.

But then, in another analysis of this, Klass wrote, "*The Oregonian*, June 10, 1950 [Partially based on recorded interview with Lou Gillette of station KMCM (bracketed statement in the original)]: 'She [Mrs. Trent] said she was first to see it. She was out feeding the rabbits in the yard alongside the garage.… She yelled to her husband, then ran into the house to fetch him.'"

In one instance, the information is taken from a quote by the witness and in the other, it is information taken from a quote by Gillette, who interviewed the witness. The discrepancy here might not be with what Evelyn Trent actually said but with the interpretation of what she said by a secondhand witness. Reliance on this sort of testimony is something that skeptics often warn UFO researchers to avoid.

Trent told Hartmann about taking the photographs. According to Hartmann:

Witness II [Paul Trent] explained that he took the first picture, rewound [advanced] the film as fast as possible, and then as the object gathered speed and turned toward the northwest, he had to move rapidly to his right to get the second picture. Both were snapped within thirty seconds, he estimated. According to an early reference: "[Witness II {Trent}] elaborated, 'There wasn't any flame, and it was moving fairly slow. Then I snapped that picture. It moved a little to the left, and I moved to the right to take another picture.…'" During this interval the object was moving quite slowly, apparently almost hovering, and it apparently shifted both its position and orientation in a complex way, changing direction and tipping just before it moved away.... However, Witness I [Evelyn Trent] described it as "not undulating or rotating, just 'sort of gliding.'" The UFO accelerated slowly during or just after the second photograph and moved away rapidly toward the west. Witness I ran into the house to call her mother-in-law, got no answer, and returned outside just in time to see the UFO "dimly vanishing toward the west."

Hartmann, in his report, added detail to the description of the craft and to the sequence of events. He said that the witnesses had said the object was very bright, almost silver, and that it was made of aluminum or silver with a touch of bronze. Evelyn Trent said that it "appeared to have a sort of super structure ... like a good-sized parachute canopy with the strings, only silvery bright mixed with bronze."

Both witnesses reported that when the craft turned and tilted, they felt a gust of wind. Evelyn thought it was quite strong and believed it was about to knock her over. Her husband described it as a light breeze.

Trent, in 1950 when interviewed and later, in 1967 when interviewed in conjunction with the University of Colorado study, said that he thought it was some sort of government experimental craft. He said that he believed that the Army knew all about them.

Trent said that they finished the film roll on Mother's Day and had it developed in town. In a somewhat contradictory statement, Trent said that he was worried that he had photographed a secret airplane, and he didn't want to get into trouble for doing that. But rather than keep the sighting quiet, he told a few friends and eventually agreed to let the pictures be displayed in the window of his bank, where Bill Powell saw them. He talked to the bankers, Ralph and Frank Wortman, and learned about Trent.

According to the tale told by Powell, he visited the Trents at home in his attempt to find the negatives. He said that he found them on the floor, where children had been playing with them. The story and pictures were published on June 8, 1950, with an Editor's Note:

> ... in view of the variety of opinions and reports attendant to the saucers over the past two years, every effort has been made to check the Trents' photos for authenticity. Expert photographers declared there has been no tampering with the negatives. [The] original photos were developed by a local firm. After careful consideration, there appears to be no possibility of hoax or hallucination connected with the pictures. Therefore, the *Telephone Register* believes them authentic....

With all that, Hartmann subjected the photographs to a variety of tests, charted the Trent's farm, and measured the distances to various tests and calculations. He determined that they showed a real object, which is not to say that it was an alien spacecraft.

Hartmann also reviewed the physical aspects of the witness testimony. They recreated the scene in the Trent yard, with Trent explaining his movements as he took the pictures. Hartmann wrote:

> I judge it reasonable that as the object allegedly drifted to the left, in danger of being lost to sight behind the garage, that the observer should step unconsciously to his right, as the photos show he did, although one might expect the observer even more reasonably to step forward, to get in front of the garage. The reason for the first response may have been that the second would put the observer close to the house, where the object might be lost to sight if it moved back to the east, while by moving away from the garage, one moves toward the open yard SE [southeast] of the house. In summary, the movement of the observer is consistent with the alleged observation.

Or more precisely, Hartmann was saying that in the recreation of the sighting, there was no glaring inconsistency. There was nothing on the photographs to suggest that Trent might have moved in a different direction, or that would suggest that a hoax had been perpetuated.

At the end of his investigation, Hartmann concluded that these were the only photographs that were left as unexplained. He wrote, "This is one of the few UFO reports in which all factors investigated, geometric, psychological, and physical appear to be consistent with the assertion that an extraordinary flying object, silvery, metallic, disk-shaped, tens of meters in diameter, and evidently artificial, flew within sight of two witnesses. It cannot be said that the evidence positively rules out a fabrication, although there are some physical factors, such as the accuracy of certain photometric measures of the original negatives, which argue against a fabrication."

"After careful consideration, there appears to be no possibility of hoax or hallucination connected with the pictures."

Remember, the overall conclusion of the University of Colorado study was that there was no real evidence of alien visitation, and further research would be a waste of time. Yet here was a case that was not explained, that did not rely solely on the testimony of the witnesses, who were described by all who knew them as sincere and honest, and that seemed to suggest something strange flying around the skies of Oregon. If it was not a hoax, and the evidence at the time suggested it was not, then it had to be good evidence of an alien craft.

But in the world of the UFO, nothing is ever final, no matter how final the answer might be. Philip Klass, who knew

McMinnville is a sleepy town in the northwest corner of Oregon. Its claim to fame was the Evergreen Aviation and Space Museum, where the *Spruce Goose* is housed. And its second claim to fame are the photos taken by Paul Trent.

that there was no alien visitation, knew there had to be a flaw in the analysis done on the McMinnville pictures. He believed, based on nothing other than his own opinion, that someone who photographs a rare event "such as a meteor or an aircraft accident, these pictures are developed promptly and made public, if only for their monetary value. It should be clear to every person intelligent enough to operate a camera that an authentic picture of a spacecraft from other worlds would be vastly more important, and more valuable, than a picture of an aircraft crash or meteor. Otherwise, why exert so much effort to get the camera and photograph the object?"

Except, of course, if you believed that you had photographed a secret military craft and might get into trouble, you might not rush to get the pictures developed. Except, of course, if you're not thinking in terms of alien spacecraft and something more terrestrial, you might not rush to get the pictures developed. And what would be sufficient speed in having the film developed? Apparently the Trents had them in hand within a month. In 1950, film was expensive, and that they waited a few days to finish the roll doesn't seem that unreasonable. This is not to mention that in 1950, it could take days to get the film back from the processor, so that the time between the event and the newspaper article isn't all that long.

Klass continued in that vein, however, suggesting that the Trents had not treated the negatives with the respect that he expected. There is something to that, though if you follow through on Paul Trent's thought it might by American military, his apparent disregard for the negatives might be understood. And while it is not necessary for the hyperbole that Klass used, the negatives were treated in a fairly cavalier way.

Klass also pointed out that the Trents were "repeaters," which to Klass was suggestive of someone whose testimony is suspect. He believed that seeing an actual alien spacecraft was such a rare event that no one would be lucky enough to see one more than once. Of course, there is the man who has been struck by lightning five times, which tells us that this extremely rare event does reoccur despite the long odds. And it could be that the Trents were just poor at identifying unusual atmospheric phenomena, and what they thought of as spaceships could be explained in other ways. The only real time they saw a spaceship was when they took the photographs. At least that is another way of looking at it.

Robert Sheaffer, a colleague of Klass', analyzed the McMinnville photographs, concluding that the two photos had been taken in the morning, not evening, and were shot several minutes apart.

While Klass was busy with his end of the investigation, his colleague, Robert Sheaffer, was beginning his analysis of the photographs themselves. Using the measurements of the Trent farm made by Hartmann, he determined that the shadows on the east wall of the Trent garage suggested the pictures had been taken in the morning rather than the evening. According to Klass, "He [Sheaffer] concluded that the pictures had been taken at approximately 7:30 A.M., not 7:45 P.M. Furthermore, his analysis indicated that the photo which the Trents claimed had been taken first had really been shot *several minutes after the other picture, and not a few seconds earlier as the Trents said*" [emphasis in the original].

Klass noted that Hartmann had also seen the shadows, but had thought they were the result of the light of the setting sun reflecting off the cloud base, given the timing of the sighting. That would have provided the illumination from the east and would explain these shadows. Klass argued that had Hartmann attempted to replicate the shadows under similar conditions, he would have not been able to do so. Sheaffer told Klass that such strong shadows could only be obtained by a "point source," or, in other words, the sun shining in the east as it rose.

Klass said that he obtained the weather records for May 11, 1950, and they revealed, according to Klass, that the sky had been perfectly clear. This was the end of the story for Klass. He wrote, "Beyond all doubt, the Trents' story that the pictures had been taken in the early evening of May 11, 1950, *could not possibly be true*" [emphasis in the original].

The weather records aren't nearly as definitive as Klass made out. According to Bruce Maccabee, he also checked the records for the date of the sighting and he found:

> The "classical" date, as reported in the initial newspaper stories, is May 11, 1950, which was a Thursday. That date is accepted here, despite the seeming contradiction between the weather reported in a newspaper story (sky overcast at 5,000 ft) and the McMinnville Airport weather report (mostly clear sky) or a sky that is uniformly overcast. (NOTE 2000 [an update to his original analysis]: although the only source for the date is the Trents themselves, there is nothing to contradict their claim.)

This suggests that there were clouds in the area and that the sky was not perfectly clear. Even a few cumulous clouds, which are the bright white, puffy clouds, would have been able to throw light on the east side of the garage. Maccabee, in his analysis, using the same sort of equipment as Sheaffer, suggested that the shadows were diffuse, meaning they weren't the heavy, dark shadows that would be expected from direct sunshine. It seems that this is a case in which the experts are at odds with one another, that the evidence isn't all that defined, but it also suggests that the Trent photographs can't be rejected by this sort of analysis. It is too vague to be conclusive.

Klass also offered an explanation for this time change in the story. He suggested that the Trents had changed the time because, at 7:30 in the morning, most farmers would be outside working and someone should have seen the object besides the Trents. But, if the photographs were taken in the evening, those same farmers would be inside eating their dinner. This explained why there were no other witnesses.

But Evelyn Trent said that there were other witnesses. At least that was what she claimed years after the fact. She said that she called her mother-in-law, who went into the house to answer the telephone, but her father-in-law remained outside and was said to have glimpsed the UFO as it disappeared.

Dr. James E. McDonald interviewed Paul Trent some nineteen years later and asked if there were any other witnesses. Trent said that his father had seen the UFO, but his father had died before McDonald asked the question.

Bruce Maccabee also asked if there had been other witnesses. In February 1976, according to Maccabee's transcripts of his interview with Evelyn, learned, "Well, the people that saw it, they're both dead."

In that same conversation, Evelyn Trent said there was a witness who lived about a mile from them, and she had seen the same object. But again, this witness was unavailable.

> ... Evelyn Trent said that there were other witnesses. At least that was what she claimed years after the fact.

There was also a suggestion that a woman, identified only as Mrs. Worth, told Evelyn Trent that she thought she had seen the same thing on the same day that the pictures were taken. Even though Maccabee wanted to interview her, and Trent said she would pass along the telephone number, by the time Maccabee finally got the telephone number and attempted to call her, years had passed. The witness had died and was no longer available.

The story, then, is that there had been additional witnesses, and their testimony would have been very important. Even if they were related to the Trents, additional witnesses in other locations would have helped establish the reality of the sighting. But none of them were interviewed, and these opportunities were lost long ago.

There was even an explanation on why it seemed the photographs showed a cloudy sky, which is in conflict with what appears in the pictures and the information developed by Hartmann during his investigation. According to Klass:

Sheaffer hit upon another possible explanation for the photometric anomalies that could have thrown off Hartmann's appraisal, and he decided to test the idea with an experiment. Sheaffer speculated that if the lens of the Trent camera had not been perfectly clear, light scattering could occur that might produce the effects like those that Hartmann had observed. The camera used by the Trents was an Eastman folding type, which sometimes needed a hard push to get it folded. The lens offered a hard point against which to push, and it might have accumulated a thin film of body oil on the lens surface. For Sheaffer's experiment, he used an ordinary streetlamp, suspended from a pole, to simulate a small model UFO at close range. He first photographed it against a bright sky using a clean lens. Then he smeared a thin layer of petroleum jelly on the lens and repeated the shot. This was followed by another, thicker layer of jelly, and still another photo. When he developed the negatives and examined them with a densitometer, the results confirmed his hypotheses. Light from the bright sky surrounding the simulated UFO had been diffused by the oily film on the lens, and this had increased the luminance of the "UFO." Using the same technique that Hartmann had employed on the Trent photos, Sheaffer could "prove" that the top of the streetlamp pole was at a much greater distance from the camera than the bottom of the same pole, even though both were actually the same distance.

The explanation, however, is loaded with speculation. If Trent pushed the camera closed using the handy lens as a strong point, then there might have been a thin layer of grime on it if he didn't clean the lens to ensure that it was clear.

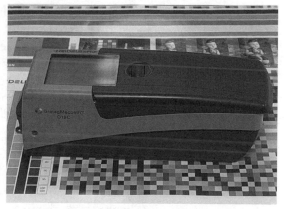

A densitometer is a device that measures the optical density of photographic material. Sheaffer used one to determine that Trent had smeared petroleum jelly on his camera lens.

Hartmann did, in fact, revise his views on the authenticity of the pictures. Once he saw Sheaffer's analysis, Hartmann apparently wrote, "I think Sheaffer's work removes the McMinnville case from consideration as evidence for the existence of disklike artificial aircraft."

Maccabee responded to all this as well. In a presentation at the 1976 Center for UFO Studies Symposium and in a posting on his website, he wrote:

> Regarding the photometric analysis (originally done by Hartmann [which Condon attempted to cover up by saying the photogrammetric analysis was useless] and repeated by me with corrections), they used measurements from a print to get relative brightnesses. (I used the negatives themselves with a gamma curve for development of the negatives.) They used as their basis for "dark" the relative brightness of the overhead wires. The problem with this is that the width of the image of the wire, unlike the width of the image of the UFO, was not great enough to "overcome" the brightening effect of the short-range veiling glare (which they mentioned) caused by the brightness of the sky surrounding the wire. Thus their conclusion that the UFO was no more than 200 feet away is not necessarily correct. My own conclusion is presented in the 1976 CUFOS symposium paper at my website.

Klass' assault on the pictures was not the last. In April 2013, IPACO (roughly translated from the French as Interactive Picture Analysis of Celestial Objects) posted two studies on their website in which they suggested computer programs they had developed found evidence of a thread holding up a small model in the Trent pictures. The software used was developed by François Louange, who had done work for NASA as well as the European Space Agency and GEIPAN (roughly translated from the French as Unidentified Aerospace

Phenomenon Research and Information Group). In their first analysis, they concluded that the geometry of the photographs was most consistent with a small model hanging from the wire seen in the pictures, but they were unable to rule out the possibility of an alien craft. To them, the more likely explanation was a small model rather than creatures from another world traveling to Earth. Specifically, in their report, *The McMinnville Pictures*, found at *http:// www.ipaco.fr/ReportMcMinnville.pdf*, they wrote:

> This quick analysis using our interactive tool confirms the following points about the object under study, whatever the final explanation:
> First picture MM1/TRNT1:
> Camera-UFO distance LESS THAN 200 feet
> Changes from the first picture to the second one:
> Different illumination conditions (or different processing conditions for the two pictures)
> Movement of the operator (as indicated on Maccabee's map)
> Increase of the camera-UFO distance by 11%
> Tipping back of the UFO by ca. 25°
> Two explanations are still open, although with very different probabilities:

Explanation 1

> The UFO is a model hanging ca. 2.3 feet under the lower power wire at a distance of ca. 15.1 feet from the camera.
> Its size (diameter of its circular base) is ca. 0.4 feet.
> It is not dark (at least its upper part).
> Between both shots, its distance from the camera increases by 1.7 feet.
> Between both shots, it has a swaying movement backward of ca. 9° in the vertical plane of the UFO's sighting axis, with a total tipping-back rotation of ca. 25° around the diameter of its circular base, which is perpendicular to its sighting line.

Explanation 2

> The UFO is an unknown object, at a distance in the order of 200 feet from the camera.
> Its size (diameter of its circular base) is in the order of 6 feet.
> It is dark.

Probabilities

> *Explanation 1* should be the final explanation with a very high probability, even if it cannot be 100% proven, because:

Explanation 1 is consistent with all measurements, without any "exotic" assumption.

Explanation 1 is quasi-consistent with Maccabee's photogrammetric study of the SLC (Sighting Line Cross).

Explanation 2 requires to assume that the UFO is moving away exactly in the direction of its sighting line, so as to explain the constant ratio of its distance from both power wires on both pictures, or—special case—that it is not moving at all (which, according to the above geometric analysis, is only consistent with the explanation by a small, very close model).

Explanation 2 requires to admit that the UFO is moving away by 11% (geometric study) from an initial maximum distance of 200 feet (radiometric study), while its radiometric darkest value (top part) decreases by 12%, which is not consistent with atmospheric diffusion effects.

Our Conclusion

At the end of this simple geometric and radiometric analysis, we conclude that the hypothesis of a small object hanging below a power wire is the most convincing.

The various contradictory photometric analyses conducted by previous investigators (Hartmann, Maccabee, Poher ...) came to the common conclusion, in the hypothesis of a hanging model, that the object could not be opaque because of the "too clear" appearance of its circular base, in spite of its short distance from the camera. According to Maccabee and Poher, the material(s) which made up the object could then only be translucent, with different characteristics for the circular base and for the upper part. The UFO could have had a composite structure, with a nonuniform translucent upper part, leaving incident light propagate down to the bottom part, which would be made of another material, also translucent but uniform and more opaque.

We propose here a different possible explanation, which has the advantage of being simpler as regards how the object might have been faked: **the object was hollow underneath** [emphasis in the original], like a dustbin lid or a lampshade. It could be light, hence bouncing about in a light breeze, like a light metal lampshade or glass fiber or plastic lid or cover.

The observed uniform dark (but not black) radiometry in the ellipse could then be explained as follows:

The undersurface of the hollow part was a matte, dark, rough, and nonreflective surface, in shadow, acting as an extremely low reflector in the optical wavebands.

The light going in to the underside of the "lid" was already quite diffuse, as it was mostly reflected up from the Earth's surface, unlike direct sunlight.

This light was, to a large degree, absorbed by the surface material itself, and the remainder underwent a large amount of reflections around within the roughness of the "hollow" shape.

Consequently, the amount of light reflected back out of the concavity could be comparatively very low indeed to ambient.

Under those conditions, we may reasonably explain the very low uniform reflectivity observed in the ellipse.

Moreover, this explanation would easily justify why a very thin (invisible) thread, such as a fishing line, had been sufficient to support this light object.

Their conclusions then were certainly ambiguous. It might have been a model, probably was, but the analysis wasn't one hundred percent conclusive. In June 2013, they revised their report as they gathered better data and analysis. They wrote:

> After the previous study, the crucial question of the evidence of a suspension thread remained pending, even though the different approaches, including the registered images shown in the epilogue, had shown that this presence was highly probable.

> Latterly, an original detection tool has been designed, developed, and integrated into the IPACO software, specifically dedicated to the search for any more or less vertical threads on an alleged UFO picture. A detailed description of the adopted logic may be found in the "Analysis Methodology" section of the website, as well as in the IPACO *User's Manual* (*Analysis* Menu).

It might have been a model, probably was, but the analysis wasn't one hundred percent conclusive.

> The basic idea is that if there are traces of a thread in a picture's pixels, above an object hanging from this thread, and if this trace is « buried in noise » within the sky's background (noise due to atmospheric diffusion and/or to the digitizing process), it should be possible to increase the signal-to-noise ratio, thus uncovering the thread by summing pixels along columns parallel to the thread. It must be stated, however, that this principle makes the tool likely to be ineffective if the sky's background does not appear uniform at all in the area above the object in the image.

Their conclusion was simple. They wrote, "The clear result of this study was that *the McMinnville UFO was a model hanging from a thread* [emphasis in the original]. The low values of the tilt angles between the suspension thread and the verticals of both McMinnville pictures are quite compatible with the presence of a soft wind on the site and with the hypothesis of a rather light, suspended object. They are also coherent with the registered images presented above."

On the National Investigations Committee on Aerial Phenomena (NICAP) website, there is a long discussion about all this, created by Bruce Maccabee and Brad Sparks. Maccabee reported it this way:

> In their most recent work, they are going for the "Holy Grail for skeptics": finding a string above the Trent UFO. They have introduced a new method of analysis for finding suspending strings (or linear features) in noisy surrounds. This new method is quite clever and requires some modern computer power to accomplish (could not have been done 35 years ago without a large research computer). Their computer program essentially allows them to create an average brightness level along any line of image pixels starting at any (lowest) point and moving along at any constant tilt angle (−30 to +30 relative to vertical on the picture). The idea is that if a thread is darker (or brighter) than the average surrounding (sky) brightness, then the average brightness level along the pixel line that contains the string image will be darker (brighter) than the average brightness along other lines that start at the same (bottom) point and have different tilts or that start at other points and have similar or different tilts.

> Using this technique, they have discovered a line of pixels starting at the top of the UFO and going upward at an 11° slant which is, on the average, a bit darker than lines of pixels going upward at other slant angles. They conclude that they have discovered "the" suspending thread which was darker than the sky. They have found this sort of line of pixels in prints TRNT1 and 2 [Trent 1 and 2] but not in a second set of prints.

> Is this convincing? It could be if they could show that the "string line" is unique in the sense that they don't get the same sort of result if they start the analysis at any other point in the picture and scan the tilt over the same range of angles. If this "dark line" is unique yet there is no string (not a hoax), one would have to ask how such a line got there in both prints.

> One should also ask whether or not it makes sense for the string to be tilted about 11° in each picture. Was the supposed model swinging left and right as it also moved forward (toward the camera) and back?

Some debunkers of the McMinnville UFO photos say it is merely a toy about five or six inches in diameter. Investigations then focused on the technical side, such as figuring out how close or far away the camera actually was from the mysterious object.

Brad Sparks, on the same NICAP web page, argued against some of the internal logic of the IPACO report. He noted, for example:

> The IPACO debunkers never consistently follow through on a numerical result throughout the rest of their analysis to see if it fits and is physically consistent. They cannot make up their collective minds whether the UFO hoax model is 0.4 ft or 0.5 ft (about 5 inches or 6 inches). It cannot be both! It is a crucially important parameter and it is based on the most accurately determined parameters in all of the two photos, namely the angular diameters of the UFO's base (1.67° and 1.46° in Photos 1 and 2, respectively). If the hoax object was 5 inches in diameter, then the closest distance to camera, which is in Photo 1, must be about 14 ft according to the geometry of the angular size (angular size is roughly the size-to-distance ratio). This is mathematically locked and cannot be fudged or adjusted or obscured—as IPACO attempts to do.

So, to make their measurements work, they must change the parameters of their investigation. In other words, the five-inch model is fine for the first picture, but the measurements fail in the second, unless the model was six inches. That seems to rule out their small model explanation, and we're all back to the most likely answer that it is a small model, but there is no definitive proof for that.

Sparks, however, has found other discrepancies in the IPACO analysis of the photographs and their claim to have found the thread supporting the small model. Sparks wrote:

The IPACO debunkers claim to have discovered something—a purported thread above the UFO—that no one else has been able to see in 63 years, including high-tech image processing by the Jet Propulsion Lab director Robert Nathan, by Bruce Maccabee and others, that never found a thing. Naturally, IPACO did not conduct a control study to see if this was just noise in the film or photoanaly-sis. They checked only 60Â°, or 1/6th of a full 360Â° circle. They did not check underneath the UFO because obviously they know it's a hoax and so it cannot be something absurd like a thread below the object. But that's how one makes scientific checks. If an absurd result emerges, then it tells you the analysis is wrong. I can already see other "threads" in their data, which would make nonsense of their findings.

But worst of all, the purported IPACO "thread"—which cannot be seen visually—would be almost 1 inch in thickness (using the half-value width as a rough thread width; it is about 0.2Â° in angular width or about 1/7 or 1/8 of the width of the supposedly 5- or 6-inch object). What kind of "thread" is that, and why wouldn't a 1-inch-thick line—more like a rope or heavy cord—not be painfully obvi-ous in the photos?

All of this leaves us where we began. There is no definitive answer for this. Debunkers seem to find evidence that the case is a hoax and report what they find. But then others who support the idea of alien visitation look at the evidence and find nothing to suggest a hoax. The Trents don't seem to be the type of people who would perpetrate a hoax, and many argue they didn't have the sophistication to have done it.

If we look at this logically, the simplest answer is that this was a hoax because it does not require alien creatures to have defeated the long distances involved in travel between plane-tary systems.

However, that alone is insufficient to rule out the possibil-ity because we don't know what the science of an alien race 100 years, 200 years, 1,000 years more advanced than us could do. A thousand years ago, there was no industrial society and trav-el was limited and slow. A hundred years ago, there were the beginnings of an industrial society; there were electrical lights, trains, steamships, and the beginnings of wireless radio. Today, the entire knowledge of the human race is available through a smartphone and the proper data plan. Who knows what we'll be able to do 100 years from now, and one of those things might be travel among the stars.

> Debunkers seem to find evidence that the case is a hoax and report what they find. But then others who support the idea of alien visitation look at the evidence and find nothing to suggest a hoax.

July 2, 1952: Tremonton, Utah

The second movie footage provided to Project Blue Book and another that was examined by those on the Condon Committee was taken by Navy Warrant Officer Delbert C. Newhouse on July 2, 1952, north of the small Utah town of Tremonton, Utah (though it has been spelled Trementon by many over the years). Newhouse provided a brief statement to the Air Force about the case that is woefully inadequate, and there is no evidence that anyone in the Air Force attempted to get something a little more comprehensive from him about the shape, size, and color of the objects. The story began, according to the Project Blue Book files available through the National Archives with Newhouse writing:

> Driving from Washington, D.C., to Portland, Ore., on the morning of 2 July, my wife noticed a group of objects in the sky that she could not identify. She asked me to stop the car and look. There was a group of about ten or twelve objects—that bore no relation to anything I had seen before—milling about in a rough formation and proceeding in a westerly direction. I opened the luggage compartment of the car and got my camera out of a suitcase. Loading it hurriedly, I exposed approximately thirty feet of film. There was no reference point in the sky, and it was impossible for me to make any estimate of speed, size, altitude, or distance. Toward the end, one of the objects reversed course and proceeded away from the main group. I held the camera still and allowed this single one to cross the field of view, picking it up again and repeating for three or four such passes. By this time all of the objects had disappeared. I expended the balance of the film late that afternoon on a mountain somewhere in Idaho.

Navy Warrant Office Delbert Newhouse reported seeing "ten or twelve objects ... milling about in a rough formation" during a road trip with his wife in 1952.

When he finished with the filming, he put the camera equipment away and they all, meaning Newhouse, his wife, and children, got back in the car to continue the trip. Then, apparently after arriving at his new duty station, he developed the film and sent the original off to Hill Air Force Base in Utah, which eventually sent it on to Project Blue Book in

The Hill Air Force Base in Utah, where Newhouse sent his photographs to be analyzed.

Dayton, Ohio. According to the Condon Committee report William Hartmann, the investigator on this case, wrote, "The witness' original letter of 11 August offers the film for whatever value it may have in connection with your investigation of the so-called flying saucers."

And while all that is interesting, it turns out not to be the most important thing in that letter. Newhouse wrote, "one (1) 50-foot roll of processed 16 mm color motion picture film."

Ed Ruppelt, the chief of Project Blue Book at the time, wrote, "When I received the Tremonton films I took them right over to the Wright Field photo lab, along with the Montana Movie [a film taken in 1950 near Great Falls], and the photo technicians and I ran them twenty or thirty times. The two movies were similar in that in both of them the objects appeared to be large, circular lights—in neither one could you see any detail. But, unlike the Montana Movie, the lights in the Tremonton Movie would fade out, then come back in again. This fading immediately suggested airplanes reflecting light, but the roar of a king-sized dogfight could have been heard for miles, and the Newhouse family heard no sound."

Ed Ruppelt was chief of Project Blue Book at the time of the Newhouse incident. He compared it to UFOs seen in Montana.

The inadequate statement provided in the letter with the film didn't tell much and according to Ruppelt, they sent a list of questions to an intelligence officer. This interview was conducted on September 10, 1952, and included not only Newhouse, but his wife, Norma; son, Delbert Newhouse, Jr., then aged 14, and daughter Anne, then aged 12. This interview did nothing to clear up the questions that researchers would have so many years later and, according to Ruppelt, "The question 'What did the UFOs look like?' wasn't one of them because when you have a picture of something, you don't normally ask what it looks like."

The answers to the questions were received by teletype on September 12 and do little to resolve the questions of today. It is unclear why certain things were not asked and why certain information is not found in the files. While Ruppelt explained why they hadn't asked what the objects looked like, it should be noted that there is no real description of the length of the film. Going through the Project Blue Book files, there are a few vague references to the film being about thirty feet long, which, given the frames-per-second rate, works out to about 75 seconds. William Hartmann, who conducted the investigation for the Condon Committee in the late 1960s, wrote, "The film contains about 1200 frames ... i.e., about 75 seconds...."

According to the teletype sent by the intelligence officer, all the Newhouses were interviewed at home, all participated in the interview, and the answers to the questions were as follows:

1. No sound heard during the observation. 2. No exhaust trails or contrails observed. 3. No aircraft, birds, balloons, or other identifiable objects seen in the air immediately before, during, or immediately after observation. 4. Single object which detached itself from the group did head in direction opposite original course and disappeared from view while still traveling in this direction. 5. Camera pointed at estimated 70 degrees elevation and described and [sic] arc from approx. due east to due west, then from due west to approx. 60 degrees from north in photographing detached obj[ect] heading in direction opposite original course. 6. Sun was approx. overhead of observer. Objects were approx. 70 degrees above terrain on a course several miles from

observer. 7. Weather conditions: Bright sunlight, clear, approx. 80 degrees temperature, slight breeze from east northeast approx. 3 to 5 mph. 8. No meteorological activity noted during that day. 9. Opinion regarding objects following CLN A. Light from objects caused by reflection. B. Objects appeared approx. as long as they were wide and thin. C. Appeared identical in shape. D. 12 to 14 objects. E. All appeared light color. F. No opinion. G. Appeared to have same type of motion except one object which reversed its course. H. Disappeared from view by moving out of range of eyesight. 10. No filters used. 11. One low hill 2 or 3 miles to right of U.S. HWY 30 dash S with observer facing north. Located approx. 10 miles north of Tremonton, Utah. 12. Other persons sighting object [names of wife, children]. Whole Newhouse family included in interview. 13. CPO [Chief Petty Officer sic s/b Chief Warrant Officer, a much higher rank] Newhouse and family have never sighted unidentified flying objects before. Newhouse stated that he never believed he would join the ranks of those reporting such objects prior to this observation…. CPO [sic] Newhouse stated he has been in the Naval service for over 19 years with service as a commissioned officer during WW 2….

From this point, the Blue Book file is filled with questions about the technical aspects of the film and the camera. On one document, in which it was revealed that Newhouse had not used a tripod, someone underscored that and added an exclamation point.

The Air Force analysis, done in the months following the sighting, did not yield any positive results. According to Ruppelt, "All they had to say was, 'We don't know what they are but they aren't aircraft or balloons, and we don't think they are birds.'"

In a document prepared by the U.S. Navy Photographic Interpretation Center on October 4, 1952, they found much the same thing but were more enthusiastic about it. This documentation provided some information that would become important later. Under references, the Navy reported that they had received approximately thirty feet of "processed 16 mm color motion picture film," which reinforces the data about the length of the film.

Under "Test and Procedures," the Navy investigators noted that the film was dry and brittle with a tendency to break. They carefully made a duplicate of that film and in the process did "some color correction … to permit better viewing of the objects."

> … the Navy investigators noted that the film was dry and brittle with a tendency to break. They carefully made a duplicate of that film and in the process did "some color correction…."

The Navy researchers explained how they determined the speed of the objects, making it clear that since they had nothing to provide them with a size which made the distance from the camera problematic, they selected a distance of five miles. Closer, they believed that the images would resolve enough for identification. According to them, the speed was 3,780 miles an hour, which eliminated anything terrestrially based.

Under the "Discussion" section, they made a comment that most have overlooked. They said, "In the analysis conducted, no attempt is made to explain the phenomena, nor are the comments tempered by knowledge of present-day science (although its influence is felt)."

There were no conclusions drawn by those conducting the research, and they had no recommendations about the film, what should be done, or what could be done. The report was signed by L. W. Keith, but there is no mention of who he was or what his role in the research might have been.

The next mention of Newhouse's experience came in January 1953, when the Robertson Panel, a CIA-sponsored study of UFOs, was made. Because there was physical evidence available, meaning the film, it was one of those reports they wanted to review. Luis Alvarez, one of the scientists involved and who would eventually win a Nobel Prize, asked that the film be run several times and then suggested that the objects looked to him like seagulls riding on thermals. The rest of the panel agreed with him, and that was the answer they appended to the case.

Nobel Prize winner Luis Alvarez was a physicist, professor, and inventor who reviewed the Newhouse film and concluded it was most likely a flock of seagulls.

Ruppelt, in his book, suggested that they, meaning those at Blue Book and ATIC, had thought of the bird explanation months earlier. He wrote, "… several months later I was in San Francisco … and I watched gulls soaring in a cloudless sky. They were 'riding a thermal,' and they were so high that you couldn't see them until they banked just a certain way; then they appeared to be a bright white flash, much larger than one would expect from seagulls. There was a strong resemblance to the UFOs in the Tremonton movie. But I'm not sure this is the answer."

In a handwritten document dated "Memorandum for Record," filed on February 11, 1953, or after the analysis by the Navy and the Robertson Panel, and because the press had somehow learned of the existence of the Utah movie, a number of those involved with the UFO investigation, including Al Chop, a civilian at the Pentagon, suggested releasing the film. Starting with the second paragraph, the memo said:

> On 9 Feb 53, Mr. Chop called that he had written the release and showed it to Col. Smith of AFOIN–2A. They believed that there would be a question asked as to the findings of the Air Force and Navy photo labs and that these reports be released. If they weren't released, the press would begin to think they contained some "hot" material and that the Air Force was holding back important data....

> The Air Force lab analysis concludes that:

> a. They are reasonably certain that the brightness of the images on the film exceeds that of any bird.

> b. The objects are not spherical balloons.

> c. The objects could be aircraft. (Note: the absence of sound almost rules out aircraft. Aircraft in a "dogfight" can be heard at almost any altitude. In addition, the area of the sighting was not a restricted airspace area, and it is doubtful that such flying would be carried on in the airways. [Note in the original document.])

> The Navy report says the objects are:

> a. Self-luminous or light sources.

> b. Could not be aircraft or balloons.

> c. No bird is known to reflect enough light to cause the images shown on the film.

> It can be noted that the Navy people deduced this from their analysis of the brightness of the image on each frame. This required about 1,000 man-hours. It was brought out by two astronomers who heard a Navy briefing on the analysis of the movies that the method used to measure the brightness of each spot was wrong; therefore, the results of the study were wrong....

> If it is deemed advisable to release the movies quickly, state that the Air Force cannot positively identify the objects but they are reasonably sure that they are balloons or gulls; consequently, no further effort is going to be put into the incident. If the Navy and Air Force reports are requested, state that due to the meager data they used, the reports must be discounted. It would be rather poor policy to state that the Navy had made an error in the beginning of their analysis....

A close reading of the document exposes the flaws in the research here. The Air Force is suggesting that the objects are not positively identified, but

One problem with saying that the UFOs might have been a flock of birds such as seagulls, said some analysts, is that birds do not reflect light in the same manner as the unexplained objects did.

they might be balloons or birds. By offering these two explanations, the Air Force is actually suggesting they have no explanation, not to mention that it would seem that birds or balloons would be difficult to confuse. They should have selected one and stuck with it. The Robertson Panel offered them the opinions of experts so their position wouldn't have been difficult to defend. The Air Force did, however, say they had no explanation and that they weren't happy with the solutions being offered by their experts.

The next time that Newhouse was interviewed about the sighting was when he met with Ruppelt as they were shooting the commercial film *Unidentified Flying Objects*, A.K.A. *UFO*. Ruppelt wrote about that meeting in his book *The Report on Unidentified Flying Objects*. Ruppelt said:

After I got out of the Air Force I met Newhouse and talked to him for two hours [in 1954, I believe]. I've talked to many people who have reported UFOs, but few impressed me as much as Newhouse. I learned that when he and his family first saw the UFOs they were close to the car, much closer than when he took the movie. To use Newhouse's own words, "If they had been the size of a B-29, they would have been at 10,000 feet altitude." And the Navy man and his family had taken a good look at the objects—they looked like "two pie pans, one inverted on the top of the other!" He didn't just *think* the UFO's were disk-shaped, he *knew* that they were; he had plainly seen them. I asked him why he hadn't told this to the intelligence officer who interrogated him. He said that he had. Then I remember that I'd sent the intelligence officer a list of questions I wanted Newhouse to answer. The question "What did the UFO's look like?" wasn't one of them because when you have a picture of something you don't normally ask what it looks like. Why the intelligence officer didn't pass this information along to us I'll never know.

Also found in the Project Blue Book files, and dated 1955, is a report, "Analysis of Photographic Material Photogrammetric Analysis of the 'Utah' Film, Tracking UFO's," created for the Douglas Aircraft Company and written by Dr. R. M. L. Baker. He provided an overview of the sighting that is consistent with the earlier reports found in the Blue Book file and other earlier sources, but then wrote, "He [Newhouse] described them as 'gun-metal-colored objects shaped like two saucers, one inverted over the other.'"

During his analysis, Baker tried several things. It had been suggested that the film was out of focus and that the objects were birds, or more specifically, seagulls. Baker wrote that examination of the film under a microscope showed that the objects were not out of focus. He wrote, "Examination under a microscope shows the camera to be well focused as the edges of the images are sharp and clear on many of the properly exposed frames."

> Baker wrote that examination of the film under a microscope showed that the objects were not out of focus.

Baker did something that the others had not. He performed an experiment to find out what the capabilities of the camera were, and he wondered at what distance the birds would be unrecognizable blobs. According to his report:

> The rectangular, flat white cardboards of the ... experiments represented very roughly the configuration of birds. The light reflected by such a surface is probably greater than that from a curved feather surface of a bird.... Many of the images on the "Utah" film have an angular diameter of 0.0012 radians (some as large as 0.0016 radians), thus they might be interpreted as one-foot birds at 600' to 800', two-foot birds at 1,200' to 1,600', or three-foot birds at 2,400' to 3,200'. At these distances, it is doubted if birds would give the appearance of round dots; also they would have been identifiable by the camera if not visually. However, actual movies of birds in flight would have to be taken to completely confirm this conclusion.

> The images are probably not those of balloons as their number is too great and the phenomenon of flaring up to a constant brightness for several seconds and then dying out again cannot well be associated with any known balloon observations.

Baker's conclusion, written on May 16, 1956, or nearly four years after the sighting, was, "The evidence remains rather contradictory, and no single hypothesis of a natural phenomenon yet suggested seems to completely account for the UFO involved. The possibility of multiple hypotheses, i.e., that the Utah UFOs are the result of two simultaneous natural phenomena, might possibly yield the answer. However ... no definite conclusion could be obtained."

But even this scientific investigation isn't without controversy. Tim Printy, at his skeptic's website, wrote:

> In 1955, Dr. Robert Baker conducted an evaluation of the film and also interviewed Newhouse again. Newhouse now added more information that seemed to disagree with his earlier testimony.

> When he got out, he observed the objects (twelve to fourteen of them) to be directly overhead and milling about. He described

them as "gun-metal-colored objects shaped like two saucers, one inverted on top of the other." He estimated that they subtended "about the same angle as B-29's at 10,000 ft" (about half a degree, i.e., about the angular diameter of the moon).

In his earliest reports he stated that he could not estimate size or distance, now he was able to do this as well as describe the shape. Newhouse suggests before filming they appeared overhead and then went off in the distance when he finally got the camera going.

A close reading of the various sources, including Ruppelt's book and the Condon Committee report, does not support the conclusion that Newhouse was giving any different answers. Baker's source seemed not to be a new interview, but what Newhouse had told Ruppelt in 1954, and that Newhouse was not saying the objects were the size of B-29s at ten thousand feet, but looked to be the size of the bomber if it was at that altitude. It was the same as a witness describing a UFO as the size of a dime held at arm's length.

> At that point, the Air Force endorsed the "birds" explanation, and that is the way it is carried in the Blue Book records.

At the same time, that is 1956, the Air Force, in response to the release of *UFO*, put together a press package to explain some of the cases mentioned in the film. At that point, the Air Force endorsed the "birds" explanation, and that is the way it is carried in the Blue Book records. The documents suggest that the Air Force was more interested in lessening the impact of the movie than they were in supplying proper solutions to the cases. In other words, their acceptance of the bird explanation was a public relations ploy.

The next analysis came when the Condon Committee conducted its investigation in the late 1960s. William Hartmann added little of importance to the case. He noted the length of the film, which coincided with the claim that the sequence was about 30 feet long or about 75 seconds. Lance Moody had suggested that if the film could be recovered now, the length could be measured, which would answer some questions that have developed in the last few years. The problem is that the Air Force file makes it clear the film had been cut. On September 15, 1952, Major Robert E. Kennedy sent Newhouse a letter saying, "The final footage of the mountain scenery will be detached and returned to you as soon as possible." This point, too, would become important later.

Hartmann reviewed all the information available, including, apparently, a complete copy of the Project Blue Book file. He provided a quick history of the investigations and did mention that during Baker's earlier investigation Newhouse provided "... substantially the same account, with the additional information: 'When he got out [of the car], he observed the objects (twelve to fourteen of them) to be directly overhead and milling about. He described them as "gun-metal-colored objects, shaped like two saucers, one inverted of top of the other...."'"

Hartmann then made his own analysis, finally concluding, "These observations give strong evidence that the Tremonton films do show birds ... and I now regard the objects as so identified."

But this comes only after Hartmann rejected the statements by Newhouse, seeing the objects at close range. Hartmann wrote, "The strongest negative argument was stated later by the witness that the objects were seen to subtend an angle of about 0.5 degrees and were then seen as gun-metal colored and shaped like two saucers held together rim to rim, but the photographs and circumstances indicate that this observation could not have been meaningful."

Baker, in 1969 and in response to the negative findings of the Condon Committee, at a symposium sponsored by the American Association for the Advancement of Science, said that while Hartmann's analysis might be appealing, "[The] motion [of the objects] is not what one would expect from a flock of soaring

Dr. James E. McDonald was a meteorology professor at the University of Arizona at Tucson and senior physicist at the Institute for Atmospheric Physics.

birds; there are erratic brightness fluctuations, but there is no indication of periodic decreases in brightness due to turning with the wind or flapping. No cumulus clouds are shown on the film that might betray the presence of thermal updraft.... The motion pictures I have taken of birds at various distances have no similarity to the Utah film."

Now the case becomes more complicated. In 1970, meteorologist and physicist Dr. James E. McDonald interviewed Newhouse over the telephone, with his wife on the extension. In a letter to Arthur C. Lundahl reproduced on the NICAP website, McDonald wrote:

It was particularly good to have Mrs. Newhouse on the phone, since she was the one who first spotted the objects and watched them for an estimated minute or so while she was trying to persuade Newhouse to stop the car for a better look....

Both of them emphasized that it must have taken two or three minutes for Newhouse to hunt through their luggage and locate the camera and film, which were in separate suitcases. In the initial period, the objects were considerably closer to them than at the time he finally began shooting, Newhouse stressed. It was his estimate that the objects lay only about 10 degrees east of their zenith when they first got out of the car. He reported his angular-size estimate that has been noted elsewhere, namely about the comparative size of a B-17 [sic; should be B-29] at 10,000 ft....

... [O]ne of the key points that I wanted to check with Newhouse concerned the description given by Ruppelt ... namely, that they appeared to be silvery-gray, "gun metal," and like two pie pans face-to-face. Both Newhouse and his wife fully confirmed that Newhouse was comparing the shape to a discus....

I asked Newhouse if it was correct that he had given that description to Ruppelt after the latter had left the Air Force. He confirmed that, saying that the only time he personally talked to Ruppelt was at a filming session for that movie entitled "UFO" produced in 1954 or 1955. He guessed that meeting must have been in 1954, and Al Chop was also present at that discussion. He brought out the important point that he had also stressed the visually observed shape in those early portions of the sighting, when he was interviewed at his duty station in Oakland by an Air Force officer. He further remarked that he saw a copy of the officer's transcript of the interview, and that point appeared in the transcript....

... A rather interesting point, which I have never seen brought out before, was mentioned, almost by happenstance. It turned out that the footage which Newhouse submitted to the Air Force was spliced from about 20 feet that he shot at the end of one 50-foot magazine, plus about 40 feet that he shot on the first part of the next magazine. In other words, he had to change magazines in the middle of that shooting....

Newhouse said that the Air Force didn't send the originals back to him at any time. He wrote ATIC when a long time had elapsed, and what they did finally send back to him was a color print, which he stressed was distinctly inferior to the original. Not only that, but he was positive that they had cut out the first 10 or 20 feet, which were shot when the objects were very much closer and appeared much sharper on the film.... The missing footage, which he seemed positive was from the earliest and best parts of his original....

I found it interesting to learn that no contacts of any sort have been made with Newhouse since that movie was made. This evidently included Baker, as well as Hartmann and the Condon Project team.

I was particularly surprised that Bob Baker had not contacted him....

There are some things that can be deduced from all this. First, strangely, in the original interviews, there is no indication that anyone asked Newhouse or his family what the objects looked like. The statement he supplied as he submitted the film is devoid of any important information other than time and location. He does not describe the objects in any way other than to say, "... that bore no relation to anything I had seen before...."

The point to be made here is that Newhouse had more than nineteen years of service in the Navy, and it is reasonable to assume that he had seen seagulls soaring in the past. It would seem that if five minutes or so passed during the sighting, which includes 75 seconds of the filming, seagulls would have revealed themselves as such at some point. If he saw the UFOs at close range, as he claims, then the seagull explanation fails completely.

Newhouse told McDonald that he had told the intelligence officer about the shape and that the description had been included in the transcript of the interview. There is nothing like that in the Project Blue Book file, which means one of two things: Either Newhouse is mistaken, or the transcript was removed from the files.

Although some believe that Newhouse didn't mention the shape until more than twenty years later when I interviewed him, it is clear that Newhouse was talking about the shape within two years. He told Ruppelt that he had told that to the intelligence officer, but there is nothing to back up the claim. The best that can be said was that he mentioned it in 1954 and was consistent in those statements from that point. His original statement does not preclude the observation, only that it can't be documented in the Project Blue Book file.

> ... Newhouse had more than nineteen years of service in the Navy, and it is reasonable to assume that he had seen seagulls soaring in the past.

The criticism that Newhouse was unable to give size, distance, and shape estimates at first but later came up with them is invalid. It is quite clear he was merely saying that the objects appeared to be the size of a bomber at 10,000 feet. The description he offered in the September interview suggests a circular object (or one that is square or diamond shaped and very thin) isn't very helpful. In fact, given that vague information, it would seem that someone, Newhouse, his wife, or children, would have said something more definitive.

The real point where this falls apart is when Newhouse began talking to McDonald about his film. Here is the one thing that is well documented in the Project Blue Book files and for the believers, there are the statements made by Newhouse himself about the film when he submitted it to the Air Force.

> But more important ... is the claim that Newhouse shot footage on two separate rolls and that there was more than sixty feet of film. The documentation ... does not bear this out.

First, when he submitted the film, he made it clear there was a single enclosure, and that was a fifty foot roll of film. The document was created by Newhouse, so there is no reason to dispute it. It says nothing about there being more than fifty feet of film or that it was a spliced film, just the whole roll that included some of his vacation pictures and that it had been processed.

Second, there is Major Kennedy's letter of September 15 addressing some of the questions raised by Newhouse as he attempted to get his film returned to him. Kennedy mentioned that the final footage of the mountain scenery would be "detached" and returned. In that same letter, Kennedy wrote, "If it is agreeable to you, a duplicate of the aerial phenomena will be made and forwarded to you in lieu of the original. It is desired to retain the original for analysis."

Third, on February 17, 1953, Major Robert C. Brown wrote, "A copy of the original movie film taken by you near Tremonton, Utah, on 2 July, 1952, is being returned."

On November 17, 1953, Newhouse wrote to the Air Force:

About a year ago I mailed for evaluation a 16 mm Kodachrome original film to the Commanding Officer, Hill Air Force Base in Utah. The film was of unidentified flying objects sighted by my wife, my children, and myself.... I gave the Air Force permission to retain the original for use in the investigation.... My copy of the film has been damaged.... If the Air Force has completed its evaluation and has no further use for it, I would appreciate the return of the original....

On January 27, 1954, Lieutenant Barbara Conners wrote, "The Air Technical Intelligence Center is attempting to locate the original of a 35 mm [sic] film of unidentified flying objects taken by a Mr. D. C. Newhouse near Tremonton, Utah...." And then on February 23, 1954, CWO R. C. Schum wrote, "We are forwarding as Inclosure [sic] 1 one copy of you [sic] Tremonton, Utah, film...."

This means the Air Force attempted to cooperate with Newhouse and that Newhouse had given them permission to keep the original. They supplied a copy, which Newhouse ruined. He asked for the original, and the Air Force attempted to comply. It is obvious from the documentation that Newhouse's discussion about all this with McDonald is in error.

But more important than this trivia about originals and copies is the claim that Newhouse shot footage on two separate rolls and that there was more than sixty feet of film. The documentation, including that written by

Newhouse himself, does not bear this out. The best estimate is that there was thirty feet of film. There is a suggestion that the film lasted about seventy-five seconds, and with a sixteen-frame-per-second use, that works out to about thirty feet of film. All the documentation agrees with this assessment, and there is nothing to suggest that the film was cut and parts of it are missing.

The exception to this is that the Air Force, in the documentation, made it clear that seventeen frames had been detached from the main body of the film. This is about one second of footage. There is nothing to suggest that this footage was missing, and it was suggested in the documentation that the frames had been reattached.

In the end, there is no good evidence that Newhouse altered his story because the original investigation lacked competence. There are hints in the September 1952 interview of what the Newhouse family had seen, but it is not very clear. It can be argued that the description is of the saucers, but it could also be argued that the description is too vague to be of any real value to determine what he meant. It could be argued that his description was vague because he didn't get a good, close-up look at the objects.

It is clear that by 1954 Newhouse was providing a description that, if accurate, eliminates the seagulls as an explanation. It also seems that others such as Baker and Hartmann took the description from Ruppelt's book but didn't attempt to verify the accuracy of the information by contacting Newhouse. This is something of an interesting point. While Baker's analysis was about what the film showed, Hartmann was reinvestigating the case. He had the resources to locate Newhouse and talk to him. It would seem that any investigation of the whole case would require an interview with the witnesses to ensure that what had been reported that they said was, in fact, what they said. That was the reason for my interview when I talked to Newhouse in 1976. He verified that he had given the description of the objects to Ruppelt, which, of course, doesn't mean that the description was accurate, only that he said it to Ruppelt.

The one point that seems to stand out here is that Newhouse made the comment in 1954 before the Air Force began pushing the seagull explanation, but after the Robertson Panel had determined, to their satisfaction, that birds was the answer.

Here it boils down to the questions about the length of the film and if Newhouse switched magazines during the filming. Given the documentation available, it seems that these new details do not reflect the reality of the situation. Newhouse himself made it clear there was but a single roll of film, that it was only fifty feet long, and that part of it was detached and returned to him. If we wish to reject the case, this seems to be a good reason to do so. It suggests that his memory of the event has been cloud-

> It is clear that by 1954 Newhouse was providing a description that, if accurate, eliminates the seagulls as an explanation.

ed by outside influences over the years. When there is a conflict, the best course is to use the earliest of the interviews.

All of the investigators seem to find the conclusions that fit their own biases. The Air Force originally said it wasn't balloons or airplanes and probably not birds. The Navy said they couldn't identify the objects. Robertson said it was birds and dismissed it. The Air Force then said it was birds and has stuck with that answer for more than fifty years. Baker said he couldn't identify the objects, and Hartmann said he could.

But Hartmann, according to his report, didn't actually investigate the film. He reviewed the file and importantly, according to what Newhouse told McDonald, Hartmann did not interview him. In keeping with the mission of the Condon Committee, Hartmann identified the objects without bothering to consult the witnesses.

When all the evidence—when what the witnesses said and did and what is on the film—is examined, it is clear that there is no satisfactory answer for what was seen by Newhouse and his family. This is a case that provided some physical evidence. That evidence could lead to proof of something unusual in the air and that terrestrial explanations don't cover all the facts, if Newhouse saw the objects close by and that they were saucer shaped. If he didn't, then the evidence is not as strong as it could be.

> That evidence could lead to proof of something unusual in the air and that terrestrial explanations don't cover all the facts....

The Condon Committee and Hartmann had an opportunity to eliminate some of the confusion about this case. Although the sighting was more than fifteen years old when they began their work, they could have interviewed Newhouse and his family, they could have reviewed precisely what both the Air Force labs and the Navy labs discovered and interviewed some of those who worked on analyzing the film for the military. They could have attempted to replicate some of Baker's experiments, and if nothing else, could have had someone film seagulls gliding on the thermals in the Tremonton area. They did none of this, content to repeat what others had said and then draw the conclusion that the Air Force wanted based on what Lieutenant Colonel Robert Hippler had told them.

Here was an opportunity to apply science to the case, but they didn't do it. Here was a case that went beyond just fifteen year-old witness testimony. It was a case that provided some interesting evidence that could be taken into the laboratory and analyzed. Instead of doing science, instead of attempting to solve the mystery, it is clear they just did their job. The real conclusion should have been, at worst, insufficient data to move toward the extraterrestrial or toward a mundane explanation. At best, it would have been unidentified.

May 15, 1955: New York City

The case was labeled as a "hoax" by the Project Blue Book officers, but that might be more of a factor of the times rather than anything that was learned about the photographs. The chief of Project Blue Book at the time was Captain Charles Hardin, who assumed the post in March 1954. It was during this time that the 4602nd Air Intelligence Service Squadron began to assume more of the investigative role concerning UFOs. According to J. Allen Hynek in *The Edge of Reality*, in a memo that Ed Ruppelt wrote, "He [Hardin] definitely doesn't believe in UFOs ... in fact, he thinks that anyone who is even interested is crazy...."

The situation there became worse in February 1955, when ATIC told the Air Intelligence Service Squadron (AISS) commander that the purpose of the investigation was to reduce the number of unidentified cases. Jerome Clark, in his *UFO Encyclopedia*, wrote, "To accomplish that, according to [David] Jacobs, 'the Air Force now broadened the identified category to include probable and possible. These vague subcategories allowed the investigators to identify a report based on their estimation of probability that the sighting was a known phenomenon. If investigators could not definitely identify a sighting, they could solve the problem, and the case, by placing it in one of these two broadly defined categories. In press releases and final Blue Book evaluation statistics, the probable and possible subcategories disappeared....'"

This can be stretched even further by recognizing the subcategory that was known as "insufficient data for a scientific analysis." In these cases, and there are thousands in the Blue Book files, the sighting was not solved, but it was not put into the unidentified category because there was a "solution" of sorts attached. It wasn't identified and it wasn't explained, but then, it wasn't labeled as "unidentified," and that was the whole purpose.

It is in this situation that the witness, whose name was redacted from the Project Blue Book files, but who was Warren Siegmond, found himself when he reported that he had not only seen, but photographed, a UFO. According to the statement he gave the Air Force, and as reported on an Air Intelligence Information Report form dated June 30, 1955, the source [Siegmond] said:

> Mr. [redacted but is Siegmond] ... was on the roof of the apartment house preparing to take pictures of Miss [name redacted but is Jeannine Bouiller] with a camera he had rented for the occasion. While he adjusted the camera Miss [redacted but clearly is Miss Bouiller] gasped and pointed at something in the sky. Mr. [redacted but is Siegmond] turned to observe. He stated that he saw a large, opaque, airborne object to the west at an elevation of 45 [degrees]. The object hovered momentarily, then moved very rapidly to the north

Model Jeannine Bouiller was the intended subject of Siegmond's camera when he instead saw the UFOs.

on a bounce. It returned to its original position with the same bouncing motion, and the process was repeated a second time. It then disappeared in the northern sky. When first sighted, the object was opaque, becoming almost translucent as it moved to the north. It gleamed in the sunlight as though metallic. At no time during the 1″ minutes of the sighting was there any sound or visible exhaust trail. Mr. [redacted but is Siegmond] utilized the rented camera to take pictures of the object in flight.

The document was signed by Major William C. van Horn, who was the officer in charge of Detachment 3, 4602nd AISS. The investigators were Captain John A. Quinn and Staff Sergeant Sylvester E. Castillo. The report was approved by Colonel John M. White, Jr.

There is a section of the report that discusses the reliability of the witnesses. It said that Siegmond was a television technician, that he had two years of college and had been an anti-aircraft gunner in the European theater during the Second World War. Under reliability, it said:

[Siegmond] was extremely cooperative, even profuse in answering questions and recounting the events surrounding the sighting. He had been somewhat disappointed that the Air Force had apparently abandoned further inquiry into the "Flying Saucers" and expressed satisfaction and enthusiasm that the investigation was to be reinstituted. He stated that as soon as the negatives of the "Saucer" were developed, he took them to the offices of *Life* magazine and to the *New York Journal-American*. Both organizations declined to publish them, the latter insisting that water vapor on the camera lens had caused the "Saucer" effect. Finally, the *New York World-Telegram* agreed to publish the pictures together with an article on the sighting. Source stated that subsequent to publication of the article, he received many requests for prints on a cost basis. In the course of conversation, Source mentioned that he had been interested in "Saucer Phenomena" for some time prior to the actual sighting. He is not participating actively, attending "Saucer Club" mettings [sic], etc. Continuing in this vein, Source demonstrated more than a cursory knowledge of the terminology and more names of "Flying Saucer" literature, e.g., Adamski, Keyhoe, Vaeth. Throughout interview, it was obvious that Source is enjoying the publicity and speculation caused by his sighting. In view of the above, and considering what might be termed a neurotic susceptibility to give credence to "Flying Saucers," Source is considered to be of extremely dubious reliability.

The reasons for rejecting Siegmond as a source seemed to be nothing more than he had an interest in UFOs and that he took his pictures to various outlets, probably in an attempt to sell them. This doesn't seem to be an unreasonable action by someone who had just taken pictures of something that he thought of being a flying saucer. *Life* had, after all, published photographs of UFOs in the past and had published articles about them as well. That Siegmond thought the news media would be interested doesn't seem to be that outrageous.

The investigation continued in that same vein. The investigators reported that Bouiller was employed by the French Government Tourist Office, but they were unable to learn any more about that. Under reliability, they wrote:

Source apparently occupies same apartment as Mr. Siegmond. She was present during the interview with the latter. She remained silent during the conversation and did not volunteer any additional, original information on the sighting. Although she appeared to be calm and confident, Source conferred with Mr. Siegmond before venturing an answer to questions posed by the investigators. She indicated a reluctance to discuss her occupation, etc., and efforts in this direction were not pressed. Her description of the sighting coincided identically with that of Mr. Siegmond. In view of her obvious "rapport" with the opinions of Mr. Siegmond, Source is considered unreliable.

Which, given the attitude of the time and of the Air Force investigators, it is not surprising that they found her unreliable. Again, there has been no evidence that they were participating in a hoax, and if the sighting had been made as described, then their memories of it would coincide.

The report continued, with the note, "Submitted the negatives of the sighting fur-

The military report concerning Siegmond as a reliable witness stated that he had been interested in UFOs and was familiar with the terminology and people involved in ufology. It was suspected Siegmond was just looking for attention.

nished by Mr. Siegmond to M/Sgt Busch, Stewart AFB Photo Lab, for inspection and evaluation. The camera was adjudged to be of inferior quality. The negatives showed no evidence of retouching. Absence of clarity and definition in the negative thought to be caused by camera motion as well as imperfect exposure."

Deeper into the report, there is finally the analysis of the photographs. The investigator wrote:

Disregarding the slight blurring effect produced by camera movement, all the buildings shown in the negatives are in focus. The water tower shown in negative #2 is not more than 300 feet from the camera lens. It is sharply outlined. The object is never in focus, nor can its shape be determined with any degree of certainty. Source [Siegmond] stated that the exposures were made with the range element of the camera set at infinity. Objects at a distance greater than 15 feet to 20 feet should be in focus. Therefore, it may be postulated that the object was less than 15 feet from the camera lens. Consequently, the object was relatively minute, probably less than 6 inches across.

That would seem to suggest, then, that the pictures were of a small model. However, Siegmond had described the object as moving, so it is possible that the blurring that so greatly worried the Air Force investigators was caused by the motion of the object rather than it being close to the camera lens. In fact, a copy of a teletype news wire story said, "An Air Force officer who was shown the pictures said, 'Whatever it was, it was moving.'"

There is a second point to this aspect. Siegmond had taken ten pictures of the UFO, but, according to the "druggist" who had developed the film, only five had come out. That means that five of the shots were no good.

The Air Force did seem to pursue a "real" investigation. They contacted both the U.S. Weather Service and Air Force weather experts, who said that the object was not some sort of cloud or "cloud activity."

> ... it is possible that the blurring that so greatly worried the Air Force investigators was caused by the motion of the object rather than it being close to the camera lens.

They ruled out other sources for the object. It was a Sunday, so it was suggested that the smoke and steam was eliminated because people wouldn't be at work. They found no flights in the area at the time, which ruled out most aircraft.

The conclusion, however, was: "The fact that the source was a 'saucer fan' and was particularly interested in publicity seems to substantiate the possibility of a hoax."

Although the Project Card suggested that the reason for the hoax evaluation was explained on the Air Intelligence Information Report, the reasons turn out to be based not on any real evidence but on the reaction of the witnesses to the sighting. There is little real evidence that the pictures are faked but given the attitude of the Air Force at this point in the investigation, it is not surprising that they labeled the case as a hoax. While it can be argued that there is no supporting evidence for the sighting, other than the pictures, and no other witnesses, at the end of the day, the label is unfair. Insufficient for a Scientific Analysis would have been a fairer label.

December 18, 1966:
Bear Mountain State Park, New York

The Air Force, after a quick analysis, decided, "Photo: Hoax. Photo does not substantiate the witnesses' description of alleged UFO."

The quick description was that the object was long with a hump on its back. The color was silver to brown. The witness said that he didn't know how big the object was, but thought it was big. He would later suggest that it was it was about twenty feet long. The object appeared to wobble, and it disappeared behind a fire tower on a 1,320-foot hill.

The official report, which was gathered within days of the sighting in a telephone interview, revealed that there was a single UFO, that there was no sound or exhaust, and that it had no wings. The pictures were taken about dusk.

First Lieutenant Thomas A. Knutson was the investigating officer. He wrote, "The initial interview was by telephone. The pictures were received 1½ weeks after the call. A second interview (personal) was conducted after receipt of the photographs and Mr. [name redacted but is Vincent Perna, 23] furnished the negative." Although it is unclear from the Project Blue Book file, Perna apparently took four pictures before the object disappeared.

This sighting would be of no real value, even with the photographs, except for the Air Force conclusion and Dr. J. Allen Hynek's response to that conclusion. On February 20, 1967, the Air Force provided its solution to the case. On the official form, located in the Project Blue Book files, Douglas M. Rogers offered his opinion:

> Examination of the negative has negated double exposure and/or retouching. The photographs appear genuine insofar as content is concerned, however, no satis-

Bear Mountain State Park in New York state, where a UFO was spotted a week before Christmas 1966.

factory explanation could be made of the unidentified object. The object appears to be circular in planform, basically flat in cross-section with a domed "superstructure." The object appears to be situated beyond the foreground trees, indicating a diameter in excess of eight inches, and the relative clarity indicates it to be substantially nearer than the background trees. The object could have a diameter as great as two or three feet. No attempt at "panning" was indicated as evidenced by the sharpness of the general scene. The object exhibits some small degree of blurriness indicating motion, the direction of which could not be ascertained.

The report was approved by Major William L. Turner, who was the chief of the photo analysis branch, and Wilber Price, Jr., who was the chief of the exploitation division.

Hynek thought that the conclusion was "completely unfounded and unjustified." He sent a letter to Major Hector Quintanilla, who was the Chief of Project Blue Book at the time. Hynek wrote:

Dear Major Quintanilla:

On re-examination I find no substantiation for the evaluation of hoax, particularly in view of the photo analysis report, No. 67–10, dated 20 February 1967, which contains no information upon which

Major Hector Quintanilla (seated), along with some of his Project Blue Book staff. Hyek wrote the major an unhappy letter after the Air Force concluded the 1966 Bear Mountain sighting was a hoax.

a hoax can be based. To the contrary, the report stated that close examination of the negative negated double exposure and/or retouching. The photographs appear genuine insofar as content; however, no satisfactory explanation could be made of the unidentified object. The lack of a satisfactory explanation of the unidentified object does not constitute sufficient reason to declare a hoax. Further, the interviewer considers the witness to be a reliable source.

After examination of the print by myself and by Mr. Beckman of the University of Chicago, we feel that the original negative should be requested for further examination. Mr. Beckman, a qualified photo analyst, disagrees with the photo analysis presented in the report as to the distance of the object. He points out that the depth of field extends much farther than indicated in the report. It will be noted, from the print, that the focus is poor in the entire periphery of the picture regardless of distance; only in the center of the picture is the focus good, and this good focus extends essentially to infinity. Consequently, no judgment can be made as to the real size of the object, if this judgment is based on the quality of focus.

The photo of the UFO was taken near Tiopati Lake. The size of the craft is difficult to judge.

My recommendation is, therefore, that the evaluation be changed from hoax to unidentified.

The letter was signed by Hynek, who was, at the time, their scientific consultant, but the recommendation wasn't followed. The "hoax" evaluation was left intact.

It could be argued, and in fact Hynek does say it, that "… the Air Force was not interested in finding out all of the possible facts—or a more thorough investigation might have been conducted."

It could also be argued that by this time, that is, early 1967, Hynek had jumped ship and was always in conflict with the Air Force. He has said that there was animosity between him and Quintanilla at that time. He might have argued with any evaluation the Air Force made.

But what about this Mr. Beckman? He isn't employed by Northwestern University where Hynek works, seems to have no stake in the case one way or the other, and he apparently agrees with Hynek's evaluation. Beckman offers a counter to what seemed to be a solid Air Force analysis that had no other mission than to evaluate a photograph of a flying saucer.

In the end, it seems like a case of picking a side and arguing the point. There is no evidence of tampering with the negative or the prints, so the conclusion that it is a genuine picture seemed to be confirmed. That evaluation, for those paying close attention, meant that no one had doctored the print or the negative. But it did not mean that the object photographed wasn't a small model suspended some distance beyond the nearest trees and the farthest. Given that the camera had a set focal length, there simply wasn't enough evidence to make a positive determination so that both sides could make claims that were hard to justify.

There is one other point to this. In 1967, the University of Colorado was beginning their investigation of UFOs for the Air Force. It would seem that a photographic case that was only a few months old would be of interest to that project. They could have talked to the witness; they could have evaluated the photograph and then would have been able to examine the camera. It was all very timely for them, but there is no evidence that they made the effort to do so. Maybe they took the Air Force conclusion as an accurate evaluation and didn't want to waste their time on a hoax. Hynek's letter wasn't sent to Quintanilla until November, which might be another reason that the Condon Committee hadn't followed that lead. Given that, they might not have thought it was worth the effort to investigate for themselves.

June 21, 1968: Flushing, Queens, New York

The Air Force would eventually label this case as "Insufficient Data" and given the circumstances, that might be the fairest evaluation possible. This is a case where there is a single chain of evidence, but that chain contains three slides of the UFOs over a bridge along the New Jersey Turnpike. The photographer, whose name was redacted from most of the case file, was Conrad Iacono, the president of an advertising agency.

According to documents in the Project Blue Book files, Iacono was traveling with a companion to Washington to take pictures of Resurrection City, which explained the camera. In a document dated August 28, 1968, Iacono is quoted as saying:

> In advertising, we are always taking pictures and we have a roomful of pictures, thus the reason for the camera. Leaving the New Jersey Turnpike when I noticed a beautiful sky and the sun was setting into it. I had the camera <u>outside the car window</u> [underlining added by a reviewing officer] and we were traveling approximately 65 mph. I was simply snapping away. My visitation [vision] was limited since we were in a small sports car. I continued to take pictures while we crossed the bridge. It was not until after the photographs were developed and we were sitting in the projection room that we say [saw] a series of very bright lights that were over the bridge. We just stopped and looked at them. There were two here and two there. I have a pilots [sic] license and have never seen anything like this before. Then then [sic] put the next photo on the

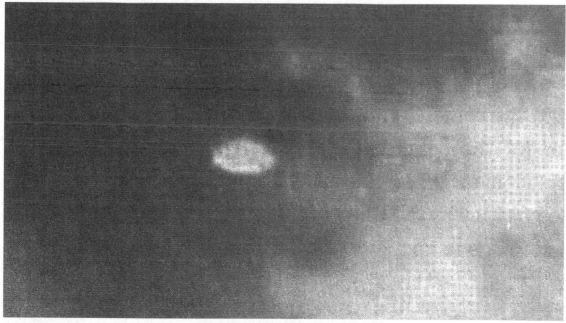

Conrad Iacono snapped this photo of UFOs over the New Jersey Turnpike in 1968.

screen. This shows the objects passing over the bridge, perhaps 2–300 ft above the bridge [underlining added by a reviewing officer]. These objects were disc shaped, with a dome with indentations. Very clear, and they look metallic. The next photo shows them leaving the bridge, going south, following the path of the river. I had decreased the lens opening, the objects are reflecting the light of the sun. There are three photographs … the first shows the outside of my car and the bridge is about 1½ miles in the distance, the next photograph we were on the bridge and the next photograph we have just left the bridge.

There are two points in the above narrative that are important. First is that he was holding the camera outside the car while traveling at 65 miles an hour. That seems to be a dangerous way to take pictures, and it would seem that it would be easy to fumble the camera.

Second is that the witness, Iacono, didn't see the objects until after the film was developed. He did answer the questions on the UFO Questionnaire that the Air Force sent. He said the objects were oval, they were a luminescent yellowish–white, and that there was "some type of shadow, indicating structure is visible." The object made no noise, and there were no contrails, smoke, or exhaust seen.

It was mentioned on the form that the objects were first seen in the photographs, but they were not the reason for taking the pictures. A note at the bottom, written by the preparing officer, probably Second Lieutenant Michael J. Conaway, said, "Mr. [redacted but obviously Iacono] saw the objects after developed slides had been returned to him. His only reason for taking photographs was to get pictures of the sunset."

Conaway, who was apparently assigned to the Suffolk County Air Force Base in New York as a public information officer, was contacted by Iacono. It is not clear from the file if Iacono had asked for him personally, meaning that he had meant Conaway in connection with some sort of public affairs project or if Conaway had an additional duty as the UFO officer. Conaway interviewed Iacono on the telephone and later in person.

The most disturbing aspect of the case, however, is a sentence in a "Memo for the Record," that is dated August 27. Conaway had called Hector Quintanilla in the middle of the afternoon on that date, with a UFO report that he, Conaway, thought was important. Conaway told Quintanilla that "… the problem was that a man had inadvertently took a photograph of a UFO while taking pictures of the sunset. The man claims they are valuable photographs and will not send them into the Air Force because they are so valuable and he has had numerous money offers [underlining in the original] from magazines."

One reason for the fuzzy quality of the photos was that they were taken from a moving vehicle.

Interestingly, the memo also said that for the Air Force to examine the photographs, they would need the original negatives, apparently not knowing that these were slides, so there would be no negatives. The original, first generation slides would be the same thing.

Then there is a statement in the memo that does show the Air Force attitude about the reality of the situation. "Colonel Quintanilla told Conaway that this man is probably trying to get the Air Force to say that his photographs are authentic. Well, all photographs are authentic, but the UFOs aren't."

While the point raised by Quintanilla in this case seems to have some validity, it is also interesting to note that the Air Force never did evaluate the photographs. The Project Card noted, "Additional photographic information was requested but was not received untill [sic] after the original photos had been returned."

In the file, in a letter dated March 12, 1969, Quintanilla wrote to Iacono, "On 10 Mar 69, we received your completed Photographic Data Sheet [which included specific photographic information such as camera type, film type, whether or not a tripod was used, etc.]. On 3 Mar 69, we returned your slides to your listed address (see attached xeroxed letter). If you left a forwarding address with the Postal Department, you should have received them by now. If, however, they are returned to this office, we will notify you that they have been returned to us and we will again submit them to our photographic department for analysis."

Given the way things were going, and given this was March of 1969, just months before the Air Force would announce the end of Project Blue Book, it is no surprise that there is no additional information about the slides. Iacono apparently never bothered to return them to the Air Force for analysis, and the Air Force made no attempt to retrieve them. It is clear from Quintanilla's letter that Iacono had moved; at the bottom of the Photographic Data Sheet, he had written that he had moved but provided the new address as well as both his home and office telephone numbers. Had the Air Force wanted to investigate further, they had sufficient information to do so. That never happened.

Copies of the slides do appear in the Project Blue Book files, but they are black and white prints that reveal little other than that the objects are saucer shaped. Iacono provided several illustrations with his original report that he had made after he and his fellows had studied the pictures and had used a projector to "blow them up." These illustrations do show an object that is saucer shaped, with what looks to be a dome on top. It also shows the indentations that could be darkened portholes or something similar.

The Air Force might have lost interest in the case simply because there was no visual sighting to go with the slides. They might have lost interest because it seemed that Iacono was attempting to get the Air Force to authenticate his slides which, if he had offers from magazines, might have increased their value. Or they might have lost interest because by March 1969, Quintanilla had to know the project was going to be dropped. The Condon Committee and other elements of the Air Force knew what results they would report, and this would enable the Air Force to stop investigating UFOs.

November 1957—USA

Although it has been suggested for years, the rapid increase of UFO sightings didn't suddenly materialize in November 1957, but it had been building slowly, beginning in the summer and finally peaking on November 6. A review of the sighting reports, as made to Project Blue Book for the year, seems to underscore this conclusion. A statistical analysis of the number of reports made show that they averaged about one a day, or about 30 a month, until July, when the number doubled to 70. They remained at about two a day until October, when the numbers jumped again. In October there were more than three a day, and finally, in November, the Air Force was receiving dozens of reports every day.

This rather rough analysis contains only the numbers for sightings reported to the Air Force officially and not those that were considered "additional sighting reports but not cases," which was the Air Force way of avoiding an investigation of them.

A few of those earlier reports suggested what was going to happen in November. On October 30, two people driving near Casper, Wyoming, saw a large, glowing, egg-shaped object. They tried to turn around, but the car engine sputtered and stalled. They finally got it started and turned, but it stalled again. When the car began to operate properly, they sped away so that they didn't see how the UFO vanished.

The next day, two couples in Lumberton, North Carolina, saw an object they believed to be 200 feet long, high up in the sky. They said that it rose straight up, spouting flames, and flew away. As it began to maneuver, the car stalled but when it was gone, they were able to restart their car.

This would become the theme for the sightings of November 1957. Dozens reported that their cars stalled, the lights dimmed, and the radios failed while the UFO maneuvered near them. Once the craft moved off into the distance or had vanished, then the car engines, the lights, and the radios began to operate properly.

November 2, 1957: Levelland, Texas

On November 2, just hours before the sightings began in Levelland, Texas, Technical Sergeant Alfred A. Calvin, along with a civilian witness who was not identified in the Project Blue Book files other than to note he was a U.S. Civil Service employee, saw a submarine-shaped object sitting on the road. It was about 30 to 40 feet long and about 8 feet high. According to an Air Intelligence Information Report dated November 4:

> The observer rounded a curve and went over a slight knoll in the road when his headlights lit an object sitting in a field just off the road. Almost immediately a flash of light appeared over the observer's automobile, and his headlights went out at this time. After bringing his car to a stop approximately 100 feet past the object, the observer started to back up to investigate the object. After putting his car in reverse, he changed his mind and started forward again. His headlights came back on at this time.

There were other details from the Project Blue Book file. The object was white on both ends, with a red area in the center. There seemed to be a white flag on the top, but it wasn't clear if the flag was attached to the object or if it

A road leading into Levelland, Texas, where the UFO landed.

was being held by a figure. They watched the object for three minutes, and it was still sitting on the ground when they left.

Air Force Captain John F. Staley conducted the investigation of the sighting on November 4. Although he had the name of the other witness, there is no evidence that Staley ever spoke to him. Instead, the conclusion drawn was that Calvin was an unreliable witness, and there seemed to be no follow-up on the sighting. That conclusion might have been based solely on the idea that Calvin had seen a humanoid figure in relation to the UFO.

Although this sighting took place in the Texas panhandle, northeast of Amarillo and not all that far from the Oklahoma border, the center of attention would shift to the southwest and to Levelland some 17 or 18 hours later. The interesting aspects of this were the claims that the UFO somehow affected the car's operation and the bright red color described by the witnesses.

In the early evening, two farmers near Pettit, Texas, working their fields, reported that both combines failed when a glowing object passed overhead. When the object was gone, the combines began to function again.

At 9:30, a single witness near Seagraves, Texas, southwest of Levelland, spotted a light on the highway. As he approached, both his engine and headlights failed. Moments later, as the light took off, his car began to function again.

It was about two hours later that Pedro Saucedo and Joe Salaz were driving just north of Levelland. Saucedo would eventually provide a statement for the Air Force investigator on this, Staff Sergeant Norman Barth. Saucedo wrote:

> To whom it may concern, on the date of November 2, 1957, I was traveling north and west on route 116, driving my truck. At about four miles out of Levelland, I saw a blue flame, to my right, front, then I thought it was lightning. But when this object had reach [sic] to my position, it was different, because it put my truck motor out and lights. Then I stopped, got out, and took a look, but it was so rapid and quite [sic] some heat that I had to hit the ground, it also had three colors, yellow, white, and it looked like a torpedo, about 200 feet long, moving about 600 to 800 miles an hour.

His passenger, Joe Salaz, who apparently was not interviewed by Barth, sat petrified with his eyes glued to the blue-green object as the glow faded into a red so intense that he couldn't look directly at it. The object rested on the ground for three or four minutes while Salaz sat still, as if motion would attract attention. Although as frightened as Saucedo, he remained where he was, and he got a very good look at the UFO.

As the UFO disappeared and Saucedo crawled from under his truck, both the lights and engine began working again,

> The object rested on the ground for three or four minutes while Salaz sat still, as if motion would attract attention.

though it is not clear if Saucedo actually started the engine or if it sparked back to life on its own. Now afraid that he might run into the object if he continued to Levelland, he drove to another town to call the Levelland police at about 10:50 P.M. A deputy sheriff identified by some as A. J. Fowler listened to his report, but laughed it off as just another flying saucer story, ignoring the obvious distress of the witness. Or, as Fowler believed at first, the caller was drunk and seeing things, and that, too, meant he paid no attention to the witness.

Also driving in that area was Newell Wright, a 19-year-old college student at Texas Tech in Lubbock. He was nearing Levelland when he glanced at his dashboard ammeter. Wright told the Air Force investigator:

> I was driving home from Lubbock on state highway 116 at approximately 12:00 P.M. when the ammeter on my car jumped to complete discharge, then it returned to normal and my motor started cutting out like it was out of gas. After it had quit running, my lights went out. I got out of my car and tried in vain to find the trouble.

> It was at this time that I saw this object, I got back into my car and tried to start it, but to no avail. After that I did nothing but stare at this object until it disappeared about 5 minutes later. I then resumed trying to start my car and succeeded with no more trouble than under normal circumstances.

Later Wright provided some additional details. He said that the object was oval shaped and that he thought it was about the size of a baseball held at arm's length. He estimated that the object was about seventy-five to a hundred feet long. One of the important facts was that he had the opportunity to get a very good look at the object, which wasn't all that far away, and it stayed on the ground for several minutes.

Barth's evaluation of Wright said, "SOURCE seemed to the investigator to be very sincere about his sighting. He was appalled at the amount of publicity given him and was anxious to have the sighting resolved. He was unhesitating in his replies; however, during the course of further questioning, he admitted uncertainty in some of his answers. SOURCE can be considered usually reliable...."

About the same time, Jim Wheeler was driving along Route 116 some four miles from Levelland when he spotted an egg-shaped object sitting on the road. He told National Investigations Committee on Aerial Phenomena (NICAP) investigator James A. Lee that the object cast "a glare over the area."

As he approached, his lights dimmed and his motor stopped. As he started to get out of the car, the UFO rose into the sky. As it disappeared, the car lights came back on and he could restart his car. He called the police in Levelland as soon as he could.

At just after midnight on November 3, Ronald Martin saw a red-glowing, egg-shaped object sitting on the road about four miles east of Levelland. As he approached to within about a quarter mile, his car engine died and his lights went out. While the UFO sat on the ground, Martin said the color was bluish-green. When he started to get out of his car, the UFO lifted off swiftly and silently. As it disappeared, Martin's car engine started again and the lights came on.

But there is a discrepancy with this report. According to NICAP records, Martin didn't say anything about the electromagnetic effects cutting off his engine. According to that report, he saw the object first in the air, but that it landed about 300 or 400 feet in front of him. He didn't report this to the Levelland Police until the next afternoon.

Almost as the police in Levelland hung up the telephone from talking with Wheeler, Jose Alvarez (or Alverez, depending on the source) near Whitharral called to report that he had seen an egg-shaped object that killed his car's engine. And, a few minutes later, Frank Williams walked into the station to report the same sort of thing.

The reaction of law enforcement in Levelland was that someone was playing some sort of an elaborate joke for some unknown reason. No one there believed that a glowing, red egg or a bluish-green oval was terrorizing the populace. Besides, the weather was poor, with mist and drizzle, and there had been thunderstorms in the vicinity, off and on all evening, at least according to what Barth would later report to his headquarters. The Air Force would claim that these facts were important.

> As he started to get out of the car, the UFO rose into the sky. As it disappeared, the car lights came back on and he could restart his car.

As the police officers discussed it and tried to laugh it off, Jesse (also identified as James) Long called to report that he was driving on a country road northwest of Levelland when he came upon a landed, bright red craft. His truck engine died, and his lights went out. Unlike the others, Long got out of his truck and started to walk toward the object. Before he could get too close, the UFO took off in a sudden burst of speed. After it was gone, Long reported that his truck engine started easily.

By this point, Levelland Sheriff Weir Clem decided that something truly strange was happening around his town. But he didn't like the idea of chasing lights in the night sky, especially with the weather as bad as it supposedly was. Thunderstorms were still in the area, again according to what had been reported since the sightings, and though it was believed they had caused some problems earlier, it was no longer raining in town. There was no excuse for not trying to find the object.

Although it was reported that Clem only saw the object in the distance and it was little more than a red streak of light, testimony from the sheriff's

Levelland's sheriff, Weir Clem, believed something strange was possibly threatening his town, and he would witness the lights himself.

family, gathered by Don Burleson several decades after the fact, suggests otherwise. He had been told not to talk about what he had seen, and Clem told those who asked him later that he hadn't seen much. But there is some evidence from 1957 to support the idea that Clem was much closer to the object than reported. In document from the Project Blue Book files, which was apparently part of a newspaper account of the Air Force investigation, the reporter wrote that Clem said, "It lit up the whole pavement in front of us [he and a deputy] for about two seconds." He called it oval shaped and said that it looked like a brilliant red sunset.

In other words, Clem said, originally, that he had seen an object that was oval shaped and that it was close enough to the ground to light up the area. This would seem to suggest that Clem, like others before him, had been pressed into changing his public tale of the sighting.

The Air Force, when their investigation was completed, would say that there were only three people who saw an object, while the others who reported their engine troubles had seen little more than streaks of light in the distance or high overhead. A review of the Project Blue Book files provided the names of more than three people who saw the object, and one report even suggested that there had been 14 witnesses.

The Air Force investigator did not find, nor did he apparently try to find, some of the other witnesses who were in Levelland on November 2 but who had returned to their homes by November 6. It is clear from the Air Force files that Barth didn't speak to Jesse Long, of Waco, Texas, who said the object had killed his engine, which wouldn't be explained by the broken rotor in Saucedo's truck, an explanation offered by the Air Force some days after the events. Nor did the Air Force investigator find or interview Jim Wheeler, Jose Alverez, Ray Jones, or Frank Williams, the farmers near Petit, or the man driving from Seminole to Seagraves, all of whom said the proximity of the object had killed their car engines and dimmed their lights.

In an unclassified message to the commander of the Air Technical Intelligence Center, it was noted about the Levelland sightings that, "Contrary to

[Donald E.] Keyhoe's [Director of NICAP] and Washington press' reports only three, not nine persons witnessed the incident. Object observed for only few seconds, not lengthy period as implied by press. Mist, rain, thunderstorms and lightning discharges in scene of incident, fact not quoted in newspaper releases."

The trouble with all this is that several of the witnesses saw an object as opposed to just a light, that they watched it for minutes rather than seconds, and reported that the close approach of the craft stalled their cars. The Project Blue Book files contain much of this information, but it was ignored because it didn't fit into their narrative. Skeptics have followed the Air Force line, repeating the inaccuracies of their investigations as if they answered the questions.

> ... several of the witnesses saw an object as opposed to just a light, that they watched it for minutes rather than seconds, and reported that the close approach of the craft stalled their cars.

In fact, the Air Force made a big deal out of the bad weather in the area at the time of the sightings, even noting that newspapers hadn't mentioned this. In a press release issued on November 15, the Air Force evaluation was "Weather phenomenon of electrical nature, generally classified as 'Ball Lightning' or 'St. Elmo's Fire,' caused by stormy conditions in the area, including mist, rain, thunderstorms, and lightning."

Dr. Michael Swords commented on the Air Force investigation in *UFOs and Government*. He wrote:

> ... the Pentagon wrote this piece based solely upon the incompetence and rushed few hours' "investigation" by Ent AFB [Air Force Base, Colorado Springs, Colorado]. Those aware of what really happened, both during the event and the field study, knew the language of the press release was so far off target as to be laughable. Beyond that, a simple check of the newspaper or any weather service would have shown that there were no electrical storms, not even rain, in Levelland that evening.... All the weather elements listed in the "Evaluation" portion of the release as "causes" were nonexistent, and the pairing of ball lightning and St. Elmo's Fire indicated an embarrassing lack of scientific knowledge, as the two phenomena are utterly different.

The Levelland sightings were the beginning of the flood of November reports that the Air Force would receive. For those who have read the file carefully, it is clear that the offered explanations simply do not explain the sightings in a terrestrial fashion. This series of sightings could have been important had the Air Force not had a policy of explaining all sightings regardless of the facts. Then, only hours after the last of the sightings in Levelland, military police at White Sands Missile Range in New Mexico would make their own sightings.

November 3, 1957:
White Sands Proving Ground, New Mexico

Part One: 0230 Hours

About the time the sightings of the glowing, egg-shaped object were ending in Levelland, Texas, new sightings began at the White Sands Proving Ground (later White Sands Missile Range) near Alamogordo, New Mexico, about 275 miles away. The witnesses, two Army-enlisted members of the Military Police (MP), were on patrol at the Proving Ground when they made their sighting. Corporal Glenn H. Toy and PFC James E. Wilbanks were "up range" on what was considered a routine "motor patrol."

According to the documentation available in the Project Blue Book files (microfilm roll number 29), and in a sworn statement given to his commanding officer written on the day of the event, Toy said:

> At about 0238–0300 Sunday Morning [November 3, 1957] I, CPL X [Toy], and PFC Y [Wilbanks] were on patrol in Range Area when we noticed a very bright object high in the sky. We were proceeding north toward South Gate, and object kept coming down toward the ground. Object stopped approximately fifty (50) yards from the ground and went out, and nothing could be seen. A few minutes later, object became real bright (like the sun), then fell in an angle to the ground and went out. Object was approximately seventy-five (75) to 100 yards in diameter and shaped like an egg. Object landed by bunker area approximately three (3) miles from us. Object was not seen again. /END OF STATEMENT

The other soldier, Wilbanks, was not interviewed by the Air Force investigator, apparently Air Force Captain Patrick O. Shere, who arrived on November 6, because Wilbanks was on a three-day pass at the time of the investigation. Shere did, however, obtain a copy of the statement given to the commanding officer, which is the next best thing. It is also important to note that the statement was taken within hours of the sighting, before the details could be contaminated by other sighting reports from that area and before the Levelland case had hit the various national networks. Wilbanks' statement said:

> I, PFC Y [Wilbanks] saw a firelike object about 0230 the 3 Nov 57 [sic] between the bunker area and South Gate, this is about all I remember seeing; it was about sixty (60) or eighty (80) feet off the ground and it started down slow, then it went out for a while, then I saw it again and it started down in about a forty (40)-degree angle. It was about three (3) miles away and was about 120 feet in diameter. /END OF STATEMENT

Looking down toward the White Sands Missile Range.

The problem here, meaning that Wilbanks was on a three-day pass and unavailable for interrogation, was that Wilbanks would have been in the local area, certainly no farther away than El Paso or Albuquerque. Military regulations limited the distance a soldier could travel on a three-day pass in an attempt to prevent traffic accidents. Keeping the soldier in the local area meant that he or she wouldn't be tempted to drive home, which might be hundreds of miles away.

The second problem is that Wilbanks wouldn't have been incommunicado during that time. He would have had to leave contact information with his first sergeant so they could have recalled him. He could easily have been made available to Shere for an interview. In an attempt to gather information, Shere should have made the effort to interview Wilbanks, if for no other reason than to flesh out his signed statement.

Shere was not impressed with the reliability of either of the witnesses. He wrote that Toy appeared to be "quite ingenuous, naïve, and impressionable." He did note that Toy was "immaculately dressed in his Army uniform and meticulously observed military courtesy." He also noted that the "Source," Toy, had already been interviewed by the press and other members of the military and discussed his sighting with another patrol that had seen something strange several hours later. While the investigator wrote that he believed Toy to be sincere, he was convinced "that this has been magnified out of all proportion." That line would appear again and again in the various documents created about the case.

In an Air Intelligence Information Report with a date of November 6, it was noted that Toy was 21; he was assigned to the Military Police and had an education that had ended in the middle of the tenth grade. There is no additional information about Wilbanks, other than he was 19 at the time of the sighting.

What the file fails to mention is that, according to Jim Lorenzen, in the January 1958 edition of *The APRO Bulletin*, the officer of the guard, who took the statements, read the soldiers the article of war, which concerned making false reports. He then had them write out the statements and sign them. Then he apparently gave the story to the press, which would negate the Air Force claim that the soldiers had been seeking publicity prior to any investigation.

The file also fails to mention that, according to Terry Clarke, who was the news director at Alamogordo radio station KALG at the time and who would be a player in the Stokes sighting the next day, Wilbanks was not on leave. He was in the base hospital. According to Clarke:

> On Wednesday [November 6], I heard a rumor through a news contact at White Sands that the boy was in the WS [White Sands] hospital suffering from radiation burns. I called the PIO [Public Information Officer] at White Sands, and, without mentioning the MP's [that is, Wilburn's] name or the rumor I had heard, asked if any more details had come out that might add to their story. The PIO man seemed rattled and immediately declared that the MP in question (whom he named but who I had NOT mentioned) had just left on leave. He said, "He had some leave time coming, and I told his commanding officer to go ahead and let him go."

Clarke said that he let it go at that but that "the next day [November 7], White Sands PIO released a story to AP [the Associated Press] that this same MP was hospitalized at White Sands 'because of a severe cold.'" He then noted that his contact at White Sands couldn't verify this because the MP was in isolation.

> Shere was not impressed with the reliability of either of the witnesses. He wrote that Toy appeared to be "quite ingenuous, naïve, and impressionable."

This, then, explained Wilbanks' absence from the discussion. If he was, in fact, in the hospital and was suffering some consequence of the UFO sighting, then the leave story covers that. If Wilbanks had some sort of visible reaction to the UFO, meaning that if he had suffered a light sunburnlike effect, that would be something to keep hidden, especially when a second case turned up just a day or two later. The James Stokes sighting, made just after noon on November 5, might have been that corroboration for what the MPs had seen.

Officially, the Air Force concluded that the two men had been fooled by the moon. According to the project record card, "On 1ˢᵗ patrol, they [Toy and Wilbanks] observed a very bright, fuzzy light to the west about the horizon, large as a grapefruit. It was cold, drizzly, windy, and cloudy."

The question that comes to mind is what would have caused these rather junior, enlisted men to believe they had seen a UFO. According to various sources, and given the timing, it is clear that neither had heard about the Levelland sightings and may not have been aware that UFOs had been reported in the southwest

> Everyone—the Air Force, skeptics, and UFO researchers—point to the young age of the soldiers as a contributing factor....

in the days that preceded their case. They were patrolling out on the range and had to have made similar patrols dozens of times. They had undoubtedly seen various types of lights in the sky, but on this night when it was cold, drizzly, and overcast, they suddenly were unable to identify the moon when they saw it.

In the end, the Air Force wrote this case off as "identified," meaning that the young soldiers had seen the moon. Everyone—the Air Force, skeptics, and UFO researchers—point to the young age of the soldiers as a contributing factor, but none of these people seem to understand that the military often places a great deal of responsibility in the hands of very young men and women. It is training that is important in these cases rather than age, and none of the sources provides any clues about the military training the soldiers had received before they were given their assignments.

The real problem with the explanation, however, is that it is impossible. Walter Webb, an astronomer who attempted to verify the explanation, found the moon was not the culprit in this. Neither of the soldiers could have been fooled by it given what they had said in their statements, the time of the sighting, and the movement of the UFO.

To complicate this further, Glenn Toy told me on December 11, 2014, that the object had landed right across the road from Wilbanks and him. Since it wasn't all that far away, they did get a good look at it and could make estimates about the size and shape. He said that "it was oval shaped." When it touched down, all the lights went out. None of this comes across in the Air Force records of the sighting.

Part Two: 2000 Hours

Some seventeen hours after the first incident was reported, two other soldiers, Specialists Third Class (E4) Henry R. Barlow and Forest R. Oaks, were driving west in a jeep near the Trinity atomic test site on the White Sands range. The night was bright with some stars and the moon visible through scattered clouds. At about the same time, they both spotted bright light in the sky they believed to be climbing slightly. In his sworn statement, SP–3 Barlow wrote:

... SP–3 OAKS and I, SP–3 Henry R. Barlow Jr., on our check at Trinity Site, at approximately 2000 [hours or 8 P.M.], we looked in the general direction of the West Impact area, and seen [sic] a bright light leave the ground and proceeding slowly into the air, we watched it for a few minutes and then proceeded to Nip Site, when were reached the Range Road, the object kept getting brighter, then going dimmer, then out, then proceed to get brighter again. On arriving at Nip Site, we sat and watched if for a few minutes, then it disappeared, we then proceeded to the PMO [Provost Marshal's Office] and notified the SGT of the Guard. On our way to the PMO, we seen [sic] the object several times and then disappear. /END OF STATEMENT

SP–3 Oaks also provided a sworn statement to his commanding officer, which was provided to the Air Force. Oaks wrote:

... SP–3 Barlow and myself, SP–3 Forest Oaks, RA 13524749, saw a large bright light hanging approximately fifty (50) feet over the bunker. It took off at a forty-five (45) degree angle and went up into the sky, then it started blinking on and off. Then it disappeared. I would say it was two or three hundred feet long. It was very bright, as the sun. We were approximately four or five miles west of the light. /END OF STATEMENT

On the form with these statements, someone had added a number of comments about the sighting. Although some of those comments are illegible and make little sense, they do provide some insight into the Air Force thinking about the sighting. Where Oaks had written that the object was "bright, as the sun," the officer had circled that and written, "at 2:30 in the morning!" which, of course, is not relevant. Oaks' sighting was just after eight in the evening, and he was describing the brightness of the light, not that the sun was actually visible during the sighting.

Also included were the interviewer's notes on these two witnesses. He wrote that they had been interviewed by other military officers and by the press, and they gave identical accounts. He added, "... [they] both impressed this interviewer as being not at all observant or competent witnesses. The general tenor of their conversation did not indicate keen insight or detail, nor did it indicate above average intelligence. In the opinion of this interviewer, SOURCE's [sic] account of the sighting has been magnified out of all proportion to its importance, and the attendant publicity has been more sensational than factual."

It is clear that the interviewer didn't think much of the two soldiers or their capabilities; he did make one relevant comment. The sighting wasn't all that important and probably would never had come to the attention of the Air

The four soldiers who saw the UFOs gather for a radio interview.

Force or the media had it not been for the Levelland sightings that happened at about the same time and so close to White Sands.

The Solutions

On the project record card, this second sighting was explained as being Venus. It said:

On 2nd patrol, they observed a pulsating light that looked "like a star" for 25 mins about 45 [degrees] above the horizon toward the SSW.

Determined that they had discussed their separate sightings among selves [sic] before rpting [sic] them (determined by AF Investigators).

This is obviously another case where rpt [sic] was influenced by famous Levelland case which took place few hrs before & was given nationwide publicity by press, radio & TV.

Sources very young (18–20) impressionable & on duty in a lonely, isolated desert post. Interviewers agreed that their statements were magnified out of proportion. Conclusions: 1st patrol sighting—moonset. 2nd patrol sighting—Venus.

Dr. Lincoln La Paz, who was at the University of New Mexico and who headed their Institute of Meteorics, apparently provided a statement for the Air Force. La Paz wrote:

The Missile Park at White Sands displays over fifty rockets for visitors, including Pershing II and Patriot missiles.

Officials at White Sands soon dampened the excitement. The description of the light that appeared at 2:30 A.M. included certain doubtful factors. The night had been overcast and so dark that the stars were not visible, although the cloud cover was broken at intervals. Since the sighting had not included any object of known distance or known size for comparison, the estimates of the UFO's distance and size were of no value. The light might have been small and close; it might equally well have been huge and far away. Under the circumstances, the most probable explanation was that the men had glimpsed the moon (then roughly half full) through broken clouds, and the apparent movement was an illusion produced by the moving clouds. The Sunday evening UFO was unquestionably the planet Venus. Then nearly at maximum brilliance, it was a conspicuous object in the western sky after sunset and inspired many saucer reports during this week of anxiety.

The White Sands incidents had reached the papers, however, and contributed to the general hysteria. By Monday afternoon, flying eggs were allegedly stopping automobiles as far north as Canada, but the Southwest was to hold the center of the UFO stage against all competition.

The one thing that is crystal clear about these sightings is that they aren't very good. In both cases the witnesses, young, enlisted soldiers, saw a light in the distance. There was no detail reported in their statements to their superiors though Toy did provide addition detail, no real maneuvers seen other than the landing across the road, and certainly no electromagnetic effects reported like those in Levelland. But then, if the sightings were inspired by the Levelland case as suggested by the Air Force, someone should have reported some kind of EM effect.

The real value in these particular sightings is not in the information about the UFOs but in the way the witnesses were treated and described by the Air Force investigator. The sightings are dismissed, not because of the information, but because the soldiers involved were young and not very highly educated. That doesn't mean they didn't see what they said they had seen, nor are the solutions necessarily correct.

November 4, 1957: Orogrande, New Mexico

About thirty-six hours after the first of the reports from the White Sands Proving Ground, and within forty-eight hours of the Levelland, Texas, sightings, another case of electromagnetic effects was reported. James Stokes, described as a retired Navy chief petty officer who had served in World War II and who was working in high-altitude research as an electrical engineer at Holloman Air Force Base near Alamogordo, New Mexico, reported that he had seen an egg-shaped craft maneuvering overhead for several minutes.

Stokes said that it was after 1:00 P.M., as he was driving between Alamogordo and El Paso, Texas, that his radio began to fade out. He reached over to turn up the volume, but the radio was dead. As this point the engine began to sputter and finally died and he saw other cars up ahead, all of them stopped with the drivers now outside, pointing up to the sky. Stokes then saw the large, egg-shaped object that was coming toward them from the northeast. He said that it had a mother-of-pearl color; it was over the Sacramento Mountains and heading, more or less, to the southwest, when it suddenly turned and passed over the highway. It made another sharp turn and again crossed the highway. It began to climb swiftly and finally vanished, not over the horizon, but apparently upward, into space.

Stokes said that when the object passed overhead, he felt some sort of pressure and a wave of heat. While standing there, Stokes took some notes so that he would have an accurate memory of what happened. He talked to two

Holloman Air Force Base near Alamogordo, New Mexico, where the "egg-shaped" craft was sighted in 1957.

of the other witnesses, one man named Duncan and the other Allan D. Baker, who might have worked at the White Sands Proving Ground. According to Stokes, Duncan was from Las Cruces and had taken some pictures of the object, but searches for these men failed. Neither was found, and no one else came forward to talk about the sighting. The pictures have never surfaced.

Once the UFO had disappeared, Stokes got back into his car. The engine started with no trouble, and Stokes continued on to El Paso. On his return, the first thing he did was call his superior at Holloman, Major Ralph Everett, whose attitude seemed to be that it hadn't happened at Holloman, Stokes hadn't been on duty, and there was nothing in the inventory that was could explain the sighting, so there was no reason for Stokes couldn't report what he had seen.

After conferring with Everett, Stokes attempted to call his friend Jim Lorenzen, who had an interest in electronics and UFOs. According to *The APRO Bulletin*, "At exactly 8:55 P.M. November 4th, the telephone rang ... and the caller identified himself as Mr. James W. Stokes, a personal acquaintance of the Lorenzens."

At about the same time, the news director of radio station KALG, Terry Clarke, who was also acquainted with the Lorenzens, had heard about the UFO sighting from sources at Holloman. He was attempting to contact Stokes. Coral Lorenzen, after hearing Stokes' story, called the radio station, and Clarke thought it would be of interest. He suggested that they come to the station for an interview.

In a December 1957 article for *Writer's Digest* about all of this, Clarke explained how he had learned about the sighting before the Lorenzens called him. Clarke made it clear that he had been searching for Stokes, based on something that Ken Prather, an old friend, told him. Prather had said that a "major mentioned something about an engineer who works for him. Said he was driving about thirty miles south of here toward El Paso and White Sands on Highway 54, and something came along and killed his car radio and engine."

Quite naturally, given the information that was circulating about the Levelland sightings, Clarke was very interested. Prather didn't know the name of the man who made the sighting, but he did come up with the name of the major. Clarke then called Major Everett and learned that it was Stokes who made the sighting. According to Clarke, Everett said of Stokes, "... he's a qualified engineer ... I reported this to the OD [Officer of the Day]."

Before Clarke could locate Stokes, Coral Lorenzen called to tell him about Stokes and the UFO sighting. Clarke suggested that the Lorenzens bring Stokes to the station for a taped interview. In the *Writer's Digest* article, Clarke published a transcript of that interview. It was conducted within hours of the sighting and before anyone, other than the Lorenzens, had talked to Stokes.

During that taped interview, Stokes said the sighting happened about 1:10 P.M. as he was driving toward El Paso. He said, "And the first indication of trouble with my car was when the radio began to fade. Then my automobile began slowing down and came to a stop. Dead motor. Ahead of me, several cars were stopped, and the people were pointing up to the sky. I immediately got out my notebook and observed this object … it was an egg-shaped-looking object … white on some kind of cream color.… As it passed over us, I experienced a warm feeling."

Clarke wanted to know if the other cars had been affected in the same way, and Stokes said that the engines of all of them had been stopped.

Stokes then provided more descriptions of the object, the speed, and the flight path. He said there was no sound and that it left no vapor trail. He said that it flew in and out of the clouds. Once the object disappeared, some three or four minutes later, Stokes returned to his car. It started with no trouble, and he continued to El Paso.

The other thing that Clarke noticed when he met Stokes was that "the engineer's cheeks were flushed, and he seemed to be suffering from a sunburn."

Clarke finished the interview, reported it on KALG and then put the story on the news wire. By six the next morning, Clarke was receiving telephone calls from all over the United States. What becomes clear here is that Stokes did not contact the media, as has been alleged. He talked to friends, the Lorenzens, who put him in touch with Clarke. Had they not done that, Clarke was already on his trail based on what he had learned from Everett at the base.

This all is in conflict with the Air Force investigator's report, which said that Stokes was a "publicity hound," and there was no evidence of sunburn when he was interviewed officially. That handwritten note appears on an intelligence assessment of the Stokes sighting,

James Stokes was a retired World War II veteran. He was on his way to El Paso in 1957 when his radio "began to fade" and his car slowed down.

> This all is in conflict with the Air Force investigator's report, which said that Stokes was a "publicity hound," and there was no evidence of sunburn....

as does another note that says, "This incident was reported the day after the Levelland, Texas … case hit the newspapers. The fact that he contacted TV, radio, & press first indicates strongly that he was a publicity seeker."

On Tuesday, November 5, Stokes was called from his duty station for a press conference about the sighting, which does seem to corroborate that statement. The truth, however, is that he was escorted to that press conference by several military officers, probably representatives of the Public Affairs Office and someone from the commanding general's office. Once he finished with that, he then met with the Air Force officer sent to get the story from Stokes.

Having satisfied himself that Stokes was a "publicity hound," Captain Patrick O. Shere, in his official report, wrote that it appeared Stokes had claimed to be an engineer but he was, in fact, a technician. He also said that Stokes didn't seem to be adverse to the "large amount of publicity which followed."

In contrast to the negative Air Force conclusions about Stokes and his reliability published in the days after the story broke, the Public Information Office at Holloman Missile Development Center issued its own press release, which said:

An electrical engineer at the Air Force Missile Development Center located near Alamogordo, New Mexico, claimed an Unidentified Flying Object sighting Monday.

46-year old James W. Stokes, an engineer with the High Altitude Test Branch here and a retired Navy Chief Petty Officer, said he spotted the mysterious object at 1:10 P.M. Monday as he was driving along U.S. Highway 54 about 10 miles south of Orogrande.

Stokes said he first became concerned when his car radio suddenly began to fade. Next, he told Air Force officials, his engine began to slow down and finally quit.

"I notice about six cars pulled off the road up ahead," Stoke related, "and people pointing to the sky. I stopped my car, got out, and began to look around also."

Stokes said the object approached out of the northeast from the tops of the Sacramento Mountains. The egg-shaped phenomenon made a shallow dive to a point about two miles in front of the observers and then sped away toward Orogrande and disappeared.

Moments later, according to Stokes, the object reappeared over the Sacramentos, made a shallow dive to a point about two miles in front of the observers, and then faded away to the north.

Stokes said when the object passed, he felt a rise in temperature. He said he had a slight sunburn Monday night, but it had disappeared Tuesday morning.

The engineer estimated the object to be about 300 to 500 feet long and traveling at a speed at least that of sound.

He said the "thing" was visible for approximately 3 minutes and was at an altitude of between 1,500 and 3,000 feet.

According to Stokes, the object made no sound and there were no vapor trails.

"The object was not spinning," he said.

Stokes has been at the Air Force Missile Development Center for the past 18 months. He retired from the Navy in 1953 after 24 years of service.

Even with the support of his superiors at Holloman, and with their suggestion that Stokes worked there as an engineer, the Air Force continued to suggest that Stokes was unreliable as a witness and focused on matters that were, more or less, trivial. In the documentation, they repeatedly noted that Stokes had said there were ten cars pulled over originally but that he later said six. In the first, taped interview, he said several rather than ten. The original sketch that he made for the Air Force and found in the Project Blue Book files showed six cars along with his. A mistake about numbers, even if Stokes had made it, seems to be a rather trivial reason for them to reject his case.

They seemed concerned about his actions after the sighting and noted that the first thing he did was to call the media. The documentation, from the Air Force at Holloman Air Force Base and from the Lorenzens, contradicts this claim. And as seen in Clarke's magazine article, the media attention was generated by Clarke rather than Stokes. In fact, had Stokes not called the Lorenzens, the story would not have remained hidden. Clarke already knew it.

Stokes had also mentioned that once he returned home, he found a slight sunburn. According to the Lorenzens and to Clarke, when Stokes arrived at the radio station, he had a slight reddening of the face. So there are witnesses to this, but by Tuesday morning, and by the time Shere arrived to interview him, the reddening was gone. Noted in the Air Force report was a handwritten note: "Hospital shows no traces of sunburn, as alleged by Stokes."

Here is a point where the Air Force claims that Stokes backtracked on a claim. Newspapers said "severe sunburn," but when

The area near Orogrande, where Stokes saw the UFO. The lens-shaped object is a lenticular cloud.

the Air Force pressed, Stokes apparently admitted that it was mild. The evidence seems to suggest that Stokes did talk of a mild sunburn, and both the Lorenzens and Clarke saw it. Newspapers do say "severe," but then, the evidence is that these articles were based on information that Clarke put over the news wire. There is no evidence that Stokes ever said it was severe.

Stokes met with the Lorenzens and other members of APRO on the evening of November 5. According to Coral Lorenzen, "Stokes told us he was scheduled for a physical examination at Holloman hospital on Wednesday morning—and then began to cautiously advance the theory that what he had actually seen was 'some kind of atmospheric phenomenon....' It was generally agreed later that Stokes had changed his story somewhat after his interview with military authorities."

The Air Force was also annoyed that Stokes was identified as an engineer, pointing out that he was only a technician. Although, according to the Air Force, Stokes had two years of college, he was not an engineer. The trouble here is that even the officers at Holloman, including his boss, Everett, referred to him as an engineer.

But that isn't the end of it. Stokes, who had been a GS–11 (a Government Service grade that is equivalent to a company grade officer in the military), was promoted and moved into the upper grades as a GS–12. His qualifications as an engineer seemed to be based on a combination of education and experience. He was employed as an engineer rather than a technician.

On November 15, the Air Force issued a press release, and in it suggested that the Stokes sighting was in a group of sightings that were "exaggerations or misunderstandings of natural phenomena." A November 17 wire service story labeled the case as a hoax suggested by the Levelland sightings. Later they would decide, because this was high desert, that mirages were a possibility. Their official conclusion would become "mirage and psychological," which was their way of calling the sighting a hoax without calling it a hoax.

The real problem with this case for UFO researchers is the claim that there were other witnesses and that one of them took photographs. Duncan was the photographer, and he had suggested that he was going to take his pictures to one of the newspapers in El Paso. If he managed to get to El Paso and if his photographs turned out, there is no evidence that they were printed in the newspaper. Given the national attention for Stokes and his story, the photographs would have been published nationally if available which might suggest there was no image on the film.

In August 1958, according to Coral Lorenzen, her son was in the hospital and she was staying with him. She was in his hospital room reading a copy of the Air Force Special Report No. 14, which, of course, deals with UFOs. The nurse asked her about that and then, according to Lorenzen, said, "I know a couple who were on the highway near Orogrande when that engineer saw that saucer last November."

Lorenzen began to press for details, but the nurse had promised the witnesses not to name them. They had seen all the unfavorable publicity directed at Stokes, and they didn't want to face that. They said that the press release that had labeled the sighting as a natural phenomenon convinced them to remain silent. Lorenzen couldn't convince the nurse to reveal the names, but Lorenzen said that she was able to deduce who they were based on the information provided.

But, of course, an unnamed source is no source whatsoever. There is no evidence that Lorenzen ever talked to them and certainly had she done so, the information, without the names, would have been published. While this little nugget is interesting, it is also virtually useless as evidence.

Aerial Phenomena Research Organization founder Coral Lorenzen

Lorenzen did provide one other bit of information that is interesting. According to her, Duncan, the man with a camera, lived in Las Cruces, and Baker said that he worked at the White Sands Proving Ground. With that information, it should have been relatively simple to find them. Neither Clarke, the radio station news director, nor the Lorenzens were able to locate either of the men. It could be suggested that the military managed to silence both of them before they had a chance to tell their story, but that is simple speculation.

Clarke did say, in a letter to Ed Ruppelt on June 1, 1959, that "I have never been able to locate the other witnesses he said saw the UFO at the same time he did. The only explanation I can find for this may have been that there is an access road to White Sands Proving Ground … and if there were other witnesses, they might have been White Sands employees and decided not to talk for fear of losing their jobs."

More Stalled Cars and Other Evidence

In the wake of the Levelland sightings, dozens of similar reports were made. One of the first came from El Paso, Texas, which the Air Force decided was an "unreliable report." According to the Air Force report, "observer's car stalled and all lights dimmed, then went out. He got out of the car to investigate and then noticed object which approached him issuing a whirring sound ... object passed over observer's car at 120 feet altitude, moved slowly on westerly heading, changing altitude at irregular intervals. On reaching Franklin Mountains, object lifted vertically."

In keeping with the descriptions of the time, the witness (whose name was redacted from the Project Blue Book files but who was described as 35 years old and a border inspector for Texas) said that the object was egg-shaped, was brownish with a bluish glow, and had a string of lights around the bottom.

Air Force investigators were not overly impressed with the sighting. On the teletype message where it mentioned the stalled car, someone circled that and wrote, "Again!"

> "It is significant to point out that this case was reported by observer one day after ... press gave story on the Levelland, Texas, and White Sands Proving Ground incidents...."

Later, on the teletype, it was noted that "observer reports car stalled and light bulbs blown out at time of sighting.... Observer appears to be positive of description provided." The "blown" is circled with a line to a question mark and two exclamation points, which suggests that this interesting piece of information was seen, but there are no indications that anyone followed up on it. Someone should have asked to see the "blown" bulbs.

Written at the bottom of the document, in a starburst, it said, "It is significant to point out that this case was reported by observer one day after [and the writer was so impressed with this he underlined "one day after" a half a dozen times] press gave story on the Levelland, Texas, and White Sands Proving Ground incidents, i.e., UFO made pass over car—ignition stalls out, etc. This object here highly suggests a balloon v.s. [sic] weather schedule indicate balloon releases at Albuquerque at 0300 Z (i.e., 0800 P.M.) [sic]."

That same officer circled the witness' description of a "brownish" object and then wrote that weather balloons are made of a tan latex, that they carry running lights, and that the winds aloft data supplied suggest the balloon would have been moving in the general direction that the witness described. But even with that, the Air Force rejected the sighting as unreliable rather than as a balloon.

On November 5, 1957, Richard Kehoe (not to be confused with Donald Keyhoe), was driving near Vista Del Mar, California, when his motor failed. Two other cars suffered a similar fate, and the drivers all got out to see what had happened. They saw an egg-shaped object that seemed to be wrapped in a blue haze. Kehoe, with the other two drivers who were identified as Ronald Burke and Joe Thomas, saw two small men exit the craft. Kehoe said they were about five-foot-five with yellowish-green skin. Other than the skin tone, they looked normal. They asked Kehoe and the others questions about where they were, what time it was, and where they were going.

When the men failed to answer any questions, the two creatures returned to their craft. It took off moments later. When it was gone, Kehoe's car started immediately, though it is not clear if it started spontaneously or if Kehoe started it himself.

This sighting was not reported to the Air Force, and there were other sightings that gained more attention. The problem might have been that Kehoe claimed to have seen creatures and spoke to them, or it might simply have been that other sightings seemed more credible. There is no evidence that either Burke, who was from Redondo Beach, or Thomas from Torrance were ever found and interviewed.

The next day, Lon Yarborough, a civilian employed at Lackland Air Force Base, was driving from Levin to San Antonio, Texas, when he claimed that his car was stalled by an egg-shaped object. The Air Force wrote:

> Oval shaped obj approximately 60 ft long. More blunt on one end. Similar to fluorescent light, but did not make a light on the surface of the ground. No trail. Observer states that he felt a gust of warm air as object left the area with a swishing sound. Radio & lights & car engine stopped. As the car slowed down, observer noticed a lighted object approx. 200 yards to the left of the road hovering near the ground. Rose vertically in a NE direction.

> Probably the result of an overactive imagination. (Following [redacted but probably Stokes'] Sighting) Duration only 5 secs [sic]. Obj has characteristics of meteor except for being stationary & hovering. Also error in time since sighting at night and 1545 [meaning 1545 hours translates into 3:45 in the afternoon, which indicates daylight but someone probably miscalculated the time when converting it into Greenwich Mean Time] not consistent. Evaluation probably meteor. Additional description considered as unreliable. Conflicting Data.

Although the witness said that the object rested for a few minutes and then took off in the direction of San Antonio and the Air Force base, in their analysis the Air Force said it wasn't a meteor because it hovered, but then seemed to believe that it was a meteor, regardless of what the witness said. The conflicting data seems to revolve around the time, but that seems to be an error made, not by Yarborough but by one of the preparing officers. None of that mattered because they had a solution that did nothing to support other sightings of the same sort of UFO. They could now ignore the data.

There were other, similar sightings made around the U.S. Near Hobbs, New Mexico, two men saw a red light, which they watched for about ten minutes. It finally took off, straight up, and after pacing the car, flew over it, and as it did the car sputtered and the engine died, and the lights went out. Once the UFO was gone, they started the car again, but the next morning the battery was dead.

Near Pell City, Alabama, a milkman saw that the sky was lit up in the distance. He drove toward the light and as he drove along a dirt road, his truck stalled. He got out and saw a huge object, 600 feet long, that was about 200 feet in the air. He said the ground was slightly scorched under it. When it was gone, he couldn't start his truck.

> He got out and saw a huge object, 600 feet long, that was about 200 feet in the air. He said the ground was slightly scorched under it.

The sightings reported weren't limited to those with some type of electromagnetic effect. In several cases, the UFOs were spotted by radar with what could be corroborating visual sightings. Although not the most impressive of those sightings, the radar contacts made on November 5, off the coast of the southern United States in the Gulf of Mexico, contained both radar contact and a visual component. The Coast Guard cutter *Sebago* was about 200 miles south of the Mississippi River delta when the radar in the combat information center suddenly showed an unidentified object about 12,000 yards away from the ship.

According to the information now publicly available in the Project Blue Book files:

Unidentified Flying Object was observed at 0510Z [GMT] ... Sebago course 023 degrees true. First contact by ship's radar bearing 290 degrees [nearly due west] at 14 miles. Target moving in north to south direction. No visual or audible contact. At 0513Z, target closed to two miles, returned up port side from south to north. Contact lost as 0514Z. Second contact at 0516Z bearing 188 degrees true [nearly due south], range 22 miles, faded at 0518Z, 190 degrees true and 55 miles. Third contact at 0520Z bearing 350 degrees true [nearly due north], range 7 miles. Target appeared stationary. At 0537Z target faded (only scope at 015 degrees true, range 175 miles. Fourth contact (only visual contact) was at 0521Z, bearing 270 degrees true, target angle 31 degrees moving in horizontal direction from south to north. Visual contact held through 270 degrees to 310 degrees for approximately three seconds. Object resembled a brilliant planet. High rate of speed.

By regulations, the captain of *Sebago* was required to file a report about the sighting. The Project Blue Book file contains little information other than the teletype messages and opinions on what might have been seen. On the teletype message someone wrote, "It should be strongly emphasized that objects were not one target—but apparently 4 distinct targets."

In a letter to then Captain Hector Quintanilla on June 5, 1963, this idea is expanded. It said that the speeds calculated for two of the three radar sightings were comparable to aircraft. It was also noted, "If the target in the third sighting actually did 'hover,' i.e., if the range remained constant, it would indicate either a balloon or a false target—probably the latter, since the contact apparently lasted only about 1 minute."

The Air Force eventually decided that the answers here were a meteor for the visual sighting and false targets for the radar returns. In 1957, however, in a press release the Air Force announced that these sightings were the result of aircraft.

In 2004, Francis Ridge received an e-mail from T. F. Kirk. He explained that he was the Thomas Kirk of the *Sebago* UFO sighting and that he had some additional information about the case. He wrote that "the USCGC [United States Coast Guard Cutter] Sebago was ordered to proceed to NAS [Naval Air Station] Pensacola instead of going to its homeport, Mobile, AL. There was a Naval debriefing at NAS Pensacola the day the ship docked. The Naval offi-

The USCG *Sebago* was an Owasco class ship that, while sailing south of the Mississippi River delta in 1963, detected unidentified objects about 12,000 yards away.

cers involved with the debriefing were not all from NAS Pensacola. I think there were some from Washington, D.C., although they were not identified as such. There were no Air Force people at the debriefing in which I took part."

What is more interesting is that Kirk wrote that he had been thinking about the sighting and with decades having passed, he wondered if they might have witnessed a test of the Navy's Regulus missile.

Some three years later, Kirk again contacted Ridge. He went over the timing of the sighting, which agrees with what the Air Force had gathered in 1957. He noted that about this time, meaning about 0520Z, Airman First Class William J. Mey and an electronics technician at Keesler Air Force Base, Mississippi, saw an elliptical UFO.

In the Project Blue Book file on the *Sebago* case, there is a teletype message that does describe a sighting that is not part of this. There is almost no information about the sighting other than that the object was egg-shaped, that it resembled a "brilliant planet," and that it traveled at a high rate of speed. Kirk added that it had disappeared into a cloud.

If this is correct, then it is another report of an egg-shaped object in the southern United States in early November. It might be seen as corroboration of those other reports, or it might just be evidence of the hysteria in the country at the time. But the situation was about to change.

November 5, 1957: Reinhold Schmidt— The Air Force Catches a Break

The number of UFO sightings had been growing, and many of the elements of one was reported in the next. The UFOs were stopping cars, seen close to the ground, and in a few cases with beings seen on the outside of the craft. The Air Force was seen as attempting to respond to sightings, but many of their explanations were falling flat, and the wave was expanding rapidly. Then Reinhold Schmidt walked into the office of Sheriff Dave Drage and asked for a minister. Schmidt had just had the experience of a lifetime, if he could be believed.

The story, as reported to the Air Force in a document found in the Project Blue Book files, began, for them, on the morning of November 6, or the day after Schmidt talked to the sheriff. According to it:

> … [T]he Air Force received a UFO report, which, within a few hours had drawn nationwide attention and was given some prominence by both the press and television. According to (unofficial) reports, a spaceship had landed on U.S. soil, was observed by a man named [redacted but obviously Schmidt], who was driving nearby, and who, upon stopping to investigate, was invited into the spaceship by its crew.

According to [redacted, but it is Reinhold Schmidt], a seed salesman, a flash of light from the ship stopped his car. It came from a nearby riverbed, on which rested an object he thought was a balloon. When he approached it, another flash of light came out of the spaceship and paralyzed [Schmidt], momentarily making him incapable of walking.

a. Two men came out and asked him if he was armed and then searched him. After the search, he was able to move and walk again, and he asked them what the ship was and what they were doing. They said they couldn't tell him. He asked to see it closer, and they said that as long as they couldn't leave for a few minutes, he might as well look at it. They started back to the ship and as they got closer, a door opened on the left side. When he got into the ship, he noticed there were four men and two women. They all spoke to him in German.

> "When he got into the ship, he noticed there were four men and two women. They all spoke to him in German."

b. The spaceship was described as approximately 100 feet long, 15 feet high, and 30 feet wide, and rested on supports or "pads."

c. [Reinhold] stated that the interior was about forty feet long. Instruments mounted on aluminum stands lined the sides of the interior. He was unable to describe exactly any instrumentation, except to say that a variety of circular dials of various sizes were noticed. Both Roman numerals and ordinary numbers were noted on the dials. [Reinhold] stated that the interior of the object was lighted from an invisible source. No noise other than the crew talking was heard. It was possible to see through the sides, bottom, and floor of the object, being perfectly transparent.

d. After 25 or 30 minutes they bid [Schmidt] goodbye and asked him to leave. The ship suddenly rose above the treetops and sped off in a southwesterly direction, without a sound being made.

[Schmidt] was taken to the scene of the sighting by Air Force Investigators. No marks where the struts of the object had rested were visible because the area had been walked by newsmen. While he had stated that the body of the object was about three feet from the ground, many dry weeds and some scrub trees of four or five feet high were unbroken in the location where the object rested. He was unable to provide a reason for this.

A spot of oil about 24 inches in diameter was found on the ground below where the object was located. The greenish oil covered the dry leaves, and it was possible to obtain a sample from the pools made on the leaves. A Veedol quart oil can was found about 30 feet from the location of the oil spot. The Veedol 10-30 can was identical to an unopened can found in the trunk of [Schmidt's] car. A beer-type can opener found in his car made identical opening marks as on the can found at the scene.

After being interviewed by Air Force and other government investigators, [Schmidt] was examined by qualified psychiatrists for approximately two hours, who found that [Schmidt] was definitely [redacted]. It was also disclosed that [redacted].

The incident was adjudged a Hoax.

There were many problems with the tale as told by Schmidt, and according to Jerome Clark in his massive *UFO Encyclopedia*, Schmidt was questioned overnight by the Air Force and Army Intelligence. "By morning, authorities learned that Schmidt had served time for embezzlement." Later, in the 1960s, Schmidt would again be imprisoned for fraud, and while this conviction might seem irrelevant to his UFO sighting, it does show a pattern of deceit that was almost unbroken.

Schmidt did end up on the contactee lecture circuit and eventually had other meetings with his pals, who had told him they were from Saturn. Schmidt rode on a ship to the Arctic Circle, where they spent some time underwater watching Soviet submarines. He also traveled into space and was given a mission by the aliens, which was that we needed to solve our problems.

Coral Lorenzen, in her 1967 book, *Flying Saucer Occupants*, seemed to weakly endorse Schmidt's claims. She wrote, "Although generally discounted by UFO researchers, probably because of the resulting publicity, the Kearney, Nebraska, 'landing' and 'contact' claim of Reinhold Schmidt is nevertheless interesting, for several reasons."

She notes that he was examined by psychiatrists and that he was then held in a mental institution for several days. She wrote, "It is generally felt that he later embroidered his original story, and this tended to discredit him." She fails to mention his criminal record, which is important, and that includes his arrests for fraud in the early 1960s, and that Schmidt had refused to take a lie detector test.

> Schmidt did end up on the contactee lecture circuit and eventually had other meetings with his pals, who had told him they were from Saturn.

It is interesting that the Levelland case, with more than a dozen witnesses, was investigated by a single NCO, but Schmidt was interviewed by officers from the Continental Air Defense Command and Army Intelligence. But they were able to say that Schmidt was delusional, at best, given the fact that he was committed in the hours after the event. They could also point to the motor oil spilled at the site, which was supposed to corroborate his story, but only added to the conclusion that it was a hoax.

This case, which also reached a national audience, damaged the reputations of those who were honestly reporting what they had seen. Schmidt talked of his engine stalling, just as those others had, and they were then lumped in with Schmidt. The revelations about his story and the problems with it were smeared across the other stories. The sightings, which had been coming in at dozens a day, dropped off quickly.

On November 7, the Air Defense Command issued a statement saying they had received some forty-six reports of UFOs, but only three of them were significant. It mentioned nothing about Levelland, Stokes, or the *Sebago*, but instead mentioned they were most interested in the Schmidt case.

> This case, which also reached a national audience, damaged the reputations of those who were honestly reporting what they had seen.

Spencer Whedon, at Wright-Patterson AFB, announced that they checked all UFO reports and that every investigation cost $10,000. That probably isn't true, and it certainly wasn't true that they investigated all UFO cases. They only investigated those reported to the Air Force, and sometimes that investigation was sending a questionnaire to the witness, with no follow-up beyond that.

As if to underscore this lack of investigation of every case, Captain Andy Beasley said that they don't investigate them all. The evidence in the Project Blue Book files actually backs up this claim. On every page of the master index, there are a number of reports noted that are listed as "Additional Reported Sightings (not cases)." That means they did not investigate every reported sighting.

In January 1958, NICAP published a front-page story in their *U.F.O. Investigator*, which included a list of mistakes or allegations the Air Force had made about the November sightings. According to NICAP:

The Air Force had labeled a Coast Guard officer and Coast Guard radar experts as incompetent.

The Public Affairs Information Officer at White Sands Proving Ground had warned all Air Force personnel of official punishment if they publicly revealed UFO sightings.

A rocket engineer at White Sands, whose story first was called "satisfactory" by the Air Force, was isolated in a hospital because of "nervous tension," after which his story was publicly labeled a hoax by Air Force Headquarters.

A Navy pilot, witness to a UFO sighting in California, had been told not to appear on a television network program.

Air Force officials had blamed the November sightings on hysteria caused by the Sputnik satellites—even the reports of CAA [FAA] tower operators, airline pilots, and members of the armed forces, whose duties require coolheaded thinking and absolute lack of hysteria....

In all fairness, it should be noted that the rocket engineer cited by NICAP was Stokes, who was not a rocket engineer, and that the man who was in the hospital was probably SP3 Wilbanks. But the Air Force press releases and the destruction of the Schmidt contact case had done its job. People believed that the simple explanations and the inadequate investigations had answered the questions. There were no UFOs, which, in 1957, was the Air Force policy.

The November Sightings in Perspective

Although the Air Force would claim that the November sightings were the result of hysteria triggered by the launch of *Sputnik II*, there is no evidence that those in Levelland had heard of the launch and were reacting to it. The Air Force also suggested that most of the sightings were a result of the publicity given to the Levelland case, which explained, to them, why others began to describe cars stalling and a description of an egg-shaped or oval-shaped object.

The launching of the Soviet *Sputnik II* (a reconstruction shown here at the Moscow Polytechnical Museum), like its predecessor, *Sputnik I*, was blamed by the U.S. Air Force for causing hysteria, leading to false "sightings" of UFOs.

The problem here is that those in Levelland, who did not have the benefit of hearing the descriptions offered by others, weren't reacting to those other reports. Each of the reports was independent of the others, and the fact that many of the witnesses provided the same descriptions is a suggestion of a real event as opposed to some sort of hysteria, hoax, misidentification, or illusion.

The Air Force dismissed these sightings by claiming that only three witnesses had seen a craft. Pedro Saucedo and Joe Salaz were together, so that doesn't count as independent verification. But the truth is that the Project Blue Book file contains the names of several witnesses, who saw an object either on the ground or close to it. In other words, the Air Force had been less than candid with their press releases about the case. Their response was to minimize the importance of the sightings around Levelland and to send a single, rather low-ranking NCO to investigate the sightings. He seemed to have introduced a number of mistakes into the case. He claimed, for example, that there had been thunderstorms in the area and that a light mist remained. Weather records gathered by Dr. James MacDonald proved that this was untrue, yet these facts are continued to be reported.

Then the sightings at White Sands that began only hours after the sightings ended in Levelland were dismissed as unimportant because the witnesses were typed as young, naïve, impressionable, and poorly educated soldiers. The Air Force would claim that the publicity about Levelland had inspired the misidentification of the moon and Venus. But again, it was a case of the Air Force misleading the public to end discussion of the UFO sightings. In fact, Walter Webb proved that Venus was not visible to the second patrol.

> The policy of downplaying the sightings and offering any sort of explanation, regardless of how ridiculous, was in place.

There is the disturbing rumor that one of the MPs had been hospitalized after the sighting. This is a rumor, as reported by Terry Clarke, and might be dismissed as a rumor because Clarke found no confirmation for it. However, it is interesting that the NICAP *U.F.O. Investigator* also carried the rumor, suggesting it was Stokes who had been hospitalized rather than the MP. The point is that the story circulated after these sightings but must be regarded as rumors without some sort of documentation. A search of the morning reports might clear it up, though responses to those requests have so far been slow in coming.

The policy of downplaying the sightings and offering any sort of explanation, regardless of how ridiculous, was in place. They harped on the fact that the witnesses were "inspired" by the events at Levelland, and the discussion of cars stalling and an egg-shaped craft proved that. On more than one file, the notation of a stalled car was underlined and marked with words such as "Again!" It didn't seem to occur to them that it was possible that the witnesses were reporting events as they happened rather than copying what they had read in the newspapers.

James Stokes is the prime example of all of this. The Air Force investigators nitpicked the case and used minor and unimportant changes in his story to suggest it was a hoax. They claimed, for example, that the first thing Stokes had done was call the press about his sighting, but it is clear that he never called the press. It was others who learned of the sighting who had done that.

The problem with the Stokes case is that he provided the names of two witnesses, and according to APRO, they both were employed by the government either at White Sands or Holloman AFB. The timing is close here. The Stokes story was on the air by ten that night but the questions, jokes, and controversy hadn't erupted until the next day.

One of the men, Duncan, had pictures and was going to El Paso to have them published in the newspaper. He apparently didn't make it because it seems unlikely that a newspaper would not publish those pictures if they had them. But it also seems that if these others had called their supervisors, as did Stokes, they might have been told not to talk about it. Air Force regulations in effect at the time required that unidentified sightings be classified, which means they couldn't talk about it. Once identification was made, once the sighting was explained, then there were no restrictions about talking.

By the next day, it might have been too late for them to talk, and there are reports that some witnesses were told not to talk about their sightings. While it seems odd that none of the other witnesses, including those named by Stokes, ever came forward or were found, the quick action of the Air Force might be the reason for it. Coral Lorenzen reported that both of those named worked either at Holloman or White Sands, so they might have been silenced. The others, with no proof of the sighting, might have decided that it was best not to say anything about the sighting.

Besides, it was on November 5 that the Air Force issued their first statement on the sightings. The nature of that press release might have been enough to keep witnesses who were leery about coming forward from doing so. Who needed that sort of harassment in their lives over something they couldn't prove?

Then came the Schmidt report, and it seemed to mimic all those others. He saw an egg-shaped object, and it stalled his car engine. When he began to talk of alien creatures and the interior of the craft, the media were there to listen. But his background seemed to say that he was not telling the truth, and if this guy was lying about the details, why should those other stories be accepted? Suddenly all the reports, regardless of who made them, what corroboration there might be for them, or what the circumstances were, were lumped into the hoax told by Schmidt. Schmidt marked the beginning of the end of the wave. The Air Force couldn't have asked for a better gift.

The sad thing is that if the Air Force had actually investigated the sightings in Levelland and other areas with the same vigor they investigated the Schmidt sighting, they might have learned something of importance. Instead, they made up answers, ignored science and witnesses, and announced answers with one purpose in mind: to convince people that there was nothing to UFOs. Schmidt made it simple for the public to follow suit, because, as a young Carl Sagan said when asked about it, there is no life on Saturn. Schmidt was wrong on that, and Schmidt became the answer to everything.

Injured by UFOs

Almost from the beginning of the modern UFO era in the early 1940s, there have been tales of pilots, soldiers, and civilians who have been killed or injured by a close approach of a UFO. There is no solid evidence that the UFOs had attacked, and it seems their responses are more defensive than offensive. From the available evidence, it would seem that the UFOs are not overtly hostile and that any injuries are the result of humans approaching too close to the alien craft.

One of the first cases of injury or death was that of Thomas Mantell, a Kentucky National Guard pilot flying an F-51. A mainstay of UFO literature from the moment the UFO was reported on January 7, 1948, near the Godman Army Air Field in Kentucky, the chase and crash of Mantell's plane has been the subject of speculation and fabrication. Radio transmissions were misunderstood, the size of the object underreported, and the sequence of events altered.

Captain Thomas Mantell, with three other fighter pilots, was on a ferry mission, taking four F-51s from a base in Georgia to their home station. Mantell contacted the Godman Tower at 2:45 P.M. A UFO that had been sighted about an hour and half earlier, at 1:20 P.M., was flying over the area. Reports had come from other towns in Kentucky and by the Kentucky Highway Patrol. Those in the control tower, which eventually included the base operations officer, the intelligence officer, and the base commander, Colonel Guy F. Hix, had all seen the object, and all were unable to identify it.

When Mantell and his flight of fighters arrived, Hix asked Mantell if he would investigate. Mantell replied that he was ferrying the aircraft but that he would he attempt an intercept. With that, he began a spiraling, climbing turn to 220 degrees and 15,000 feet.

Once he was at that altitude he radioed the tower, but the records of that transmission are in dispute. According to the official records, Mantell did say that the object "is above me and appears to be moving about half my speed." Later he would say that it was "metallic, and it is tremendous in size." With the UFO above him and moving away, Mantell said that he would continue the climb and the pursuit.

At 22,000 feet, two of the wingmen turned back. One of the pilots was reporting trouble with oxygen and at that altitude, they could easily and rapidly lose consciousness. Lieutenant B. A. Hammond radioed Mantell that they were turning back, but Mantell failed to acknowledge that transmission. Mantell did say that he was going to continue to 25,000 feet and if he was no closer to the object, he would abandon the intercept.

At 3:10 P.M., Mantell was the only pilot continuing the pursuit. He was passing through 23,000 feet and still climbing. He made no more radio calls and by 3:15 P.M., everyone had lost both radio and visual contact with him.

Just after 5:00 P.M., the wreckage of Mantell's plane was found. His body was inside, and it was clear that he had not attempted to bail out. Although the aircraft was seen by witnesses on the ground to break up, Mantell, apparently unconscious, rode the plane to the ground.

Captain Thomas Mantell was flying an F-51 to a Georgia base in 1948, when he reported an unidentified object flying above his jet.

According to the Air Force Report of Major Accident, "When last observed by the wingman, Lieutenant Clements, Captain Mantell was in a maximum climb at 22,500 feet, the aircraft in perfect control. Captain Mantell was heard to say in ship-to-ship conversation that he would go to 25,000 feet for about ten minutes and then come down. Transmission was garbled, and attempts to contact Captain Mantell by his flight were unanswered. Lieutenant Clements was the only pilot equipped with an oxygen mask."

The report said that Mantell had lost consciousness at about 25,000 feet, with his aircraft trimmed to continue to climb. The aircraft levelled out at about 30,000 feet and then began a gradual left turn, caused by engine torque. This slowly increased the angle of bank, which caused the aircraft to begin a spiraling dive and an increase in speed. The forces of the dive caused the aircraft to disintegrate somewhere between 10,000 and 20,000 feet.

The problem here was that the Air Force now had an accident in which the pilot was killed and he was chasing a flying saucer. The last thing they wanted was the publicity surrounding the event and quickly determined that Mantell had been chasing Venus, which was bright enough to be seen in the daylight if someone knew where to look. They also suggested a weather balloon and then two weather balloons and Venus.

The solution was, however, in the file, had they understood it in 1948. Drawings of the UFO, provided by those in the tower, showed an object that looked somewhat like an ice cream cone. Although it was classified in 1948, there was a project launching huge balloons known as "Skyhook." They could reach altitudes of 80,000 to 90,000, were made of polyethylene, which gave them a metallic sheen in bright sunlight, and were large enough to be seen by those on the ground, even at that extreme altitude. This is the solution that

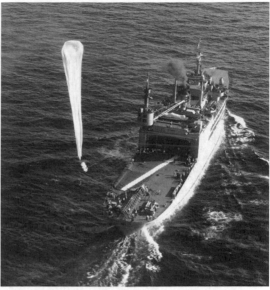

Classified in the 1940s and 1950s was a U.S. Navy project known as "Skyhook" that involved large balloon soaring to elevations of 90,000 feet (Skyhook Ballon 93 is shown here launching from the USS *Norton Sound AV-11*).

makes the most sense. It was a tragic accident, caused by hypoxia, which is a reduced level of oxygen in the blood, causing a variety of symptoms and eventually unconsciousness. At the altitude that Mantell reached, he would lose consciousness rapidly and never know what happened.

While the Mantell case is probably resolved by these factors, there are other reports in which people were injured by the close approach of a UFO. The James Stokes case, as detailed in the November 1957 chapter, is just one of the cases. There are many others, though some are not quite as clear-cut as others.

November 4, 1957: Fort Itaipu, Brazil

Dr. Olavo Fontes Teixeira, known as Olavo Fontes in the United States, was the one who originally investigated the sighting and provided the information to his colleague, Coral Lorenzen. Although he provided the preliminary information to Lorenzen within weeks of the event, it would not be mentioned in the UFO literature until 1959 and then first appeared only in the *Bulletin* of APRO.

According to an article published in *The APRO Bulletin* in September 1959, and written by Fontes:

> On November 4th, 1957, at 2:00 A.M. ... something sinister took place at the Brazilian Fortress Itaipu.... It was a moonless, tropical night.

Everything was quiet. The whole garrison was sleeping in peace. Two sentinels were on duty on top of the military fortifications.... Then a new star suddenly burst into searing life among the others in the cloudless sky, over the Atlantic Ocean, near the horizon. The sentries watched the phenomenon. Their interest increased when they realized it was not a star, but a luminous flying object. It was coming toward the fortress. They thought at first it was an airplane, but the speed was strange—too high ... there was no need to alert the garrison, however. In fact, so tremendous was the object's speed that the two soldiers forgot their patrol just to observe it....

> "The sentries were frozen on the ground, their eyes wide in surprise, the Tommy guns hung limply from their hands like dead things."

In just a few seconds the UAO [APRO's term for a flying saucer, which is Unidentified Aerial Object] was flying over the fortress. Then it stopped abruptly in midair and drifted slowly down, its strong, orange glow etching each man's shadow against the illuminated ground between the heavy cannon turrets. It hovered about 120 to 180 feet above the highest cannon turret and then it became motionless. The sentries were frozen on the ground, their eyes wide in surprise, the Tommy guns hung limply from their hands like dead things. The unknown object was a large craft about the size of a big Douglas [aircraft], but round and shaped like a disk of some sort. It was encircled by an eerie, orange glow. It had been silent when approaching, but now, at close range, the two sentries heard a distinct humming sound coming from it. Such a strange object hovered overhead, and nothing happened for about one minute. Then came the nightmare....

The sentinels were startled, unable to think what to do about the UAO. But they felt no terror, no premonition, no hint of the danger. Then something hot touched their faces (one of them thinks he heard a faint whining sound he could not identify at that same moment). In darkness, this would have been horrifying. But the UAO was bright, and they could see that nothing had changed. Then came the heat. Suddenly, an intolerable wave of heat struck the two soldiers.

One of the sentries said later that, when the heatwave engulfed him, it was like a fire burning all over his clothes. The air seemed to be filled with the UAO's humming sound. Blind panic yammered at him. He staggered, dazed, heatwaves filling the air around him. It was too hot.... He went stumbling and lurching, his whole conscious purpose that of escaping from that invisible fire burning him alive. He fought, and gasped, and beat the air before him. He was suffocating. Then he blacked out and collapsed to the ground—unconscious.

The other sentry got the horrible feeling that this clothes were on fire. A wave of heat suddenly enveloped him. Horror filled him, and he lost his mind. He began to scream desperately, running and stumbling and crying from one side to another, as a trapped animal. He did not know what he was doing, but somehow he skidded into shelter, beneath the heavy cannons of the fortress. His cries were so loud that he awoke the whole garrison, starting an alarm all over the place.

Inside the soldier's living quarters, everything was confusion. There was the sound of running footsteps everywhere, soldiers and officers trying to reach their battle stations, their eyes wide with shock. No one knew what could explain those horrible screams outside. Then just a few seconds later, the lights all over the fortress collapsed suddenly, as well as the whole electrical system that moved the turrets, heavy cannons, and elevators. Even the ones supplied by the fortress' own generators. The intercommunications system was dead too. Someone tried to switch on the emergency circuits, but these were dead too. The strangest thing, however, was the behavior of the alarms in the electric clocks, which had been set to ring at 5:00 A.M.—they all started to ring everywhere at 2:03 A.M.

The fortress was dead, helpless.... Inside it, confusion changed to widespread panic, soldiers and officers running blindly from one corner to another along the dark corridors. There was fear on every face—fear of the unknown—hands nervously grasping useless weapons. Then the lights came on again, and every man ran outside to fight the unexpected enemy, who surely was attacking the fortress. Some officers and soldiers came in time to see an orange light climbing up vertically and then moving away through the sky at high speed. One of the sentinels was on the ground, still unconscious. The other was hiding in the corner, mumbling and crying, entirely out of his mind. One of the officers who came first was a military doctor and, after a brief examination, he saw that both sentries were badly burned and ordered the men to take them [the injured soldiers] to the infirmary immediately. They were put under medical care at once. It became clear that one of them was a severe case of heat syncope; he was still unconscious and showing evident signs of peripheral vascular failure. Besides this, both soldiers presented first and deep, second-degree burns of more than 10 per cent [sic] of body surface—mostly on areas that had been unprotected by clothes. The one that could talk was in deep nervous shock, and many hours passed before he was able to tell the story.

The nightmare had lasted for three minutes....

The next day the commander of the fortress (an army colonel) issued orders forbidding the whole garrison to tell anything about the incident to anyone—not even to their relatives. Intelligence officers came and took charge, working frantically to question and silence everyone with information pertaining to the matter. Soldiers and officers were instructed not to discuss the case. The fortress was placed in a state of martial law [which, of course, would be a natural state for a military installation anyway], and a top-secret report was sent to the Q.G. [headquarters] (at Rio or Sao Paulo). Days later, American officers from the U.S. Army Military Mission arrived at [the] fortress together with officers from the Brazilian Air Force to question the sentries and other witnesses involved. Afterwards, a special plane was chartered to bring the two burned sentinels to Rio. It was an Air Force military aircraft. At Rio, they were put in the Army's Central Hospital (HCE), completely isolated from the world behind a tight security curtain. Two months later, they were still there. I [Fontes] don't know where they are now.

> "One of the sentinels was on the ground, still unconscious. The other was hiding in the corner, mumbling and crying, entirely out of his mind."

Three weeks after the incident, I was contacted by an officer from the Brazilian Army, a friend who knew about my interest in UAO research. He was at the Fortress of Itaipu the night of the incident. He was one of those who questioned the two sentries. He told me the whole story exactly as it was described above. His name was suppressed from this report in order to protect him. The reasons are obvious; he told me something he should not tell. As a matter of fact, this officer has asked me to forget his name, and he wasn't laughing. He was too frightened.

I was aware, however, that the information was not enough, despite the fact that it had come directly from one of the witnesses. The case was too important. On the other hand, to get more information through the security ring built by Army Intelligence would be an almost hopeless task. The only way was to attempt to break the secrecy around the two soldiers under treatment in the Army's Central Hospital. As a physician, I might perhaps contact some doctors from the hospital and even examine the two patients if possible. However, all my attempts failed. The only thing I was able to determine was the fact that two soldiers from the Fortress of Itaipu were really there under treatment for bad burns. Only that.

The case remained in my files until two months ago [July 1959], when the final proof was finally obtained. Three other officers from the Brazilian Army who had been at the fortress on the night of the UAO were fortunately localized and contacted. They told the same story. They confirmed the report transcribed above in every detail.

Looking at the testimony offered here, there are many problems. There are no names associated with any of these statements. The sentries are not identified, the officer who was Fontes' source is not identified, and neither are the three others who apparently corroborated the sighting.

Since Fontes did not have the opportunity to interview the two men who were so badly burned, his speculations about their reactions upon sighting the UFO are just that, speculations. He is suggesting that they panicked, that their terror overwhelmed them, and that they were unable to function as sentries. Their duties were forgotten because the orange disc hovered above them. This is a little difficult to believe, and it seems to be more hyperbole than actual fact.

Secondly, the same could be said about the reactions of the other soldiers in the fort. Both the officers and soldiers awoke confused, dashed about without a thought of what should be done, and panicked when the lights all went out. This too seems to be hyperbole to increase the suspense in the story, rather than actual details found through interviews.

This story has been widely circulated in the UFO literature, but nearly every bit of it originated with the same source, that is, Dr. Fontes. No one seemed to question the accuracy of his statements about what went on in the fort, nor in his failing to mention the name of a single witness. In the late 1950s and the early 1960s, most of those engaged in UFO research and reporting didn't bother with worrying about such things. Instead, they relied on the credibility of those who were reporting the sighting. Fontes was deemed credible by Coral Lorenzen, who herself was deemed credible by nearly everyone in the UFO community.

And there was one document that seemed to lend credibility to the case. It came from the Office of the Air Attaché, Brazilian Embassy in Washington, D.C. There is no date on it, but it uses a zip code, which means it probably came about after the U.S. Post Office started using them widely in 1963. It said:

At two o'clock on the morning of November 4, 1957, in Fort Itaipu, located in the vicinity of Santos, Sao Paulo [Brazil],

Dr. Olavo Fontes Teixeira

according to a Report by Dr. Olavo Fontes, two guards where [sic] on watch duty at the top of the highest lookcout [sic] tower facing the ocean. Suddenly an orange color light appeared and quickly positioned itself at approximately 50 meters about the guards. With inoperable automatic weapons, they watched the starange [sic] glow and high pitched noise emerging from the strange object. Suddenly the two guards were hit by an intolerable heatwave, knocking one of the guards unconscious. The other thought himself to be in flames and screamed to alert the others. The troops in the Fort quickly became alarmed due to a failure of all the power systems, including lights, elevators and weapons. Three minutes later the power returned, with many officers claiming to have seen the strange object rapidally [sic] climb toward the sky. The two guards sustained first- and second-degree burns over 10% of their bodies. The alarm system and the automatic electric clocks were originally set for 5 am, went off at 2:30 of the same morning. After the incident the Fort was shut down and investigations by the Brazilian Secret Police and afterwards by North American Officials was conducted. The results were not made available.

> All sources consulted and statements obtained discard the information that "soldiers were burned by the heatwave caused by [the] UFO."

This statement added nothing new to the tale, except for the mention of the Brazilian Secret Police. The story is the same as told by Fontes, but does not corroborate Fontes because he is the source. Had the document suggested someone other than Fontes, this would have been valuable confirmation of the tale, but as it is, it seems to be little more than a summation of the case by a Brazilian official, based on information that came from Fontes.

The Project Blue Book files for November 1957 mentioned this case as "Other reported sightings (not cases)." This meant they had information about it but hadn't investigated it; since it was a foreign sighting, this isn't surprising. They had received a news clipping about it, but that clipping was missing from the file. Nothing could be learned about when they received the case, what they knew about it, or where they got the clipping. It is just another dead end.

But that isn't the end of the story. Thiago Luiz Ticchetti, a Brazilian UFO researcher and a coeditor of *Revista UFO* and Coordenador da Revista UFO Brasil, www.ufo.com.br, investigated the case. According to him:

> It was recorded [that there was] a blackout, but there may have been a momentary power interruption, which characterized the case as being CE–2 [a close encounter of the second kind, that is, one in which the UFO manifests some sort of effect on either an animate or inanimate object, such as causing a power failure].

However, I found no evidence so far to say that there was indeed a blackout or power outage during the episode. Thus, considering only the sighting of an enigmatic light by the military and even witnessed by the commander of the fort, one would classify this as a simple case of CE-1. All sources consulted and statements obtained discard the information that "soldiers were burned by the heatwave caused by [the] UFO." And the testimony of [a] veteran UFO researcher confirms information, making it clear that Dr. Olavo Fontes Teixeira added fraudulent data to an authentic narrative and even mounted an "official" document to the American Embassy....

Unfortunately, over 50 years, many told and published this partial lie so often in books, journals, and conferences in various countries of the world that [it] became true. I suppose after the news have returned from abroad to Brazil, years later, in the form of books, websites, etc., the military ended up adding new details untrue.... Both military [officers] did not know the provenance of that information, just repeated it because they have heard from others the same story.

What is being said is that there had been a UFO sighting, but it was of a somewhat distant object. There was no close approach, no heat ray or microwave radiation that burned the soldiers, and no blackout of the fort. In fact, it is difficult to think of a way that a mechanical weapon, whether a rifle or submachine gun, could be rendered inoperative. Other than the sighting, the other elements of the case seem to have been manufactured.

There is one interesting coincidence that might explain the added details. On November 2, 1957, as noted elsewhere in this book, there was the sighting of an object around the Levelland, Texas, area that caused car engines to stall and radios to fade. On November 4, 1957, James Stokes reported that he and several others watched a UFO maneuvering near Orogrande, New Mexico, and after the sighting, Stokes had a mild "sunburn." While there is nothing to suggest this speculation is true, it seems that Fontes, who was a close friend of Coral Lorenzen, might have embellished the case to make it conform with the reports she was investigating in and around Alamogordo, New Mexico. It was a case with some corroborative detail.

The one fact that seems to stand out, based on the documentation available in *The APRO Bulletin*, is that Fontes communicated this information to Lorenzen not long after it happened, but nothing was reported until September 1959. And while he said that he investigated, he never spoke with the injured soldiers, never was able to identify them, and didn't name any of the other witnesses or the officers who supplied him with the information. Those facts seem to suggest that part of the tale is not true.

February 28, 1959: Near Cedar City, Utah

In another case that comes down to a single source and was traced back to APRO, Army PFC Bernard G. Irwin, known as Gerry, was returning to his duty station at Fort Bliss, near El Paso, Texas, in February 1959. At Cedar City, Utah, he turned from the major highway to another road that was less traveled but provided a shorter route to El Paso. He was about six miles from that turn when the ground brightened. A glowing object that had some kind of unidentifiable shape came from the right, crossed the highway in front of Irwin, and then disappeared behind a ridge. He had the impression that it was in a shallow dive. As it disappeared, there was a bright flash and then it was gone.

Irwin thought he might have seen an airplane crash. He wasn't sure what to do and believed that returning to Cedar City for help would take too long. He thought there might be survivors and that the aircraft had burst into flames. He thought he needed to get to the scene as quickly as he could.

So he decided to write a note saying that he had gone to investigate a possible aircraft accident and put it on the steering wheel of his car. After that, he pulled his Army overcoat from the passenger's seat, picked up a flashlight, and got out. At that point he realized that no one would stop, so he returned to his car. In a zippered duffle bag, he found some shoe polish and printed "STOP" on the side of his car.

When he saw the glowing object making a shallow dive over Utah, PFC Bernard G. Irwin at first thought it was a plane crashing into the desert.

According to Coral Lorenzen's account of the case in *Encounters with UFO Occupants*, it was about thirty minutes later that a "fish and game inspector" stopped at Irwin's car, saw the note, and reported it all to the Cedar City sheriff, Otto Pfief [spelled Fife in the newspaper]. Newspapers from the time, including the *Salt Lake Tribune*, reported on February 22, 1959, that the fish and game inspector Sanders Clark found the note. With volunteers some 24 hours later, Pfief headed out to search the area. They found no evidence of a plane crash, but they did find Irwin. He was facedown and unconscious but with no sign of any injury.

Irwin was taken to the Cedar City Hospital for treatment. He was still unconscious but in a state that resembled sleep, except no one could wake him. Once he was identified as a soldier and his commander at Fort Bliss was alerted, attempts to awaken him ceased, at least according to Lorenzen. She wrote that a doctor named Broadbent diagnosed Irwin's condition as a result of hysteria. There are a number of doctors named Broadbent who live in Utah as of 2014.

From the description offered by Lorenzen, it seemed that Irwin awakened on his own. He looked around the room and asked the doctor, "Were there any survivors?"

Instead of answering, the doctor asked Irwin how he felt. He again asked if there had been survivors and was told that there had been no plane crash. He didn't believe it at first, even when told the same thing by the sheriff. Although he asked them what he had seen, no one had an answer for that.

> After he was finished working one day, and as he walked back to his barracks, he fainted.... He had no history of fainting, and he recovered quickly.

As he was gathering his personal property, he found that his sports coat had disappeared, along with about thirty dollars he had in his pocket. His Army overcoat and the rest of his belongings were returned. His car, driven into Cedar City by one of the searchers, was left on the street, where the cooling system failed and the engine block cracked.

According to Lorenzen, when he was released from the hospital, a general's plane from Fort Bliss was sent to pick him up. This seems to be something of a stretch. Fort Bliss is home to Biggs Army Air Field, which means there were many other aircraft based there. While the Army probably did send an aircraft to pick him up, it probably wasn't one that was reserved for use by a general.

When Irwin arrived back at Fort Bliss, he was taken to the Beaumont Army Hospital and after a preliminary exam was assigned to Ward 30. Lorenzen wrote that this was the "psycho ward." He was there for four days before he was returned to duty. But his security clearance was revoked, and he was assigned to work as a file clerk. Interestingly, while he had been on leave just prior to the UFO sightings, he was promoted to Spec 4, one grade above a PFC. There is nothing in his military record to validate this claim.

After he was finished working one day, and as he walked back to his barracks, he fainted. According to what he told Lorenzen, and apparently what he told the military, he couldn't remember what happened. He had no history of fainting, and he recovered quickly.

Then, on March 11, 1959, he was "contacted by telephone by Mrs. Lorenzen, who was investigating the case for APRO," though it is unclear how she learned of it. At the time, Lorenzen lived in Alamogordo, New Mexico, which was only an hour or two away from El Paso, with a good, two-lane highway all the way. It made it easy for her to get into El Paso to interview Irwin in person.

Irwin agreed to meet Lorenzen at his barracks on Friday, March 13. He made no secret that he was now interested in UFOs, and his experience had aroused his interest. Lorenzen, her husband, Jim, and another APRO member were at Irwin's barracks at the agreed-upon time. Jim Lorenzen entered to meet Irwin, but Irwin was not there. They waited for about an hour and then left without seeing him.

Irwin called them that night to apologize, claiming that he had been required to return to the hospital. He had tried to call, according to what he said and what Lorenzen wrote, but there had been no one at "APRO headquarters" to take the call. He said that a lieutenant had questioned him, apparently about the fainting episode. The Lorenzens made arrangements to meet Irwin at a later date.

On Sunday, March 15, Irwin was in downtown El Paso when he fainted again. He was taken, unconscious, by ambulance to the Southwest General Hospital and was again a man asleep that couldn't be awakened by the doctors. At about 2:00 A.M. the following morning, he opened his eyes. According to Lorenzen, the first thing he said was, "Were there any survivors?"

When it was established to Irwin's satisfaction that he wasn't in Utah and it wasn't February, he was skeptical. He claimed his last memory was rushing up a hillside in Utah. An ambulance from the military hospital arrived in the morning, and he was taken back to Beaumont Hospital and back to Ward 30.

He was in the hospital for another 32 days. He was told it was for observation, but he was given several psychiatric tests. Again according to Lorenzen, the evaluation was completed by a Captain Valentine, who said that Irwin was normal and cooperative.

The final test was with sodium amytal, a hypnotic that is sometimes called a "truth serum." Irwin remembered nothing that came out during the session and was told that it hadn't worked. Valentine said that Irwin would continue to be held for observation, but two days later was returned to duty. The only explanation for the strange behaviors, the fainting spells, and the amnesia might be something that was bothering Irwin at a subconscious level. In today's world, some UFO researchers would suspect an abduction, but there is no evidence that such was the case.

Within a day or two of his discharge, according to what he told Coral Lorenzen, he felt the urge to return the site of the UFO in Utah and his adventure near Cedar City. He said, as reported by Lorenzen:

> I felt the urge to return to the location of my original experience, and I proceeded to follow this urge. Although I can remember everything that happened, it all seems more like a dream than an actual memory. I just seemed to know that I was going back—I didn't know why, and I didn't question it. That's why I say that it seemed like a dream. In a normal state of mind, I would have questioned my motives.

Irwin climbed onto a bus in El Paso, got off in Cedar City on Sunday afternoon, April 19. From there, he walked out to where he thought he had seen the UFO. He left the road and walked up into the hills. According to Lorenzen, he walked directly to where his jacket was hanging on a bush. In one of the buttonholes was a piece of paper wrapped around a pencil. Irwin didn't look to see if there was a message on it. He just burned the paper. That last wisp of smoke shook him back to reality, and he couldn't explain why he didn't read the message.

At this point, Irwin seemed to realize that he was AWOL, that is, absent without leave. Had he been able to return to El Paso by Monday morning, there wouldn't have been problem, but he was in Utah, not all that close to Cedar City, and with a bus ride that wouldn't have gotten him back to Fort Bliss in time to avoid any trouble.

He dropped his jacket where he had found it and began to walk back to town. When he reached town, he turned himself in to the local police who, apparently, threw him in jail overnight. On Monday morning, Irwin called the local sheriff, Otto Pfief.

> According to Lorenzen, he walked directly to where his jacket was hanging on a bush. In one of the buttonholes was a piece of paper wrapped around a pencil.

Although Pfief recognized Irwin, at least according to Lorenzen, Irwin didn't recognize the sheriff. Irwin began to remember some of the incidents that had been lost to him; he just never recovered a memory of the sheriff. At no time did anyone mention the car with the cracked block. Instead, they all seemed to worry about the AWOL.

They, Irwin and the sheriff, contacted a local recruiting sergeant, who told them to call Fort Ord, California. It would seem that Irwin would have called his own First Sergeant to let him know what happened. While he was, technically, AWOL, something could have been worked out. Instead, he sat around Cedar City for three days waiting for the MPs, who escorted him to Fort Ord so that they could then arrange for his return to Fort Bliss.

Finally back at Fort Bliss, Irwin met with the company commander and was given an Article 15, that is, a nonjudicial, company punishment. Although he claimed that his departure from Fort Bliss was at some strange compulsion, Irwin was reduced in rank to PFC. But he was also sent back to the hospital for another evaluation.

Captain Nissen interviewed Irwin, asked him many questions, and wrote the answers on a sheet of paper. Nissen's assessment was that Irwin was a "gold-bricking" soldier who was attempting to avoid work. He remained a PFC since the doctor apparently didn't believe the story of the compulsion to return to Utah.

The Lorenzens, still in contact with Irwin, though periodically, arranged for an El Paso medical doctor skilled in the use of hypnosis to meet with Irwin.

Fort Bliss, which spreads from Texas, near El Paso, to New Mexico, is the second largest U.S. military installation and is near White Sands.

They called for Irwin at his company orderly room and went to dinner. During the meal, Irwin provided much of the information that Lorenzen related in her book. They mentioned the hypnotic regression session, and Irwin seemed to be enthusiastic about it.

The appointment was set, but on the Wednesday afternoon, Irwin found himself assigned to extra duty, which meant he couldn't leave Fort Bliss. He attempted to trade it with another soldier, but the sergeant in charge didn't want to allow it. From the information supplied by the Lorenzens, it was not clear if this was the company first sergeant or merely the sergeant in charge of that detail.

Irwin again found himself in front of the company commander, who warned him about his continued "stirring things up." Why not just forget about it and tend to his military business? If he continued, he might find himself spoiling what had been a good record up to that point. Of course, that point could be argued. He had gone AWOL, been reduced in rank, and had been confirmed to the psychiatric ward of the post hospital—at least according to what Lorenzen was reporting. That is not exactly the best record. Though, upon transfer, the record of the Article 15 would be expunged from his personnel file.

For the next two weeks, Irwin was assigned additional duties every evening, apparently teaching him a lesson, so he was unable to meet with the civilian doctor. Annoyed with his treatment, Irwin met with the inspector general, who apparently told him that if the military doctors had anything on the ball, they'd be out in the civilian world, which, of course, is a comment that could have been directed at the IG as well. If he had anything on the ball, he'd be out in the civilian world as some sort of professional rather than advising soldiers of their rights.

According to Lorenzen, "The last time we saw Gerry Irwin was May 30, 1959. He spent the weekend at our house in Alamogordo, New Mexico."

The investigation by the IG, again according to Lorenzen, "... rattled down the chain of command and he [Irwin] was scheduled to re-enter William Beaumont Army Hospital on July 10th." That means that Irwin had left the Lorenzens about six weeks before he was sent back to the hospital.

Lorenzen wrote, "We never saw him again. He had agreed to keep us informed, but we heard no more from him. Some months later, we checked with his orderly room. From August 1, 1959, he had failed to report for duty. On August 30, 1959, he was dropped as a deserter." This seems to mean that the Army listed him as a deserter as opposed to merely AWOL. Desertion is a much more serious charge.

Remembering that this all began in 1959, and *Encounters with UFO Occupants* was published in 1975, it seems strange that Coral Lorenzen never thought about an alien abduction. Her analysis, published in 1975, said:

> In evaluating this case, we can fairly assume, first of all, that Irwin had a real experience—the twenty-three-hour period of unconsciousness seems to confirm this.
>
> Reconstructing the incident, we can say that somewhere over that ridge, he saw something which prompted him to leave another note. He removed his jacket, left the note in the buttonhole, and hung the jacket on a bush to attract the attention of eventual searchers.
>
> Amnesia is often brought on by an experience which the subject for some reason cannot face or accept. What did Irwin see? He had climbed the ridge, thinking he was investigating a plane crash; presumably, the second note furnished additional information; its very existence suggests a fear on Irwin's part that he might no longer be around when help arrived. We have the distinct feeling that Gerry somehow came under some bizarre influence which caused his hysteria—and later, amnesia.
>
> If we accept the foregoing cause for his amnesia, it would follow that the ensuing fainting spells and progressive amnesia were trig-

gered by attempts to get at the cause of his original hysterical condition. Possibly his eventual desertion was subconsciously brought on by the continued probing of the army medics. In all fairness, we must point out that Gerry's conscious attitude was quite another thing. On the conscious level, he was quite anxious to find out what had happened, about what was wrong with him.

Now what about the trek back to the scene of the original incident to burn the crucial note? It shouts post-hypnotic suggestion, or should we say post-amytal suggestion. Our first reaction was to suspect the army of deliberately sending Gerry back to destroy the evidence, but we now feel that there are many things wrong with this idea. It's too messy and unpredictable, for one thing, and it's just not the army way. Under amytal, suggestions can be given inadvertently. For instance, a suggestion that he eliminate things that were bothering him, if carelessly worded, could conceivably produce this result.

> "If we accept the foregoing cause for his amnesia, it would follow that the ensuing fainting spells and progressive amnesia were triggered by attempts to get at the cause of his original hysterical condition."

The army way would be to detail a group of men to search the area. We can imagine Army Intelligence resorting to post-amytal suggestion, but we find that Irwin went into the truth-drug session with only the doctor and a regular medic present. And only these two were present when he came out.

It is our opinion that the army did not take the Irwin case seriously during any phase of its development. The men in the barracks generally considered that Gerry was "bucking for a discharge." The approach of the medics seem to be "What makes this guy tell these ridiculous stories and have these fainting spells?" It may have been this attitude that drove him eventually to desertion—or possibly further probing by the medics brought on another amnesia seizure and an excursion from which he never returned.

But all this is speculation based on the assumption that there was a real event that triggered it. There are no other witnesses who saw the UFO, no witnesses to anything unusual other than Irwin's behavior, and frankly, at this point, no medical records to corroborate the tale. The Lorenzens did see Irwin at Fort Bliss and did see him in the Army environment.

This story is beyond bizarre and makes no sense. The Army reactions as reported by Lorenzen seem to be consistent with a soldier who has mental problems, and they tried to solve them in the best way they could. They provided medical assistance, they provided psychological evaluation, and seemed bent on helping the soldier. Instead, he told a tale that simply had no corroborative evidence, was extremely bizarre, and actually, has no UFO component to it.

The military record of Irwin paints a somewhat different picture. He was assigned to Fort Bliss in January 1959 and was in training throughout this period. There are no indications that he was ever a deserter, though there are indications that he was in some sort of trouble with the Army. He was apparently discharged as a sergeant in 1966.

> In fact, it could be argued that Irwin was dodging the meetings because he had invented the tale.

It should be noted that he claimed to have fainted on a number of occasions, and the Lorenzens have taken this at face value. There are no medical records to corroborate this, which would be considered private without Irwin's permission to review them. While the Lorenzens seem to believe this case, it is, at best, problematic. In fact, it could be argued that Irwin was dodging the meetings because he had invented the tale. He got in too deep and used the Army to get out of it. He couldn't keep the appointments because of extra duty or because of orders from his superiors. It is clear, however, that he had not deserted.

In the next sighting, there are official documents and analyses that are available. That makes it much a stronger case.

March 8, 1967: Leominster, Massachusetts

There have been many cases of people affected by UFOs and in some of those cases, that evidence was manifested in burns that resemble sunburns. James Stokes had a light sunburn, and as will be noted later, Manuel Amparano's burns were documented by his fellow police officers and the medical records that were available.

There have been many cases in which the effects were temporary and invisible. People have reported that upon a close approach of a UFO, or their close approach to a craft, they have experienced a form of paralysis. Such is the case reported by William and Joan Wallace in 1967.

According to various documents, including those included in the Project Blue Book files which are labeled, "No case. Info only," Wallace and his wife had been driving out in the country to see the snow cover from recent storms. Wallace, in his own handwriting, on a form that was originally sent to Ray Fowler, wrote:

> On the night in question, my wife [Joan] and I was [sic] out riding to see the changing trees in the country following a snowstorm, we were on our way home, at [deleted here because that was his address decades earlier]. We have to pass the area on [the] way home. As we passed the cemetery, I noticed what looked like a large bright light

to my left. I asked my wife if she saw anything, and she said no. I was certain I had and decided I would look again. On the second pass my wife saw it also. I then lowered our windows and came back again. I also got excited and told my wife, I think we have something here, and returned to [the] point of light. I came to a halt [,] got out of my car. Upon getting out I pointed at the object, my car stalled, lights went out, and radio stopped playing. I was unable to move. My wife was in a panic. My mind was not at all effected [sic], just could not move, felt like shock or numbness. I was there 30 or 40 seconds before [the] object moved away. It moved quickly, at increasing speed, not instantly. I was able to move again, and I got in the car. I turned my car around after starting it, my electrical system came on again and seemed normal. My reactions were slow and sluggish. I hit my doors on the way into the driveway. It [was] 15 to 20 minutes before I felt able to move right with good coordination.

Joan Wallace was frightened by what had happened. She had remained in the car when her husband got out, so her perspective was different than that of her husband. In her handwritten statement, she wrote:

We were on our way back home when we suddenly came across a very thick fog, which we had to slow our car to a real slow speed…. We rode right through [though handwriting is difficult to read and she might have used the wrong form of through] it, so we turned around to investigate why this was there. [Redacted but probably Bill or Billy, her husband's name] spotted a light at this time over the cemetery, so we turned back again, and by this time I saw it…. This time we stopped the car. [This is a sentence that has been crossed out by Joan Wallace.] Bill [last name redacted] got out, which I was very much against. When he got out of the car, everything went dead. I tried to reach him threw [sic] the open window…. My attention was, from there on, on Bill and not the object. I was very aware of a noise but unlike anything I could explain. When the car went dead, I was yelling for Bill to get back into the car, but he did not move from where he was standing. I then slid across the seat and reached for him. It was about this time that the lights and the radio came back on. Bill jumped back into the car and turned around in the middle of the road, and we came right on home.

Once they got home, they were both agitated and didn't stay there long. Joan Wallace called her mother at about 1:30 A.M. According to the documentation in the Project Blue Book files, she was noticed that her daughter sounded so upset that she, the mother, told her daughter to come right over. According to Fowler, who provided the report in the Blue Book files, "Her [the mother's] account of what they told her checked out perfectly with what the witnesses had told the investigator [Frank] Pechulis [of NICAP], with a few details (minor) that had not been mentioned."

There were some additional details that came from the interviews conducted in the days that followed the sighting. Fowler filed a report for NICAP, with a copy to be sent to Project Blue Book, that "I received a telephone call from a Mr. [name redacted] of Leominster, Massachusetts, regarding the sighting in question. The *Leominster Daily Enterprise,* dated Friday, March 10, 1967, carried a small item on the local sighting.... I [Fowler] dispatched NICAP MASS investigator Frank Pechulis to investigate. His interviews with the witnesses and the police department took place on April 1, 1967."

His investigation added some details that hadn't been mentioned in the forms that the Wallaces had filled out. Pechulis noted the fog and that it had been localized around St. Leo's Cemetery. He mentioned that both had seen the bright light hovering over the cemetery. In what is an important piece of information, Pechulis reported that as the automobile lights, radio, and engine failed, Wallace had felt an electrical shock and that his body was numbed and immobilized.

As Wallace had gotten out of the car, he pointed at the light, and that was when he was suddenly paralyzed. That arm was forced back sharply and slammed into the roof of the car, where it left an imprint in the ice and snow. He said that once the UFO was gone and the paralysis ended, he felt sluggish for another fifteen or twenty minutes.

> "Her [the mother's] account of what they told her checked out perfectly with what the witnesses had told the investigator [Frank] Pechulis [of NICAP]...."

Joan yelled for him to get into the car and said that she leaned across the seat to tug at his jacket through the open window. She said that she had felt no shock, and she felt no paralysis.

Fowler, in his rather comprehensive report, said that the car was a 1955 Cadillac with an eight-cylinder engine. Just before the systems failures, the car was in neutral with the engine running. The lights and radio were on, and Wallace had put on the emergency brake. Once the UFO was gone, the lights and radio came back, and he had no trouble starting the car.

In a point that might have some relevance, it was noted that Wallace did have a police record and that he was known to the local police. According to Pechulis, "I talked with Lt. Matteo Ciccone ... [who] showed me a card indicating the police record.... He also showed me the record-card of the police officer who questioned Mr. [redacted, but this is Wallace] after the sighting. The Lieutenant knows Wallace pretty well and feels that he was telling the truth about the UFO."

As was pointed out in these reports, Wallace's police record in this case seemed to work for him. The last thing that Wallace would want was contact

Joan and Bill Wallace were driving a 1955 Cadillac by St. Leo's Cemetery near Leominster, Massachusetts, when the engine, radio, and lights failed. When Bill got out of the car, he was suddenly paralyzed.

with the police. That he felt it important enough to contact the police suggests that the report is authentic.

The Air Force had a file on the case, but only because Fowler had submitted it to them. They just filed it away without further investigation. Given that there were only two witnesses and they were together when the sighting took place, that translates into a single source of information. There was nothing on the ground, and nothing on the car, to verify the sighting. However, as Wallace drove down the driveway, his reflexes were still slow, and he hit the garage door. Evidence of that was still visible, and while it seems that someone faking a UFO sighting would not go so far as to cause that damage, it does not prove that there was a UFO.

There were no lasting effects of the paralysis, no burns or other visible injuries, and no way to confirm that it had happened. Michael Swords, in the *International UFO Reporter* of May 2011, wrote, "The two witnesses told their stories promptly to a variety of persons, plus there was a relatively timely UFO investigation. (And because it occurred in Massachusetts in Raymond Fowler's heyday, its credibility goes way up....) There are a variety of ways to interpret this, but it could be a hint of some kind of technology that can induce involuntary movements."

May 20, 1967:
Falcon Lake, Winnipeg, Canada

Stefan Michalak considered himself a part-time prospector looking for quartz in the Falcon Lake region of Manitoba, which is a large wilderness area, at about noon on May 20, 1967. He told investigators that it was at about 12:15 P.M. when he heard geese in the area making noise, and he looked up from his work. He saw two red objects that he thought were cigar-shaped. They approached at high speed. As they neared, he thought the shape was more disclike than cigar. The one farthest from him stopped to hover off the ground, while the other landed on a large, flat rock.

According to Michalak, he got a very good look at the closest object, which was saucer-shaped with a dome or cupola on top. It was changing colors as he watched from his place in the bushes.

The other object hovered for a few seconds and then took off, climbing away at high speed. It changed colors from red to orange to gray, until it disappeared in the clouds in the west.

He watched the remaining UFO for thirty minutes as it sat radiating heat in "rainbowlike colors." He said that it had been red as it had come in but once it landed, it had the appearance of stainless steel.

While in hiding, Michalak sketched the UFO. After twenty-five or thirty minutes, a hatch with rounded edges opened and a "fantastic," purple light could be seen. He put on his welding glasses and could see flashing, red, green, and blue lights inside the craft but couldn't see where they were located. In a self-published book about the case, Michalak wrote:

> Placing green lenses over my goggles, I stuck my head inside the opening. The inside was a maze of lights. Direct beams running in horizontal and diagonal paths and a series of flashing lights, it seemed to me, were working in a random fashion, with no particular order or sequence. I took note of the thickness of the walls of the craft. They were about twenty inches thick at the cross-section.

At the same time, he heard a high-pitched whine that reminded him of a motor operating at high speed and a whooshing sound that resembled air being taken in and expelled. He also caught an odor of ozone.

After so long, with nothing happening, Michalak decided to get closer. As he approached the craft, he could feel heat radiating from it. He also said that he heard voices from inside, and believing it was something from the United States, some sort of experimental craft, he shouted at them in English. When there was no response, he tried a number of other languages, including German, Polish, and Russian.

> According to Michalak, he got a very good look at the closest object, which was saucer-shaped with a dome or cupola on top.

The motor stopped at this point, and he again heard the voices. Before he could react, the hatch closed. Now that it was closed, he could not see where it had been. There was no seam or crack. He reached out to touch the craft, but his leather gloves slipped off the surface. He would later say that the surface was highly polished, and the light bounced off it as if it was colored glass. The object began to spin, and he was blown back by a blast of hot air or gas. His clothes caught fire and he ripped off his shirt and undershirt, throwing them to the ground.

Now fearing that the burning shirts might start a larger fire, he stomped on them, smothering the flames. The outer shirt was nearly burned, but he did pick up his undershirt. He noticed that in the area where the UFO had landed, there was a fifteen foot circle that had been swept clean of the pine needles and soil.

As he picked up the rest of his gear he began to get sick. He had a headache and he began to vomit. He started the walk back to his motel but had to stop frequently to rest, vomit, and then start walking again. He finally reached the highway, and at about 3:00 P.M. saw a Royal Canadian Mounted Police (RCMP) car coming toward him, according to documents available. He flagged down the Mountie, but the officer thought he was drunk and refused to help him. However, a report filed by that officer, Constable Solotki, on June 18, 1967, seems to refute this. It said:

> This subject, upon seeing the police car, began waving his arms excitedly. I turned around on the highway and drove back to see what he wanted. He shouted at me to stay away from him. I asked him why, and he replied saying that he had seen two spaceships. He said I might get some sort of skin disease or radiation if I came too close. He seemed very upset....

> The exhaust or some sort of hot substance came off the spaceship, burning his shirt, chest, and hat. The spaceships remained a while, how long he was not certain, then flew away. He left the bush to get medical treatment.

> MICHALAK showed me his cap, the back of which was burnt. I wanted to examine his shirt, however, he would not let me, and kept backing away every time I got close to him.

> As far as I was able to determine, the back of MICHALAK's head was not burnt. It appeared to me that MICHALAK had taken black substances, possibly wood ashes, and rubber his chest. At no time during my conversations with MICHALAK would he allow me close enough to him to definitely see whether or not he was injured. I asked him why his hands were not burnt if he had touched the spaceship, and he would not answer me. At my request he drew a diagram of the spaceship, which appeared to be saucer shaped.

> I could not smell the odour [sic] of liquor on MICHALAK. His general appearance was not dissimilar to that of a person who has overindulged. His eyes were bloodshot and when questioned in detail could or would not answer coherently. I offered to drive him to Falcon Beach and arrange for someone to treat him, but he declined, saying he was all right.

The object began to spin, and he was blown back by a blast of hot air or gas. His clothes caught fire and he ripped off his shirt and undershirt, throwing them to the ground.

It did seem unlikely that a member of the law enforcement establishment, seeing someone in obvious distress, would refuse to offer aid. The report Solotki wrote seemed to demonstrate that those suggesting that he ignored Michalak were in error, though it does seem that Solotki wondered if Michalak was drunk. In a report dated May 26, 1967, two other members of the RCMP visited with Michalak at his home in Winnipeg. They repeated Solotki's observations in their report and then noted that when they arrived at the house, J. B. Thompson of APRO was there but left before they began their interrogation of Michalak. This wouldn't be the last time that the RCMP would participate in the investigation.

When Solotki left Michalak there on the highway, Michalak walked on to the motel, but then didn't enter. He was afraid that he was "contaminated." Instead, he walked over to the park headquarters, but the office was closed. He returned to the motel, walked into the coffee shop, and asked where he could find a doctor. He was told the nearest doctor was nearly fifty miles away. It would be quicker to go home.

While waiting for the bus, he called the *Winnipeg Tribune*. He explained what he had seen and told the reporter that if he would come to pick him up and take him to the doctor, he would provide a full account of the story. The reporter declined the offer.

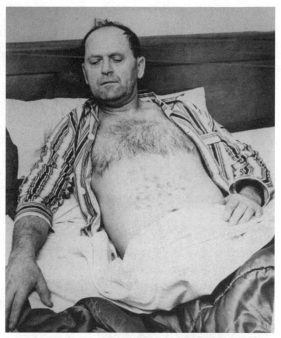

Michalak showing the burns after his UFO encounter.

When he finally got back to Winnipeg, he called his wife and asked her to have their son drive him to the hospital. Once there, he said that he had been burned by the exhaust of an airplane. He was given a sedative and sent home. There, he took a bath and fell asleep.

The next day, he was feeling no better. He couldn't eat, and he smelled terrible. That evening he saw his personal doctor, R. D. Oatway. Several months later, Oatway wrote:

> He complained of bandlike headaches, hot forehead, anorexia, and nausea, feeling of blacking out. On examination, he appeared rather depressed, dazed, apathetic, but rational and coherent. There was singeing of the hair on the forehead at the hairline and over the lower sternal and upper abdominal region. Over the upper abdomen, in the midportion and especially to the left of the midline, there were numerous reddish, slightly irregular, oval-shaped, slightly raised lesions, arranged with their long axes mainly in a transverse direction. These lesions seemed to be consistent with a first-degree burn. As I recall, they were painful and tender, but not severely. I also observed the burnt undershirt, which had holes with charred (or blackened) edges corresponding to the site of the burn.

Those weren't the only symptoms. Michalak said that he had lost twenty-two pounds in the week after the sighting. He fainted several times and continued to periodically vomit, but eventually started feeling better.

According to *The APRO Bulletin*, "Mr. James B. Thompson of Winnipeg initiated the investigation on behalf of APRO, assisted by Edward Barker and Brian Cannon … Mr. Thompson did an exceptionally thorough documentation of the incident and forwarded Mr. Michalak's glove, with which he touched the UAO, and a piece of burned shirt to APRO early in the investigation."

The RCMP did continue to investigate. According to their reports, between May 26 and May 30, they visited Michalak daily, hoping he would feel well enough to accompany them back to Falcon Lake so that they could find the landing site. On May 30, though Michalak was still ill, he provided them with a description of the area and a sketch of the terrain.

"As well as the air search we examined areas by foot, but we were unsuccessful in coming up with anything worthwhile."

Accompanying the RCMP constables in their attempt to find the landing site was a Canadian Air Force (RCAF) officer, Squadron Leader Paul Bissky. To make the search easier, Bissky arranged for a helicopter. In the official RCMP report, it said, "We took this course of action, hoping to able to find the spot MICHALAK described without his being there. The reason for us doing this was our belief that vegetation and growth in the area would be such that it would make the place very difficult to find if it was left much longer."

The official documents of that search, available on the Canadian government website, said:

Cst. [Constable] ANDERSON and myself travelled to Falcon Lake on the morning of May 31ˢᵗ and were met there by a group of R.C.A.F. personnel, headed by Squadron Leader [Major] BISSKY. The R.C.A.F. personnel had travelled by automobile, as did we. A Canadian Army helicopter from Rivers, piloted by Captain Bruce MUE-LANDER, arrived from the Rivers Air Station at about noon on May 31ˢᵗ. A search was conducted from the air by Squadron Leader BIS-SKY and myself with the helicopter pilot, and we were unable to locate any area that resembled that sketched by MICHALAK. In his description to us of the area, he described a flat piece of rock approximately 300' by 100' wide, and such outcroppings of rock that size are very rare in the Falcon Lake area. As well as the air search we examined areas by foot, but we were unsuccessful in coming up with anything worthwhile. The search was continued until nearly dark on May 31ˢᵗ and then called off for the day. We discussed the situation with Squadron Leader BISSKY, and we decided to continue; without MICHALAK being there to give us some idea of directions it would be futile, and we decided to return to Winnipeg and attempt to convince him he should come down for at least one day. Cst. ANDERSON and I returned to Winnipeg in the late evening of May 31st, and we went directly to MICHALAK's residence and spoke to him. He agreed to make the trip with us, and arrangements were made to pick him up early the following morning.

That search, with Michalak in the helicopter, failed. According to Michalak, the terrain looked different from the air than it did on the ground. Michalak told the RCMP constables he was not able to recognize the landmarks from the air. Back on the ground, Bissky reported:

> The search then continued with him leading the ground party, with the helicopter monitoring the proceedings from the air. With the aid of RCMP portable radios, an air/ground ... and this greatly assisted in directing the ground party.... Following a frustrating afternoon and evening search.... Mr. Michalak insisted the ground party had been very very close to the sought-after location....

There is a problem here. According to Brian Cannon, a member of CAPRO, which was associated with APRO, Michalak knew right where the site was. Cannon wrote, "The area of the landing was investigated approximately a week to ten days later."

The suggestion is that Michalak had found something that made the area valuable to him, and he didn't want to reveal the exact location until he filed a claim to mine. If that was true, it would explain his reluctance to return to the area.

The University of Colorado's Air Force-sponsored UFO investigation was underway at the time of this sighting, and Roy Craig, with Mary Lou Armstrong and a reporter from *Life*, also attempted to find the landing site, with Michalak's assistance. He failed this time as well.

Then, according to official RCMP documents, they learned that Michalak had found the site. According to that report, dated August 10:

> On the evening of June 26th, I received a telephone call from Sqdn/Ldr Paul BISSKY, who advised me that MICHALAK had just contacted him to tell him that he had been to the Falcon Lake area on the weekend of June 24/25 and had found the landing place. He was accompanied by one Gerald HART, who he claimed was now a partner of his. [Three lines of the report are redacted.] MICHALAK told Sqdn/Ldr BISSKY that he had recovered his shirt remnants and his steel tape from the scene, as well as dirt and moss samples, and had brought them back to Winnipeg. He said that under no circumstances would he take anyone to the scene at this time until he had filed mineral claims that he was staking in the area.

REF. AUTRES DOSSIERS	DIVISION "D"	DATE 18 June 67	REF. DOSSIERS ORG. 67D-700-130
	SUB-DIVISION · SOUS-DIVISION Winnipeg		67-700-8
			67-700-2
p.c.r. 26-5-67	DETACHMENT · DÉTACHEMENT Falcon Beach		67WS-700-2c

RE: OBJET:

Stefen MICHALAK – Report of Unidentified Flying Object,
Falcon Beach, Man.   20 May 67

26 May 67

1.   On even date a telephone call was received from Cpl. C.J. DAVIS, G.I.S. Winnipeg, requesting that enquiries be made at the Falcon Hotel in Falcon Beach, Man. Persons having had contact with MICHALAK the evening prior to his sighting of the U.F.O., were to be interviewed.

2.   The first person approached at the Hotel was Mr. William HASTINGS, a bar tender. He stated he had attended to the bar until 8.00 P.M., on 19 May 67, but hadn't seen MICHALAK or a man of his description. At 8.00 P.M. he stated that ▇▇▇▇▇▇▇▇▇▇, manager of the Lounge and dining room, had taken over the bar. Mr. HASTINGS at this time left for home for the evening.

3.   ▇▇▇▇▇▇ was located and interviewed. He stated that MICHALAK was in the lounge at the time he took over and that he had served him 3 bottles of beer up until 9.30 P.M. at which time MICHALAK left the lounge. It may be noted that this conflicts with MICHALAK's given statement. ▇▇▇▇▇▇ went on to say that MICHALAK returned at approximately 11.00 P.M. and had two more bottles of beer in the licenced dining room in the Hotel. It was at this time that MICHALAK had some conversation with ▇▇▇▇▇. MICHALAK asked whether many prospectors worked the area North of Falcon Beach. ▇▇▇▇▇▇ answered that many men try their luck. When asked about MICHALAK's condition at the time, ▇▇▇▇▇▇ stated that he thought MICHALAK was feeling the effects of alcohol. However, he did think that MICHALAK was strange in that he was so sure that he'd find something in the bush. After drinking the beer he left the Hotel and wasn't seen by ▇▇▇▇▇ again.

4.   A check was then made with Antje POLDERVAART, the maid responsible for cleaning MICHALAK's room in the morning. She stated that she hadn't found any liquor bottles in the room but thought it unusual that none of towels or soap had been used. This would seem to indicate that he hadn't washed. It was found that MICHALAK had occupied unit 17, not 13 as stated.

5.   Mrs. Martin BUSECK, wife of Hotel owner, stated that MICHALAK approached her in the early afternoon on 20th May 67, on the Hotel parking lot. He was holding his jacket closed across his chest and asked for a doctor. He was advised that there wasn't one available and wouldn't be until the 1st July. She told him that if something was wrong to see the R.C.M.P. This would be the time he saw Cst. SOLOTKI at the Police Office. Mrs. BUSECK stated that a short while later MICHALAK appeared again and this time requested the use of a telephone in order that he might make a collect call to Winnipeg. She referred him to a telephone nearby and didn't see him again.

Michalak's description of what he saw as written in the report for the Canadian Mounted Police on May 26, 1967.

It was at this point that some of the inconsistencies that worried the RCMP developed. According to them:

I would like to point out that MICHALAK's actions are inconsistent with previous arrangements made with him and previous statements made by him. From the outset of this investigation, he pointed out to us that he was concerned about too many people knowing where his claims were, and he wanted to confine the knowledge to the R.C.M.P. and R.C.A.F. members who were working on the case. At no time did he indicate any unwillingness to take our members and Sqdn/Ldr BISSKY to the scene, and in fact on a number of occasions he told us how anxious he was to do so. The inconsistency occurs in that he was apparently contacted by telephone by HART, whom he claims to have never met personally before the weekend of June 24/25, and he agreed to let HART accompany him on his search for the scene, a search which was ultimately successful. The other point that is irregular is that I made it clear to MICHALAK, on more than one occasion, that if he decided to look for the scene on his own and found it, he should not remove evidence, such as the burned shirt and steel tape, from the site before our investigators had had the opportunity of conducting an examination of the site. This conversation between MICHALAK and me was in the presence of Sqdn/Ldr BISSKY and Cst. ANDERSON, who both verify what was said and heard MICHALAK agree to comply with my request.

This actually isn't much of an inconsistency, and while Michalak might have agreed with the requests, they were, in fact, requests. That Michalak apparently returned to the area with someone other than members of the government isn't all that important, and if this is the extent of the inconsistencies with the story, then it isn't much of an excuse to reject it.

According to Michalak and Hart, when they inspected the landing site, they found that the leaves on the trees had withered and died. They found a clear outline of the spacecraft on the ground, and they found Michalak's tape measure and parts of his shirt. They picked these up and took samples of the rock and soil, separated into separate plastic bags, which they took back to Winnipeg. This is, of course, one of those inconsistencies. Michalak collected samples before the RCMP had a chance to survey the site.

According to an outgoing message prepared on July 24, 1967, that is apparently the results of the examination of the items recovered by Michalak and reported by him to the RCMP:

Laboratory tests here indicate earth samples taken from scene highly radioactive. Radiation protection Div. of Dept. of Health and

Welfare concerned that others may be exposed, if travel in area not restricted. Suggest you close off area completely. Radiation Protective Div. are sending one Stuart Hunt, radiation expert to Winnipeg, and will contact CPL. Davis for assistance. Date and time of arrival not known at this time. Suggest you contact Manitoba Dept. of Health and determine what action they have taken in this matter. No publicity to be given to this matter. Determine whether Michalak has been examined medically from radioactive exposure aspect.

The next day, there was another unclassified message prepared by S/Sgt. L. H. Winters, and it was noted:

Soil samples, steel tape, and burned clothes obtained from Defence Research Board Lab in Ottawa 18 Jul 67. Articles apparently forwarded to DRB by S/L Bissky, who recovered them from Michalak on 26 Jun 67. Tape also radioactive. Report submitted by S/L Bissky indicates that Michalak located alleged scene of landing on 25 Jun when accompanied by one Gerald A. V. Hart … who has a cottage in the Falcon Lake area. Michalak also reported to have photographed the scene, with showed indications of burned circle 15" diameter.

What all this seems to mean is that the official investigators, whether with the RCMP or the Canadian Air Force, found that there was excess radiation in the area, and they seem to be confirming the existence of photographs of the landing site. Bissky, writing in an official report, acknowledged that there was clear evidence of the circle at the site. And, he also acknowledged that Michalak's illness and burns were not easily explainable.

> They found a clear outline of the spacecraft on the ground, and they found Michalak's tape measure and parts of his shirt.

Roy Craig, the investigator with the Condon Committee, did make some observations that are troubling. There were fire towers in the area, and one of them was within two miles of the site of the landing. Since these towers were manned at the time of the sighting, rangers in those towers should have been in a position to see something. Even the smoke from Michalak's burning shirt should have been seen. In Craig's analysis of the sighting, he wrote:

According to Conservation Officer Jim Bell, the fire lookout towers were manned on this date from after 9 A.M. A ranger with Officer Bell indicated that the forest was dry at this time. Both rangers felt that a fire capable of burning a man would have started the forest burning. They commented that watchmen in the towers generally notice smoke immediately from even a small campfire and felt that a small fire in lichen and moss, such as Mr. A. [Michalak] said he tramped out when he threw his burning shirts to the ground, would have been seen by the watchmen, had they been present for even a fraction of the time Mr. A. claimed. Watchtowers are 8' × 8'. About six other towers are visible in the distance from the tower near the alleged landing site. Although a 35–40 ft. metallic saucer only –2 mi. away should have attracted the watchman's attention, nothing unusual was noted from the watchtower.

It could be suggested that the fire was of such a fleeting nature, and of such a small size, that the smoke never rose high enough to be seen by the rangers in the towers. The other point that is made, however, is that if two saucers of the size claimed by Michalak had been in the area, had hovered close to the ground or landed, and then took off, climbing out, they should have been observed by the rangers. This is a disturbing point and not easily dismissed.

Countering all that are the reports of radioactivity in the area. Although this is wrapped in controversy, according to Craig in the Condon Committee report:

> ... massive pieces of radioactive material in a fissure of the rock within the 'landing circle.' This ... consisted of two "W"-shaped bars of metal, each about 4.5 in. long, and several smaller pieces of irregular shape. These items were said to have been found about 2 in. below a layer of lichen in the rock fissure ... the two fragments each consisted of a central massive metal portion, which was not radioactive. One of these was 93% and the other 96% silver. Both contained copper and cadmium and had a composition similar to that found in commercially available sterling silver or sheet silver. The metal was coated with a tightly adhering layer of quartz sand, similar to that used as a foundry sand. This also was not radioactive. The radioactivity was contained in a loosely adhering layer of fine-grained minerals containing uranium. This layer could be removed steadily by washing and brushing. The minerals were uranophane and thorium-free pitchblende, characteristically found in deep deposits.

Bissky, writing in an official report, acknowledged that there was clear evidence of the circle at the site. And, he also acknowledged that Michalak's illness and burns were not easily explainable.

This evidence, such as it was, is in dispute. Others suggest that these items, found long after the landing, should have been recovered in earlier searches of the landing site. Although some labs seemed to indicate unusual radiation found at the site and in the samples, others did not. Chris Rutkowski, considered by many to be the leading authority on the case, reported that the original soil samples did not contain anything other than natural background radiation. But then, radium 226 was found by some investigators; however, this might have been an error. Rutkowski did write, "The metal samples ... are definitely mysterious and do not appear natural."

Chris Rutkowski, an authority on the Michalak case, asserted there were no unusual amounts of radiation in the soil at the purported UFO site.

While the official Canadian investigations "were unable to provide evidence which would dispute Mr. Michalak's story," the Condon Committee was not quite so generous. Craig wrote, "Attempts to establish the reality of the event revealed many inconsistencies and incongruities. Developments subsequent to the field investigation have not altered the initial conclusion that this case does not offer probative information regarding inconventional [sic] craft."

Strangely, however, Craig noted, "If Mr. A's [Michalak] reported experience were physically real, it would show the existence of alien flying vehicles in our environment."

As noted, these "inconsistencies and incongruities" were mostly made up of trivia that actually provided no real insight into the case. They are mostly the sorts of things expected as someone is required to provide statements about an event over and over, none of which suggest that Michalak was lying. And, as noted, in one case it was Michalak's "violation" of his verbal, yet nonenforceable, agreement with the RCMP.

To make the conclusion by Craig even stranger, and as mentioned by Rutkowski, Michalak's character was described by Craig as " ...very reliable.... He had convinced representatives of the RCMP and the RCAF, two of the several physicians involved, as well as his family, that he was telling the story of a real event. During the project, [Condon Committee] investigator's [Craig] interview, he seemed honest, sincere, and concerned. His presentation of his story was convincing."

There were also the physical effects, that is, the burn marks on his body that just didn't look as if they were self-inflicted. There was a pattern there that persisted for quite a while, and photographs of them do exist. These have not been explained.

Those burns, however, do not seem to be the result of hostile intent by the crew of the craft, but rather a result of Michalak's close approach to it. Had he not approached, then he probably wouldn't have been burned. If the craft was alien, it seems that the injury was an accident.

May 13, 1978: Kerman, California

Dr. Michael Swords has suggested that this case disproves the claim that there is nothing substantial to investigate in UFO sightings. While there is not a bit of metal to take into the laboratory, there are the physical reactions of the witness, police officer Manuel Amparano, a veteran of five years on the force. Had the situation developed differently, there was research that could have been conducted, but wasn't.

According to the information available, Amparano was on late night/early morning patrol when he spotted what he thought was a fire in the distance. He thought it might be youngsters setting palm trees on fire, but as he neared an intersection saw that it was something else.

According to Swords, "... at 3:32 A.M., when he observed a reddish glow ahead of him ... he drove to the site and pulled off the road by a cotton field near railroad tracks in time to see an unusual source of illumination ... up in the southern sky."

Coral Lorenzen reported that "the object was hovering, was a 'silver aluminum, round' craft, which the witness approached fairly close."

Amparano later said that the oval-shaped object was twice as wide as it was high and that it was a bright crimson, about half as large as the full moon. He said that it was about one hundred to one hundred fifty feet off the ground and twenty-five to fifty feet in diameter. He was close enough to it and it was large enough that there was no question that it wasn't some sort of conventional craft.

As it hovered overhead, it glowed with an intensity that did not hurt his eyes. He watched it out of the side window of the car for about four minutes until a bright blue beam shot out of the craft that Amparano described like that of a flash from a camera. The UFO then climbed out silently toward the southeast and finally disappeared straight up in seconds.

Although he felt a slight tingling, he thought it was the result of the cold night. He drove back to the station. There he met several fellow officers and the police chaplain, who mentioned that he looked as if he had been sunburned. According to Swords, the sunburn lasted for about four hours before fading, which is reminiscent of that suffered by James Stokes.

Strangely, Swords wrote that at 7:00 P.M. that night, Amparano went to the hospital for treatment of second- and third-degree burns to his face, neck, and arms. The trip to the hospital was documented in various hospital records and because of the injury, he applied for, or his boss, the chief of police, applied for, worker's compensation. That too was documented.

> As it hovered overhead, it glowed with an intensity that did not hurt his eyes. He watched it out of the side window of the car for about four minutes....

It would seem that something that large, that bright, and that close to the ground would have been seen by someone else. Although it was very early in the morning, there were others who might have seen the same thing. Lorenzen reported:

Lisa Harrison's husband had driven his cement mixer truck to Los Angeles for an overnight job and she wasn't able to sleep, so she was watching the late show on television. She was sitting next to the living room window of her apartment in Kerman.... Suddenly, at 3:30 A.M., she heard a strange, loud, whirring noise, and the house began to vibrate. She took three quick steps to the front door to see what was happening. Looking toward the northwest, she saw two lights moving toward the South at treetop level. The leading light was white and the rear light was reddish, but "not like the red lights on airplanes." She described the lights as large, but couldn't estimate how large. Mrs. Harrison ran back into the house after the object went out of sight behind some houses to the south.

Harrison isn't the only other witness to be found. Amparano, on his way back to the station, had stopped at a parking lot near Highway 145 and Interstate 80 for a few minutes. There he found Phil Mahler, who was delivering newspapers for the *Fresno Bee*. Mahler said that he had seen what he called "a reddish ball in the sky."

UFO incidents have also occurred in the Central Valley of California, such as the report made by Lisa Harrison in the farming town of Kerman.

There were still other, somewhat ambiguous reports. According to something referred to as "a Seattle-based phenomenon research center," an astronomer in Fresno reported a "reddish ball" close to the ground.

At about the same time, someone called the Fire Department to report a fire that was in a direct line from where Amparano saw the UFO. The Fire Department said that they found no evidence of a fire.

After Amparano's sighting was reported, Ken Westbrook, Jr., who had been raking hay at the Gilory Farm west of Kerman, said that he had seen a glowing "orange ball" at treetop level. He watched it for some thirty to forty seconds as it "just kind of drifted around a little bit."

At the station, Amparano called the Air Guard, the Fresno Airport, and the weather bureau, wondering if they had anything on their radarscopes or if there had been any other reports. While he was making the telephone calls, police officers A. J. Byington and Bob Muller saw the burn marks on his face. They then discovered that Amparano had been burned through his shirt as well. At that point, they all returned to the cotton field, but there was nothing there to be seen.

According to other sources, it was at 5:00 P.M. that Amparano woke and was feeling sick. That was when he went to the Fresno Community Hospital emergency room. There, his burns were noted and listed as coming from an unknown source. It was also noted his blood pressure was high, and later a private doctor said that he suffered from exposure to a "high-intensity, fluorescent pipe light or a gamma ray."

> It was also noted his blood pressure was high, and later a private doctor said that he suffered from exposure to a "high-intensity, fluorescent pipe light or a gamma ray."

What is important here is that these injuries, regardless of source, were documented by the hospital authorities, and there was that worker's compensation claim that was also filed, which further corroborated the injuries.

At this point, Police Chief James Van Cleaf decided that he wanted nothing about the sighting to be released to the press or to UFO researchers. He told Amparano not to talk to them. According to Lorenzen:

> A reporter went to the Amparano home after learning the identity of the officer but was told that Amparano wasn't available for an interview. Mrs. Amparano said that Chief Van Cleaf had told her husband not to talk to anyone about the incident, least of all out-of-town reporters. She thought that her husband would be willing to talk—he had nothing to hide—but only if the Chief said it was all right. But Van Cleaf was adamant—no interviews.

This order also seemed to apply to members of other law-enforcement agencies. On June 26, 1978, this was a sheriff's department memorandum that was sent to Amparano: "Saw the article and was impressed ... one of our sgts. [M]ike

Soderberg experienced much the same thing as you did … no burns, however … no one really knows at this point what really exists out there in space!!!"

While interesting, it's not clear if the sighting was at the same time and exactly what Soderberg saw, other than it was similar. This could be further corroboration of the sighting, but at this point no one has followed-up on it.

In July 2014, Jason Marzek, writing for *Fringe Republic*, contacted Amparano, who responded to him. In that e-mail, Amparano wrote:

The UFO … was behind the trees lining the west side of Del Norte Avenue and near the ground hovering midway below the treetops, which gave the impression the tree was on fire.… The UFO was first sighted at Trinity and Shaw Avenues by a Fresno County resident, who called the North Central Fire Department, Kerman Station, and reported a grass fire in a field.… The firemen arrived on the scene and found no evidence of a fire.… A short time later, Thomas Addis was working in a vineyard … when he observed a fireball moving at treetop level.… Also five Kerman Police Personnel observed my physical appearance when I reported for duty and confirmed that I was not sunburned prior to going on patrol. Officers A. J. Byington, Bob Muller, Bill McKinney, Jon Crouch, and Chaplin Tom Johnson were with me inside a well-lit police station. Fresno Community Doctors Allen Mau and T. T. Shigyo reported that [I] had a sunburnt condition when examined at community hospital. Dr. Shigyo said that microwaves can burn the flesh through clothing without damaging the cloth. Chief Van Cleaf requested workman compensation for on-the-job injury.

> Unlike the Stokes case, there were additional witnesses interviewed about the red object in the sky at about the time that Amparano made his sighting, which creates a chain of testimony.

This case becomes important, because it has multiple chains of evidence. There was the physical effect, which was the burns suffered by Amparano, documented by the hospital records, and observed by his fellow police officers. Unlike the Stokes case, there were additional witnesses interviewed about the red object in the sky at about the time that Amparano made his sighting, which creates a chain of testimony.

Had the chief of police reacted with a more open response, some of that additional testimony might have been documented as well. Tests could have been conducted on the police car, which might have yielded some interesting evidence. Unfortunately, as has happened all too often, the chief was probably afraid of adverse publicity, and his response was to limit access to the witnesses.

As has happened all too often, the opportunity was lost. With the Rendlesham Forest case, which happened only two years later, that opportunity might not have been lost.

December 26–27, 1989:
Rendlesham Forest, England

There is some confusion about the dates of the sightings, and one of the witnesses who claims involvement probably wasn't there for the sightings. But there is documentation for the events, a solid roster of those who did participate, and an ongoing struggle over the medical records of two retired U.S. Air Force NCOs who may have been injured when they approached too close to the UFO.

These events began in the early morning hours of December 26, 1980, when Airman First Class (A1C) John Burroughs saw strange lights in the Rendlesham Forest, which was near the U.S. Air Force base at Bentwaters in England. These lights were red and blue, the red above the blue, and they were flashing. Following military protocol, Burroughs called his immediate supervisor, Staff Sergeant Bud Steffens. Both saw the lights, and neither knew what they were. Their best guess, at that moment, was that it was a civilian plane crash.

Together they left the air base, drove out into the forest, and saw a white light that seemed to be coming at them. They couldn't identify the light and Burroughs, who had been stationed at Bentwaters for some seventeen months, was familiar with the lights that were found around the base.

They thought they should report what they were seeing and returned to the air base so that they could use the landline, which was more secure than the radios they carried. It meant that civilians couldn't listen in, as they could with radio transmissions. Burroughs talked to Sergeant McCabe, known as "Crash," who suspected some sort of joke. But Steffens confirmed what Burroughs had said. McCabe bucked the problem up the chain of command to Staff Sergeant John Coffey, who in turn called Staff Sergeant Jim Penniston.

Penniston decided to go look for himself. In a vehicle driven by A1C Edward Cabansag, he joined Burroughs and Steffens at what was known as East Gate. Burroughs and Steffens told Penniston what they had seen and that they had gone out into the forest to search but had turned back. They were still operating under the impression that what they had seen was a civilian aircraft accident.

John Burroughs prepares to testify during the 2012 Citizen Hearing on Disclosure.

It was then, according to what Nick Pope published in the book he wrote with Burroughs and Penniston, *Encounter in Rendlesham Forest*, that Steffens said, "It didn't crash. It landed."

Still believing that it was an aircraft accident, even after Steffen's strange comment, Penniston called the flight chief, Master Sergeant J. D. Chandler. Chandler checked to see if any military aircraft had been lost but found that all were accounted for. Instead, he learned that some fifteen minutes earlier there had been a radar contact with an object or aircraft that seemed to have disappeared from radar near Woodbridge, a base colocated with Bentwaters. Penniston asked for backup, and now Chandler decided that he'd go out himself.

Three of them, Penniston, Burroughs, and Cabansag, drove out to the forest. This time, as they entered the forest, they saw blue, red, white, and yellow lights. There is some disagreement among the various witnesses, with Cabansag suggesting that Chandler had already arrived, but the others thought he joined them after they had left the gate. Such a discrepancy is of little importance.

As they moved deeper into the forest, all the radios malfunctioned. They attempted to set up a radio relay, with the men separating so that they could maintain radio contact with the operations center.

Now Burroughs and Penniston pushed deeper into the trees. They said that the air was filled with static electricity and that their hair was standing on end. They found it difficult to walk, but they could see the lights ahead of them.

They continued toward a clearing that was brightly lit and as they neared it, there was an "explosion" of light. Both men dropped to the ground but then, seeing nothing dangerous, Penniston stood up. Now he saw that Burroughs was engulfed in light, and the ball of light that had been in front of him faded until he saw there was a craft in the clearing.

According to Pope in *Encounter in Rendlesham Forest*, "Penniston took stock of the situation. In the clearing was a small, metallic craft. It was about three meters [11 feet] high and maybe three meters across at the base. The craft was roughly rectangular in shape and appeared to be either hovering just above the ground or perhaps resting on legs at each edge of the object, as if it was on a tripod.... It had a bank of blue lights on its side and a bright white light on the top."

Penniston inched forward and touched the object. According to Penniston, the surface of the object was smooth, like glass. He could detect no seams or imperfections. There were some symbols on the craft, and they were rough, or as he said, "like running my fingers over sandpaper."

As he touched the symbols, the white light at the top of the object flashed brightly, temporarily blinding him. When he let go, the light dimmed, and the feeling of panic that had nearly overwhelmed him lessened. It was at this time that the craft began to lift off, maneuvering carefully to avoid the trees, and once clear, shot up into the night sky.

Burroughs, who had remained behind Penniston, was confused about exactly what had happened and would later suggest that he was "in the light" while Penniston was examining the craft. Once the object had taken off, they tried to spot it and reported more lights. They thought it might be going to land again, but that didn't happen.

Eventually Burroughs and Penniston headed back and crossed the clearing where the UFO had been sitting. On the ground they found indentations, which suggested something heavy had been resting there. These indentations seemed to form an equilateral triangle.

They left the clearing and found Cabansag, Chandler, and other members of the security team waiting for them. They all returned to the base and learned they had been gone longer than they thought. But their shift was nearly over, and they had to turn in their weapons, fill out the paperwork, and undergo a shift-change briefing. With the others asking what had happened in the clearing, Penniston and Burroughs simply wanted to get off duty and get to bed.

At the time, Lieutenant Colonel (later Colonel) Charles Halt was the deputy base commander. He learned of the events when he reported for work that morning. He heard the story of the lights in the woods, but he was reluctant to label them as UFOs. Instead, he opted for the less provocative "unexplained lights." And since the events were unusual, he said that the various logs should reflect that information.

Sometime on the morning of December 26, Major Edward Drury, who was Deputy Squadron Commander, and Captain Mike Verrano, the on-duty shift commander, interviewed both Penniston and Burroughs. Had it not been for the radar report of the night before, neither officer would have thought much of the story being told. Now they decided to inspect the clearing and landing area, taking Burroughs and Penniston with them. They also took along Master Sergeant Ray Gulyas to make the measurements.

They followed the same route that had been used the night before, first in vehicles and then on foot. It didn't take long for Burroughs to find the indentations he'd seen. Penniston

Jim Penniston (left) and Nick Pope (right), seen here at the Citizen Hearing and Disclosure, cowrote the book about the UFO landing in Rendlesham Forest.

briefed the officers about what he had seen, though that briefing was not as detailed as it could have been. It was only later that both men would remember more of what happened to them.

Once they had gathered the information, they returned to the base, and Burroughs and Penniston signed off duty. However, the officers were ordered back into the field with English police officers to search the area once again.

During that day, Halt interviewed those who had been involved. He also said that he was going out to look for evidence. Everyone seemed to accept the idea that the airmen had seen something in the woods, especially when they learned about the radar reports. No one was sure what it might have been, but something had been out there.

> There was something that appeared to be hovering over a carpet of yellow debris in the forest. There was a red light on top and a series of blue lights around the middle.

All this is somewhat confusing because there are various chains of command as well as various law-enforcement organizations involved. Not only that, the bases, while designated as Royal Air Force (RAF), actually belonged to USAF. The law-enforcement functions and Status of Forces agreement allowed the Americans to work off base, and there were English police involved. And finally, there were two national governments that would eventually get involved, both seeming to want to hand the problem off to the other.

When the day was done, many of those involved in the base command structure were at an award dinner that evening. Both the base commander, Colonel Ted Conrad, and Charles Halt were there. During that ceremony Lieutenant Bruce Englund, who was the on-duty shift commander, arrived, pulled Halt aside, and said, "It's back."

"What's back?" asked Halt.

"The UFO is back, sir."

Halt conferred with Conrad, and for whatever reason, Conrad ordered Halt into the field. Halt authorized an investigation into these new sightings of the unexplained lights. It meant that the men would again leave the base and would again search through the Rendlesham Forest.

There was something that appeared to be hovering over a carpet of yellow debris in the forest. There was a red light on top and a series of blue lights around the middle. There also seemed to be some kind of electrical field that was affecting the men.

This time they radioed the base for more instructions. Halt, who had returned to the base, told the men to wait at the edge of the forest. He said, "I'm on my way with more people."

It was now just after midnight and Halt, with the additional manpower, had arrived on the scene. They had a number of vehicles with them, and this included the "light-alls," that is, large, independent lights used in the field to light aircraft and other equipment for maintenance or any other purpose that required a great deal of light at night.

Halt ordered the lights erected, but there were various problems and malfunctions. Rather than use the trucks to pull the lights into the forest, they had to manhandle them because of the terrain. As they were set up near the area where the triangular indentations had been found, the lights would switch on and then back off, seemingly by themselves. There was no reason found for these malfunctions, though Halt believed that they were low on fuel.

The men were spread out through the forest. They were searching for anything that could explain the lights seen earlier. As they moved deeper into the trees, Halt began to record his thoughts and observations on a small, handheld tape recorder. It was Halt's habit to use the recorder at all times in his job as the deputy base commander. Other voices, adding to that perspective, can be heard in the background on the tape.

At 1:48 A.M., the first voice heard said, "We're hearing strange sounds out of the farmer's barnyard animals. They're very, very active, making an awful lot of noise.... You just saw a light...?"

Another voice said, "Right on this position. Here, straight ahead in between the trees.... There it is again. Watch. Straight ahead off my flashlight, sir. There it is."

Halt then said, "I see it too. What is it?"

"We don't know, sir."

"It's a strange, small, red light. Looks to be maybe a quarter to a half mile, maybe farther out," said Halt. "I'm gonna switch off. The light is gone now. It was approximately 120 degrees from our site. It is back again?"

"Yes, sir."

Then someone else said, "Well, douse the flashlights, then. Let's go back to the edge of the clearing so we can get a better look at it. See if you can get a better look at it. See if you can get the star[light] scope [an image-enhancing device that uses the available ambient light to illuminate an area] on it. The light's still there, and all the barnyard animals have gone quiet now. We're heading about 110, 120 degrees from the site out through the clearing now, still getting a reading on the [Geiger counter] meter.... We're about 150 or 200 yards from the site. Everywhere else is just deadly calm. There is no doubt about it. There's some type of strange, flashing, red light ahead."

"Sir. It's yellow."

Halt said, "I saw a yellow tinge in it too. Weird. It appears to be maybe moving a little bit this way? It's brighter than it has been. It's coming this way.

It is definitely coming this way. Pieces of it are shooting off. There is no doubt about it. This is weird."

"Two lights," said someone. "One to the right and one light to the left."

"Keep your flashlights off," ordered Halt. "There's something very, very strange. Keep the headset on. See if it gets any.... Pieces falling off it again."

"It just moved to the right."

Another voice said, "Yeah. Strange. Let's approach to the edge of the woods up there. Okay, we're looking at the thing. We're probably about two to three hundred yards away. It looks like an eye winking at you. Still moving from side to side. And when you put the star[light] scope on it, it's like this thing has a hollow center, a dark center, like the pupil of an eye looking at you, winking. And it flashes so bright in the star[light] scope that it almost burns your eye.... We've passed the farmer's house and across into the next field, and now we have multiple sightings of up to five lights with a similar shape and all, but they seem to be steady now rather than a pulsating or glow with a red flash. We've just crossed a creek, and we're getting what kind of readings [Geiger counter] now? We're getting three good clicks on the meter and we're seeing strange lights in the sky."

> "Okay, we're looking at the thing. We're probably about two to three hundred yards away. It looks like an eye winking at you."

The next time check on the tape is at 2:44 A.M. Halt said, "We're at the far side of the second farmer's field and made [a] sighting again about 110 degrees. This looks like it's clear off to the coast. It's right on the horizon. Moves about a bit and flashes from time to time. Still steady or red in color. Also, after negative readings in the center of the field, we're picking up slight readings. Four or five clicks now on the meter."

About twenty-one minutes later, Halt added, "We see strange, strobelike flashes ... well, they're sporadic, but there's definitely some kind of phenomenon.... At about ten degrees, horizon, directly north, we've got two strange objects ... half-moon shape, dancing about with colored lights on them. That ... guess to be about five to ten miles out, maybe less. The half moons are now turning full circles, as though there was an eclipse or something there, for a minute or two."

Ten minutes later, at 3:15 A.M., Halt added, "Now we've got an object about ten degrees directly south, ten degrees off the horizon. And the ones to the north are moving. One's moving away from us."

Someone corroborated Halt's observation, saying clearly, "It's moving out fast."

A third man said, "They're both heading north. Okay, here he comes from the south. He's coming toward us now. Now we're observing what appears to be a beam coming down to the ground. This is unreal."

Fifteen minutes later, Halt said, "One object still hovering over Wood-bridge base at about five or ten degrees off the horizon. Still moving erratic and similar lights and beaming down...."

This was the essence of what Halt recorded and for years, everyone thought that Halt had released all the tape he had recorded. However, according to Pope in *Encounter in Rendlesham Forest*, "In late 1999, Charles Halt told author and investigative journalist Georgina Bruni that he had four or five hours of tape—unlike the eighteen minutes in the public domain—nobody would be allowed to hear. When she pressed him for details of what was on these tapes and why the material couldn't be made available, Halt refused to elaborate."

But there is more evidence. There is more than just the audio tape of witnesses talking about strange lights in the forest near the base which, of course, makes this an intriguing case. It isn't very often that a senior Air Force officer makes a recording as he's chasing unidentified lights and objects through the woods near a NATO base where there were nuclear weapons stored. And this isn't the end of it. About two weeks after the event, Halt sent a letter to the Royal Air Force Commander, detailing the events of the day. It said:

This is where the UFO was said to have landed in Rendlesham Forest in Suffolk, England.

1. Early in the morning of 27 Dec 80 (approximately 0300L [meaning three o'clock in the morning, local time]), two USAF security police patrolmen saw unusual lights outside the back gate [also known as the East Gate] at RAF Woodbridge. Thinking an aircraft might have crashed or been forced down, they called for permission to go outside the gate to investigate. The on-duty flight chief responded and allowed three patrolmen to proceed on foot. The individuals reported seeing a strange, glowing object in the forest. The object was described as being metallic in appearance and triangular in shape, approximately two to three meters across the base and approximately two meters high. It illuminated the entire forest with a white light. The object itself had a pulsating red light on top and a bank(s) of blue lights underneath. The object was hovering or on legs. As the patrolmen approached the object, it maneuvered through the trees and disappeared. At this time, the animals on the nearby farm went into a frenzy. The object was briefly sighted approximately an hour later near the back gate.

2. The next day, three depressions 1‴ deep and 7" in diameter were found where the object had been sighted on the ground. The following night (29 Dec 80), the area was checked for radiation. Beta/Gamma readings of 0.1 milliroentgens were recorded with peak readings in the three depressions and near the center of the triangle formed by the depressions. A nearby tree had moderate (.05—.07) readings on the side of the tree toward the depressions.

3. Later in the night, a red, sunlike light was seen through the trees. It moved about and pulsated. At one point, it appeared to throw off glowing particles, and then broke into five separate white objects and then disappeared. Immediately thereafter, three star-like objects were noticed in the sky, two objects to the north and one to the south, all of which were about 10 [degrees] off the horizon. The objects moved rapidly in sharp, angular movements and displayed red, green, and blue lights. The objects to the north appeared to be elliptical through the 8–12 power lens. They then turned to full circles. The objects to the north remained in the sky for an hour or more. The object to the south was visible for two to three hours and beamed down a stream of light from time to time. Numerous individuals, including the undersigned [Lieutenant Colonel Halt], witnessed the activities in paragraphs two and three.

Here we have the statement of a senior officer, made through official channels to the Royal Air Force commander. It described events that are difficult to put into a mundane framework. That they have been documented in an official letter is also quite important. While it does not say that the lights or object was of alien construction, it does confirm the events as they transpired and suggests that there are multiple witnesses and physical evidence. There is no suggestion in the letter that anyone was injured by a close approach to the object, whatever it was.

Skeptics have dismissed all these sightings and evidence as various misinterpretations. The lights seen were either low-hanging stars seen through the thick atmosphere, which gave them a strange appearance, or the flashing beacon of a lighthouse some miles away. It wasn't explained why that beacon didn't cause confusion for the airmen on other occasions.

The Orfordness Lighthouse, which was decommissioned in 2013, is several miles from the Rendlesham Forest, but some still speculated that the light from the tower was somehow mistaken for a UFO.

The holes, that were in what Penniston suggested was a perfect triangle, were identified by the skeptics as rabbit burrows. The radiation found at the site was normal background radiation and nothing more, again according to the skeptics.

Those who had seen something strange on the second night were confused and excited by the discussions held during the day. Lights that had been there for years but were unnoticed were now interpreted as a craft from another world. The skeptics were satisfied with their explanations.

There are a couple of problems here, however. First, what events precipitated the first night's "hysteria"? These men were security police, whose job it was to guard the military base. They were responsible for the security of the installation, even in time of war. They should have been aware of stationary lights and other features of the terrain around them. It would have been part of their job.

This means that it is difficult to believe that the security police, other airmen and NCOs, and the officers at the Bentwaters base would be fooled by something as mundane as a flashing light from a lighthouse that had been there for years. It is difficult to believe that they wouldn't have seen that same light the next night and the night after that and that someone wouldn't have followed the light to its source. It is difficult to believe that a high-ranking officer would then write a letter to be passed up the chain of command describing the incident without first determining if the lighthouse might not have been the source of the light.

These skeptical answers simply do not satisfy. That doesn't mean that there was an alien craft in the area; it simply means that the skeptics have not solved the case. And to accept their explanation, it is necessary to overlook some of the facts.

It is clear that the men involved, particularly Burroughs and Penniston, got a very good look at the light in the clearing. Penniston said that he touched it. He was that close to it, and if we accept that, then those other explanations are eliminated. There is no reason to reject what Penniston had to say about it, and there is evidence that his close approach, as did that of Burroughs, resulted in physiological injury.

> Penniston said that he touched it. He was that close to it, and if we accept that, then those other explanations are eliminated.

None of this, however, came out in the first round of investigations into the case. There were other issues that got in the way, not the least of which was the claim that some of the interrogation of the witnesses had been heavy-handed.

There were some hints about it, but no one was talking about the sightings until Larry Warren, who had been assigned as a part of the security section in December 1980, just weeks before the sightings were made, spoke up. There is confusion about Warren's role, and even Halt has disputed some of what Warren said, but the fact seems to be that he was the initial whistleblower on the case. Even if he wasn't there to see what had happened, he had heard enough about it that he could tell the story to Barry Greenwood and Larry Fawcett.

Warren's involvement in the tale has been challenged by many. In a videotaped interview conducted by documentary filmmaker Russ Estes in the 1980s, Warren said that for the first two days of the events in England, he had been on a pass in Germany. He returned in time for the events on the third night, if, in fact, there was a third night. But from his descriptions and his discussions with Charles Halt, it seemed that he was saying that he'd been there on the second night.

In a tape-recorded conversation on February 16, 1993, Warren explained that he wanted to set the record straight. He said, beginning with Fawcett and Greenwood's book, that he had seen distortions, apparently forgetting that these distortions were the result of his telling the story several different ways.

Halt was asked during the conversation if he knew that what Warren had alleged were his experiences. Halt, in answering, explained that he had agreed to help Fawcett understand the case. Halt said, "All I know is what I have gained from two or three tapes that Larry [Fawcett] and somebody, I don't even remember now who, shared with me. In fact, one time I agreed to cooperate with Larry [Fawcett] … I provided him a lot of information and then he sent me a tape…."

Warren then began to explain that he was working on a book and that he just wanted to tell the story. Halt interrupted him and said, "You're aware that the story you've told or the stories you've told through the years don't fit in with what I recollect and other witnesses recollect...."

Warren responded by saying, "Oh, yes." But quickly added, "I have statements from other guys that were right next to me in certain elements of this thing.... It's like being at the scene of an accident, where all the different people say some variation of [the] thing...."

Warren then changed the conversation to talk about the problems he had with his military records. He mentioned that he had been working with his congressman, apparently trying to locate his records.

> [Warren] said, beginning with Fawcett and Greenwood's book, that he had seen distortions, apparently forgetting that these distortions were the result of his telling the story several different ways.

Halt, later in the conversation, asked Warren a number of questions about the story. "Where did the story come from that, number one, Gordon Williams was there.... Where did the little green men come from?"

Warren interrupted, and parroting a line that was attributed to Mack Brazel of Roswell UFO crash fame, said, "They weren't green." But after chuckling, he said, "There was something there that was alive."

Halt said, "There are two nights there that are intertwined. Are you aware of that?"

At this point Halt was trying to end the confusion. Halt said, "You have events from the first night in the second, or in the third, night rather intertwined together. It's very confusing."

Warren asked cautiously, "What are the events that are intertwined?"

"The actual confrontation with a craft, or whatever you want to call it."

"You don't feel there were several...."

Halt interrupted again to say, "No."

"I have witnesses I've talked to from the third night that say there were (unintelligible) lights...." Then Warren, keeping with his third-night theory, said, "Sounds like a lot of minds were jerked around with, then."

Until Warren had introduced the third night, the thinking was that there were events on two nights, and if that was true, then Warren's role was nonexistent. His knowledge would have come from talking with other members of his unit who had been directly involved. That makes for a simple way to dismiss Warren, but it is not that simple.

Jim Penniston, who was clearly there and deeply involved, has said there were only two nights of activity. But John Burroughs, who was also clearly there and also deeply involved, said that there were three.

> ... those who had participated were subjected to some sort of interrogations that left them with few conscious memories of what happened.

And when Warren said that it "sounds like a lot of minds were jerked around with, then," he might not have been far from the truth. There is a growing body of evidence that once the events were over, those who had participated were subjected to some sort of interrogations that left them with few conscious memories of what happened.

Peter Robbins, who was also there during the conversation between Warren and Halt, said, "I have a question for you. Let's say there were real, unexplainable events that happened, and they were taken advantage of.... That if certain men, Larry and Adrian, to name two, remember certain things that were a mixture of what happened and what was programmed for them to remember for other purposes. Larry remembers Colonel Halt being there...."

Warren interrupted to correct Robbins. "Colonel Williams...."

Robbins agreed and continued, "Could that have been part, for some reason, to keep this...."

Robbins didn't finish the question. Instead, Warren said, "Okay. Fair enough."

"When I took the tape on the following Saturday morning," said Halt, "it was the day after. I ran into Gordon Williams in the hallway of the office.... I was going into the office to pick up some papers, and he was coming in to do something similar ... we stopped in the corner to talk, and I told him about it. And I told him about the tape. He said, 'Do you have the tape?' and I said, 'Yeah. It's in my office.' He said, 'I want to take it down and play it for the general....' He was totally surprised by the whole thing. He had a very keen interest. Took the tape down and played it and brought the tape back and I said, 'What happened?' He said, 'Nobody knew what to do.' He said, 'I played it at the staff meeting and [the general] asked, 'Is Halt credible?' ... He brought the tape back and said, 'Call me the next time. I want to be there too.'"

Warren, after a few minutes, said, "I'm not married to anything I say. All I have done, or tried to do through the years...." He then talked about telling his mother, who, according to Warren, could tell whether he was lying or not. From Warren's point of view, his mother had believed him.

Halt interrupted this to ask, "Do you remember two separate, distinct nights, or were you involved in one night?"

"One. But what I remember on that night ... I can remember people with me and that whole bit ... I can remember that is real or created or God knows now, but that's fine...."

Warren is in effect suggesting that his memories of the events might have been created by someone else, or to be clear, implanted during an interrogation. But if Warren wasn't involved in the sightings in the forest, then why would he be interrogated? Further, if there was no reason to interrogate him, why did he know that they had taken place?

The Warren intrusion into the case might be a complete invention by Warren, but he did have inside knowledge. It could be based on what others said after the events, but he knew that something had happened and he knew that there had been interrogations. The problem for Warren is that Burroughs has said that he knew who was there, and Warren wasn't among them. Warren's role, then, was more of a whistleblower than a participant.

Jim Penniston, who apparently approached closer to the object than anyone except John Burroughs, told the former members of Congress at the Citizen Hearing in May 2013 that he had undergone an interrogation. He had been questioned by two men he didn't know, who administered sodium pentothal.

As he attempted to get treatment for medical problems that happened while on active duty, John Burroughs was told that his civilian doctors had been told that there were no records of his service between 1979 and 1982. While many former members of the military have difficulty in retrieving records, it is interesting that Burrough's records have disappeared covering the critical period.

This was clarified in the publication of *Encounter in Rendlesham Forest.* Penniston wrote, in Chapter 19, "Final Thoughts from John Burroughs and Jim Penniston:" "I have had difficulty with what I saw and was exposed to out there that night. Within weeks after the incident I was being treated for new ailments I had not had before: vertigo, headaches, and then memory issues and unknown infections: all treatable but always reoccurring."

This establishes that Penniston had reported to the military doctors, that he was having some health problems that were probably related to the events in the forest. Even if a direct connection couldn't be established, the injuries happened while on active duty and should have been covered by the military and by their health care providers after discharge. There was an obligation by the government to pay for the treatment. Of course, with the military medical records missing, then there was no obligation to pay the costs, because it couldn't be established that the injuries had been sustained while on duty.

From the left are Nick Pope, John Burroughs, and Jim Penniston, preparing to testify at the Citizen Hearing on Disclosure.

That's not all. Warren had suggested that some kind of interrogation had taken place and now, both at the Citizen Hearing in 2013 and in the book, Penniston was confirming that. He wrote, "I often think, so if my memory was messed with, then the obvious question is why? ... I am sure that information could have been extracted under drugs or in other parts of the interrogation, as described in my one and only hypnosis session.... When I was taken into the building for debriefing and sodium pentothal, the agents revealed nothing.... I do take medication that curtails the nightmares and flashbacks from the night."

The most frightening part of this section is that Penniston was having serious heart issues and that his doctor needed to see his military medical records. They contacted an attorney, Pat Frascogna, and Senator John Kyl, who attempted to help. According to what Penniston wrote in *Encounter in Rendlesham Forest*, "Senator Kyl's first attempt to get my records was denied by the U.S. VA [Veteran's Administration]. They told him that I [Penniston] needed to file a VA claim for disability, and then came the most stunning part of the letter: they told him they felt my records could be located in the VA classified records and that if they were, it would be up to the USAF to release those records to the Senator and my doctor for treatment or even allow the VA to treat me."

This establishes that Penniston suffered serious injury because of his close approach to the UFO. John Burroughs also suffers from a variety of maladies as a result of the incident in the forest. Both men have used various means to gain access to their records and have failed. This indirectly establishes that something they came into contact with on those nights has affected their health, and because of the nature of the event, the U.S. government seems to believe that it is more important to keep that incident buried in a fog of denial than it is to treat the service members who were injured.

There was a change in the status, at least for Burroughs, in March 2015. Burroughs learned that his claims for disability had been approved. He would receive compensation for the injuries that he sustained while on active duty. While this does not lead directly to the conclusion that the VA was confirming the UFO sighting, it does provide another piece of evidence.

Analysis

It would seem, based on the evidence and the investigations conducted by those in Brazil, that the injuries reported to have been inflicted on the soldiers at Fort Itaipu in 1957 didn't happen. The best that Brazilian UFO researchers, including Thiago Luiz Ticchetti, could say was that there might have been a UFO sighting at the time. Reports of the injuries were exaggerated by Dr. Olavo Fontes, some saying that he was attempting to get his name in front of an American audience. The research done by others in later years simply did not bear out the facts he claimed. Add to this that he didn't name a single source, and most researchers, if not rejecting the case outright, find it highly dubious.

The case of Army PFC Bernard G. Irwin is equally bizarre. There are names associated with it, and Jim and Coral Lorenzen believe that it happened. There are aspects of it that are quite strange, but the reason to reject the case in today's world is because Irwin disappeared from the UFO scene. Irwin's actions, when looked at in a dispassionate light, make no real

> There is no physical evidence to support the story, but then, there is actually no reason for it to be invented, especially at that time.

sense, unless he was attempting to find a way out of the of the investigation being conducted by the Lorenzens. It is clear from his record that he remained at Fort Bliss long after Lorenzen thought he had gone. His fainting spells and periods of unconsciousness are suspicious, but in the end, the case is single witness, not to mention that there isn't much in the way of a UFO sighting.

The one aspect of the case that is interesting is that in today's world, researchers would be wondering if Irwin had experienced an alien abduction. There are the clues there, but in 1959, no one was thinking in those terms, and with Irwin gone long before the Lorenzens began their research into abductions, there was no way to follow up on the idea.

The Leominster, Massachusetts, case sounds like many of those that came out of the 1957 events. It is a report of a stalled car and then a brief paralysis of one of the witnesses. Again, the case is based on the testimony of the two witnesses, but their credibility is in question. There is no physical evidence to support the story, but then, there is actually no reason for it to be invented, especially at that time. UFOs weren't quite the hot topic they had been in November 1957, when there were literally dozens of reports of stalled cars and the occasional report of slight injuries.

This case would be simple to ignore, except for the criminal record of one of the witnesses. He had been in trouble with the police, and they knew who he was. It just seems unlikely that someone would invent such a wild tale and then go to the police with it, given his background. Ironically, in this case, it seems that what might have been considered a disqualifying factor in the case supports, to some extent, the validity of it.

It is the Falcon Lake, Winnipeg, Canada, case that involved Stefan Michalak that is on much more solid ground. While it is again a single-witness case, there are the unexplained burns in a somewhat geometric pattern on his body. There are the other unexplained reactions to his close approach to the UFO. Given the nature of the witness, the nature of the case, and the limited physical evidence, the case is a very good one.

Chris Rutkowski, who does believe the case is good, acknowledges the flaws in it. If the fire towers were manned as they were required to be, then someone should have seen the craft that Michalak said he saw. If, on the other hand, those rangers, for whatever reason, weren't there at the proper time, then this isn't a major problem. Michalak's story did check out, for the most part, and the criticisms leveled at it by official investigators might be based more on personal opinion than observed fact.

The Kerman, California, case is even better. It is a multiple-witness case, meaning that people in a number of locations saw the UFO in the air. The burns seen on the police officer had not been there at the beginning of his shift and were observed by a number of his fellow officers after the sighting. There is documentation that confirms the physical effects reported by the police officer. This seems to be one of those cases where there are multiple chains of evidence, documentation, and observed effects. Properly investigated at the time, this case could have provided some very interesting evidence and might have suggested some answers, if it hadn't been shrouded in the mantle of UFO.

And finally, there is the Rendlesham Forest case. Again, it is multiple witness, there were landing traces, there were aftereffects on some, possibly all, of the witnesses, and it was documented not only by the tape of Colonel Halt, but the memo he wrote, as well as other files. But this case became an international hot potato, with the English saying that it happened to American service members, who were stationed at the base next to the forest, and the Americans saying that it had happened outside the base perimeter on English soil. Neither side seemed to want to handle it.

The service members involved have provided some very interesting details; it does appear that officials from both governments did, in fact, investigate, and there is evidence of interrogations, as opposed to debriefings, of those directly involved. There are also reports of physical effects from the close approach of the UFO. These ongoing health problems seem to be a result of the UFO, but those interested in obtaining their military medical records have been denied access to them because they were classified until recently.

This is not to mention the tape made by Halt as he explored the woods on the second night. While that is certainly interesting and provides an insight into what the men felt as they approached the lights, the more important aspect is the hint that there is more tape of the encounter. Without being allowed to hear it, researchers can only speculate about what it might reveal; however, if the information was benign, the tape would have been allowed to enter the public arena.

The last thing to be noted is that it doesn't seem that the injuries suffered by so many are of a hostile nature. While it could be suggested that the soldiers at Fort Itaipu were attacked, the investigations of Brazilian UFO researchers suggests that the attack didn't take place.

And others seem to have suffered injuries as a result of their actions. They approached the UFOs and were burned simply by that proximity. There is no evidence that the UFOs intended to injure them and that the actions of the UFO crews might be seen as resulting from the actions of the people involved. Had they not approached, they probably wouldn't have been injured. The burns and other maladies suffered are more of a side effect than a direct, hostile action. That doesn't mean that the witnesses are to blame for their curiosity or for doing their duty. The police officer and the Air Force service members were checking out a situation that might have been of immediate importance.

> The last thing to be noted is that it doesn't seem that the injuries suffered by so many are of a hostile nature.

There is one important fact that is evident in many of these cases and something that has been mentioned before. There were opportunities for some real, scientific investigation in these cases. Unfortunately, there were artificial roadblocks erected. In the Kerman, California, case, the chief of police didn't want his officers talking to anyone about what had happened. That prevented the opportunity for some real research.

The Rendlesham Forest case had two governments arguing about jurisdiction, each claiming the other had it. The information was hidden behind a shield of security, and the opportunity for some real research was lost. Now the argument is about the physical evidence, and the service members injured are at the mercy of military protocol and national security.

The point is that there have been many opportunities to learn something about what is being seen, but rather than attempt to do that, the witnesses are ridiculed, governments prevent research, and the opportunities are lost. All that can be said now is that the evidence suggests there is no overt hostility, and given the problems with UFO research, that might be the best that can be said.

Lights in the Night Sky

August 25, 1951: The Lubbock Lights

The first well-publicized UFO sighting that involved a series of lights seen over several days took place in Lubbock, Texas, beginning on August 25, 1951. Several professors from the Texas Technical College (now known as Texas Tech University) watched a group of dully glowing lights pass overhead in a matter of seconds. None of the men got a very good look at the lights, and none were sure what they had seen. The lights had been in sight for only two or three seconds.

The professors, W. I. Robinson, A. G. Oberg, and W. L. Ducker, discussed the sightings and tried to determine what they would do if the lights returned. About an hour later they had another sighting, and this time they were ready.

The lights were softly glowing bluish objects in a rough "U" formation. During the first sighting, the lights had been in a more structured formation, or rather, that was the impression the professors had. They weren't sure of numbers of lights, only that they silently crossed the sky.

Their next move, they decided, was to try to find anyone else who had seen the lights. Ducker called the local newspaper and spoke to the managing editor, Jay Harris, who wasn't interested in the story. Ducker, however, wasn't to be denied. Harris argued that he would only run the story if he could use the names of the professors. Ducker wasn't sure he liked that idea and at first refused. He then called back and agreed, but only if Harris would contact the public relations department of the college.

The details were worked out, and the story ran in the Lubbock *Avalanche-Journal*. There were others who had seen the lights on the same night.

Two of the witnesses to a strange formation were in Albuquerque, New Mexico. According to the Project Blue Book report, a man, Hugh Young, and his wife, he being a security guard for the Atomic Energy Commission at Sandia and who had a "Q" security clearance, said they had seen a flying, winglike craft that was only eight hundred to a thousand feet overhead. There were dark bands running from the front to the back, and the lights on the trailing edge were glowing blue-green. It made no sound. The object disappeared to the south in a matter of seconds.

The Air Force linked the sightings. In a letter that had once been classified and addressed to the Inspector General at Kirtland AFB, it was noted:

1. Reference is made to your Spot Intelligence Report of 27 August 1951, subject give above [Unconventional Type of Aircraft Sighted].... It is not known whether or not you are familiar with a report from OSI [Air Force Office of Special Investigations] District Office No. 23, Carswell Air Force Base, Fort Worth, Texas, in which a similar sighting over Lubbock, Texas, on 25 August 1951 is reported....

2. Also inclosed [sic] are four photographs taken by Mr. Carl Hart, Jr., on 30 August 1951, which are supposedly very similar to those seen over Lubbock, Texas, on 25 August 1951. It is requested that these photographs be shown to Mr. Hugh Young and obtain his opinion as to whether or not this is what he saw over Albuquerque....

Carl Hart in a photo taken in 1951.

There was a response on November 14. It said, "On 10 November 1951, Mr. and Mrs. Hugh Young were shown the photographs inclosed [sic] with referenced letter and stated the formation of lights appeared similar to the lights they had observed on the trailing edge of the unidentified object they saw...."

There are those who also believe that this object, with its V-shaped formation of lights, was what the professors saw hours later. And, once the newspaper published the story, there were others who said they had seen the same thing that night. One of those was Joe Bryant from Brownsfield, Texas, who said that he had been sitting in his backyard when a group of lights flew over. He said that they had a kind of glow and were bigger than a star but were not in any sort of formation. He saw a second group a little later, and there was a third flight. This time they dropped down and circled as if for a landing, but then one of them chirped. According to Bryant, these were plover. If he hadn't been able to identify them when one chirped, he would have been as puzzled as the men in Lubbock.

The professors, unaware of Bryant's identification of the objects, set out to obtain additional information. They were joined by others, were equipped with a two-way radio, and had a measured baseline for calculations of height, speed, and size, and they began to wait. The problem was that those who were off along the baseline never saw anything, though the wives, who had remained at the house, did see the lights.

All this probably would have faded away, except that on August 31, 1951, Carl Hart, Jr., a nineteen year-old high school graduate who was going to enter Texas Tech in the fall and who was an amateur photographer, took five pictures as the lights flew over his house.

Hart said that he had seen the lights flash by. He knew that they sometimes returned, so he got his camera ready in case they did. When the lights reappeared a few minutes later, he managed to take two pictures of them and not long after that, he had the chance to take three more.

Although Hart didn't approach the newspaper, Harris learned about the pictures from a photographer on the staff. Harris was the one who suggested that Hart bring in the pictures, but Harris still feared a hoax. With William Ham, the newspaper's lead photographer, Harris interviewed Hart for the next several hours. Harris asked Hart if he had faked them, and Hart denied it. Nearly forty years after the incident, when I asked Hart about that, he said that he still didn't know what he had photographed.

Ham told Air Force investigators, specifically Edward Ruppelt, that he had tried to replicate the pictures. Standing on the top of the *Avalanche-Journal* building, he tried to photograph birds as they flew over at night. Although he could see, barely, the birds flying over, nothing registered on the film. From his attempts to duplicate Hart's pictures, he concluded that Hart couldn't have photographed birds under any circumstances.

Air Force investigations continued throughout the fall, and they interviewed Hart more than once. They did everything they could think of to get him to admit the hoax, if it was one, including informing him of his rights under the Constitution, but he told them that he had taken pictures of the objects as they had flown overhead. Ruppelt, in his report, wrote, "Hart's story could not be 'picked apart' because it was entirely logical. He [Hart] was questioned on why he did certain things, and his answers were all logical, concise, and without hesitation."

The Air Force again talked to the professors. They said that the pictures taken by Hart did not match what they had seen. The objects in Hart's

The offices of the *Lubbock Avalanche-Journal*. Hams stood on top of this building to try to take better photos of the lights.

photos were flying in a V formation, but what they had seen was more of a U formation.

During the investigation, Air Force officers found a number of other sightings in the area. Prior to August 25, J. Russell Heitman, who was the "head of tech journalism," said that he had seen a "string of beads" fly over.

On August 31, several witnesses, including S. E. West and J. F. Woolsey, watched lights in V or U formations fly over. On the same night, T. E. Snider saw a formation of lights fly over the Westerner Drive-In, but he said that they were definitely ducks.

The next day Mack Forester and W. S. Bledsoe, in two separate sightings, saw formations fly over. One, Forester, said they were too fast for ducks, and they were flying in a U- or V-shaped formation. Bledsoe, a radio engineer, said that they definitely were ducks. The sightings took place about two hours apart.

On September 5, another group of professors from Texas Tech had a sighting that was reported to the Air Force. According to the official file:

The 5 September 1951, sighting was observed by a group of people with scientific backgrounds from the Texas Tech faculty. The group was unnamed but included six men with Ph.D. degrees. They observed three flights and supposedly made measurements. Their counter to the migratory fowl theory is that:

a. There would not be enough light from reflections to obtain photographs of birds in flight at night. (Comment: Substantiated by the Photo Section at WADC.)

b. The speed is too great, a 120-degree-arc in 3 seconds....

c. The object was sighted by Big Spring Texas Airport officials from the airport, which was not lighted, so there could be no light to reflect.

d. In regard to the 120-degree arc, one flight was observed over a cloud that was at 2,000'. The professors calculated that if the object were at 2,000', the speed would be greater than 600 mph....

In an investigation conducted privately in 1993, experts at Texas Tech said that there were ducks in the Lubbock area that flew in V formations, but they had dark breasts that don't reflect light. There are migratory birds that fly over Lubbock, but that happens later in the year. What this proves is that whatever was photographed, it was not birds.

Joe Bryant claimed that he saw the lights and then he saw them close enough to identify them as birds. There is no reason to debate his identification. He saw birds. But from Bryant, the Air Force investigators extrapolated that all the Lubbock sightings could be explained by birds. In their final analysis, they wrote all the sightings off as birds, even the photographs. They wrote, "It was concluded that birds, with street lights reflecting from them, were the probable cause of these sightings.... In all instances, the witnesses were located in an area where their eyes were dark-adapted, thus making the objects appear brighter."

There is one other aspect to this that becomes important. The Air Force officers, in the course of their investigation, discovered another sighting of the flying wing made just hours after the sighting by Young and his wife. A man told the Air Force investigators that his wife had been in the back, taking down the wash, when she came running into the house. He said that she was white as a ghost and was shouting about a giant, "winglike" aircraft that had just flown over the house. It moved silently and had several bluish lights on the trailing edge.

There were two important points about this. First, because of the timing, there was no way that the woman had heard of the Albuquerque sighting. Second, the flying wing being developed by Northrop was not flying anywhere in that area at that time.

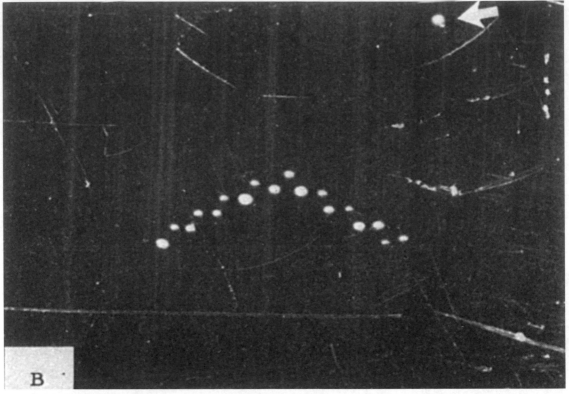

This photo of the lights taken by Carl Hart has become quite famous among UFO enthusiasts.

These other sightings, including those in which an object was seen, didn't persuade the Air Force. The opinion continued to circulate that birds, flying in loose formations and reflecting the streetlights, was the solution, and that is how the sightings are carried in the Project Blue Book files.

Ruppelt, however, didn't seem to agree. In his book, *The Report on Unidentified Flying Objects*, he wrote:

Personally I thought that the professor's lights might have been some kind of birds reflecting the light from mercury-vapor street lights, but I was wrong. They weren't birds, they weren't refracted light, but they weren't spaceships. The lights the professors saw—the backbone of the Lubbock Light series—have been positively identified as a very commonplace and easily explainable natural phenomena [sic].... It is very unfortunate that I can't divulge exactly the way the answer was found because it is an interesting story of how a scientist set up complete instrumentation to track down the lights and how he spent several months testing theory after theory until he finally hit upon the answer.... But he fully convinced me that he had the answer, and after having heard hundreds of explanations of UFOs, I don't convince easily.... With the most important phase of the Lubbock Lights "solved"—the sightings by the professors—the other phases become only good UFO reports.

But a solution that isn't offered is no solution whatsoever. Eventually, however, that explanation would be learned. According to Ruppelt's notes and records on the sighting and available to researchers after his death, that final answer was fireflies. That still does not explain the pictures taken by Hart.

But even all this doesn't cover the whole event. The *Amarillo Daily News* of August 27, 1951, reported that several people in Amarillo had seen two groups of objects fly over. The objects over Amarillo had appeared twenty hours after the professors had seen the lights in Lubbock. According to the newspaper, "This [the lights moving at incredible speed] jibed with the report by Bill Coons ... one of the observers here, who said they were 'flying faster than any jet I've seen.'"

> The first group was made up of two objects, which looked as if they had been stacked one on top of the other. The second group of five flew over about five minutes later.

According to Coons, the first group was made up of two objects, which looked as if they had been stacked one on top of the other. The second group of five flew over about five minutes later. All the objects had a pale pink glow and moved without a sound. His wife watched them until they disappeared behind the drive-in theater screen.

On September 2, 1951, the Amarillo newspaper reported that "Mrs. Ross DeFries ... said she saw about 100 saucers between 9:40 and 9:45 o'clock. She said the objects were flying at high speed in formations of about ten each." It was also reported that she had seen flying saucers every night for the last week.

On September 4, 1951, the *Odessa* [Texas] *American* reported, "String of Beads Is Seen Again in Sky by Odessans." According to the story, J. W. Horton reported that he and his wife, on September 3, spotted what they said "appeared to be a lit 'flock of geese' traveling at great speed from east to west...." Horton said that the objects were flying in a V formation and were at least 2,000 feet overhead.

That story also mentioned that Bill Winston said that he had seen something similar two days earlier while at a drive-in movie.

There is no way to prove that these sightings and the one from Albuquerque are directly related to what was seen in Lubbock and what was photographed by Hart. There are descriptions of formations that match one another generally; they are associated in time, taking place in the same two-week period; and there were multiple sightings of multiple objects—all of which suggest a relation.

In the end, if everything is taken into account, there seem to be some solutions to some sightings, but only those in which the witnesses actually saw birds. In other sightings, including the one from Albuquerque, there is no simple solution. There are multiple witnesses, there are photographs of the lights over Lubbock which are not identified, and there are witnesses in other cities around Texas. Birds do not explain these sightings.

Lubbock, however, is not the only location in which there were multiple sightings of lights in the night sky. One of the best known of these took place over Belgium in 1989 and 1990.

November 1989: The Belgian Triangle

The beginning of this series of sightings is marked by a case from Eupen, Belgium, on November 29, 1989, when 120 people, including thirteen police officers, saw a UFO at close range. The object had shining lights and made no sound. Although there were multiple witnesses and there were discussions of a triangle shape behind the lights, this case was little more than a report of nocturnal lights. It is important, not because of the number of witnesses, but because it seems to mark the beginning of a series.

According to Major General Wilfried De Brouwer, as reported by Leslie Kean in *UFOs: Generals, Pilots and Government Officials Go on the Record*, two of the thirteen police officers, Heinrich Nicoll and Hubert Von Montigny, were on patrol near the German border at 5:15 P.M. They saw a field light up with an intensity that would have allowed them to read a newspaper in their

Witnesses said the triangular UFO hovered by Belgium's Lake Gileppe for about an hour, plenty of time to get a good look at it.

car. Over the field, they saw a triangular object with three lights surrounding a single red light. It moved silently toward the German border and then turned back toward Eupen. It remained over the town for about thirty minutes.

The object then began to move toward Lake Gileppe, where it stopped again and hovered for about an hour. The police officers, Nicoll and Von Montigny, saw the UFO flash two red beams with a ball on the end. When the beams disappeared, the red balls returned to the craft. The cycle repeated itself several times, each cycle lasting several minutes.

Over 90 minutes later, a second craft appeared. This time they got a better look at the object when it tilted, showing the top of the UFO. There seemed to be a dome on top with lit, rectangular windows. It eventually disappeared, flying to the north.

Then the first craft stopped emitting the red balls and it too departed, but moving toward the southwest. These were not fleeting glimpses of an object, but prolonged observations of them. Both officers had time to study them and determine that they were something strange rather than some odd, natural phenomenon.

When the objects left, they learned over the police radio that two other officers, Dieter Plummans and Peter Nicoll (who is no relation to Heinrich Nicoll) watched the craft coming from the direction of Eupen. They stopped near a monastery. The craft had three strong spotlights and a bright, flashing red light in the center. They believed they were within 300 feet of it and that it was hovering about 250 feet in the air, or, in other words, they were close enough to get a very good look at it.

This object also began to emit a red light ball from the center. It dropped straight down and then turned so that it was flying horizontally. It disappeared behind some trees as the craft moved to a position directly over the police car and flew toward the northeast. They followed it for nearly five miles before they lost sight of it, but Heinrich Nicoll and Hubert Von Montigny could still see it.

Thirteen police officers in eight locations around Eupen saw the UFO. Dozens of others also made reports of something strange that night. It seemed that like the reports from Levelland, Texas, in November 1957, this object was seen at a low level and moved slowly enough that many of the witnesses had the opportunity to get a good look at it. Of all these sightings, seventy of them, according to De Brouwer, were investigated, but no conventional craft explained the sightings.

Two nights later, Francesco Valenzano (a Belgian weather specialist at the time) and his daughter were walking through Ans, in Liege province, when his daughter shouted at him. In the sky overhead was a triangular-shaped object that was drifting slowly above the buildings in the town square at a low altitude. Valenzano said that he saw the triangular shape with three lights at the corner and a rotating, red light in the center, a description that matched, to an extent, the object that had been reported earlier. Finally, it flew off toward another village.

On December 11, a lieutenant colonel (later colonel) in the Belgian Army, Andre Amond, reported that as he was driving with his wife, he spotted a slow-moving, strangely lit object at a low altitude. He said that it had three large light panels with a flashing, red light. He had been driving faster than the object was moving, so he stopped the car and got out. A searchlight from the craft approached to within about 300 feet of them, and Amond's wife wanted to leave. As he opened the car door, the object turned, and three other lights appeared, forming a triangle with a flashing light in the center. It made no sound, and they couldn't see any structure. The UFO accelerated suddenly and disappeared.

> Valenzano said that he saw the triangular shape with three lights at the corner and a rotating, red light in the center, a description that matched, to an extent, the object that had been reported earlier.

The next day, SOBEPS (the Société belge d'étude des phénomènes spatiaux, or Belgian Society for the Study of Space Phenomena), several police officers, and members of the Belgian Air Force held a press conference in Brussels. According to Peter Gutierrez in an article in *The Bulletin*, the Defence Minister, Guy Coeme, had ordered the Belgian Air Force to investigate. He would later eliminate a number of the suggested solutions for the sightings, including an AWACS (large plane filled with radar and communications gear) aircraft and other aircraft, including the F-117 stealth fighters, that would be blamed by some journalists.

In fact, a few days after the press conference, on December 18, 1989, it was reported that the "most plausible explanation" for the sightings were flights of the F-117. But there was no documentation to corroborate the theory, and the sightings continued.

The most spectacular of these new sightings and the ones that seemed to underscore the importance of the wave took place on March 30 and 31. This time, the sightings resulted in the scrambling of Belgian Air Force F-16 fighters. Dozens of witnesses, including several police officers, reported that the triangular-shaped object was back. The fighters were launched to chase it down.

According to one account, the fighter pilots had no visual contact with the UFO, but the on-board radar locked on to a target. It moved slowly, only about twenty-five miles an hour, and then it would suddenly accelerate to high speeds, described as "fantastic." It was traveling at 7,500 feet and then dropped to 750 feet.

The fighters locked on to the target three times, but each time the UFO evaded them. Eventually, both the fighters and the UFO left the area. But one of the pilots had photographed his radarscope so that a record of the intercepts had been kept. Auguste Meessen, a physics professor at the Catholic University of Louvain, and scientists associated with SOBEPS had the opportunity to review the evidence. In June, SOBEPS released the results of their examinations. They found no conventional explanation for the sighting.

At the same time, Major P. Lambrechts of the Belgian Air Force general staff released the official report. All conventional explanations—and he listed all of them—had been rejected by their investigation. According to Michael Swords in *UFOs and Government*, "The report was of the opinion that the performance characteristics of the objects, particularly with regards to their speed in change of altitude and the lack of sonic boom, precluded their identification."

That wasn't the end of the sightings. Although these sightings were less than exciting, from an evidence point of view, they did underscore the continuing nature of the events. On May 4, 1990, an archaeologist walked out of his

Not only did witnesses on the ground see the UFO triangle, but it was also spotted by two F-16 jets using radar.

greenhouse, closed the door, and heard the neighborhood dogs howling. He saw a huge object in a field about five hundred feet away.

Although he wanted others to see this, only his wife was available. They described a cone-shaped object with a top that had a mushroomlike appearance. After several minutes, they went into the house, but the man came back out. The UFO had moved and now was only 100 to 150 feet away.

It had made no noise, or rather, none that he had heard. The center was bright and opaque; the center was white, and the edges were yellowish. The UFO was twenty-five to thirty feet in diameter at the base and seemed to be about eighteen feet tall.

The mushroom tip detached and began to climb. As it did, it turned bright orange and then after a few minutes, it began to descend. It reattached itself, and the colors returned to their original hues.

Both the man and his wife returned outside to watch the UFO for a few minutes longer but could find no other witnesses. Their son went out the next day to where the UFO had been. He found and measured four circular impressions in a rectangular shape about twenty-five by thirty feet. In the grass in each of the markings was a yellow powder.

While the sightings continued, media in various countries came up with explanations for the sightings. The French magazine *Science and Life* took an anti-UFO view, suggesting, again, that the sightings were the result of secret American flights of the F-117. The aircraft does have a shape, especially when seen from the ground, that is triangular. But again, both American and Belgian sources rejected that explanation, and no evidence was found to support it. Meessen found the source of that rumor. According to an article published in the *International UFO Reporter* in the May/June 1991 issue:

> It turned out that the "explanation" was only speculation, put forward by the Flemish paper *Het Laatste Nieuws*. I [Meessen] phoned the journalist who wrote the article that triggered off a rumor, which is still causing much ink to be spilt. He explained that he had just read an article on the F-117A and wished to pass on such information to his readers. To make his article more interesting, he had suggested (gratuitously, with no reference to the actual sightings) that there might be a possible connection with the recent sightings in Belgium. In the meantime, I had learned from Lt. Col. De Brouwer, Chief of Operations of the Belgium Air Force, that the Air Force had sought information from the American Embassy to help them explain the reports. This should not have been necessary if the sightings were caused by secret exercises, as De Brouwer routinely would have been informed of any such overflights.

In October 1990, with the stealth fighter explanation rejected by American and Belgian officials, the magazine claimed that the sightings were caused by American experimental aircraft, flown by American pilots, without telling the Belgian officials about it. But there is no evidence for this either, nor is it explained why the experimentation would take place over Belgium rather than the remote areas of the U.S., where there would be little chance of observation by civilians or secret agents.

Even with explanations being trotted out, the sightings continued. On October 21, a Sunday, two people were returning to Bastogne when they spotted two lights descending toward them. One of them shouted, "They're coming for us."

Looking at this F-117 fighter jet from underneath certainly demonstrates why one theory about the Belgian UFO was that the triangular shape belonged to a military plane.

They lost sight of the object but it reappeared, now behind a hedge on the right side of the road. They thought this might be a reflection on the glass, but when they rolled down the window, the light was still there. Now it was about fifty feet from the car.

As they drove along, they thought that the UFO was pacing them. When they slowed, it slowed; when they stopped, it stopped, and when they accelerated, so did the craft. When they reached the end of the roadside hedge, they stopped again. The UFO appeared to be a dark mass more than forty-five feet in diameter. It then climbed into the sky silently. On the bottom was a ring of seven or eight lights.

About two days later, at 5:30 A.M. on October 23, a young woman identified only as Regine was awakened by her alarm clock. Through the window of her residence on the outskirts of Athus, near Luxembourg, she saw two bright lights hovering about a quarter mile away. Between those two lights was a dimmer, smaller, bluish light. After ten minutes, they rose into the sky and began to move silently toward her. The lights flew over the house, and she ran into the dining room so she could keep watch.

The object kept flying in the direction of Athus but then veered to the left, turning toward Luxembourg. It disappeared at that point. No other witnesses have come forward.

On the same day, in an event that apparently was unrelated, four teenagers watched an object that lifted off from behind a hill. They said it was about a quarter mile away and had bright lights on the lower side that were

They thought this might be a reflection on the glass, but when they rolled down the window, the light was still there.

directed toward the ground like searchlights or landing lights. Centered among these lights was another dimmer light.

They described the craft as pyramid shaped, with the apex pointing to the front. At the base were two red lights. They said they watched the UFO for about thirty seconds, until it disappeared behind another hill.

These sorts of sightings continued on throughout the rest of the year, and the New Year changed nothing. On January 6, 1991, two separate groups saw a low-flying object described as a circular plate. There were many lights on the UFO. According to one witness, the craft was about 250 feet long and forty to fifty feet high. The underside bulged outward and was dark gray. This witness said that there were fifteen lit portholes. The rear was flat and seemed to have fins.

After so much time, the press lost interest, which means only that they stopped reporting the sightings, not that the sightings had ended. The stories were becoming the same. Witnesses were seeing brightly lit, mostly triangle-shaped objects, floating silently above the ground. There were no real cases of any type of physical evidence, including photographs.

That changed on April 4, 1990, when a woman walking her dog said she saw spotlights of the UFO hovering over her house. She told her partner, who shot two slides of the UFO. He only had two exposures left on the film. Once he had shot the pictures, the UFO banked to the left and flew out of sight. The witness, identified only as Patrick, held on to the pictures for months before releasing them.

The photos were examined by a number of experts, who said that they found nothing on them to suggest hoax. Skeptics complained that the pictures held nothing but the object, so that no measurements could be made. There was no foreground or background detail and for them, this suggested that the pictures might be a hoax. No real conclusions were drawn. The investigation of the pictures disintegrated into the standard debate between believers and debunkers.

That all changed on July 26, 2011, when Patrick was revealed to be Patrick Marechal, and he said in an interview on Belgian TV that he had faked the pictures. He demonstrated how it was done.

But nothing is ever simple in the study of UFOs. Some of those in the UFO community claimed that the admission of a hoax was a hoax in itself. As late as May 2014, claims were made that no evidence had been presented to prove the hoax. Patrick was supposedly still identified only as Patrick, and no details were given. The Belgian TV report seems to refute this with Marechal launching the Styrofoam model he used to fake the pictures as evidence of what he had done.

It should be noted that those who had hoaxed UFO photographs eventually admitted to the hoax. Some of the photographs that were considered among the best have eventually been admitted to be hoaxes. There is no reason here to reject the idea. It seems clear that the photograph is a fake.

That in no way means that all the other sightings of a triangular object in Belgium are faked. There are dozens of interesting sightings, and they remain unexplained. In July 2008, at the 39th Mutual UFO Network (MUFON) Symposium, retired Major General Wilfred de Brouwer said:

> ... I was the Chief Operations in the Air Staff when an exceptional UFO wave took place over Belgium.... Belgium had no official focal point for reporting UFO observations. Nevertheless, in my function of Chief Operations, I was confronted with numerous questions about the origin and nature of these craft. In the first instance [November 29, 1989], and in consultation with other NATO [North Atlantic Treaty Organization] partners, I could confirm that no flights of stealth aircraft or any other experimental aircraft took place in the airspace of Belgium. In addition, the Civil Aviation Authorities confirmed that no flight plans had been introduced. This implied that the reported object(s) committed an infraction against the existing aviation rules.
>
> The Belgium Air Force tried to identify the alleged intruder(s) and, on three occasions, launched F-16 aircraft. On one occasion, two F-16[s] registered rapid changes in speed and altitude which were well outside of the performance envelope of existing aircraft. Nevertheless, the pilots could not establish visual contact, and the investigation revealed that specific whether [sic] conditions may have caused electromagnetic interferences and false returns on the radar screens. The technical evidence was insufficient to conclude that abnormal activities took place during that evening [March 30–31, 1990].
>
> In short, the Belgium UFO wave was exceptional, and the [Belgium] Air Force could not identify the nature, origin, and intensions [sic] of the reported phenomena.

The Belgium sightings are now in the realm of eyewitness testimony, with very little evidence to support the idea of an alien craft flying overhead. However, there is no good explanation for the sightings that cover all the events, and that is often where the UFO cases end, not so much with a bang as with a whimper.

The lights seen over Phoenix seem to underscore that. There are all sorts of eyewitnesses in many locations reporting a triangle or V-shaped formation flying over Arizona, with almost as many explanations as there are witnesses.

Some of the photographs that were considered among the best have eventually been admitted to be hoaxes.

March 13, 1997: The Phoenix Lights

In an interesting parallel to the other cases, the sighting of lights over Phoenix gained national publicity, but it was the sightings of an object that could be described as a flying wing with lights in a V formation that were made first in Nevada, rather than Arizona. Just before seven (Pacific Standard Time), a man living in Henderson, just outside of Las Vegas, said that he saw a V-shaped object that he thought was about the size of a Boeing 747 and that it sounded like the rushing of wind. There were six lights on the leading edge. He watched as it flew to the southeast, eventually disappearing over the horizon.

Had this been the only sighting in that area that night, it would have been just another UFO report. A little over an hour later, at 8:15 P.M., a former police officer said that he and his family saw a cluster of lights in a V formation near Paulden, Arizona. He described them as red-orange balls of light. He said that there were four lights traveling together, with a fifth bringing up the rear. He said that the lights were in sight for about two minutes and that they made no sound. He thought that each of the lights consisted of two parts. When he returned home, he watched them through binoculars until they vanished over the horizon.

Others reported the lights as they flew from northern Arizona to the southern corner, a distance of about two hundred miles in about thirty minutes, or at about four hundred miles per hour. The speed is not outside that of conventional aircraft.

The Sky Harbor Airport in Phoenix, Arizona, received multiple calls from pilots on March 13, 1997 about strange lights.

At the control tower at Phoenix's Sky Harbor Airport, the air traffic controllers received a large number of reports from pilots. The controllers, including Bill Grava, said he had no idea what everyone was seeing. To him, the lights were "weird, inexplicable." He thought there might be a military explanation, but he had no real answers.

Dana Valentine, a laser printer technician, said he was sitting in his yard when he saw the lights. He ran inside to alert his father, an aeronautical engineer, and both saw the lights, an estimated five hundred feet above them. They could also see a mass behind the lights. Neither could see a definable shape, just the formation of lights with a wavy, gray mass behind them. Neither of them could explain what they had seen.

Peter Davenport and his National UFO Reporting Center (NUFORC) received dozens of calls from witnesses in Arizona that night. According to him:

> One group of three witnesses, located just north of Phoenix, reported seeing a huge, wedge-shaped craft with five lights on its ventral surface pass overhead with an eerie "gliding" type of flight. It coursed to the south and passed between two mountain peaks to the south. The witnesses emphasized how huge the object was, blocking up to 70–90 degrees of the sky.
>
> A second group of witnesses, a mother and four daughters near the intersection of Indian School Road and 7th Avenue [in Phoenix], were shocked to witness an object, shaped somewhat like a sergeant's stripes, approach from over Camelback Mountain to the north. They report that it stopped directly above them, where it hovered for an estimated 5 minutes. They described how it filled at least 30–40 degrees of sky and how it exhibited a faint glow along

> its trailing edge. The witnesses felt they could see individual features on the ventral surface of the object, and they were certain that they were looking at a very large, solid object.
>
> The object began moving slowly to the south, at which time it appeared to "fire" a white beam of light at the ground. At about the same time, the seven lights on the object's leading edge suddenly dimmed and disappeared from the witnesses' sight. The object moved off in the general direction of Sky Harbor International Airport, a few miles to the south, where it was witnessed by two air traffic controllers in the airport tower and reportedly by several pilots, both on the ground and on final approach from the east.
>
> After this point in the sighting, the facts are somewhat less clear to investigators. It is known that at least one object continued generally to the south and southeast, passing over the communities of Scottsdale, Glendale, and Gilbert. One of the witnesses in Scottsdale, a former airline pilot with 13,700 hours of flight time,

"The object began moving slowly to the south, at which time it appeared to 'fire' a white beam of light at the ground."

reported seeing the object execute a distinct turn as it approached his position on the ground. He noted that he witnessed many lights on the object as it approached him, but that the number of lights appeared to diminish as it got closer to overhead. Many other witnesses in those communities reported seeing the object pass overhead as it made its way toward the mountains to the south of Phoenix.

Other sightings occurred shortly afterward along Interstate 10 in the vicinity of Casa Grande. One family of five, who were driving from Tucson to Phoenix, reported that the object that passed over their station wagon was so large that they could see one "wingtip" of the object out one side of their car and the other "wingtip" out the other side. They estimated they were driving toward Phoenix at approximately 80 miles per hour, and they remained underneath the object for between one and two minutes as it moved in the opposite direction. They emphasized how incredibly huge the object appeared to be as it blocked out the sky above their car.

Many witnesses, located throughout the Phoenix basin, allegedly continued to witness objects and peculiar clusters of lights for several hours following the initial sightings. One group of witnesses reported witnessing a large disc streak to the west over Phoenix at a very high speed. Others reported peculiar orange "fireballs," which appeared to hover in the sky even hours after the initial sightings.

One of the more intriguing reports was submitted by a young man who claimed to be an airman in the Air Force, stationed at Luke Air Force Base, located to the west of Phoenix in Litchfield Park. He telephoned the National UFO Reporting Center at 3:20 A.M. on Friday, some eight hours after the sightings on the previous night, and reported that two USAF F-15c fighters had been "scrambled" from Luke AFB and had intercepted one of the objects. Although the presence of F-15s could never be confirmed, the airman provided detailed information which proved to be highly accurate, based on what investigators would reconstruct from witnesses over subsequent weeks and months. Two days after his first telephone call, the airman called to report that he had just been informed by his commander that he was being transferred to an assignment in Greenland. He has never been heard from again since that telephone call.

What all this demonstrates is that there were more sightings than have been reported by most of those commenting on the lights. More importantly, some of the explanations offered in the days that followed did not account for the variety of sightings.

An air force pilot stationed at Luke Air Force Base west of Phoenix contacted the National UFO Reporting Center and claimed that jets had been scrambled and intercepted one of the UFOs.

But the sightings didn't end, they just became more controversial and produced a number of videotapes. These were lights that inspired the investigations as well as the media attention, because nothing excites the media like a good visual. One of the tapes, shown repeatedly on local, national, and cable television, was analyzed using an impressive-looking array of computers and some very sophisticated software. The conclusions drawn in those early investigations were that the lights were not natural phenomena and did not exhibit any of the features of manufactured lights. In other words, they were unique.

Quite naturally, the Air Force was questioned about this and the official spokesman said, as usual, that the Air Force no longer investigates UFOs. Most people in Phoenix were unhappy with that answer and believed that the Air Force was hiding the truth about this.

Others, including private researchers, began to gather the stories of the lights that had moved across Arizona, some of them believing that all the sightings were related. There were those who claimed to have seen a triangular-shaped object and others who claimed to have seen individual lights in a triangular or V-shaped formation. Some thought the lights were white, others red, and still others saw various faded colors in the lights.

Couple this with the hundreds of witnesses to the formation of lights that were videotaped over Phoenix, and an impressive case begins to emerge. But there are problems with the sighting. For example, an amateur astronomer, Mitch Stanley, who was interviewed by Tony Ortega of the *New Times*, said that he had seen the lights in the sky and turned his telescope on them. He said that he could see that they were airplanes. He saw them flying in a loose V formation.

He wasn't the only one who saw airplanes in formation that night. Tim Printy, on his website www.astronomyufo.com, reported that another witness to the formation was Rich Contry, who was driving west on I-40 north of Prescott when he saw the lights. According to an e-mail published by Printy, Contry wrote:

> I was on my way from Flagstaff to Laughin [Nevada] Thursday when I saw the light formation reported on the radio the other night. I'm a pilot and was in the U.S. air force [for] years. Being in the mountains on highway 40, the night was clear and still. As the formation came toward me, I stopped my car and got out with my binocs to check out what this was. As it came towards me, I saw 5 aircraft with there [sic] running lights (red and green) and the landing lights (white) on. They were also flying fairly slow and in the delta formation. As they went over me, I could see stars going between the aircraft, so it could not have been one large ship. The flying was like that of the Blue Angels or the thunderbirds demo team. Also as they went by, their jets were not very loud because of the low throttle setting for flying slow, but I did hear the jets as they went away toward the south.

One of the witnesses, Rich Contry, said the objects were flying like the Blue Angels in a delta formation like in this photograph.

Printy goes on to analyze the statement made by Contry, pointing out that Contry's original posting was made within days of the sighting. Printy wrote:

Rich gets many things right in his observation, which was posted a short time after his sighting.… He properly identified the number of craft in the videos of this formation (5) and also gets the direction correct (flying south). It was obvious to him that the objects were aircraft, but did anyone else see aircraft? When I contacted Rich, he confirmed to me that the aircraft came from a westerly direction (he could not recall specifics since I talked to him in January 1998) and appeared to head toward Prescott. Rich's memories of the events seem a bit faded by time since he had problems recalling if there was a moon that night. This is expected, since I am asking him to recall specifics almost 9 months after an event. His initial posting was made just a few days after the event and can be considered factual for the night in question. He told me that he felt they were military aircraft and could see the landing lights. He also felt they were low altitude and had their engines at a low throttle setting. He could not identify the aircraft but felt they may have been F-22s (I could not get a positive identification, and he was not sure) and saw one of the landing lights illuminate the front landing gear. He used 10 × 50 binoculars and felt they were several hundred feet apart in the formation. Most of the specifics are hard to get from Rich, since he could not recall (once again emphasizing how important those initial reports are). However, I am satisfied that Rich could have seen a formation of aircraft that night that may have produced the lighted V formation of lights.

It would seem that Federal Aviation Administration (FAA) regulations concerning flying in formation and could present some issues with the claim. But it comes down to an agreement by the aircraft commanders in each aircraft . There are some other requirements, but there was nothing to prevent civilian aircraft from flying in formation, especially as loose as the formation was described here. Military regulations cover formation flying by military aircraft, but again, there is nothing to prohibit it. Any suggestion that it couldn't have been a formation of aircraft because of either FAA or military regulations is wrong. And, if Contry saw F-22s, it is even more likely that this formation was aircraft.

The one piece of evidence needed to prove this to an exact degree would be for those flying in the formation to identify themselves. Given the publicity of the sightings, it would seem that one of those pilots would have mentioned that they were responsible for the sightings. If they had been military (which is the most likely possibility, given the speed), it would seem that the military would have had records to prove this and would have offered them as soon as the controversy started.

One of the things that came out of all this was that Captain Stacey Cotton from Luke AFB said that they had been asked if they had seen anything unusual that night and she said, "No." But she added that a formation of five aircraft traveling at high altitude over Sky Harbor would not have been considered unusual. Or, in other words, had they been seen on the military radar, no one would have given them a second thought.

There is no radar data available for any of this. According to those at Sky Harbor, these high flights would not be monitored on their radar. It would be controlled by FAA radar in Albuquerque. If such a flight had been made, it would have been represented by an asterisk, but since the flight would have been far above their control zone, they would not have been concerned about it. Radar records would have been kept in Albuquerque, but since no question about the radar displays was raised within two weeks, the tapes were reused. The record had been erased.

It might also be said that this is where things become confusing. There is good testimony that one formation of lights was identified as airplanes. While those in the UFO community were talking of multiple formations, it was reported by Steve Wilson of *The Arizona Republic* that they might be right. He interviewed four people who saw the lights and whose testimony suggests there was more than a single formation. He reported:

Dr. Bradley Evans, 47, is a clinical psychiatrist from Tucson. He and his wife, Kris, were driving north on Interstate 10 to a swimming meet in Tempe. They watched the lights for 20 minutes or so move slowly south in a diamond formation and pass over them at an estimated 1,500 feet. Even then, with the car's moonroof open, they heard not a sound from the sky. He was "awed" by the experience and has no idea what he saw. Kris said she couldn't explain it either and guesses it was "something military."

Contry believed he saw an F-22. When a jet plane is going at super-fast speeds, condensation can form around the body of the plane, making for an unusual appearance.

Trig Johnston, 50, is a retired commercial airline pilot who lives in north Scottsdale. His 22-year-old son was looking for Comet Hale-Bopp that night when he noticed the lights and told his dad.

"I looked up and remember saying out loud, 'I'm going to chalk this up to an illusion.' It was the size of 25 airliners, moving at about 100 knots at maybe 5,000 feet, and it didn't make a sound.

"I've flown 747s across oceans and not seen anything like I saw that night," Johnston said.

… Max Saracen, 34, is a real estate consultant who lives in north Phoenix. He and his wife, Shala, were driving west on Deer Valley Road when they saw a huge, triangular craft. They pulled off the road, got out, and watched it pass overhead. "It was very spooky—this gigantic ship blocking out the stars and silently creeping across the sky. I don't know of any aircraft with silent engines."

These reports don't sound as if they are observations of a formation of aircraft flying high. Evans and his wife, if their timing is accurate, watched the lights too long for them to have been aircraft flying at four hundred miles an hour. Johnston, as an airline pilot, should have recognized aircraft; he, of all the witnesses, would have been the most qualified to estimate size, speed, and altitude. True, without some way to scale size, meaning that the objects were in the sky without an object of known size close, he could have been badly mistaken.

> The local—and later, the national—media jumped on the tape, showing it over and over. It turned out that there was more than one tape....

The point is that these sightings don't seem to fit with some of the others and suggest that there might have been two objects or sets of lights seen that night. Those identified by Contry and Stanley as aircraft probably were aircraft. But other sightings don't seem to be that easily explained.

But it was the videotape of the lights over Phoenix that gained the most attention. The local—and later, the national—media jumped on the tape, showing it over and over. It turned out that there was more than one tape and that the others provided some interesting clues about the identity of these particular lights. These lights were not airplanes, and they weren't flying in a V-shaped formation. Here was some physical evidence that could be analyzed.

The Air Force was asked if they had been dropping flares in the area on March 13, and the official spokesman said that there were no flight operations that could have been responsible for the lights, so, by inference, there were no flares being dropped by the Air Force.

Village Labs in Phoenix, run by Jim Dilettoso, obtained a copy of one of the tapes and ran tests on it. He provided various local television, syndicated, and cable shows with his analysis claiming that he had proved that the lights, whatever they were, were not flares. The spectral analysis of the light was the deciding factor.

Other analysis, however, suggested the lights were exactly that—that is, videotape of airborne flares. Although the local Air Force units, including those at Luke AFB and Davis-Mothan AFB near Tucson, had said they had nothing flying that night to drop flares. But a visiting unit from the Maryland Air Guard was using the firing range that night, and their jets did drop flares. The confusion came about because the local units said they flew nothing and didn't mention the visiting unit.

Adding to this was an investigation by Arizona MUFON investigator Richard F. Motzer, who studied "all the videos I could find and interviewed other witnesses," outlined in his research in the July 1997 (number 351) issue of the *MUFON Journal*. He wrote:

The key to the solution was also the biggest mystery. Why did all videos of 3–13–97 at 10:00 P.M. have a different number of lights, different order of starting and decay, and shapes?

It was really dependent upon the observation point of the witness in the Phoenix area and, most important, how high their viewing point was. It turned out that the lights were not over Phoenix, but near the Estrella Mountains to the southwest. This determination was made after viewing all the videotapes and going to all but one of the sites and shooting 35 mm film in daylight. Using the point marked by the pilot, I drew a line from each of the sites where the Estrella lights were taped. On the Rairden tape there are nine lights, but only eight lights on the Moon Valley footage, and just in the early part you see a light form briefly, which then goes out, but did it really? No, something must have blocked it out, but it was still there in the Rairden footage. As the lights drifted downward, some lights were blocked out by the many small peaks making up the Estrella range.

… what I wanted to find was footage where a tripod was used and the zoom lens was left in one spot. To my surprise, there were several clips that met these specifications. What I did next was to mark each segment of the ground on a monitor and the ending position of each light. When I ran the editor video deck in reverse, I could see each light rise in altitude and drift to the right or to the left. In all the video clips, the results were the same. Just before each light went out, there was an increase in the descent of each light.

The Estrella Mountains are a small range surrounding Phoenix. MUFON investigator Richard F. Motzer believed people merely saw a group of flares burning against these mountains.

What this suggested to Motzer was that the lights were, in fact, flares. The witnesses believe that the lights were in front of the Estrella Mountains, but the video showed they were not. He learned that the Army had been firing flares that night and that these were parachute flares. The heat generated by the flare helps to slow the rate of descent of the flares, but as the flare begins to die out, the rate of descent increases. But there should be smoke visible, and some of the witnesses said they had seen no smoke. Motzer reported that the control tower crew at Sky Harbor had seen the smoke.

With that, including the confirmation by the Army National Guard that they were firing flares that night, that they were firing them at

8:30, 9:25, and 10:00 on March 13, and that the evidence on the tapes suggests flares, that seems to end the questions. Contrary to the reports from Village Labs, the evidence available suggests flares as the most logical and best solution here.

But this does not explain the V formations that some people reported. Given the timing of some of the reports and given the length of time that some of the V formations were visible to witnesses, it seems that there might have been more than a single event. That would mean that both Stanley and Contry saw airplanes, but some of the others might not have.

> They turned toward the light and when they did, it seemed to respond to them. It climbed suddenly, stopped, and then hovered, and both officers saw that it seemed to be rotating.

While this seems to be where the March 13 events remain—with the videotapes showing flares, some of the V formations were identified as aircraft, and the possibility of another flight of lights as something else—that wasn't the end of sightings in the Phoenix area. Jim Kelly, of Arizona MUFON, has investigated many of these later sightings.

One of the best of these, according to Kelly, involved two police officers in a helicopter, who had seen a strange, green light off in the distance on the evening of October 12, 1999. They said that it was about twice the size of Venus and might have been about four miles away from them. They could see no object behind the light.

Kelly, who interviewed the officers, said that they had been surprised and upset by what they had seen because they hadn't seen anything like that before. They turned toward the light and when they did, it seemed to respond to them. It climbed suddenly, stopped, and then hovered, and both officers saw that it seemed to be rotating. The smooth maneuvering suggested to the police officers that the light was under intelligent control rather than some sort of natural phenomenon.

As they tried to identify the source of the light, they wondered if it was some sort of reflection from the instrument panel but quickly eliminated that possibility. They turned and looked at the light through the open doors on the side of the helicopter. They had a clear view of it.

Kelly checked with the FAA in search of a possible radar contact, but the limited information he was able to recover suggested there was no radar contact. All that means is that limited search records show no radar contact, which doesn't mean the light wasn't there or had no substance. Given the nature of radar operations conducted by the FAA, this is not an unusual situation.

The police officers thought the light was several miles from them, but they were looking up at it, so distances and sizes, without some sort of reference, made judging these things difficult, if not impossible. They watched the light for ten or fifteen minutes but then were dispatched for a police call. When they returned, the light was gone.

The trouble here is that there was nothing seen other than a green light. It seemed to maneuver, it seemed to respond to them, but in the end, it was just a light seen at night. This is the classic definition of a nocturnal light.

In a case that is reminiscent of the original Phoenix Lights, Kelly said that he had learned of a videotape of three lights taken on July 4, 1999. They were flying with one another in a loose formation. His investigation, however, showed that several vintage aircraft were flying that night, and the videotape showed the lights of these aircraft. This, like those tapes made in 1997, showed manmade objects.

July 15, 2001: The New Jersey Lights

Telephone calls to police and to Peter Davenport's National UFO Reporting Center (NUFORC) began while the objects were still visible on July 15, 2001. According to the information Davenport provided, witnesses claimed that as many as one hundred cars and trucks were stopped along the highway of the New Jersey Turnpike just after midnight. They were watching a V-shaped formation of as many as thirty orange lights crossing the sky.

One of the first of those sightings reported to Davenport's hotline was made at 10:00 P.M. from Manhattan by five witnesses. The somewhat generic report said:

> I was on the Throgs [Neck] Bridge, going to New York, off Interstate 95 … about 10:00 to 11:00 P.M. I encountered seven lights in the New Jersey skyline on my right side. Six of [the] objects were very close together and seemed as if they were not moving. The largest object was by itself, and it was bright and appeared bigger than the rest of the objects encountered. As I moved over the bridge, my vision of the objects had disappeared, and I could no longer see the objects. The next day I heard on a radio station about the same encounter I had seen, and this is what made me report this sighting.

Connecting the Bronx and Queens over the East River, the Throgs Neck Bridge is where some drivers were commuting when they saw the V-shaped arrangement of mysterious lights.

The New Jersey *Star-Ledger* began its coverage of the sightings in an article written by Dore Carroll that featured a different aspect of this case. That story said:

A drowsy mother in Carteret [New Jersey] saw the flickering, golden lights in the sky and ran for her camera. A hard-boiled Navy veteran traveling the New Jersey Turnpike spotted the slow-moving, bright-yellow V formation and pulled his car to the shoulder to get a better look.

Police officers on patrol at 12:40 A.M. yesterday couldn't believe their eyes.

Within the hour, the Carteret police dispatchers said they heard from at least 15 callers reporting strange, orange flares blazing high about Arthur Kill. The eerie glow had people at backyard barbecues mesmerized, with heads upturned and mouths agape. Almost 75 vehicles pulled over on the New Jersey Turnpike to watch the spectacle.

"About 75 cars stopped on the highway to view the lights, and 15 people in different locations noticed it independently of each other and called the Carteret police department."

But no one seems to know what caused the luminous vision.

From that point, there are various quotes from various people about what the lights were not. The police had no explanation for the lights. Someone at the National Weather Service said there was nothing in the atmosphere that would have caused the lights, and an airman at McGuire Air Force Base said that they had no planes in the air at the time.

Carroll quoted Steven Vannoy, who had pulled over to watch the lights with his girlfriend. He said, "It wasn't fireworks, and it couldn't have been a hot-air balloon, not at night near the airfield."

Davenport's NUFORC continued to draw reports of the lights. In what he labeled as "Report #2," Davenport described a single object and stated that there were more than 90 witnesses. This one said:

It was a diamond-shaped craft but more of a V on one end, hovering over Arthur Kill River, Carteret, NJ, and between the Amoco Oil plants and the Elizabeth Consolidated Energy Plant. Object seemed to glow and hover about 500–1,000 feet in the air (not accurate). Lights were pulsating from orange to bright yellow and had no noise. Object seemed six to eight times larger than the size of regular aircraft flying through at their regular height. Witnesses include 80–90 people pulled over on the NJ Turnpike between exits 12 & 13. Carteret residents on northern end of West Carteret and Carteret may have seen it.

In Davenport's report on the sightings, he included a recap of those sightings in New Jersey. The report said:

I wish I had seen it too. Anyway, I would like to recap the facts presented by different people so far in regards to these observations.

The sighting was collective. About 75 cars stopped on the highway to view the lights, and 15 people in different locations noticed it independently of each other and called the Carteret police department. According to reports, police officers themselves saw the lights as well.

Whatever this was, it must have been close to the ground, as only people at Perth Amboy, Raritan Bay, and Carteret, NJ, but not in the neighboring towns, saw it.

The descriptions all point to orange-reddish, radial, self-contained lights in a V-shaped formation and then a diamond V-shaped formation. This does not convincingly correspond to any possibility of projected light from the ground or Aurora Borialis [sic], as some suggested....

Suggestions about what was seen ran the gamut from meteors to balloons. Meteors fail because of the duration of the sightings, but balloons, especially hot-air balloons built out of those lightweight bags from dry cleaners, do not. The balloon theory, however, does have some merit.

Tim Printy offered an analysis of the situation in the days that followed that suggested balloons. He wrote:

1. There were 15–30 lights that were independent of each other over Carteret, NJ, at roughly 12:30 A.M. on the morning of the 15th. They were independent of each other since most of the witnesses do not report seeing the dark shape that Filer [George Filer, a retired Air Force officer, who has published *Filer's Files* for many years, which is often featured in the *MUFON UFO Journal*] keeps talking about. They also were reported in different formations/formations that shifted.

2. Direction of travel seems to have been to the east (some witnesses at NIDS [National Institute for Discovery Science, a privately funded organization that investigated various areas of the paranormal] seemed confused about their directions). The NIDS interviews were not very good at "fleshing out" the important details such as this. The easterly direction was in the same direction of the wind.

3. The color of the lights seemed to be amber/yellowish/gold.

4. Almost all witnesses described the lights as simply "fading away" or "disappearing." Several described small lights leaving the main light prior to it disappearing (witness #2 and #7 on NIDS). One witness (#3 on NIDS) reports seeing smoke.

5. Duration was about 5–15 minutes for most witnesses.

Compare these remarks to those from the Condon Report, case 18 [which involved college students launching hot-air balloons made of dry cleaner bags and heated with a small candle].

1. Triangular formations were reported. Others reported a straight line.

2. Motion was in the direction of the wind.

3. The color of the lights seemed to be orange/reddish/gold.

4. Witnesses described the lights as "fading away" or "disappearing." Two of the nine saw "sparks" leaving the lights.

5. Duration was about 5–15 minutes for most witnesses.

Also note Hendry's [Allan Hendry, who at one time was the full-time investigator for the Center for UFO Studies and wrote *The UFO Handbook*] remarks concerning balloon pranks: "The important symptom of burning, dripping candle wax, and conformance to wind direction prevail here." (*The UFO Handbook*, 47–8)

Interesting parallels in these cases that should not be ignored. Also interesting to note is Hendry's remarks about positively identifying the source: "Only once did I ever have the luck of finding out exactly who launched one, and then only because the police caught him." (*The UFO Handbook*, 47)

While the "garbage bag balloon" hypothesis is not proven (and may never be based on Hendry's remark), it seems to be the most likely source of the lights that evening.

While that explanation does make some sense, and the descriptions match, in a gross fashion, some well-known launches of these sorts of balloons, It doesn't explain everything that was reported. In the late 1960s and the early 1970s, there were many cases that were solved when those who launched the balloons came forward with the evidence or when the culprits were caught launching similar events.

Another of the problems is that a candle in a dry-cleaners bag is usually dim and hard to see, yet these lights were reported over a relatively large area, and photographs were taken. That tends to negate the explanation of hot-air balloons.

Analysis

All these cases have things in common. They are of lights in a formation and sometimes the suggestion of lights on a single object. They were witnessed over a limited geographic location but were seen by dozens of witnesses. There is a limited photographic record for the sightings and in one case, Belgium, that photograph is an admitted hoax.

It is also true that in each of the cases, there are sightings that are explained by the mundane, with the exception of the New Jersey sightings. In each of the cases, there is a core of unexplained sightings that suggest something that is unusual, strange, and probably extraterrestrial.

In Lubbock, for example, there were people who reported the lights, and some of those sightings were clearly birds, which was the Air Force explanation for all the sightings. It fails because it doesn't explain the photographs. They do not show birds, and Carl Hart, Jr., even after more than forty years, said that he didn't know what he photographed.

In the end, there are the photographs of the lights which show the V formation, and there is no explanation for them. We can write off some of those sightings but not the pictures.

Scientists and UFOs

It has long been suggested that professional scientists, especially astronomers, don't see UFOs, and by UFOs they mean alien spacecraft. There have been many skeptic UFO sites which repeat this as if the fact somehow negates the reports of pilots, police officers, school teachers, high school dropouts, and the thousands of others who have reported UFOs. In fact, it seems, according to the available statistics, that the higher the level of education and the longer the sighting, the less likely it is to be identified as something natural, man-made, or mundane.

A case that was reported to Project Blue Book about a "flying saucer" sighting on December 16, 1953, demonstrates that highly trained people do spot UFOs and do report them. What is appalling about this case is that the Air Force wrote it off as a lenticular cloud, even though there seemed to be no evidence that such was the case.

December 16, 1953: Agoura, California

According to the documentation found in the Project Blue Book files, Lieutenant General D. L. Putt wrote to Colonel George L. Wertenbaker, telling him about the chief engineer of Lockheed aircraft, who in turn told him that some of his associates had seen a flying saucer. The Lockheed people had created a report, "reluctantly," about their sighting. Putt was forwarding it for what it was worth.

The first report, written by the witness, was dated on December 18, 1953, or two days after the sighting, and was addressed to the "Air Force Investigating Group on Flying Saucers." It said:

On Wednesday, December 16th, 1953, my wife and I went out to our ranch, which is three miles west of Agoura, California, [which is how it is listed in the Blue Book files, rather than by Lockheed engineers] and one mile north of Ventura Blvd.... At approximately 5 o'clock (within two minutes' accuracy), I was looking at the sunset through a large picture window when I noticed above a mountain to the west what I first thought was a black cloud. The sun had gone down and the whole western sky was gold and red, with several thin layers of clouds or haze at fairly high altitude. I wondered why this one object was so dark, considering that the sun was behind it. I immediately thought that some aircraft had made an intense smoke trail, so I studied the object closely.... Thinking it was a lenticular cloud, I continued to study it, but it did not move at all for three minutes....

When it did not move or disintegrate, I asked my wife to get me our eight-powered binoculars, so I would not have to take my eyes off the object, which by now I had recognized as a so-called "saucer." As soon as I was given the glasses, I ran outside and started to focus the glasses on the object, which now was moving fast on a heading between 240 [degrees] and 260 [degrees]. When I got the glasses focused on the object, it was already moving behind the first layer of haze. I gathered its speed was very high because of the rate of foreshortening of its major axis. The object, even in the glasses, appeared black and distinct, but I could make out no detail, as I was looking toward the setting sun, which was, of course, below the horizon at this time.

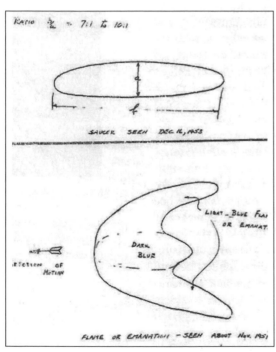

The witness who wrote this report, and whose name had been redacted by the Air Force, said that he had seen the object hover and watched as it accelerated. He saw a shape which in one view he drew looked like a long, flat pill but from a different perspective had a boomerang shape that was reminiscent of the stylized drawing offered by Kenneth Arnold of the objects he'd seen in 1947.

This is a standard UFO report in that it is basically, at this point, single witness. True, the man's wife saw the object, but she adds only a little value to it. That he saw it through binoc-

Drawing of the UFO seen by Kelly Johnson in 1953.

ulars and that it was in sight for several minutes adds to the value. He didn't take a photograph but did supply a drawing of it.

Of course, there are some other facts that raise the value. The sighting was made, according to the documentation in the Project Blue Book files, by the man who was the chief engineer at Lockheed. Though he is not identified in the files because the Air Force took the names of witnesses out of the reports prior to releasing them into the public domain, they neglected to eradicate his initials that showed he had written the report but someone else had typed it. Finding out who this was based on the initials CLJ wasn't all that difficult. It was Clarence Leonard "Kelly" Johnson, who would become famous at the Skunk Works and in the development of new-generation military aircraft.

There is an aside to this that makes for interesting commentary. Inside the world of UFOs, someone who reports a UFO or flying saucer more than once is labeled a "repeater." Philip Klass, in *UFOs Explained*, said, "Experienced UFO investigators, even those who believe in extraterrestrial space-ships, are suspicious of reports that come from 'repeaters'—a term applied to persons who claim to see UFOs frequently."

Johnson, in his report to the Air Force, wrote, "I should also state that about 2 years ago, Mrs. Johnson and I saw an object which I believed at the time, and still do, to be a saucer, flying west of Brents Junction, California, on a very dark night. I did not see the object itself but saw a clearly defined flame or emanation.... This object was travelling from east to west at a very high speed and with no noise. The flame or emanation was a beautiful light blue, having extremely well-defined edges. My first impression was that it was an afterburning airplane, but the lack of noise and the pure spread of the flame eliminated that possibility completely."

But given Johnson's credentials, given his training, it would seem that his sighting of flying saucers twice does not reduce the importance of the sighting. It turns out that Johnson was not alone in what he saw during that second sighting.

The next morning, additional testimony was discovered. Johnson was at work and talking with Rudy Thoren when Thoren mentioned something he had seen the day before. This sighting was described in the Blue Book file, in the words of Thoren:

On Wednesday, December 16, 1953, I participated in a test flight ... taking off at

Aviation pioneer Clarence Leonard "Kelly" Johnson.

4:29 P.M. The flight crew consisted of [names redacted but are Roy Wimmer as the pilot, Thoren as the copilot, Charles Grugan as flight engineer, and J. F. Ware as the flight test engineer].... Somewhere between 15,000 and 20,000 feet [redacted but is Wimmer] said to me, "Look out, there's a flying saucer." I looked out the windshield toward where Roy was pointing and saw some sort of an object at approximately the altitude that we were flying. I made a slight turn heading right toward this object, expecting to overtake it so that we could look at it more closely. I maintained this heading for roughly five minutes, looking at the object all the time.

[Redacted] and myself viewed this thing for at least five minutes, discussing what we thought it might be. [Redacted]'s first impression was that it was a small cloud. After studying it for several minutes, though, I deduced that it was not a cloud, because it had too definite, sharp edges, and its appearance stayed constant. It looked to me like it was flying right directly toward us, and at about the same elevation as a very large flying wing airplane. I would estimate at this time that I was somewhere between 17,000 and 18,000 feet.

Although the object appeared to be absolutely stationary, we did not seem to be closing the gap between us and this object, even though we were flying at some 225 miles per hour. The object then seemed to be getting smaller, and my attention was diverted from it for a minute or so, but Wimmer [the Air Force, in their attempt to redact the names, overlooked this, so that it is apparent who was in the cockpit] mentioned that the object was disappearing. In probably an elapsed time of somewhere around a minute, the object had reduced in size to a mere speck and then disappeared.

It is clear from the above that they were watching an object that they could not identify. Unlike Johnson, Thoren thought they might have been watching a flying wing, though there were no versions left flying at the time. What is important here is that Thoren reported that the object seemed to be shrinking, which meant it was moving away from their aircraft and disappearing in the distance.

Roy Wimmer, who was the pilot, also provided a report, dated January 12, 1953. He wrote:

On Wednesday, December 16th, I made a test flight in Constellation 4301. The crew in the cockpit consisted of myself as pilot, R. L. Thoren as copilot, Charles Grugan, flight engineer, and J. F. Ware as flight test engineer.

I took off late in the afternoon and ran some tests during the climb to 5,000' and then made a level run for a few minutes.

The Lockheed crew that was testing a plane in 1953 when they reported seeing an unusual aircraft flying near Agoura, California.

I then started to climb to 20,000' and turned the controls over to Rudy Thoren. We continued our climb in a southeasterly direction, and somewhere in the vicinity of Long Beach or Santa Ana between 16,000' and 20,000', we made a right turn onto a west heading. The sun had just set, but the air was very clear and the light was real good toward the west. I noticed a cloud layer in the west starting somewhere east of Santa Cruz Island at about our altitude. Above this cloud layer, well out in the clear air, I saw what I thought was a small cloud. Just for the fun of it I said, "Boy, look at the flying saucer!"

After watching it for a few minutes, we decided that it wasn't a cloud but some kind of object. It had a definite shape, which appeared to me like a crescent. Others on board described it as a huge flying wing. I could not detect any details other than the shape of it. I estimated the distance from us to be at least 50–60 miles and possibly much further. In the clear air like that, it is very hard to judge distance.

We flew directly toward it for about 5 minutes, and our relative position did not appear to change. I do not recall our exact speed, whether we were still climbing or whether we had leveled off during the time.

As Rudy was flying the airplane, I had nothing else to do but to watch the object. After about 5 minutes, I suddenly realized it was moving away from us, heading straight west. In the space of about one minute, it grew smaller and disappeared. I was watching it all the time, so I was able to see it for several seconds after the rest of

Lockheed flight engineer Phil Colman was one of the witnesses to the 1953 UFO.

the crew lost sight of it. Right up until the time it disappeared, it maintained its sharp outline and definite shape, so I know it was not a cloud that dissolved, giving the appearance of moving away.

I might add that I have had considerable experience, while doing radar bombing on P2V's, of estimating distance where there is very little to judge by, and I am convinced this was a large object some distance away.

There was another man in the cockpit. That was J. F. Ware, Jr., listed as a section supervisor. He was not piloting the aircraft but in a position to see everything. He wrote:

On December 16, 1953, I was aboard a WV-2 airplane, LAC 4301, with [redacted but clearly is Roy Wimmer] as pilot, [redacted but is Rudy Thoren] as Co-Pilot, and [redacted but is Charlie Grugan] as Flight Engineer. [Redacted but is Phil Colman] was also in the cockpit.

At about 5:00 PM we were over the Catalina channel area (between Avalon and Palos Verdes hills) at 15,000'–16,000', on top of a scattered to broken overcast. The horizon was well defined by the rays of the setting sun, and the sky above the overcast was clear.

Our attention was drawn to what looked like a large airplane off to the right. We were roughly paralleling the coast at the time and Roy, I think, mentioned, "There's a flying saucer." We have kidded Roy a good deal about flying saucers since the night about two years ago when he and Bob Laird were in 1951S and sighted some lights over Catalina. These lights reportedly stood still for a while, and moved around over the island, and finally disappeared.

I was standing between the pilots and observed the object out of the copilots window in the 4301. [Redacted but is Phil Colman's] attention was also drawn to the object. Rudy [the Air Force missed this name in their attempts to redact all names], who was flying at the time, turned around and headed toward the object. During this time, it seemed to be stationary, although we did not appear to overtake it at all. My first thought was that it was a large airplane, possibly a C–124, but after looking more closely, it seemed to look more like a large object without wings with a maximum thickness in the middle tapering toward either side; I could not distinguish front or rear on the object. It seemed to be somewhat above us and to the West, over the water, possibly in the vicinity of the Santa Barbara Islands.

After looking at the object off and on for about five minutes, it became apparent that it was moving away from us, and in just a minute or two it completely disappeared. As it was disappearing, I looked at it off and on, and gradually I could not see it at all. Roy watched it continuously and could see it after I had lost sight of it—he actually observed it continuously, I believe. It disappeared in a generally westward direction (toward the setting sun).

I've been interested in flying saucers particularly ever since one evening during the 1951 Christmas Holidays. I was putting up a TV antenna on my roof when I looked up toward the north over the hills behind our home and saw a large, circular object, apparently stationary. The time of day was about dusk, and I watched the object for several minutes and called Leslie and a neighbor, Mr. Murphy, who also looked at it. I continued working on my TV antenna, glancing at the object now and then, with more and more time between glances, and finally the object was gone.

There is a small airstrip at Giant Rock, and I have visited the group of people there who have devoted their life to flying saucers. They have many photographs and books on the subject and figuratively eat and sleep saucers.

The Air Force and the skeptics would take note of the last paragraph in Ware's report to suggest that a prior interest in UFOs makes the testimony less credible. But it is also interesting that Johnson claimed to have seen a flying saucer on another occasion, and Ware has been to Giant Rock, which was the home of George van Tassel, one of the contactees of the era. Van Tassel claimed to have made contact with people on Mars.

It was noted in some of the information about the case that the aircraft was equipped with two types of radar. There is no indication that either of the radars had been turned on, and no data had been collected from them, which would have made the case that much stronger.

> There is no indication that either of the radars had been turned on, and no data had been collected from them, which would have made the case that much stronger.

The important facts in this case, other than the stature of the men making the report—all highly trained engineers who had been around aviation for years and who were familiar with not only the military aircraft in the inventory but also with that under development—was that the object was independently observed. Johnson on the ground saw it without knowing that his colleagues in the air were seeing it. This seems to suggest that if Johnson had been fooled by something as mundane as a lenticular cloud, those in the aircraft would have been able to identify it as such. Or, if the men in the aircraft had been fooled by that cloud, Johnson might have been able to identify it from the ground.

This Project Blue Book file contains the reports prepared by the Lockheed personnel, but the project card doesn't provide much in the way of a clue as to the caliber of the witnesses. It said, "First appeared as a black stationary cloud, then rapid movement in long, shallow climb." The solution is simply "lenticular cloud."

January 16, 1951: Artesia, New Mexico

Johnson and his fellows at Lockheed weren't the only engineers who reported UFOs to Project Blue Book. On April 24, 1949, Charles Moore, who would gain fame as one of the Project Mogul engineers who launched balloons that he said were responsible for the Roswell UFO crash, reported a UFO while tracking balloons near Arrey, New Mexico. Moore would describe the object as "ellipsoid … white in color, except for a light yellow of one side, as though it were in shadow." The Air Force did not explain the sighting, and it is listed as "Unidentified" in the Project Blue Book files. The whole story appeared in *Alien Mysteries, Conspiracies and Cover-ups*, published in 2013.

Nearly two years later, near Artesia, New Mexico, engineers working with another balloon project spotted a UFO. The official file is somewhat confusing because there is a problem with the date, but it seems that the sighting took place on January 16, 1951. According to the Project Blue Book file:

> Two members of a balloon project from the General Mills Aeronautical Research Laboratory and four other civilians observed two unidentified aerial objects in the vicinity of the balloon they were observing. The balloon was at an altitude of 112,000 ft. and was 110 ft. in diameter at the time of the observation.
>
> The objects were observed twice, one from Artesia, New Mexico, and once from the Artesia Airport. In the first instance, one round object appeared to remain motionless in the vicinity but was apparently higher than the balloon. The balloon appeared to be 1½ inches in diameter and the object 2½ inches in diameter (ratio 3:5), and the color was a dull white. This observation was made by the General Mills observers.
>
> A short time later, the same two observers and four civilian pilots were observing the balloon from the Artesia Airport. The objects

at apparently extremely high altitude were noticed coming toward the balloon from the northwest. They circled the balloon, or apparently so, and flew off to the northeast. The time of observation was about 40 seconds. The two objects were the same color and size of the first object. They were flying side by side. When the objects appeared to circle the balloon, they disappeared, and the observers assumed they were disc-shaped and had turned on edge to bank.

The writer of the Blue Book analysis, who didn't sign it, mentioned that it was unfortunate that they didn't report the sighting until April 5 and that it didn't reach Air Technical Intelligence Center (ATIC) until April 16, or two months afterward. Because of the time lapse, he contemplated no further investigation, and he reached no conclusion about it.

Eventually the Air Force would label the case as "insufficient data for a scientific analysis," and part of the reason might have been the length of time between the sighting and the eventual gathering of the statements. But they note that four of the witnesses are civilian pilots, and although they attempted to redact the names, two of them were reinterviewed, and the men were identified as Alvin H. Hazel and A. V. Swearingen. Hazel was the manager of the Artesia Municipal Airport, and Swearingen was the manager of the Goodyear Tire Company there.

> "The objects at apparently extremely high altitude were noticed coming toward the balloon from the northwest. They circled the balloon, or apparently so, and flew off to the northeast."

Although unidentified by name in the various Blue Book documents, one of the men from General Mills was described as an aeronautical engineer. He provided some very important information about the objects, and unlike some sightings that had no point of reference, he knew that the balloon was drifting at 112,000 feet, and at that altitude would have been 110 feet in diameter. That meant that he could estimate the size of the objects to a reasonable degree.

The sighting lasted long enough for them to get a very good look at the UFOs and to realize that they matched nothing in aviation, either civilian or military. Given their training, jobs, and backgrounds, it was clear that they saw something that was not readily identified.

November 22, 1961: Grafton, North Dakota

Melvin C. Vagle, Jr., a metallurgist for Honeywell in Minneapolis, told National Investigations Committee on Aerial Phenomena (NICAP) investigators that on a clear, starlit night, at about 7:00 P.M., he and his wife were on U.S. Highway 81, nearing Grafton. They saw a red light in the west and then other lights near it that made them believe they were seeing some kind of aircraft. As they got closer, they pulled to the side of the road and saw that a cigar-shaped

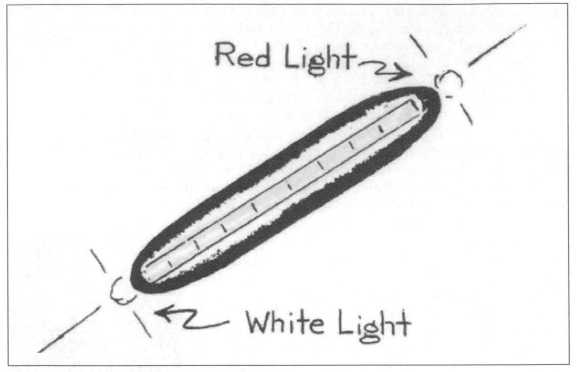

Red Light

White Light

Illustration of the UFO seen by Melvin Vagle, Jr.

craft was hovering over a farm field at a 45-degree angle. At the lower end was a bright, flashing, white light, and at the other end was a steady, red one. There was a row of square-shaped portholes that were lit by a yellowish-white light, but they saw no movement behind the windows and no sign of a crew.

The UFO hovered over the field, but when Vagle's son began to cry, they started to drive away. The UFO then slowly moved across the highway, heading to the west. They lost sight of it then.

There is a suggestion that a sighting report was forwarded to the Air Force, but there is nothing in the Project Blue Book files to confirm this. A search of the database did produce a sighting from September 26, 1961, from Grafton. The information suggests the object was disc-shaped and had a red glow. It was seen from a car and was descending toward the horizon and moving away from the witness. It was in sight for twenty-five minutes. To confuse the issue, the information suggests that the first sighting took place one mile west of Grafton, and the second was four miles east. The witness is listed as a resident of Grafton, while Vagle lived in Minneapolis.

The Air Force file said there was no explanation for the sighting, that no unusual objects were detected by the Grand Forks Air Defense Sector personnel, and that the investigation was a single telephone interview with the witness. The Air Force file eventually listed the sighting as that of a weather balloon, though there seems to be no evidence to support that conclusion.

Clearly, this is not the sighting made by Vagle and his wife. In the search for additional information, there is a reference in the NICAP *UFO Investigator*. The single paragraph about the sighting provides nothing new, but they noted that five farmers in the area had also seen the UFO.

According to Richard Hall in *The UFO Evidence*, "Accompanying Mr. Vagle's report to NICAP was a letter from the farmer confirming the basic points of his sighting, which occurred at sunset. The farmer could see no 'ports,' only a dull, reddish glow from the UFO. The object vanished behind a dark cloud after about ten minutes."

This sighting has been presented by a single witness with a hint that there are others in the area. It becomes important because it is clear that Vagle was an educated man, and while metallurgy is not as important to the identification of UFOs as aeronautical engineering, it does suggest someone who should be able to identify aircraft and natural phenomena.

February 9, 2005: Owing Mills, Maryland

Frank Griffin is described as a Lockheed Martin software engineer who reported he had seen a triangular-shaped object fly over as he was lying on his trampoline looking at the stars. He could see no lights and heard no sound. According to what Griffin told WUSA 9 News, "I noticed that some of them [stars] were disappearing almost directly above me. There was a very faint V shape that I could see moving north to south."

Griffin said that there was a broken cloud layer at about a thousand feet, which gave him a reference point. With the city lights reflecting from the clouds, he saw that the object was triangular, or as he said, "almost equilateral."

It was black, with a slight gray V shape on the bottom. There were no lights, which meant that it wasn't an aircraft. He thought it looked like a stealth fighter from below, but a fighter would have been required to have navigation lights and an anticollision beacon or strobe. It wouldn't have been flying completely blacked out over the United States. Griffin said that he'd seen stealth fighters on the ground and doing flyovers, so he knew that the object wasn't one of them.

Griffin told WABC, "I am very familiar with all known civilian aircraft and all known military aircraft in the current inventory. I work for Lockheed Martin, and I have had that interest since childhood. The absolute total silence of it was spooky, along with the slow airspeed."

""I am very familiar with all known civilian aircraft and all known military aircraft in the current inventory.... The absolute total silence of it was spooky, along with the slow airspeed."

What is interesting about this sighting is the shape of the craft. There seems to have been something of an evolution in the shapes of UFOs since the Arnold sighting in June 1947. Although Arnold's original drawing was of a craft with a blunt nose and could be described as heel-shaped, his later, more professionally drawn illustration is of a crescent-shaped craft with a scalloped rear. William Rhodes took a photograph in July 1947 that showed something that was close to what Arnold reported, and in 1953 Clarence Leonard "Kelly" Johnson saw something that was disc-shaped.

In the last two decades or so, there have been more reports of triangular craft. These are large, usually dark colored, and travel relatively close to the ground. Some have lights at the points of the triangle, and some do not. The influence might be the development of the stealth technology, which is of military aircraft that take on the triangular shape. This is not to suggest that any alien creatures are mimicking the military development here, only that this is an interesting coincidence. An important point, however, is that witnesses were reporting the triangular craft before the current military designs were well known outside the closed research in secret locations.

It is also important to note that those seeing these UFOs reported here are highly trained engineers, many who are in the aviation industries and who are familiar with the designs, structure, and capabilities of those aircraft. In other words, they would be able to spot a military aircraft, even if it was in limited production and design, without suggesting something from another world.

Astronomers and UFOs

As noted, it has long been suggested that astronomers don't see flying saucers, meaning alien spacecraft. They do report UFOs, which means something that is unidentified and flying but not something that is necessarily created by an alien intelligence.

Dr. J. Allen Hynek, who for many years was the scientific consultant to Project Blue Book, interviewed astronomers about their interest, belief, and theories about UFOs. The vast majority of them didn't want their names associated with something like UFOs and were not identified in Hynek's August 6, 1952, report. They offered their opinions, most of them ill-informed, and went on their way.

Hynek provided an introduction to the report and under a section called "Purpose of Interviews," he wrote:

The desirability has been established of inquiring of professionally trained astronomers of considerable scientific background as to whether they had ever made sightings of unidentified aerial objects. At the same time, it is felt that it would be profitable to obtain the informal opinions and advice of high-ranking astronomers on the entire subject of unidentified aerial objects, of the manner in which the investigation of these objects was being conducted by the Air Force, and of their own inner feelings about the possibility that such objects were real and might constitute either a threat to national security or a new natural phenomena worthy of scientific investigation.

Accordingly, it was planned that a tour would be made of several of the nation's observatories, not in the guise of an official investigator, but rather as an astronomer about to discuss scientific problems. It was felt that this mild deception was necessary, that an artificial barrier to communication might not be set up, which would invalidate the assumption that truly representative opinions were being obtained. Therefore, to maintain good faith, the names of the astronomers interviewed are withheld from this report.

> In the report, Hynek then ranks them as observers and as professional astronomers. Only six were rated as "excellent" as astronomers, while most were not ranked at all.

In all, 45 astronomers were interviewed, nearly always individually, except in a few cases where this was impossible. Eight observatories were visited, and the National Meeting of the American Astronomical Society in Victoria, British Columbia, was attended on June 25 to June 28.

Because of the confidential and highly personal manner in which the interviews quoted below were made, and to keep faith with the many astronomers interviewed, who, generally, were not aware that anything more than a personal private talk between astronomers was going on, the names of the astronomers will be withheld. They will be assigned letters, but the code will not be included in this report.

In the report, Hynek then ranks them as observers and as professional astronomers. Only six were rated as "excellent" as astronomers, while most were not ranked at all. Nine of them were ranked as average observers, and again, many were simply not ranked. Without the names, these statistics mean very little, and what is important here are the opinions about UFOs.

Many of the astronomers answered that they had never seen anything and knew of no associates, colleagues, or friends who had seen anything. Some expressed a mild interest in the topic, and others thought of it as nonsense not worthy of any additional thought.

There were cases in which the astronomer claimed to have seen things that others would call flying saucers but things that could be explained. For example:

Astronomer B has made sightings of things which people would call "flying saucers" but hasn't seen anything that he couldn't explain. He has seen birds at night flying in formation illuminated by city lights, but probably not bright enough to have been photographed because they were traveling "pretty fast." [This is a clear reference to the Lubbock Lights case, in which birds were used to explain some sightings but could not account for the photographs taken by Carl Hart, Jr.] Astronomer B wonders if some of the sightings are not due to Navy secret weapons, since only the Navy has officially said nothing about flying saucers. [Clearly he was unaware of a top secret Navy study, in which it was concluded that the flying saucers were not secret Navy weapons.] Astronomer B was quite outspoken and feels that past methods of handing the subject have been "stupid." He feels pilots should not be hushed up and that secrecy only whets the public appetite.

Astronomer EE has never seen any unexplainable objects. He has seen a phenomenon which most people would have said was a "flying saucer." This turned out to be a beacon light describing a cone of light, part of which intercepted a high cirrus cloud. This led to a series of elliptical lights moving in one direction and never coming back.

There were also those who reported their own sightings when asked. Although most remained anonymous, a few did allow their names to be associated with the sightings. According to Hynek's report:

Astronomer R has personally sighted an unidentified object, a light which loomed across his range of vision, which was obstructed by an observatory dome, much faster than a plane and much slower than a meteor. If it had been a plane, then its rapid motion could be accounted for only by closeness, but since no motors were heard, this explanation was essentially ruled out. Light was steadier than that of a meteor and was observed for about three seconds. Astronomer R does not ascribe any particular significance to this sighting.

Astronomer FF has seen none himself, but recently received a report from a ranger who said he was an amateur astronomer; he reported a bright light but said that it was not a meteor. Astronomer FF said his recitation of the incident was very dramatic. Astronomer FF suggested sending up a control "flying saucer" to see how many reports come back [something that has been done in the past].

Astronomer II, with an adequate professional rating, has made two sightings personally. The sightings were two years apart. The first sighting, which was witnessed also by an astronomer not interviewed on this trip, occurred in this manner: A transport plane

The Alvan Clark Dome at the Lowell Observatory in Flagstaff, Arizona. On May 20, 1950, an object was observed just after noon from the grounds of the observatory.

travelling west made quite a bit of noise and Astronomer II looked up to watch it. He then noticed, above the transport and going north, a cluster of five ball-bearing-like objects. They moved rapidly and were not in sight very long. Two years after this sighting, he sighted a single object which disappeared from sight by accelerating, probably turning, but not by going up quickly.

Astronomer OO is a meteor observer at the Harvard Meteor Station in New Mexico. Although relatively new on the job, he observed two lights while on watch at 1:30 a.m. that moved much too fast for a plane and much too slow for a meteor. The two lights were white and moved in a parallel direction.

A meteorologist at the Lowell Observatory is identified here as Astronomer PP [who was Seymour Hess]. He was not interviewed, but a clipping was obtained from a Flagstaff newspaper covering his observations.... The object was observed between 12:15 and 12:20 p.m. on Saturday, May 20, from the grounds of the Lowell Observatory. The object presented a bright, visible disc to the naked eye

The object that was described by witnesses was always said to be disc-shaped and did not resemble any kind of known Earth-based craft.

and passed moderately rapidly in front of a fractocumulus cloud in the northwest. Upon passing in front of the cloud, its appearance changed from that of a bright object to a dark object, due to the change in contrast. No engine noise was heard, nor was there any exhaust. It seems that this might have been a weather balloon, but in this case it would be strange if this meteorologist would become confused by it. He reports that it was not moving with the wind, but across the wind.

These sightings add little to the knowledge of the subject, and it could be suggested that while they are of UFOs, they are not of alien spacecraft. Lights in the sky are difficult to resolve into spacecraft. However, five objects described as ball bearings, that is, bright, metal, ball-shaped objects, are certainly more than some sort of natural phenomenon and certainly are not like anything that was manufactured on Earth. It could be suggested that while the astronomer himself might not have called it an alien spacecraft, if the sighting is accurate and not some sort of delusion, then there is little else that it could have been.

The sighting by Astronomer PP suffers from the same problem as that of Astronomer II. He describes a disc-shaped craft, which is not any kind of Earth-based aircraft. In fact, Hess, when interviewed for the newspaper, said, "I saw the object between 12:15 and 12:30 P.M.... It was extremely prominent and showed some size to the naked eye ... it was not merely a pinpoint.... I could see it well enough to be sure it was not an airplane ... nor a bird. I saw no evidence of exhaust gases nor any markings...."

Hess had a very important career as a planetary scientist. In 1948, he developed an interest in planetary meteorology. His Ph.D. dissertation was *Some Aspects of the Meteorology of Mars.* Two years later, he became part of the meteorology department at Florida State University and served as the department chair twice. Most importantly, he helped design the meteorology package for the Viking 1 Mars lander, and on July 21, 1976, he made the first-ever weather report for another planet, giving the atmospheric conditions at the Chryse Planitia on Mars.

July 13, 1959: University of Brazil

Other astronomers on the observatory grounds have seen UFOs, and in some cases actually suggest that what they had seen were alien spacecraft. Such a sighting was made in Brazil on July 13, 1959, and that was reported to Project Blue Book. The Blue Book file was nothing more than a translation of three articles that had appeared in Brazilian newspapers, with the names of the witnesses redacted in the translations but left in the original articles. These translations also identify a third man as Captain Silio (as opposed to Silvio, named in *The APRO Bulletin*) of the Technical School of the Army. That article said, in part:

> "Very excited, the professor said, that the disc transversed 130 degrees in 20 minutes, but he was not able to calculate the linear velocity...."

> The object presented itself in the field of the binocular with the aspect of a disk with a conical protuberance in the central part and a set of green lights, separated, forming optically a [redacted] cross with six lights in each arm, totaling 24 points of green light. The object could not, by its characteristics and movement, be confounded with any known celestial body.

> The astronomer [redacted but Mario Diaz Ferreira] told us that the cupula [sic] of the object had a metallic aspect, and the set of green lights was similar to the indication of the masts of ships. The "disk" also emitted an orange-colored jet from its extremity, giving the impression to the naked eye that it was divided into two parts.

> The astronomers were unanimous in affirming that the object would be at a distance of at least more than 30 kilometers from the earth.

More information was provided by another article that is also part of the Project Blue Book files. This said:

> Three astronomers of the observatory of the University of Brazil [now the University of Rio de Janeiro] yesterday accompanied [sic] through binoculars from 10:10 to 10:30 P.M. the trajectory of a flying disk at the elevation of the Alia constellation, moving toward the astral triangle on the Southern Cross until it was lost in the base of the horizon. Two public statement was [sic] by Professor Luis Eduardo of the National Facility of Philosophy, and he added that that the astronomers [redacted but is only one astronomer, Mario Ferriera Diaz] and Captain [redacted but is Sirio Vas, as noted in the newspaper clipping] of the Technical School of the Army supported him.

> "I have no doubt whatever but that it was a flying disk," said Professor [redacted but is Luis Eduardo]. "We are used to making these observations, and we would not be confound the apparatus with any celestial body, balloon, [translation is confusing here] or interplanetary rocket."

> Very excited, the professor said, that the disc transversed 130 degrees in 20 minutes, but he was not able to calculate the linear

velocity, because at that hour their measuring instruments had been put away.

After confirming Luis' declarations, Captain Sirio added that the flying disc would be seen by the naked eye and that its size was twice that of the planet Venus, which appears in the evening. Its green light was steady and not twinkling like that of the stars.

The apparatus, which was also seen through a telescope of soldiers or the guard of the observatory, projected almost vertically upward a reddish light, approximately about one-fifth of its size.

The press gives prominent place to the announcement of this strange phenomenon. It is worth emphasizing that this is the first time in the world that a flying disc has been seen by an observatory. However, the speed with which it traversed the trajectory did not allow for the taking of pictures. No rotational movement was observed in it—only a translation (forward) movement.

The third article in the file repeats most of what is in the first two articles, although it does mention that several pilots had seen the "flying disk." There is no additional information that I can find, and note that the astronomers and other witnesses refer to the object as a flying disk as opposed to a UFO.

Looking at *The APRO Bulletin* article, it uses the term "flying saucer" as opposed to "flying disk," either of which could mean they meant an alien spacecraft. Coral Lorenzen, in the article she published about it, used "flying saucer." Given that the original articles are in Portuguese and the translations might not be completely accurate, there is room for some speculation about what the astronomers meant to say. By 1959, flying saucer usually referred to an alien craft, while UFO generally meant something that was unidentified.

However, when the articles are studied carefully, and given that the astronomers took pains to list a number of astronomical phenomena that have been eliminated, it seems reasonable to believe they were talking about a spacecraft. Their use of the term "flying disk" does suggest more than does the more generic UFO.

The problem is that all the information comes from the newspaper articles, which do name names, but there are no follow-up investigations. It is listed as "Insufficient Data" in the Project Blue Book files, which seems to be a legitimate solution. In the end, it is another case in which there is a body of testimony but with no physical evidence, such as the photographs. There is little more to be learned, even if there was a way to follow up on it.

The World of Official UFO Studies

U.S. Studies

While nearly everyone suggests that the modern era of UFO sightings began in June 1947 when Kenneth Arnold reported nine mysterious objects flying rapidly in formation in the distance, the truth is that there had been official studies of these phenomena for years. During the Second World War, the Allies were concerned with strange objects and lights that seemed to be buzzing their aircraft and were sometimes seen by service members on the ground. Such was the concern for the Foo Fighters, as they were called, that an official, high-level, classified investigation was begun.

In *Government UFO Files*, the Foo Fighter investigation is examined, and it is noted that although investigators were highly motivated to find an answer because of fear of enemy secret weapons, they failed to find any solution. There were reports of solid objects and not just lights following aircraft. Some service members fired on the lights and objects without results. Sometimes the rounds seemed to pass through the lights, and other times it seemed that these rounds were absorbed by the Foo Fighter.

Keith Chester, in his massive work about Foo Fighters, *Strange Company*, tracked all the documentation from the various theaters of the war and provided a real look at the concern about them. It is also clear that when the war ended, the Allies no longer cared what had been observed. The enemy was defeated, and the Foo Fighters no longer presented any threat to the military operations.

While the sightings were interesting and many of them clearly mirror those that would be reported later, no one cared to follow up on them. The Foo Fighters became a topic of little interest to anyone.

Kenneth Arnold standing next to the plane he was flying when he saw UFOs in June 1947 over the Cascade Mountains.

Less than a year after the war ended, Scandinavia began seeing the Ghost Rockets. It wasn't until the summer of 1946 that the wave peaked with dozens of sightings of cigar-shaped objects, many of them reminiscent of the German V-2 rockets. Many believed that the Ghost Rockets were some sort of Soviet experiment or attempt to intimidate the Swedish government with displays of power.

There was an official investigation made, but by December, the number of sightings had tapered, especially after a news embargo imposed by the various Scandinavian governments. There was no solution, though it seemed that many believed the Soviets were behind it. When the Soviet Union collapsed and many of their records became available to historians, there was nothing found to indicate that the Soviets were behind the Ghost Rockets.

These were the first two official studies in the modern era of these sorts of phenomena. Neither of them came to a satisfactory conclusion, and both sort of fizzled out as the priority dried up. The war ended, and the number of reports of the Ghost Rockets fell when the newspapers stopped reporting on them.

That didn't stop the U.S. interest in these sorts of things. Colonel Howard McCoy had been part of the Foo Fighter committee, attempting to learn more about them. When the Ghost Rockets started to fly, McCoy was there gathering information, though not in an official capacity. His was an unofficial interest. In December 1946, six months before Kenneth Arnold reported the objects near Mount Rainier, McCoy was ordered to set up an unofficial investigation at Wright Field, now part of the large Wright-Patterson Air Force Base complex (for a more comprehensive examination of this material, see *The Government UFO Files*, published in 2014 by Visible Ink Press).

According to UFO historians Wendy Connors and Michael Hall, this was a single room with a good lock on the door. Access was limited to a very few people. McCoy and others spent their time gathering stories of the Foo Fighters and more specifically, the Ghost Rockets. There were some sightings of unusual phenomena in the United States, such as the series of sightings from Virginia.

On April 1, 1947, near Richmond, Virginia, a member of the U.S. Weather Bureau would see something strange that began the case. This would later become Incident No. 79 in the Project Grudge final report. Although it is referenced in the Project Blue Book files, it has disappeared from those files as they were released to the public in 1976. According to the report:

> A weather bureau observer at the Richmond Station observed on three different occasions, during a six-month period prior to April 1947, a disclike, metal chrome object. All sightings were made through a theodolite while making pibal [balloon] observations.
>
> On the last reported sighting, the balloon was at 15,000 feet altitude, and the disc followed for 15 seconds. It was shaped like an ellipse, with a flat-level bottom and a domelike top. The altitude and the speed were not estimated, but the object, allegedly through the instrument, appeared larger than the balloon.
>
> Another observer at the same station saw a similar object under corresponding circumstances, with the exception that her balloon was at an altitude of 27,000 feet and possessed a dull, metallic luster. There was good visibility on days of observation. Report of this sighting was not submitted until 22 July 1947.
>
> AMC [Air Material Command] *Opinion:* There is no readily apparent explanation. If there were only one such object, it seems amazingly coincidental that it would be seen four times near the pibal of this station only. On the other hand, there would have to be a great number of these objects to rule out coincidence, and as the number of objects increases, so do the chances of sightings by other witnesses.
>
> *Project Astronomer's Opinion:* There is no astronomical explanation for this incident, which, however, deserves considerable attention because of the experience of the observers and the fact that the observation was made through a theodolite, and that comparison could be made with a pibal balloon. The observers had, therefore, a good estimate of altitude, of relative size, and of speed—much more reliable than those given in most reports.
>
> This investigation would like to recommend that these and other pibal observers be quizzed as to other possible, unreported sightings.

"On the last reported sighting, the balloon was at 15,000 feet altitude, and the disc followed for 15 seconds."

This series of reports, made by Walter Minczewski, are not mentioned in the Project Blue Book Index, which lists only a couple of reports made prior to the Kenneth Arnold sighting of June 1947. All were reported after the press coverage of the Arnold sighting, so there is no way to document the actual date of the sighting, except for Minczewski's reports.

This is one of the reports that McCoy gathered during his unofficial investigation of what would become UFOs. Somewhere along the line, these reports fell out of the system but are mentioned in some of the documentation. What isn't known today is how McCoy learned about them or how they ended up in the Project Grudge final report, when there is no documentation for them in other parts of the Blue Book files.

McCoy's unofficial investigation ended in June, when Arnold made his sighting. At some point after that, McCoy's investigation became official and in September 1947, Lieutenant Nathan Twining (who was later a general and chair of the Joint Chiefs of Staff from 1957 to 1960) ordered an investigation setup. This would become Project Sign, the first official investigation into what would eventually be called "flying saucers."

Sign began its official investigations on January 22, 1948, and most of these investigations were conducted by officers from the closest Air Force base to the sighting. In the important cases, officers from Wright-Patterson would be sent out to make the investigations.

These investigations led to the creation of an Estimate of the Situation, which is an intelligence method of consolidating, coordinating, and analyzing a great deal of information. In this case, they were attempting to learn something about the flying saucers, and they concluded, based on the evidence, that they were alien spacecraft, or to put it in the terms of the time, interplanetary craft.

Nathan Twining was a lieutenant in 1947, when he ordered an investigation into UFOs that would become Project Sign.

The Air Force Chief of Staff, General Hoyt S. Vandenberg, read the estimate and decided that the case was not proven. In the fallout of that report, those who had held the belief that these things were built on another world found that their careers had been derailed. Project Sign, which had worked at finding an answer, learned that no one cared about them any longer. The pressure from the top in the summer of 1947 had disappeared when no alien invasion fleet arrived. Those who remained behind at Sign, the lowest ranking members of the team, were just going through the motions.

In February 1949, the Air Force announced that they had ended their investigation of UFOs. A report entitled *The Findings of Project Sign* was eventually written. It outlined the motivation behind Project Sign, who the players were, and the results of their research. In the summary, it was noted that the data in the report were "derived from reports of 243 domestic and thirty foreign incidents. Data from these incidents is being summarized, reproduced, and distributed to agencies and individuals cooperating in the analysis and evaluation.... The data obtained in reports received are studied in relation to many factors, such as guided missile research activity, weather and other atmospheric-sounding balloon launchings, commercial and military aircraft flights, flights of migratory birds, and other considerations, to determine possible explanations for sightings."

> ... the Air Force thought that if there was an article in the popular press debunking the idea of alien visitation, then people would lose interest in the subject.

Rather than ending the investigation as they announced, they merely changed the name. On February 11, 1949, Project Grudge was officially created and though it retained the rather high priority of Project Sign, the theory of those on the project was that there wasn't much to flying saucers. Those working on Project Grudge were just going through the motions.

Interestingly, and in a belief that seems to still be alive today, the Air Force thought that if there was an article in the popular press debunking the idea of alien visitation, then people would lose interest in the subject. The two-part article appeared in the *Saturday Evening Post* and suggested that UFOs were hoaxes, misidentifications but not alien spacecraft. The plan didn't work because in the days that followed the article, the number of sightings reported to the Air Force spiked.

In August 1949, the officers assigned to Grudge issued a huge report, and although they reported that some 23% of the sightings were unexplained, the recommendation was that the project be reduced in scope. They also mentioned a belief that they would revisit in the future, that enemy forces could somehow disguise a missile or bomber attack with UFO reports. With the report finished and published, and with the conclusion that there was nothing in these reports, very little work was being done at Grudge.

To make it worse, if possible, Bob Considine wrote an article for *Cosmopolitan* that also mentioned a belief that is still alive today that UFO witnesses are "screwballs" and "true believers." With that, Grudge was reduced to one investigator, which is not to say it was a result of the article, but it certainly didn't change any attitudes inside the Air Force, especially at the highest levels.

At around that same time, there was a series of sightings involving UFOs and radar at Fort Monmouth, New Jersey, that began on September 11, 1951, at 11:10 A.M., when a student radar operator demonstrating the radar functions picked up a fast-moving object. The object was southeast of Monmouth and seemed to be following the coastline. He thought that it was moving at 700 miles an hour, which was as faster than most conventional aircraft of the time.

Twenty-five minutes later, the pilot of a T-33 jet trainer, Lieutenant Wilbert S. Rogers, along with Major Edward Ballard, spotted a silver object that was about the size of a fighter. He thought it was flying at 900 miles an hour. Rogers told the Air Force investigators:

> When first sighted, I would judge that it was between 5 and 8,000 feet over Sandy Hook [New Jersey].... It appeared to be descending when I first saw it at Sandy Hook and appeared to level out in flight just north of Red Bank, New Jersey, and continued on at the same altitude until it disappeared. At the point of our first sighting of the object, I started a descending, 360–degree turn to the left from 20,000 feet to 17,000 feet, gaining air speed from 450 mph to 550 mph on a course paralleling that of the object until it was lost from sight.

> In our training and daily practice as intercept pilots, we must note accurately the times at which the object of the interception is first sighted. I did this automatically when I first sighted the object over Sandy Hook and noted the time to be approximately 1135 EDT, 10 September 1951. Although we were on a direct course for the destination at Mitchell, AFB [New York] at 20,000 feet at the time of the sighting, I was so amazed at the speed of the object that I immediately started the turn to the left and waited for Maj. Ballard to get through with the radio conversation he was having ... so I could point the object to his attention, and we both watched it make a 90–degree turn to the left and kept it under observation together while it covered approximately 20 miles and disappeared out to sea. The object appeared to be banking as its course, described a radual [sic] 90–degree turn to the left.

Several hours later, at 3:15 P.M., a second sighting was made by radar. This was a slow-moving object and was identified as a balloon. The next day, at 10:50 A.M., two radars picked up an object moving too fast to be tracked automatically. It was a very strong return, and the radar operators believed that the object was moving at 1,000 miles an hour.

At 1:30 that afternoon, that is, September 11, radar picked up another object. Radar showed that it was 10,000 yards away (just over five and two thirds miles). They tracked the object as it climbed vertically at a high rate of speed and then flew off so fast that it was lost to the automatic tracking, a point on which the skeptics would hang part of their analysis. At one point, when it seemed the object was hovering, they did go outside to look for it, but it was overcast. They couldn't see anything visually. Project Grudge investigators would conclude that the sighting was caused by "anomalous propagation," which is a fancy way of saying it was caused by the weather.

As noted, at the time of these sightings, no one assigned to Grudge was doing much of anything. The belief was that there was nothing to UFOs, or flying saucers, and there was no reason to waste resources on the investigations of them. The chief at ATIC [Air Technical Intelligence Center], General Harold Watson, and the man running Grudge, James Rodgers (not to be confused with the T–33 pilot), were telling Major General Charles Cabell, the chief of Air Force intelligence in Washington, that the investigations were ongoing, but the truth was something other than that. What Watson and Rodgers did when they received a report was ridicule it without asking any questions about it and then in military tradition, they filed it.

A problem arose here because Bob Ginna was doing research for an article for *Life* and saw that the project was doing virtually nothing. Watson was so embarrassed by what Ginna found that he reassigned Rodgers and put First Lieutenant Jerry Cummings in charge of the UFO project. Ginna should have noticed, and probably did, that Cummings, while having the proper academic credentials, was a very low-ranking officer. If the project was to gain any sort of prestige, it should have been led by a field grade officer.

> They tracked the object as it climbed vertically at a high rate of speed and then flew off so fast that it was lost to the automatic tracking....

With all this sort of intrigue going on, the Monmouth report, a somewhat detailed analysis of the sightings, was given to Watson's chief of intelligence, Colonel Bruno Feiling, who sent the report not to Cummings or Cummings' superior, Lieutenant Colonel N. R. Rosengarten, but to Captain Roy James, a radar expert. This report eventually found its way to Rodgers.

At some point Rosengarten heard that some significant report had not found its way to him and he complained to Feiling, who in turn saw that he received a copy of the report. Cummings then saw the report it and he went to see James and Rodgers, who were laughing about the sighting. They had already solved the mystery. The radar operators were just a bunch of kids who were not that experienced, and the T–33 crew had been fooled by a reflection. Watson had endorsed that solution.

There was, according to Edward Ruppelt who would become the chief of Project Grudge, an argument in Feiling's office, and it ended when they placed a call to Cabell. Unfortunately Cabell wasn't there, but his assistant was surprised that there wasn't a team of investigators on their way to Fort Monmouth already.

With that, Cummings and Rosengarten were ordered to New Jersey, and they spent September 13 interviewing the witnesses. But, more importantly, once they finished the interviews, they flew on to Washington to brief General Cabell personally.

There was a meeting already in progress about what was going on at Fort Monmouth. There were high-ranking officers in the room as well as a man, Robert Johnson, who was there to suggest that a group of scientists and businessmen believed that the Air Force program dealing with UFOs wasn't a very good one.

Those best known for their role in UFO investigation in the early 1950s. From the left to right, they are Al Chop, who ran the UFO publicity out of the Pentagon; Dewey Fournet, the Pentagon UFO Liaison Officer; and Edward Ruppelt, the Chief of Project Blue Book.

At this point, Cabell asked Cummings to tell him what was going on with the UFO investigations. Cummings, according to a private wire recording of the meeting that Ruppelt listened to several times before it was destroyed, said that the meeting was acrimonious. A portion of this was published in Jerome Clark's *UFO Encyclopedia:*

Jerry [Cummings and not Clark] told me that he looked at Rosy [Rosengarten] and got the OK signal, so he cut loose. He told how every report was taken as a huge joke; that at the personal direction of Watson, Rogers [meaning Rodgers], Watson's #1 stooge, was doing everything to degrade the quality of the reports; and how the only analysis consisted of [Rodgers'] trying to think up new and original explanations that hadn't been sent to Washington before. [Rodgers] couldn't even find half the reports.

This, of course, suggests that many of the solutions that had been appended to sightings prior to this meeting were of no value, and other, possibly good, sightings had been lost in the process of "investigating" them. It suggests that while the Air Force was pretending to investigate the sightings, they were ignoring them, and if they couldn't ignore them, they belittled them.

Cabell, upon hearing this, was furious. He wanted to know, "Who in the hell has been giving me these reports that every decent flying saucer sighting is being investigated?"

As the discussion continued, Cabell's outrage increased. He yelled, "I've been lied to ... I want an open mind.... In fact, I order an open mind. Anyone who doesn't have an open mind can get out now."

Cummings and Rosengarten were sent back to Wright-Patterson and ATIC with orders to revitalize the UFO project. Cummings was about to leave active military service and Ed Ruppelt, who had been studying the Soviet air order of battle, found himself drafted into the UFO program, something that he had been watching unofficially.

Even with the renewed interest in the UFO project and with a mandate to complete the investigations in an unbiased fashion, the ultimate solution to the Monmouth case, according to the files released decades later: "Extensive investigation revealed that the target on 10 Sept was caused by a Balloon. Targets on 11 September were attributed to Anomalous Propogation by Radar analysts [sic]."

Skeptics, including Curtis Peebles in *Watch the Skies!*, believed the case was eventually solved. He wrote:

> It took time to sort out the Fort Monmouth sightings. The first radar sighting was due to the student's error. He had not followed the correct procedure for putting the radar on automatic tracking. The target was an ordinary airplane. (The only "proof" the object was flying at high speed was the inability of the radar to automatically track it.) The T-33 sighting was caused by a balloon. The second radar sighting was also a balloon. The frantic phone call from headquarters was to settle a bet on how high it was. The two radar sightings on the second day were caused by another balloon and by weather. A layer of warm, humid air over one of cool, dry air can cause radar signals to bend, strike the ground, and be reflected back. The objects also seem to travel at high speed. This illusion was completed by the operator's belief that something strange was going on.

Peebles cited Ruppelt's book, *The Report on Unidentified Flying Objects*, but the page numbers Peebles used didn't track with the edition held by others. However, Ruppelt did write essentially the same thing about the Fort Monmouth case in his book. But Ruppelt also noted in that wire-recorded interview that the two pilots thought those at ATIC were nuts for the solution, and the Grudge Special Report No. 1 explained the sighting as "probably a balloon."

There are, however, a few disturbing things in the Air Force report on these sightings. It is clear that even though this was supposed to be an unbiased investigation, there is a tone that suggests otherwise that isn't revealed in Ruppelt's book. It is clear that even though Cummings and Rosengarten were dispatched at the insistence of General Cabell, there were problems with the investigation. In one of the reports, in discussing the telephone call from a higher headquarters to the radar station, they suggest it was to settle a pool about the altitude of a balloon. It involved seven officers who each put a dollar into the pool,

Releasing weather balloons is a common military practice, and such balloons are often blamed for false reports of UFOs.

according to the official documents. But the attitude can be seen in the final line of that paragraph. It said, "So much for Item 2, Paragraph 2."

The possible identification of the UFOs in the Fort Monmouth case is not the important feature. It was the briefing that was given to Cabell and his reaction to learning that he had not been receiving the reports that he thought he had been. He was not pleased to learn that the information was being filtered and that the investigation was virtually dead. Cabell ordered a change.

That change was slow to be implemented. As noted, Ruppelt was appointed to lead Grudge and began to streamline the system. He reviewed the prior investigations, organized the files, and even hired a clipping service so that they would receive reports that hadn't been reported to the Air Force through any other channel. He was the one who invented the term "UFO," though others before him had called the flying saucers "Unidentified Flying Objects." He was interested in learning what was going on as opposed to explaining every sighting that was submitted to them. But Ruppelt's tenure lasted less than two years.

> Slowly, under various officers, Project Blue Book became little more than a public relations operation.

In January 1953, the CIA sponsored a panel to "investigate" UFOs. After the five-day meeting, the Robertson Panel, as it was known, offered a number of suggestions including that the mystique of the UFO be stripped from them by "debunking." They believed that proper investigation would lead to answers or solutions for every sighting. This was the end of investigations that searched for answers; it was the beginning of the search for any solution that sounded plausible.

Slowly, under various officers, Project Blue Book became little more than a public relations operation. They issued press releases designed to explain everything and regulations were written, first Air Force Regulation (AFR) 200-2 and then AFR 80-17, which ordered members of the military and those who investigated UFOs to release information if there was an explanation but if there was none, then no information could be released.

By the middle of the 1960s, the Air Force was pushing to get out of the UFO business. They were being hammered by the media, civilian research organizations, and the general public. The solution to their problem was to find an impartial organization, a university, to study UFOs and then conclude it the way the Air Force wanted. The idea was to have them claim that there was no threat to national security, that the Air Force had done a good job, and recommend that Project Blue Book be closed.

Dr. Edward U. Condon of the University of Colorado accepted the grant and began the scientific investigation. Although it was wrapped in the trappings of science and alleged impartial research, the truth is that all of that had been laid out in a letter from Lieutenant Colonel Robert Hippler to Dr. Robert

Low of the university (see Chapter 1 for the text of both the Hippler letter and Low's response to him). It was clear what was going to happen.

On December 17, 1969, the Air Force announced that it was closing Project Blue Book. After twenty-two years, they have found no evidence that UFOs were a threat to national security and that nothing of a scientific nature could be learned by further study. By January 1970, there was no Project Blue Book.

But then there was Moon Dust.

This was a project that began shortly after the first artificial satellite was launched in October 1957. By December of that year, Moon Dust had been created to recover returning space debris of foreign manufacture or of unknown origin. While it could be argued that there was nothing in the mandate that concerned UFOs, the fact is that "unknown origin" covered that point. To make the connection stronger, there are four cases from September 1960 found in the Project Blue Book files that are labeled as Moon Dust. None of the four are very good, and it is obvious from the case files that one or two of them can be resolved by meteors.

When the Air Force was approached by U.S. Senator Jeff Bingaman (D-New Mexico), who was assisting Cliff Stone of Roswell, New Mexico, in learning more about Moon Dust, the Air Force denied that there was such a project. The Congressional Inquiry Division responded with a letter signed by Lieutenant Colonel John E. Madison that said, "There is no agency, nor has there ever been, at Fort Belvoir, Virginia, which would deal with UFOs or have any information about an incident in Roswell. In addition, there is no Project Moon Dust or Operation Blue Fly. Those missions never existed."

Madison probably could have gotten away with the first statement that there was no agency at Fort Belvoir that dealt with UFOs, though other information suggests that units there did have an additional mission of UFO investigation. But Madison got into trouble when he denied that there was no such project as Moon Dust. Bingaman and Stone responded with a number of documents from the Department of State that were labeled as Moon Dust. This was before the Project Blue Book files were found that also referenced Moon Dust.

The next response was from Colonel Mattingley, who wrote, "Upon further review of the case ... we wish to amend the statements contained in the previous response to your inquiry." He said that the missions did exist but "these teams eventually disbanded because of lack of activity; Project Moon Dust and Opera-

Project Moon Dust was headquartered at the Air Force Missile Development Center at Holloman Air Force Base in New Mexico.

tion Blue Fly missions were similarly discontinued.... Although space objects and debris were occasionally reported and recovered by United States citizens and subsequently turned over to Air Force personnel for analysis, such events did not require the assistance of an intelligence team."

That too seems to be in error. Robert G. Todd, using the Freedom of Information Act, attempted to learn more about this. In an Air Force letter dated July 1, 1987, he was told the "nickname Project Moon Dust no longer exists officially." According to Colonel Phillip E. Thompson, Deputy Assistant Chief of Staff, Intelligence, "It [Project Moon Dust] has been replaced by another name that is not releaseable [sic]. FTD's [Foreign Technology Division] duties are listed in a classified regulation that is being withheld because it is currently and properly classified."

What all this means is that the United States began with an unofficial interest in these things in 1946. This eventually became Project Sign in 1948, but the Air Force announced that their investigation had ended and they found nothing of interest, certainly nothing that affected national security. This was not true. The code name was changed to Grudge, and they kept right on collecting the information.

Eventually they announced that Grudge investigators found nothing to suggest that UFOs were interplanetary as opposed to interstellar, that there was no threat to national security, and the project would be closed. This was not true. The name was changed to Blue Book, and they kept on collecting the information.

General Charles Cabell tried to reinitiate the investigation, but the Robertson Panel squashed it.

As anyone who has looked at the history of the American UFO project will tell you, at first, in the summer of 1947, the upper echelons of the military and the government were concerned about the UFOs. When it became obvious that no invasion fleet was waiting to attack and it was clear that the UFOs, whatever they might be, were not of Soviet manufacture, the pressure was off. When General Vandenberg declared that the evidence didn't support the conclusion that some UFOs came from other worlds, the fire went out of the investigation.

General Cabell rekindled it, but in January 1953 the Robertson Panel, a group of high-level scientists, looked at the evidence, deemed it incomplete at best and useless at worst, and the fire went out again. Ruppelt had set up a good investigative effort in late 1951 and into

1952, but by the time of the Robertson Panel, Ruppelt was gone, and so was any sort of in-depth analysis.

Project Blue Book continued under a series of project leaders, but for the most part, they believed there was no need to investigate and that they were wasting their time. The University of Colorado study was not an investigation of UFOs, but rather the Air Force attempt to end the unclassified and very public Project Blue Book. That plan was successful, and Blue Book was closed.

But, of course, there was Moon Dust, which did have a UFO component, as declassified documents proved repeatedly. When asked about it, the Air Force lied, though a kinder spin would be that those answering the inquiries about Moon Dust were simply not cleared to know of its existence. Moon Dust lasted until 1986, when the name was compromised and then changed. No one has been able to crack the new code word nor find documents relating to what it might be called today.

The fiction is that the United States does not investigate UFOs. They have found nothing to threaten national security and found no compelling evidence to prove they are anything other than mistakes, delusions, illusions, hysteria, and hoaxes. Other countries, however, have launched their own investigations and seem to have come to other conclusions.

Australia

The Australian government seemed to follow the path outlined in the United States, which is not to say that they were overly influenced by the USAF. When Project Blue Book closed in 1969, it hardly made a blip in Australia. They kept their investigation going for decades after that.

But as you wind your way through the maze that is the official Australian attitude on UFOs, you see them beginning to mirror what was happening, or had happened, with the investigation in the U.S. It degenerated into a case of worrying about national security, collecting the data on a covert level, and instances in which the official position as given to the media wasn't precisely what the official position actually was.

In May 1952, according to the evidence presented by Michael Swords in the massive *UFOs and the Government*, the Commonwealth Scientific and Industrial Research Organisation (CSIRO) suggested that the flying saucers were one of three things. They were products of the imagination, meteors, or sunlight glinting off aircraft at high altitude. Of course, as is often the case, such an attitude is subject to change, and one of those changes was triggered by Don Keyhoe's *Flying Saucers from Outer Space*.

In fact, on August 14, 1952, with the United States buried in UFO reports from a wide variety of sources from all over the country, William

Don Keyhoe was the author of the influential *Flying Saucers from Outer Space* that sparked interest in UFOs around the world.

McMahon, the Minister for Air, told the Australian Parliament that the flying saucers were nothing more than "flights of imagination." Even with that, he believed that a thorough investigation was warranted.

That didn't do much to change the situation. On November 20, 1953, McMahon suggested that the UFO question was one that belonged to the psychologists rather than the defense authorities. He wrote, "The Royal Australian Air Force has received many reports about flying saucers, as have the Royal Air Force and the Royal Canadian Air Force, but the phenomena have not yet been identified.... The Royal Australian Air Force has informed me that, so far, the aerodynamic problems relating to the production of flying saucers have not been solved."

The response was a "Note of Action" that indicated that "all reports are still being investigated closely and recorded as an aid to further research into future reports of this nature." Or, in other words, they thought the sightings should be investigated and the Royal Australian Air Force was the responsible agency. But, as was the case in the United States, they simply weren't investigating all the reports.

According to what Swords reported, based on the work of Australian Bill Chalker, there was another Australian government agency involved in some of the UFO research. The Department of Civil Aviation (DCA) was actively collecting UFO reports in the early 1950s. One of the best cases, again according to Swords, was the report from Captain Bob Jackson and the crew of an Australian National Airways aircraft on May 10, 1953, near Mackay.

Jackson, echoing a sentiment that other airline pilots around the world expressed, delayed his report, fearing ridicule. About the report, he said:

I was flying toward Mascot, near Worinora Dam [New South Wales] about 11 P.M., when suddenly I saw a flash of light. I watched the thing with an orange-coloured light at the tail flash toward the coast, near Wollongong. Naturally, the first thing I did was call Mascot control to ask if any other planes were in the vicinity. They replied [that] their radar proved negative. About two minutes later, the thing appeared again. It made a complete circle around us and vanished again toward the coast at a terrific speed. I can't explain it. All I know is it was nerve-wracking. I mentioned to control that if their radar failed to pick up an object—and it was a definite object—then it must be a flying saucer. They laughed, so I've kept quiet about it.

There was an additional sighting that related to this. At 6:08 P.M., Captain B. L. Jones was in an Australian National Airways DC-3 passenger plane and reported that he had seen a "strange object, like a lit glass dome" as it maneuvered around his aircraft. He, along with his copilot, watched the object for about five minutes as it climbed and dived at speeds estimated between 200 and 700 m.p.h. There was no vapor trail or tail of sparks. The UFO finally crossed in front of the airplane and disappeared, traveling to the west.

A formerly classified document created in 1954 suggested the object was a "light like [a] star." It was first seen in the east, and it maneuvered around the aircraft. According to the report as published by Swords, that report also said:

> The description given by Captain Jones is indicative of a UFO. Anticipatory vectoring on an internal light reflection may possibly have produced the circling movement, but it would not give the impression of flashing overhead. In any case, a pilot is well aware of illusions produced by light reflections, and there was ample time to check various possibilities as to the origin of the light.

And there was more. Mr. W. Overell, the officer in charge of the control tower at MacKay Airport, said there were no other aircraft in the vicinity and, more importantly, said that he saw the light climbing in the west until it vanished.

There was another sighting, this one by Frank Hines, a radio operator, at three in the morning. He said that he turned off the lights to see better, and the light shot straight up at a tremendous speed and disappeared

And there are other circumstances that seem to match. On October 30, 1953, an "Unexplained Aerial Object" was photographed over New Guinea, and those photographs were forwarded to the Directorate of [Royal Australia] Air Force Intelligence (DAFI), but the file was lost. There were a number of searches over the decades. As with the USAF, many of the files or cases are listed as missing, with only the vaguest of ideas what those files might have contained.

It wasn't until 1954, when Italy was in the middle of a wave of sightings, as were other parts of Europe, that the situation changed. Casey used his connections in intelligence to query others about flying saucers, including the American ambassador to Italy, whose Air Attaché reported that the Italians were receiving up to fifty "unexplaineds" a week and that many of the reports were of cigar-shaped or clipped, cigar-shaped craft about two hundred feet long.

Mr. W. Overell, the officer in charge of the control tower at MacKay Airport, said there were no other aircraft in the vicinity and ... that he saw the light climbing in the west until it vanished.

Casey sent Keyhoe's book to his Chief of the Division of Radiophysics, Dr. E. G. Brown, along with a note that suggested he had also seen the USAF statements about "'Unexplained Air Objects,' which are always carefully worded and are at pains to explain that the greater part of the 'sightings' are explainable as natural phenomena or on some other grounds."

Bowen wasn't too impressed with the information. He wrote that he "found the book by Major Keyhoe intensely amusing and entertaining ... I am far from convinced by any of the anecdotes or arguments." He also claimed that he knew many scientists involved with defense matters in the United States and that they rejected Keyhoe's suggestions.

> ... Bowen believed that Keyhoe's book, while entertaining, would eventually lead to the conclusion that there was nothing to the tales of flying saucers.

In keeping with a belief held at high levels, Bowen believed that Keyhoe's book, while entertaining, would eventually lead to the conclusion that there was nothing to the tales of flying saucers. The public would eventually become disillusioned with the UFOs, and that would be the end of it. Of course, that didn't turn out to be the case.

It might be said that all of this caused a change in the way the Australians dealt with the UFO problem. Melbourne University's O. H. (Harry) Turner was asked by the DAFI to undertake a classified study of the early investigations held in their files. It could be said that this was the Australian equivalent to the Robertson Panel in the United States: respected scientists studying the data that had been collected about UFOs. The outcome was certainly different.

According to Swords, based on information recovered by Chalker, Turner, in his detailed report, recommended greater official interest with a concentration on radar-visual reports. One of his conclusions was, "The evidence presented by the reports held by the RAAF [Royal Australian Air Force] tend to support ... the conclusion ... that certain strange aircraft have been observed to behave in a manner suggestive of extraterrestrial origin."

In what can only be considered a case of irony, Turner cited Keyhoe's *Flying Saucers from Outer Space*, using the reports he described as coming from the USAF. Turner did qualify his report, saying "if one assumes these Intelligence Reports are authentic, then the evidence presented is such that it is difficult to assume any interpretation other than that UFOs are being observed."

Given that Turner had used Keyhoe's reports of what official USAF reports and intelligence documents said, the DAFI did communicate with the USAF to confirm the accuracy of Keyhoe's statements. The response from Washington, D.C., was, "I have discussed with the USAF the status of Major Keyhoe. I understand that his book is written in such a way as to convey the impression his statements are based on official documents, and there is some suggestion that he has made improper use of information to which he had access while he was serving in the Marine Corps. He has, however, no official status whatsoever, and a dim view is taken officially of both him and his works."

As a result of this, the report was weakened. The Department of Air concluded, "Professor Turner accepted Keyhoe's book as authentic and based on official releases. Because Turner places so much weight on Keyhoe's work, he emphasized the need to check Keyhoe's reliability. [The Australian Joint Service Staff] removes Keyhoe's works as a prop for Turner's work so that the value of the latter's findings and recommendations is very much reduced."

The problem here was that the RAAF and the DAFI believed the information that was provided by the USAF. In the Levelland, Texas, sightings in November 1957, the Air Force and Keyhoe got into another such battle, with the Air Force suggesting that Keyhoe was wrong about the number of witnesses. Keyhoe had claimed there were nine, but the Air Force said there were only three who had seen an object. A study of the case, including an examination of the Project Blue Book files, shows that both were wrong. There is good evidence that witnesses at thirteen different locations saw something, and there is a very good possibility that the sheriff was one of those who saw a craft. (See Chapter 3 for additional information.)

> ... the USAF was not a fan of Keyhoe, so when the Australians asked for an analysis of Keyhoe and his book, they got a biased report that was not based on the evidence.

The relevance here is that the USAF was not a fan of Keyhoe, so when the Australians asked for an analysis of Keyhoe and his book, they got a biased report that was not based on the evidence. It is now evident that the Air Force had engaged, as Swords wrote, "an act of either conscious or unconscious misrepresentation on the part of the U.S. Air Force. They were engaged in a campaign to undermine the popularity of Donald Keyhoe's books. While Keyhoe may have slightly overstated his USAF data, the intelligence reports quoted by Keyhoe and used by Turner to support his conclusions to DAFI were authentic. Eventually the Air Force admitted that the material Keyhoe used was indeed from official Air Force reports."

Or, in other words, the USAF was able to manipulate the investigation being conducted in Australia to match their conclusions. If nothing else, it should be obvious based on this that after the negative conclusions of the Robertson Panel in 1953, the Air Force was actively attempting to implement the various debunking recommendations and were not interested in gathering UFO information. They were more interested in convincing everyone that there was nothing to UFO reports.

In a move that looks like a copy of what the USAF did, the RAAF, seeing that the UFO investigations were becoming a bigger problem, tried to get rid of them by pushing them to another agency. When the Director of Air Force Intelligence, Group Captain A. D. Henderson, learned that the Joint Intelligence Bureau (JIB) had a scientific intelligence division, he decided that the UFO investigations belonged there. On April 1, 1957, Henderson wrote to JIB director Harry King that they received many reports from civilians and that they received many more from civilian UFO clubs. He also mentioned that they had been able to identify many of the reports as mundane objects but there were other reports that remained unexplained. JIB rejected the idea.

Again, following the pattern of the UFO investigation in the United States, the Australians had a number of high-profile cases. In October and November 1960, an area of Tasmania was in the middle of a "spectacular wave of sightings," according to Swords. An Anglican priest, Reverend Lionel Browning and his wife made a sighting from their dining room in the Cressy Anglican rectory on October 4, 1960. As happened during the Washington National sightings in July 1952 in the United States, these sightings put the RAAF in the same position as the USAF. The public was very interested in what had happened.

Given that, the RAAF was forced to interview Browning and his wife on November 11 at their home. Wing Commander Waller conducted the inter-

Rev. Lionel Browning described the UFO as being slightly longer than a Viscount aircraft, such as the one pictured here.

view and provided a written statement that was based on Browning's comments. It said:

> He and his wife were standing in the dining room ... looking out through the window at a rainbow over some low hills approximately 8 miles to the east. The hills, the highest of which are approximately 800 feet, were partially obscured by low cloud[s] and rain.... [His] wife drew his attention to a long, cigar-shaped object, which was emerging from a rain squall.
>
> The object was a dull greyish colour, had 4 or 5 vertical, dark bands around its circumference ... and had what looked like a short, aerial array which projected outward and upward from the northern-facing end of the object. The object seems to be slightly longer than a Viscount aircraft, which Mr. Browning frequently sees flying in that area, and he therefore estimated the object's length as about one hundred feet. The outline of the object was well defined and was even more so a little later, when it had as a backdrop the tree-covered slopes of a rain-free area of the hills....
>
> The object, after emerging from the rain squall, moved on an even keel in a northerly direction at an estimated speed of sixty to seventy MPH and at a constant height of approximately four hundred feet....
>
> It moved approximately one and a half miles north ... and then abruptly stopped. Within seconds, it was joined by five or six small, saucerlike objects, which had emerged at high speed from the low cloud about and behind.... [They] stationed themselves at positions around the cigar-shaped object at a radius of one-half of a mile and then, after an interval of several seconds, the cigar-shaped object, accompanied by the smaller objects, abruptly reversed back toward and then into the rain squall from it which it had emerged.... In all, the cigar-shaped object had been visible for approximately one minute.

Had they been the only witnesses, the case might have faded from sight, but a Mrs. D. Bransden said that she had seen the same thing. She said that it "looked like a lot of little ships flocking around a bigger one."

On November 14, 1960, the director of DAFI operations reported that a "preliminary analysis indicates that the sighting was of some form of natural phenomena associated with the unsettled weather conditions." Such a nonsensical explanation was used to explain the sightings at Levelland, Texas, in 1957, and later by the Condon Committee, who claimed that a sighting had been caused by a natural phenomenon so rare that it had never been seen before or since.

Waller wrote to Dr. James McDonald that he found the couple to be mature and stable, "who had no cause or desire to see the objects in the sky other than objects of definite form and substance."

One rather hard-to-believe explanation for UFO sightings is that witnesses mistake the moon for an alien aircraft. That's what the Australian Air Force attempted to state.

The quality of the witnesses and the observations about them by a high-ranking Australian Air Force officer apparently made no difference. The sighting was rejected as "a phenomena (caused by) a moon rise, associated with meteorological conditions at the time.... The presence of 'scud'-type clouds, moving in varying directions due to turbulence in and around a rain squall near where the objects were sighted, and the position of the moon or its reflections produced the impression of flying objects."

Browning, however, said that during his interview with the RAAF intelligence, he had not been asked about the clouds. He said, "At no time was there cloud or scud when I saw the objects.... The rain cleared in front of us, although it was still raining near the mountains. I saw the objects in the sky, where there was no rain, and the rain near the mountains provided the backdrop...."

Although there were other sightings being made, including one by a USAF bomber crew on November 15, it was the Browning sighting that seemed to cause the uproar. According to Swords, Browning's federal member (meaning the equivalent to a congressional representative) identified as Mr. Duthie, asked a question that was relevant. He asked:

> Has the Minister for Air read the reports of unidentified flying objects sighted in Australia in the last two years, especially the detailed description of such an object at Cressy in my electorate by the Reverend Lionel Browning and his wife two weeks ago, and twice this last weekend? Incidently [sic], the reverend gentleman was my Liberal opponent at the 1951 and the 1954 elections. Does the Minister accept responsibility for investigating these sightings? Has the Minister any information about them that may be of interest to the people of Australia?

The Minister of Air, Mr. Osborne, gave the answer that sounded as if it could have come from the USAF, and that set the policy for the RAAF for more than ten years. He said:

> I have read the press reports of these sightings in Tasmania, and in accordance with the usual practice, all the information that is available concerning them has been furnished to my department and is

now being examined. The Department of Air does obtain information about all well-reported cases of unidentified flying objects. The department not only receives information about them but also exchanges it with the Royal Air Force and the United States Air Force. There is a regular exchange of information on these matters. I can tell the honourable member from Wilmot that although reports of this sort have been investigated very carefully for years, nearly all of them are explainable on a perfectly normal basis. Sometimes they are found to be weather balloons, high-flying aircraft, or even stars. On one occasion, it was established that a reported spaceship was the moon. Of all these reports, only 3 percent, or 4 percent, cannot be explained on the basis of some natural phenomenon, and nothing that has arisen from that 3 percent or 4 percent of unexplained cases gives any firm support for the belief that interlopers from other places in this world, or outside it, have been visiting us.

While the statement actually explained nothing and attempted to reduce the UFO problem to extremely small and therefore irrelevant numbers, the sightings continued. But this attitude was slowly eroding and on February 27, 1965, at what was billed as Australia's first UFO convention, the RAAF made an appearance. The RAAF representative was B. G. Roberts, Senior Research Scientist of the Operational Research Office, Department of Air, Canberra. He was accompanied by two officers of the RAAF, who had a hardware display with them.

"Of all these reports, only 3 percent, or 4 percent, cannot be explained on the basis of some natural phenomenon...."

Roberts gave a presentation about the term "UFO" and said that there were some objections to it, suggesting instead "unidentified aerial sightings," which removed the qualifications, suggesting that these things were flying and that they were objects. This term just suggested some sort of a phenomenon in the air. Roberts went on to say:

> ... the assessment of reports of unidentified aerial sightings in Australia and the territories is the responsibility of the Department of Air, Canberra. There is no hidden implication in this allocation of responsibility. The Department is simply the most appropriate authority for the task, which is performed to determine whether or not a threat to the security of the nation is involved....

> The number of sightings which the Department is unable to identify from the information available has remained fairly consistent at around two a year. Indeed, given sufficient time and effort, the number of unidentified sightings probably could be reduced further. One has to assess, however, whether the required additional time

and effort is warranted. The Department of Air believes that there is, and always will be, a small number of sightings (due to high-altitude phenomena, which are strange to the untrained eye) for which available information will never be sufficient to enable an identification to be made. In other words, it is just not possible to achieve 100% record of successful identification. The ideal can be approached but not achieved, simply because the inaccuracies inherent in this type of work militate against its achievement.

Which is essentially the same argument made by the U.S. Air Force. They would claim that no matter how hard they tried, they simply couldn't identify everything. The argument does make some sense when it is considered. A lone pilot in a private plane flying across a city at three in the morning with the landing lights on might confuse a witness on the ground. If there is no sound associated with it because of wind direction, it might be impossible to identify the craft, and the sighting remains unidentified.

> "I would like to make it clear that the Department of Air never has denied the possibility that some form of life may exist on other planets in the universe...."

The flip side of the argument would be that an honest sighting of an alien craft, because of its performance and its design, could not be identified in the conventional sense. It just might be that the number of actual alien craft flying around the world is extremely small, and these sightings would be lost in the suggestion that everything could be identified as conventional if those making the search got the right breaks. Or, in other words, the small residue left when the investigations were completed could be of alien spaceships.

Roberts, in his discussion at the meeting, continued, and did address part of this issue as well. He said:

> The number of unidentified sightings each year in Australia does not warrant such great effort or expense. Only where there is evidence that a threat to the security of the nation is involved (e.g., the possibility of foreign aircraft infringing our air space) would this attitude be reversed. The Department of Air believes that there always will be aerial sightings of high-altitude phenomena, which are strange to the untrained eye, and that of these some will not be identified.

> Finally, I would like to make it clear that the Department of Air never has denied the possibility that some form of life may exist on other planets in the universe.... However, the Department has, so far, neither received nor discovered in Australia any evidence to support the belief that the earth is being observed, visited, or threatened by machines from other planets. Furthermore, there are no documented files or dossiers held by the Department which prove the existence of "flying saucers."

This, too, seemed to be the argument used by the U.S. Air Force. There was no real responsibility to investigate these sightings unless they posed some sort of threat to national security. By the middle of the 1960s, after two decades of UFO reports from the Foo Fighters to the Ghost Rockets to the fly-ing saucers, no case could be made of a threat. They were up there, probably some sort of high-altitude phenomena that those untrained would mistake for something else, and the investigating agencies could do nothing about them. It was a waste of time, money, and resources to chase down every report the Department of Air received, and it was clear that they weren't receiving reports of every sighting made.

Added to this was a Department of Air memorandum from February 1966 that pointed out there were no "written responsibilities for the (RAAF) Operational Command in the UFO field." There was an "ad hoc" system to deal with the UFOs, meaning there was no real official structure to it, and that seemed to be working. In March 1966, DAFI issued an order written by Group Captain I. S. Podger for the Chief of the Air Staff to the Operational and Sup-port commands that said:

> The main purpose of the investigation of any UFO is to establish whether or not the subject of the report poses a threat to the secu-rity of Australia. The identification of the cause of the UFO report and its classifications as aircraft, balloon, missile, astronomical body, or phenomena, etc., is of minor importance and mainly for the benefit of the members of the public, whose interest may have been aroused by the report....

> No attempts should be made to answer public enquiries at unit or command level. Requests by members of the public for information on UFOs in Australia and for the RAAF assessment of their origin, etc [sic] should be referred to the Department of Air, where they will be dealt with by the Directorate of Public Affairs.

This was the path that was being followed by the USAF. They were attempting to move UFO investigations from the Air Technical Intelligence Center to the Public Affairs office. They believed that the ATIC letterhead added weight to the belief in UFOs, but if the less prestigious letterhead of the Office of Public Affairs appeared, people would be inclined to believe that there was nothing important to UFO sightings.

In the course of the discussion at the upper levels of these departments, the Director of Public Affairs also noted:

> In summary: by continuing with the old policy of playing our UFO cards close to the chest, we only foster the incorrect (but neverthe-less widely held) belief that we have much vital information to hide. On the other hand, by maintaining a current "Summary"

"... by continuing with the old policy of playing our UFO cards close to the chest, we only foster the incorrect (but nevertheless widely held) belief that we have much vital information to hide."

(which the DPR [Director of Public Relations] is prepared to do, with your continued help) we dispose, in one blow, of the UFO enthusiasts' belief that:

(a) he is not being taken into the RAAF's confidence;

(b) the RAAF is desperately determined to suppress UFO information to prevent national panic....

This sort of discussion continued, just as it had in the United States, with confusion at various levels of the government. The Director of Public Relations wrote to the Director of Air Force Intelligence, saying, "While security is not DPR's affair, our relations with the general public (cranks and all) certainly are, and I feel strongly, from the PR point of view, that we are handling this whole UFO business in an unnecessarily rigid and unimaginative way."

Swords, writing in *UFOs and Government*, confirmed the confusion. A memorandum from the DAFI, dated October 12, 1966, said:

There appears to be some confusion concerning Department policy over UFOs ... on file ... there is ministerial statement to the effect: "Anyone who is interested in sightings of UFOs can apply to the Department of the Air for information on the subject and is welcome to a synopsis of UFO sightings, which includes a very brief assessment of the probable causes."

This statement was made in answer to ministerial representation. It would appear, however, that the policy represented by this statement may not have reflected the view of DAFI, despite earlier, although inconclusive, evidence.

Then to underscore this confusion and the communications among the various agencies:

DAFI has proposed to DGPP [Director of General Plans & Policy], who in turn referred to [the Director of Civil Aviation Safety] that our approach to UFO reports be liberalised. It does not appear that either DGPP or DCAS were aware of the Minister's statement. In my opinion, we must either comply with the terms of that statement or inform the minister of our "new" approach, if it is not intended to provide the synopsis of sightings, and on this I am not altogether clear from reading the files....

It would also appear that there is some need for rationalization of our files on this subject. There are at least 4 different files which contain a confusion of policy, reported sightings. and requests for information. Three of the files are classified, two of which are

SECRET, although there appears to be nothing in the files consistent with this classification. Could DAFI and DPR consider rationalizing these files please…?

As happened with Project Blue Book in the United States, there was a series of "Summary" statements that were issued on a regular basis, but as happened with the Blue Book Status reports, these summaries slowly became erratic.

Harry Turner, who had written the 1954 report that was of a positive nature, reappears in 1969. He had asked for access to the DAFI's reports, and that was granted. He thought that the reporting form should be redesigned, and he was working with other scientists to create a rapid intervention team to investigate cases of UFO physical evidence. Unfortunately, this was not going to happen.

In 1969, a new UFO flap broke out in Western Australia and involved a radar-visual sighting at Cloverdale. The radar was in Kalamunda on May 23, 1969. Since the "Rapid Intervention Team" had not been formed, Turner was asked to assist. His report said:

On the 23rd May, 1969, (Mrs. C___'s) 13-year-old son, who has an interest in the night sky, noticed from the front door of their house

… that to the south and about 10 degrees above the horizon, there was a moving light, which he first took to be an aeroplane. As it approached to the SE of the observer, it became apparent to him that its behaviour pattern differed considerably from that of an aircraft. He called his mother, who observed … in an easterly direction a steady, red light on top of a more diffused blue-white light and darting haphazardly in a zigzag pattern, but in general travelling toward a northerly direction until it disappeared behind the house. The two witnesses proceeded to the NW side of the house, where they observed a luminous object against the clear starry sky at an elevation between 10 and 15 degrees and at a bearing of 015 degrees.

The light observed was circular—about half the diameter of a full moon. It was steady in position and intensity for some 15–20 minutes. It no longer had a red light on top and had the brightness of a fluores-

This illustration is based on a description by Shirley Ryall and her brother, Bevan Adam, who saw a UFO near Barmedman, New South Wales, in 1970. It was cigar-shaped just like the one seen by Rev. Browning and his wife.

cent streetlight. The edge was not clean cut but was somewhat hazy, even though the night air was perfectly clear. The time at which the object was first sighted was estimated at being 1835 hours [6:35 P.M.] … shortly before 1900 hours [7:00 P.M.], the object moved at extremely high velocity, away from the observers, in a general N to NE-ly [sic] direction.

Mrs. C____ … telephoned the shift operator on site. [He] was still talking to Mrs. C____ when a request came from the meteorological radar situated near Perth Airport as to whether he could check out an unidentified echo seen on the meteorological radar.

The Kalamunda radar operator had not been watching his screen as no aircraft were in the vicinity, but on checking the P.P.I. [Plan Position Indicator] screen, he observed a large echo some 9 miles away at 300 degrees from his position, which placed the echo some 2½ miles north of Mrs. C____'s position. Initial contact was made at 1901 hours [7:01 P.M.] and held for only 30 to 40 seconds. The echo which reappeared for short durations on 5 further occasions was twice the size of a large aircraft at that position. The echo has not been seen since it finally disappeared at 1942 hours [7:42 P.M.]

One unusual feature of the Kalamunda report is that the radar is equipped with a Moving Target Indicator (MTI), which suppresses all permanent echoes and all targets moving at speeds less than an estimated 6 knots…. The night in question was clear and calm, and there is no justification for an MTI breakthrough in the region of the target. Despite the operations of the MTI, the unknown target was clearly visible, even though there was no displacement of its position. The operator had never before met an apparently stationary target that was recorded so clearly, despite the operation of the MTI. [The operator] paid particular attention to this echo over the whole period of 41 minutes that it occurred because it was a potential traffic hazard to two aircraft in circuit about that time, and they had to be warned to avoid the area of the unknown target…. The operator is quite sure … that the echo's appearance never lasted more than a minute at any one time….

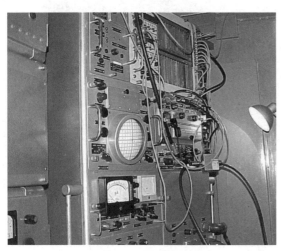

A moving target indicator (MTI) like this one was installed at the Kalamunda radar. The MTI removes false signals of echoes and slow-moving targets such as birds.

[Just] before 1900 hours, the object moved away from the observer, disappearing from sight in a fraction of a second, and it is possible that it correlates with the stationary echo on radar at 1901 hours. The unusual features of the echo are:

(a) size;

(b) the fact that it was seen, despite the operation of the MTI; and

(c) the spasmodic appearance.

It is not possible to readily conceive of an explanation for these observations. All observers were obviously sincerely puzzled individuals with an aversion to publicity.

Turner thought that the meteorological returns might have a mundane explanation but that neither the Kalamunda radar observations nor Mrs. C___'s sighting could be easily explained. He did make one mistake in his report and that was to mention the DAFI system's lack of assistance to the "on-the-spot" Air Force Intelligence officer. The Air force didn't like that, and Turner's access to the DAFI UFO files was terminated.

At that point, the idea of the rapid-intervention team was dropped and to make the situation even worse, in July 1971, the Director of Air Force Intelligence, Group Captain R. S. Royston, provided his opinion on the matter of UFOs. According to a memo he wrote:

Although I am directly concerned with any possible threat to Australian security, I am not particularly interested in the subject of UFOs, even though my directorate devotes valuable time to this problem. I accept the U.S. assessments without question and consider that it would be a complete waste of time for we, here in Australia, to spend valuable time and money in further detailed investigations. However, should the Department of Supply wish to undertake such studies, the records of this directorate would be freely available. It would have to be pointed out to Supply, however, that the RAAF could provide no additional assistance in the matter and Supply would have to undertake all the facets of the further investigation.

What this does is answer one of the questions about how such a worldwide problem could be contained. The Australian military wanted no part of a UFO investigation. Believing that there was no threat to Australian security, they could fall back on the USAF assessment and the University of Colorado study, which had concluded there was nothing to the UFO sightings. Why expend Australian resources when there was a clear-cut answer, or rather one that they believed to be clear-cut?

But Turner, the man who had been driving most of the interest in UFOs in the Australian government for decades, wasn't about to give up. He contin-

Dr. Jacques Vallée (right), shown here with Dr. J. Allen Hynek in an undated photo.

ued to produce papers about UFOs and used Jacques Vallée's book, *Passport to Magonia*, which contained a thousand worldwide UFO reports, as one of his sources. He suggested that there could well be a threat to Australian national security.

But even with this and an agreement by some of those inside the Joint Intelligence Organisation (formerly JIB) that such an investigation might yield results, there just weren't the resources available to do it, and it would require "considerable backup." Or, in other words, yes, it might be valuable, but we can't do it, or maybe more accurately, we just don't want to do it.

It becomes apparent, in the documentation uncovered by Chalker and reported by Swords, that the RAAF lost interest in UFOs after 1977. In response to Bill Chalker, they wrote:

> My Directorate is charged with the responsibility for UAS [also known as UFOs] investigation and reporting. It has been a contentious issue for many years, with opinions varying from a questioning of a need for monitoring such sightings to the organisational area most appropriately placed to deal with them.... The only advantage I see in retaining UAS investigation responsibilities are:
>
> a. It allows a security oversight of unusual events which, on the odd occasion, may bear some military implication, and
>
> b. it provides "cover" if we wish to investigate some incident, not necessarily related, in more details, and....
>
> I seek your views on whether the RAAF should continue to carry the responsibility for the investigation of UAS....

By this time, however, it is clear that the RAAF was no more interested in UFOs than the USAF was. There was a wave of sightings in 1983 in Australia, but these seemed to be nocturnal lights. In what the RAAF called Operation Close Encounters (probably for the reason everyone thinks), they ordered RAAF aircraft on standby to intercept any verified radar sightings, but apparently the aircraft were never launched to chase UFOs.

While there were some interesting radar sightings at the Sidney Airport, none were confirmed by visual sightings. The press attention was used by the RAAF to convince the public that they were doing something substantial with their investigations, but that just seemed to be the public face of it. The RAAF realized there was no coherent threat and decided this was the time to end their public involvement in UFO investigation.

In a letter dated January 4, 1994, the RAAF reported, "The number of reports made to the RAAF in the past decade had declined significantly, which may indicate that organisations such as yours [that is, Chalker's civilian group] are better known and are meeting the community's requirements."

The new policy also noted, "For many years the RAAF has been formally responsible for handling Unusual Aerial Sightings (UAS) at the official level. Consideration of the scientific record suggests that, whilst not all UAS have a ready explanation, there is no compelling reason for the RAAF to continue to devote resources to recording, investigating, and attempting to explain UAS."

While much of that is true, the real point was that there were no national security implications and the RAAF could, in good conscience, ignore the sighting reports. But it is also true that there were some truly inexplicable sightings that deserved proper investigation, just as there had been in the United States. The mission of these investigations seemed to be to absolve the military of any responsibility for investigating them. The obvious answer in Australia, as it would be anywhere, would be for a proper scientific investigation to be conducted, but it always seems to get lost in the bureaucratic infighting. Nothing is ever really done.

> The press attention was used by the RAAF to convince the public that they were doing something substantial with their investigations....

France: GEPAN to SEPRA

Like so many other countries, France, in 1977, began what was described as a "quasi-official" investigation of UFOs. As will become clear later, during the examination of COMETA (Comité d'Études Approfondies, or Committee for In-Depth Studies), the police officers of the Gendarmerie Nationale began to record sightings of UFOs made to them in the 1950s. These were then reported to the French Air Force, and because the gendarmes' chain of command runs upward to the Ministry of Defense, it was natural for them to pass these reports over to the Air Force.

According to Gildas Bourais, writing in the *International UFO Reporter* during these early years, there were some military personnel who were interested in the flying saucers. One of those was General Lionel Max Chassin, who encouraged those efforts, and once he retired, he became involved in a civilian group known in France as GEPA (Groupe d'Étude des Phénomène Aériens, or Group for the Study of Aerial Phenomena).

Bourais wrote that Jacques Vallée had suggested that some French scientists were interested in UFOs, and Vallée said that he had given some of the

It was France's President Charles de Gaulle himself who sent down the order to create a research team to study the possibility of UFOs and extraterrestrials.

best of the Project Blue Book cases to Yves Rocard, who had been instrumental in the creation of the French atomic bomb, or, in other words, he was one of the top physicists in France. It was at about the time of Vallée's visit to France that an interest had been expressed in undertaking a UFO investigation, though it is not clear if Vallée's visit had sparked the interest or not.

Jean-Luc Bruneau, the former inspector general at the Commissariat a l'Energie Atomique (CEA), told Bourais that he had been asked to make a proposal for the creation of a research group on extraterrestrial life and UFOs. Interestingly, the idea came from the military staff of France's president at the time, Charles de Gaulle. According to Bourais and Bruneau, de Gaulle had been worried about a sighting in Madagascar, which was also covered in the COMETA study. De Gaulle was interested in France having its own UFO study that was independent of what the USAF was doing.

In 1967, about the time that the Condon Committee was being created at the University of Colorado, Bruneau's confidential study was approved. Again, according to Bourais, he had three objectives. They involved experts in the probability of the existence and search for extraterrestrial intelligence, what human relations could be with them through space, and what was going on in the terrestrial environment, or, in other words, an investigation of the unidentified aerospace phenomena (UAP).

Bruneau was careful in his wording because he believed that the phenomenon, that is, the UFO, could include both material and nonmaterial objects. He told Bourais that at the time of his study, the opinions of the scientists were divided about equally between those who thought there was something real and observable going on and those who thought it was all nonsense. Bourais noted, parenthetically, that no one in France in the 21st century would dare to hold such opinions.

While all this sounds good, events on the ground, as they have in other countries, overtook the formation of the investigation, and it was postponed. The opportunity to reignite it never appeared. According to Bourais, Bruneau still believed it could work, but again, the scientific environment and the world of the UFO has changed radically since the idea was conceived.

In 1973, there was another series of sightings that attracted the media and a French radio reporter, Jean-Claude Bourret, produced a successful series of reports for a French national network. Bourret interviewed the French defense minister, Robert Galley, who said that there were some very interesting and unexplained reports in the files of the gendarmes, and he recommended "keeping an open mind" on UFOs.

It was also about this time that J. Allen Hynek's book, *The UFO Experience*, was translated into French. It was defended on French national television by astronomer Pierre Guerin when it was attacked by some skeptical French reporters.

Then, in 1974, it was decided to systematically gather the reports that had been made to the gendarmerie at the national level. Copies of the reports were to be made for Centre National d'Etudes Spatiales (CNES). It was that same year, 1974, that a committee of the Institut des Hautes Études Defense Nationale (IHEDN), chaired by French General Robert Blanchard, recommended the study of the UFO data.

As if that wasn't enough support, an engineer, who was the chief of the systems and projects division at CNES, Claude Poher, who was already studying the UFO question on a personal level, completed a statistical study of UAPs. He had been surprised to learn, after reading the Condon Committee report, that many of the cases investigated by the committee had not been explained.

In 1976, he made proposals to the director of CNES and was supported by INEDN for the creation of a UFO study group. According to Bourais, Poher had been promised the full cooperation of the French Air Force, the gendarmerie, French civil aviation, and the national meteorology office. This was the sort of thing that should have been established decades earlier in many different countries.

A year later, 1977, the government asked CNES to create a permanent group for the study of UFOs. That was done in May 1977, with the creation of Groupement d'Étude des Phénomènes Aerospatiaux Non-identifies (GEPAN). Poher would be the director.

Bourais reported that in the first session, the president of CNES, Hubert Curien, asked GEPAN to make the study with an open mind.

French radio reporter Jean-Claude Bourret produced a series of reports for national broadcast about UFOs in 1973.

> **Cases labeled as "perfectly identified" or "probably identified" made up twenty-six percent of the sighting reports.**

A scientific council was created with the idea that GEPAN would report to them once a year. There was solid support for the study from others, including the inspector general of CNES, M. Gruau.

During the first couple of years, GEPAN had a staff of six to seven, but it also had cooperation from others inside and outside of GEPAN. One of the first tasks was to analyze the reports coming in from the gendarmerie. They started with the three hundred that were already in the files, and they were gathering another hundred a year. According to Bourais, that number eventually dropped to fewer than twenty a year.

In December 1977, there was the first meeting of the Scientific Council, and they were given a two-volume report of 290 pages that included, according to Bourais, three general presentations, three reports on detailed investigations, an analysis of two alleged photographs of UFOs, and five statistical analyses of samples and various cases. The council recommended that GEPAN take on additional studies, and these were presented in a five-volume report of 670 pages. As before, these contained detailed field investigations, a summary of the investigations written by Poher, and information on other cases that had not been subjected to the intense study of the detailed cases. Unfortunately, according to Bourais, these studies were never published, but the information might still be hidden in classified files somewhere.

The statistical analysis presented was interesting. Cases labeled as "perfectly identified" or "probably identified" made up twenty-six percent of the sighting reports. Those labeled as "insufficient data" made up thirty-six percent, and most importantly, the "unidentified" cases made up thirty-eight percent. That unidentified category is interesting because it is close to the statistical summary of the Condon Committee, in which a large number of the cases investigated did not have a mundane solution.

In 1979, Poher concluded that UFOs were real, and he presented his findings to the Scientific Council of GEPAN. The French media resisted this conclusion, according to Bourais, but that didn't change Poher's mind. He did take a year off to sail around the world and then he returned to CNES. Since then, according to Bourais, Poher has made no additional statements about UFOs, but he is still interested in the topic.

Also in 1979, a new man, Alain Esterle, was appointed to the top position in GEPAN. He expanded their resources and increased the staff to ten. During this time, there were a couple of important sightings, including a physical trace case at Trans-en-Provence in 1981. The case was reviewed in the COMETA report that would follow years later.

The cases were carefully investigated, but no solutions were found; they were considered too provocative. The funding for GEPAN was reduced, though the study of the cases might not have been the whole story. According to Bourais, CNES was also having money trouble, and that was the deciding factor in cutting support for the UFO investigation. In the years that followed, the Scientific Council no longer met.

In 1988, GEPAN was closed. A new organization, Service d'Expertise des Phenomenes de Rentrees Atmospherriques (SEPRA), or in English, Atmospheric Re-entry Phenomena Expertise Department, was created. It didn't refer to UFOs directly. The new name seemed to be aimed at satellite and rocket debris, which is the same sort of description often made about Project Moon Dust in the United States. Both organizations continued to exhibit an interest in UFOs, but their main purpose seemed to be aimed in the terrestrial rather than in the extraterrestrial.

According to Bourais, the Scientific Council was silenced, and no technical notes were published. The new leader found that he had other duties and could only spend part of his time in UFO investigation. This low-profile policy, again similar to that of Moon Dust, remains in effect in the 21st century. It seems that those in France who have studied UFOs come to the conclusion that something real is going on. Those on the outside seem to suggest that there is nothing to the UFO phenomenon.

But all this controversy led to the creation of COMETA and a report that strongly suggested that UFOs were of extraterrestrial manufacture. COMETA wasn't an official study, but it did look at the phenomena closely on a world-wide scale, and as had happened so often in the past, it was opposed by those who know there are no extraterrestrial visitations. It's just the evidence that gets in the way.

The COMETA Report

Although the report was created by former high-ranking military officers, government officials, and former members of the official French UFO study, COMETA (Comité d'Études Approfondies, which translates as Committee for In-depth Studies) was a private investigation of UFO sightings and doctrine. It was intended for only the highest level of the French government and was never intended for public consumption. The participants in the study were men who had attended advanced workshops at the Institut des Hautes Études Defense Nationale, or the Institute of Advanced Studies for National Defense. The IHEDN is a French organization that is somewhat analogous to the top-level war colleges of various American military services, and has a mission of providing advice to the French government on matters of national security.

This was something of a departure for the French, who had never been overly concerned with the issue of UFOs. Even in the past, when it seemed that the majority of the interesting UFO sightings were being reported in France or in Western Europe, there was no organized effort to assemble case files, gather evidence, or study what was happening. But when the U.S. Air Force announced the end of Project Blue Book, the French Minister of Defense, Robert Galley, promised that the UFO "problem" would be studied. This was done with the formation of a committee made of up "auditors" from IHEDN. Robert Blanchard, a member of the gendarmerie, was given the job as chairman.

A year or so later, their report led to the formation of Groupe d'Études des Phénomènes Aerospatiaux Non-Identifies (GEPAN—Unidentified Aerospace Phenomena Studies Group) on May 1, 1977. This was part of the French National Center for Space Studies (CNES, Centre National D'etudies Spatiales, which is the French version of NASA). Unlike Project Blue Book and

The National Center for Space Studies in Paris, France.

the various other U.S. Air Force public investigations into UFOs, GEPAN was engaged in serious research but suffered from poor funding. Unlike the UFO investigations in most other countries, this was not part of a military operation. There were public and comprehensive reports issued that were available to the both government officials and civilian researchers.

What this all means is that various entities in the French government were interested in UFOs and that the study of UFOs was not considered to be a dead end. The history showed who was investigating UFOs, what their status in the government was, and that they took it all seriously. It followed naturally that those who had been involved in the earlier investigations would join together to again study UFOs, and that was the genesis of COMETA.

With the support of those still involved with the French military and government, particularly General Bernard Norlain who was, in 1995, the director of IHEDN, the COMETA group moved forward. The group was chaired by retired General Denis Letty, who had also been part of IHEDN.

Letty was important to the overall UFO picture. Although he had seen nothing himself, he had spoken to French air force pilots, who had seen something. It was the sincerity of the pilots that left an impression on Letty, and as they began their investigation, those reports were an important part of it.

Letty also spoke to Professor Andre Lebeau, who was a former chairman of CNES, and he provided a forward to the final COMETA report. In what he called "stripping the UFO phenomenon of its irrational layer," he wrote:

> It is not looked on highly in certain scientific circles to be preoccupied with phenomena that are deemed to come under the heading of popular mythology or that are, at any rate, outside the realm of science....
>
> Phenomena of this type pose a preliminary problem for the scientific approach: Does a scientific fact exist?
>
> When the phenomenon is a matter of experimentation, the criterion to be used is simple; the reproducibility of the experiment is the touchstone and furnishes the fact that must be interpreted. But the situation is more difficult when the phenomenon is not open to experimentation, when repeated observation is the only basis on which one can go, as is the case in astronomy and for the most part geophysics. However, when the fact, albeit rare, is collectively and indisputably visible, it is easy to elevate it to the status of scientific object.... Thus collective and simultaneous observation plays the same role as the reproducibility of experiments.
>
> This is not true when the event is not only rare, but discrete as well, and when there is a very small amount of evidence at each occurrence, which opens the door to various suspicions. Unidentified flying objects, or UFOs, fall into this category. One runs up against additional difficulties in the case of UFOs, firstly that of how many human activities, especially since the beginning of the space age, have generated atmospheric phenomena, the origin of which is not immediately ascertainable by those who observe them. In any case, UFOs, the origin of which cannot be attributed to either a human source or a natural mechanism that has not been identified by science, are mixed in with a background of noise, the origin of which, although difficult to identify, is not all mysterious.
>
> Moreover, and above all, the existence of unexplained manifestations, both in the atmosphere and occasionally on the surface of the earth, inevitably gives rise to a fundamental question: are we alone in the universe? Could some of these phenomena be the work of extraterrestrial beings? This question gives the UFO issue a sociological, media-related, and even religious dimension in a domain that is not that of science and scientific methods. And it is the very existence of this dimension that elicits reactions of rejection in the scientific community.

> "This report [COMETA] is useful in that it contributes toward stripping the phenomenon of UFOs of its irrational layer...."

However, a dispassionate examination of the situation should lead those who believe in the value of scientific method to consider that the very existence of a strong irrational environment is another reason to apply the precepts of this method to the issue of UFOs....

This report [COMETA] is useful in that it contributes toward stripping the phenomenon of UFOs of its irrational layer.... What a scientist believes is important in the conducting of his research because this is what motivates and drives him. But his belief is not important to the results of his research nor does it have any effect on those results if he is meticulous.

What he is suggesting is that a study of UFOs should be conducted as other scientific research is conducted. It should be dispassionate, it should be meticulous, and it should be free of bias. All too often, as seen in the Air Force investigations and later in those conducted at the University of Colorado, the results were driven by influences outside the investigation. The need to resolve the issue of national security was important, but once that had been established, then the investigation should have moved into a new arena. Instead, a need of security drove the investigation. Here, with COMETA, the driving feature seemed to be a desire to learn what was happening without those outside influences.

The first part of the COMETA report is "Facts and Testimonies." According to them, "it seems worthwhile to us to present several facts and testimonies that in themselves justify the interest of the in-depth study that we are going to develop below: three testimonies of French civilian and military pilots ... five major aeronautical cases in the world ... three sightings from the ground ... four cases of close encounters in France."

Two of those cases were those that had come to the attention of General Letty and convinced him of the importance of the study of UFOs. As Letty would report later, he was impressed with the sincerity of the men who related the stories. It should be noted as well that there was no motivation for them to invent the tales, they weren't seeking some sort of momentary fame, and such a story, told to a superior, could have an adverse effect on a pilot's career. Tales of pilots grounded after a UFO report, or moved to a less responsible assignment, are told throughout the world. In these cases, the reports impressed the superior.

March 7, 1977: France

The first sighting that intrigued General Letty was that of Major, later Colonel, Hervé Giraud, who was flying a Mirage IV fighter on March 7, 1977. According to the documentation available, it was about 8:34 P.M. on a night navigation training exercise, flying at about 32,000 feet, when they noticed a brilliant light coming at them. Both the pilot, Giraud, and the navigation officer, Captain Jean Paul Abraham, saw the light out at about their three o'clock position. They contacted ground control at Contrexeville but were told that the radar there had no other traffic in the area. The ground controller suggested they check their oxygen supply, seeming to believe that they might be hallucinating because of an oxygen deficiency.

The object appeared to be flying toward them at high speed, at their altitude, and looked as if it was on a collision course. Giraud turned right and left to be sure that he wasn't seeing some sort of reflection on the canopy of the aircraft. It was obvious to both of them that it was a solid object. Giraud said later, "I had the impression of a shape and an important mass behind us, much larger than my Mirage."

> The ground controller suggested they check their oxygen supply, seeming to believe that they might be hallucinating because of an oxygen deficiency.

According to the COMETA report, Giraud maneuvered his aircraft and then returned to a course toward the airfield at Luxeuil. He had the impression that he was being watched and said to the navigator, "You wait and see, it's going to come back."

But with the object still in sight and with what he considered to be a real threat—which is to say that anything that is flying toward a fighter is considered a threat until identified—Giraud made a tight, high-G turn. The light followed and took up a position directly behind the fighter. Giraud continued to maneuver, and the light disappeared again. Still, there was no radar contact with it.

The COMETA report claimed there were two points that were important and should be emphasized. According to it:

> ... only combat aircraft could have performed comparable to that of A1 and A2 [the fighter and the object] (speed and maneuverability). In the case, C [meaning the radar controller] would have had radar contact on this aircraft, especially at that altitude, a contact that he would have seen all the better since there was no other traffic in the vicinity of the Mirage IV.

> ... given the apparent maneuvers of A1 and A2, regardless of whether or not they were the same craft, their speed could only be supersonic, which, in the case of combat aircraft, would be manifested on the ground by a very loud sonic boom due to the phenomenon of the focusing of the shock wave generated by the bank. This would have been noticed in the surrounding area, especially since it was nighttime. But no sound was heard in the region.

Given the training of the aircrew and their familiarity with the aircraft of various nations, and given the length of time the UFO was in sight, the case is quite puzzling.

March 3, 1976: France

The second report covered by the COMETA is also from a fighter pilot. Although he had requested his name not be used, he later reconsidered, and he has been identified as Colonel Claude Bosc. According to the COMETA report, he was a student at the combat flight school at Tours and was on a solo night training mission in a T-33, which is a jet trainer:

> The mission consisted of navigating at an altitude of 6000 m [19,500 feet], following a Rennes-Nantes-Poitiers itinerary, then landing at Tours. Several aircraft were following the same itinerary at 5-minute intervals. The night was dark but cloudless, and the towns could be detected very clearly at the flight altitude in question. Visibility was greater than 100 km [60 miles]. While he was flying stabilized at an altitude of 6000 m, at a speed of 460 km/h, [Bosc] first saw straight ahead, very far off in the distance (at the detection limit of lights on the ground), what he at first thought was the launching of a green signaling flare.
>
> In 1 or 2 seconds, this flare exceeded the altitude of this aircraft by 1500 m [about 5,000 feet] and seemed to level off in space before descending in his direction. It approached at a dizzying speed on a collision course with the aircraft and filled the entire front windshield of the cockpit. Thinking that impact was inevitable, [Bosc] let go of the joystick and crossed his arms in front of his face in a reflex protection gesture. The aircraft was completely enveloped in a very bright and phosphorescent green light. [Bosc] saw a sphere (S) that avoided his aircraft at the very last moment and passed over his right wing, grazing it, all within a fraction of a second. [Bosc] retained the following memory of the incident:
>
> - was not very large (1 to 2 m in diameter [3 to 6 feet]).
> - was extended by a tail, which was comparable to that on a comet, that was also a fluorescent green in color.
> - the center of S consisted of a very bright white light (magnesium-fire type).
> - the sighting lasted a total of less than 5 seconds.
>
> [Bosc], who was very shocked by this phenomenon, informed the radar controller, ensuring the control of the mission on the ground; the controller had not detected anything on his radarscope. Upon return, two other pilots who had followed the same itinerary as [Bosc] stated they had seen the phenomenon, but from a distance.

"Thinking that impact was inevitable, [Bosc] let go of the joystick and crossed his arms in front of his face in a reflex protection gesture."

Although not mentioned in the COMETA report, the sighting is reminiscent of the Foo Fighters of World War II. Often they were reported as glowing balls of light or spheres that seemed to be attracted to the aircraft. They sometimes followed the formations of bombers or fighters, seemed to buzz them and then flash off into the distance. No explanation for the Foo Fighters was found after the end of the war. They were not German secret weapons, and there were no anti-aircraft weapons that would account for the sightings. Foo Fighters were reported in all theaters of the war and in many cases were reported as solid objects that were larger than the light reported by Bosc.

January 28, 1994: France

The last of the sightings from France in the COMETA report is from an Air France flight, AF 3532, which was commanded by Jean-Charles Duboc, with Valerie Chauffour as the copilot. They were on a Nice-to-London flight when, at 1314 hours [1:14 P.M.] and flying at 11,900 meters [39,000 feet] near Coulommiers in Seine-et-Marne the chief steward [flight attendant] saw what he thought was a weather balloon. According to the COMETA report:

> His sighting was immediately confirmed by the copilot, [Duboc], who in turn saw it was an aircraft banking at a 45-[degree] angle. Very quickly, however, all three agreed that what they were seeing did not resemble anything they knew of. The excellent visibility and the presence of altocumulus clouds permitted [Duboc] to estimate the phenomenon was at an altitude of 10,500 m [about 34,000 feet] and at a distance of approximately 50 km [30 miles]. Taking into account its apparent diameter, they deduced that the craft was large. They were struck by changes in the shape of the craft, which first appeared in the form of a brown bell before transforming into a chestnut-brown lens shape, then disappearing almost instantaneously on the left side of the aircraft, as if it had suddenly become invisible. [Duboc] reported to the Reims Air Navigation Control Center, which had no information on any mobile air presence in the vicinity. However, following the existing procedure, Reims informed the Tavery Air Defense Operations Center (CODA) of the sighting made by the crew and asked [Duboc] to follow the "Airmiss" [known as a "Near Miss"] procedure upon landing.

"They were struck by changes in the shape of the craft, which first appeared in the form of a brown bell before transforming into a chestnut-brown lens shape...."

If that was the whole story, it could be easily dismissed as some sort of phenomenon that fooled the flight crew. But CODA had corroborative data from the radar at Cinq-Mars-la-Pile that showed something in the air near the

Air France aircraft at the location and time of the sighting. It showed that the object had crossed the path of the flight. The records showed that there was no flight that corresponded to that radar return that had filed a flight plan and that the return disappeared from the radar screens at the same time the flight crew lost sight of it.

According to the COMETA report, "The investigations conducted by CODA enabled both the hypothesis of a weather balloon to be ruled out and the precise crossing distance of the two trajectories to be determined, consequently bringing the approximate length of the craft to 250 meters [about 800 feet] in length. It should be noted that the Northern Regional Air Navigation Center (CRNA), which handles 3,000 movements per day, has investigated only three cases over the last seven years, one of which was that of flight AF 3532."

The importance of this case is that there was a visual sighting, corroborated by three of the flight crew, and that the evidence was available from the instrumentality, meaning the radar. It proved that something solid was in the sky and provided information about the size of the object, its location, and its maneuvers. This wasn't a case of a flight crew seeing something but a case where their observations were confirmed by an outside source.

The COMETA report then went on to explore what they labeled as "Aeronautical Cases Throughout the World." It was their thought to again concentrate on cases in which there was both radar and visual sightings and on one case in which there were multiple witnesses.

August 13–14, 1956:
Bentwaters/Lakenheath, United Kingdom

This case was reported to Project Blue Book, but it seemed that those conducting the investigations were uninterested in finding answers. They were more interested in explaining the sightings than in a proper investigation. Here they claimed the explanation was false radar returns and a sighting of Mars.

The case began, according to the Project Blue Book files, at 2130Z, or at 9:30 P.M., when Technical Sergeant Elmer L. Whenry, a GCA (Ground-Controlled Approach) radar operator for the USAF's 1264th Airborne Air Control Squadron (AACS) at RAF Station Bentwaters, England, spotted twelve to fifteen blips on his radarscope. These were not correlated to any of the aircraft known to be flying in the area at the time.

According to the Project Blue Book file:

This group was picked up approximately eight miles southwest of RAF Station Bentwaters and were tracked on the radarscope clearly until the objects were approximately fourteen miles northeast of

The dozen or so UFOs converged to form a large object that was described by Sergeant Whenry as several times larger than the B-36 pictured here.

Bentwaters. At the latter point on the course of these objects, they faded considerably on the radarscope....

At the approximate forty-mile range, individual objects ... appeared to converge into one very large object, which appeared several times larger than a B-36 aircraft due to the size of the blip on the radarscope. At the time that the individual objects seemed to converge into one large object, the large object appeared to remain stationary for ten to fifteen minutes. The large object then moved NE [northeast] approximately five or six miles, then stopped movement for three to five minutes, then moved north, disappearing off the radarscope.

At about this same time, Airman Second Class (A2C) John Vaccare, Jr., another of the radar operators at the base, spotted a single blip twenty-five to thirty miles to the southeast. As he watched, the target seemed to be moving on a 295-degree heading at a very high rate of speed. After about thirty seconds, when the blip was fifteen to twenty miles from the radar installation, it disappeared. According to the figures developed at the site, the object was moving, conservatively, at 5,000 miles an hour.

Thirty minutes later, at about 10:00 P.M., and about five minutes after Whenry's first sighting ended, he saw another blip on the radar, located some thirty miles east of the base. Although the blip was on the screen for only sixteen seconds, it moved to a point where it was west of the station and then faded. Calculations suggested that it moved about 12,000 miles an hour.

From the Bentwaters control tower, others, including Staff Sergeant (SSGT) Lawrence S. Wright, reported a bright light, according to the Project Blue Book file. It was the size of a pinhead held at arm's length, which meant it was quite small, and it rose slowly from a point about 10 degrees above the horizon. It remained in sight for about an hour, appearing and disappearing. Nearly everyone who has looked at the official file and then checked the various star charts and maps has concluded that this object was Mars.

As Whenry was tracking the object on radar, a flight of two T-33 jets from the 512th Fighter Interceptor Squadron returned from a routine mission. The two pilots, identified in the Blue Book files only as Metz and Rowe (other data revealed they were First Lieutenant Charles V. Metz and First Lieutenant Andrew C. Rowe), were asked to try to find the objects. Although they searched the area for forty-five minutes, vectored by the radar operators, they failed to find anything. They broke off and landed at about 10:15 P.M.

Forty minutes later, at 10:55 P.M., another target was spotted about thirty miles to the east and heading west at only 2,000 to 4,000 miles an hour. It passed directly overhead and disappeared from the radarscope, about thirty

An early evening sky showing the moon, Venus, and Mars (circled at upper right) gives one a good idea how ridiculous it is to claim that a pilot would mistake Mars for a UFO.

miles away. This time, however, there was an airborne observation. A C-47 pilot saw the object flash beneath his plane. To him, it looked like little more than a blur of light.

The pilot wasn't the only person to see the light. On the ground several people, looking up, saw the same bright blur. The problem is that they provided little in the way of a useful description of the object.

Just as Mars had been identified as the source of the control tower sighting, there were those who believed that this segment of the sightings could be explained in the mundane. UFO debunker Philip Klass speculated that the C-47 pilot saw a meteor, one of many that could be seen during the Perseid meteor shower. Atmospheric physicist Dr. James McDonald disagreed with Klass. Using the ground observations and the pilot's sighting, he suggested that the object was between ground level and 4,000 feet. Klass failed to mention that there were ground observations of that object. But even if Klass was correct, doubtful as that might be, there were other sightings that were not so easily explained.

The sighting by the C-47 pilot and those on the ground was the last of the events at the Bentwaters base. The action shifted to the west-northwest as

A C-47 was flying near Bentwaters when its pilot also saw the UFO.

the Lakenheath Air Force Base radars detected the objects. Ground personnel saw a luminous object approach from a southwesterly direction, stop, then shoot off toward the east. Not much later, two white lights appeared, "joined up with another, and both disappeared in formation together." Before they vanished, the objects had performed a number of high-speed maneuvers. All of this was seen on two separate radarscopes at Lakenheath.

The Project Blue Book files noted, "Thus two radar sets [that is, Lakenheath GCA and the Radar Air Traffic Control Center (RATCC) radars] and three ground observers report substantially the same thing ... the fact that the radar and ground visual observations were made on its rapid acceleration lend credulance [sic] to the report."

But Klass, in his analysis of the case, found what he believed to be the fatal flaw here too. He seized on the point that the blip stopped to hover. He wrote:

> With the radar operating in the moving-target indicator (MTI) mode, *only moving targets* should appear on the scope—IF the MTI is functioning properly. In radars of that early vintage, MTI was a relatively new feature and one that often caused problems. For example, the instruction book for the MPN–11A [the designation of that particular radar set design] radar, which also had MTI, specifically warned radar operators and maintenance personnel of the possibility of *spurious signals* being caused by an MTI malfunction. In chapter 5, page 12, the Technical Order (as the instruction book is called) warned that MTI "circuits are complex; the stability requirements are severe; the tolerances are close." And on page 18 of chapter 4, the same manual warns operators of still another potential source of spurious signals that can result from what is called "extra-time-around signals."

What Klass was suggesting, without going into a complex and detailed discussion of the workings of the radars that are now more than fifty years old, is that "this condition can arise during anomalous-propagation weather conditions when echoes from distant, fixed targets on the ground far beyond the selected maximum radar operating range defeat the MTI functions. Under this condition, the Tech Order warned, 'the signal from this distant fixed target may appear as a false moving target....'"

Klass is arguing, based on the technical specifications of the radars in use, that the blips during the first sighting are anomalous propagation. In other words, the returns were not caused by real craft but a "phantom" created by weather conditions outside and the electronic characteristics of the radars being used. But it is based on speculations by Klass and doesn't take into account the experience of the radar operators or the actual weather conditions at the time.

About midnight, one of the operators at Lakenheath called the chief fighter controller at the RAF station at Neatishead, Norfolk, England, and

The RAF station at Neatishead scrambled a Venom night fighter like this one (shown at a 1952 air show) to intercept the unknown aircraft.

reported a strange object buzzing the base. F. H .C. Wimbledon would later say, "I scrambled a Venom night fighter from the Battle Flight through Sector, and my controller in the Interception Control team would consist of one Fighter Controller, a Corporal, a tracker, and a height reader. That is, four highly trained personnel in addition to myself could now see the object on our radarscopes."

Project Blue Book files, which can be confusing, suggested that it took the two-man fighter between thirty and forty-five minutes to arrive at Lakenheath. As the aircraft approached, according to the documentation, "Pilot advised he had a bright light in sight and would investigate. At thirteen miles west, he reported loss of target and white light."

Immediately afterward, the interceptor was directed to another target over Bedford, and the navigator locked on it with his radar. He said it was the "clearest target I have ever seen on radar."

The radar contact was broken, and the Lakenheath controllers reported that the object had passed the Venom fighter and was now behind it, that is, in military terminology, at the six o'clock position. The pilot acknowledged the message and tried various maneuvers to reverse the situation and get behind the UFO. Unable to do so, or shake the object from his tail, he asked for assistance.

Now low on fuel, the pilot decided to return to his base. According to the Project Blue Book documents, "Second Venom was vectored to other radar targets but was unable to make contact." The second aircraft returned to the base, and no other fighters were scrambled. By 3:30 A.M., all the targets had vanished from the radarscopes.

When the Condon Committee began, one of the controllers who had been on duty that night at Bentwaters sent a letter describing these events. Although it had been nearly a dozen years since it happened, the memory seemed to be well etched in his mind. Naturally, there were some discrepancies, but nothing of a significant nature.

The man pointed out that he had not told anyone of the events because he was "pretty sure it is considered (or was) classified, and the only reason I feel free to give you details is because you are an official government agency."

His long letter then described most of the events that night. He provided a detailed look at the attempted intercepts. He made a number of interesting observations in the letter, including information about these intercepts. He wrote:

> The first movement of the UFO was so swift (circling behind the interceptor), I missed it entirely, but it was seen by other controllers. However, the fact that this had occurred was confirmed by the pilot of the interceptor. The pilot of the interceptor told us he would try to shake the UFO and would try it again. He tried everything—he climbed, dived, circled, etc., but the UFO acted like it was glued right behind him, always the same distance, very close, but we always had two distinct targets. Note: Target resolution on our radar at the range they were from the antenna (about 10 to 30 miles, all in the southerly sectors from Lakenheath) would be between 200 and 600 feet probably. Closer than that, we would have got one target from both aircraft and UFO. Most specifications say 500 feet is the minimum, but I believe it varies, and 200 to 600 feet is closer to the truth.

What all this means is there was a series of radar observations of objects that displayed characteristics that were outside the capabilities of the aircraft of the day. In at least one of the reports from Bentwaters, the radar sightings coincided with visual observations on the ground and by a pilot in a C-47 (which is the sighting that Klass identified as a meteor). This should not be confused with the observation of Mars by the control tower personnel. That aspect of the case has been resolved to the satisfaction of nearly everyone, whether a believer, a skeptic, or an Air Force investigator.

On the ground at Lakenheath were witnesses who saw two luminous objects in fast flight. They witnessed the course reversals and the dead stops. The maneuvers rule out meteors, which some have suggested were responsible for the sightings.

Dr. James McDonald, in his paper, "Science in Default," published in *UFOs—A Scientific Debate*, wrote:

> The file docs, however, include a lengthy dispatch that proposes a series of what I must term wholly irrelevant hypotheses about Perseid meteors with "ionized gases in their wake which may be traced on radarscopes," and inversions that "may cause interference between two radar stations some distance apart." Such basically irrelevant remarks are all too typical of Blue Book critique over the years.

While the Perseid meteor showers do occur during August, Dr. James McDonald believed that such attempts at an explanation were "basically irrelevant."

He also pointed out that "not only are the radar frequencies here about two orders of magnitude too high to afford even marginal likelihood of meteor-wake return, but there is absolutely no kinematic similarity between the reported UFO movements and the essentially straight-line hypersonic movement of a meteor, to cite just a few of the objections to meteor hypotheses."

Two separate radars at Lakenheath, having different radar parameters, were concurrently observing movements of one or more unknown targets over an extended period of time. One of the ways that the reliability of a return on one radar is checked is to compare it to another. If they are operating on different frequencies, then an inversion layer, if affecting the returns, will be different on the two sets. Or one will show it, and the second will not. It eliminates the possibility of a spurious target.

That is not to mention the fact that the Project Blue Book files suggest that some of the two-radar sightings were coincident with the visual observations of those on the ground. In other words, not only were the objects seen on multiple radars, but there were people outside who saw them in the sky.

Klass, in his analysis, attempting to dismiss the case as anomalous propagation, wrote, "If it were not for the incident involving the first Venom pilot's reported radar-visual encounter with the UFO, this case would deserve scant attention because of the erratic behavior of the radar—UFO is so characteristic of spurious targets...."

Klass then goes on to explain the cockpit configuration of the Venom fighter, reporting, accurately, that it is set up so that the pilot sits on the left, and the radar operator sits on the right. Controls for the radar, and for the screen, are situated so that it would be difficult for the pilot to both fly the plane and work the radar. He suggests, based on the reported communication between the pilot and the ground, that there was no radar operator in the cockpit. This, Klass believed, explained why there seems to be a radar-visual sighting. The pilot, doing double duty as both the pilot and radar officer, was "overwhelmed" by the workload and made a simple mistake.

This, however, is speculation by Klass, based on his observation that "never once did the words 'we' or 'radar operator' appear in the reports; only the words 'I' and 'pilot.'"

This was a "scrambled" intercept mission. It is unlikely that the aircraft took off with an inadequate crew in the cockpit. Regardless of the speculations by Klass, there would have been a man sitting beside the pilot, operating the radar. If this was the case, then Klass' whole theory is in error and should be rejected.

Even if he was correct in his assumption about there being a single occupant in the cockpit, that does not explain the other visual sightings at the scene. The case is made of more than a single misidentified blip on the radars. It is a complex case that demanded careful research.

The Condon Committee did investigate the case but in a very limited fashion. They suggested that their investigation was hampered by receiving the case late in their project. It wasn't until the letter from the controller arrived that they even began to study it. Only then did they request a copy of the Air Force file.

One of the interesting aspects is that Klass criticizes some researchers for relying on the twelve-year-old memories of the controller, preferring to rely on the reports written within days of the sighting. The investigators for Condon, however, noted:

> One of the interesting aspects of this case is the remarkable accuracy of the account of the witness as given in the letter … which was apparently written from memory twelve years after the incident. There are a number of minor discrepancies, mostly a matter of figures (the C-47 at 5,000 feet was evidently actually at 4,000 feet), and he seems to have confused the identity of location C with B [as noted in his letter]; however, all of the major details of his account seem well confirmed by the Blue Book account.

This, of course, negates Klass' contention that the controller's memories were in error. They match, with accuracy, what appears in the files so that the twelve-year-old memories are corroborated by the files created at the time.

After their review of the case, the Condon Committee, which was financed by the Air Force, reported, "In conclusion, although conventional or natural explanations certainly cannot be ruled out, the probability of such seems low in this case, and the probability that at least *one genuine UFO was involved* seems high."

J. Allen Hynek, in a "memorandum for record" found in the Project Blue Book files, wrote:

> The Lakenheath case could constitute a source of embarrassment to the Air Force, and should the facts, as so far reported, get into the public domain, it is not necessary to point out what excellent use the several dozen UFO societies and other "publicity artists" would make of such an incident. It is, therefore, of great importance that further information on the technical aspects of the original observations be obtained, without loss of time, from the original observers.

There is no evidence that anyone from the military did any sort of follow-up investigation. Even the Condon Committee scientists, who by the time this case arrived were predisposed to believe that UFOs were nothing more than misidentifications, imagination, and illusions, wrote that they believed there was a genuine UFO involved in the case.

The COMETA report concluded its section on this sighting with a quote from Gordon Thayer, who had served as the radar expert for the Condon Committee and who wrote an article in the journal *Astronautics and Aeronautics*, "If one considers the strong credibility of the information and the coherence and continuity of reports, as well as their high degree of 'strangeness,' this UFO case is certainly one of the more troubling cases known to date."

July 17, 1957: The RB-47 Case

According to the Condon Committee report, they learned about the RB-47 incident at a "project-sponsored conference for air base UFO officers held in Boulder in June 1967." The aircraft commander of the flight, Major Lewis Chase, who was assigned as the UFO officer at Malmstrom Air Force Base in 1967, mentioned his sighting that occurred in 1957. Roy Craig, who was the investigator for the study on this sighting, wrote:

> According to the officer, a Major [Chase] at the time of the encounter, he was piloting a B-47 on a gunnery and electronic countermeasures training mission from an AFB [Air Force Base]. The mission had taken the crew over the Gulf of Mexico and back over South Central United States, where they encountered a glow-

ing source of both visual and 2,800 mHz. electronic radiation of startling intensity, which, during the encounter, held a constant position relative to the B-47 for an extended period. Ground flight control radar also received a return from the "object" and reported its range to the B-47 crew at a position in agreement with radar and visual observations from the aircraft.

Craig tried to find the report in the Project Blue Book files or in the Defense Command records but failed. He did mention that the most important members of the crew, in relation to the sightings, were the pilot, Chase, copilot 1st Lieutenant James McCoid, and the Electric Countermeasures Officer, known as a "Raven," in the Number-Two position, Captain Frank McClure. Those interviewed were surprised that there was no report in the Project Blue Book files, and it was clear from those interviewed that a report had been made by the base intelligence officer Captain E. I. Piwetz, the crew was debriefed at length, and the aircraft commander, Chase, had filled out the forms being used at the time for UFO reports.

> While on the east–west leg of the flight, the pilot spotted a bright white light that he believed was coming right at the aircraft.

During the investigation, Craig gathered additional information from the crew members he could locate and who were not serving in Vietnam at the time of his work. Craig learned that there were a series of incidents that began when the RB-47 crossed the coast of Mississippi, and McClure picked up a signal on his scope. McClure was surprised to see it move "up scope," which wasn't supposed to happen. His job was to find ground-based radar stations emitting signals at around 3,000 MHz. Since these were ground-based stations, the signal would, naturally, move down scope as long as the aircraft was flying straight and level. McClure thought, at first, this was an equipment malfunction and didn't mention it to either the other Ravens with him or to the aircraft commander.

Near Meridian, Mississippi, they turned toward the west, heading for Louisiana and eventually the Dallas–Fort Worth area, where they would again turn, this time to the north, toward their home base. While on the east–west leg of the flight, the pilot spotted a bright white light that he believed was coming right at the aircraft. According to the Intelligence Report created by Piwetz in the hours after the encounter:

> At 1010Z [that is, 5:10 CDT], aircraft commander [Chase] first observed a very intense light, white light with light blue tint, at 11 o'clock [position] from his aircraft, crossing in front to about 2:30 position, copilot [McCoid] also observed passage of light to 2:30 o'clock, where it apparently disappeared. A/C [aircraft commander] notified crew, and the ECM [Electronic Counter Measures] operator nr 2 [McClure] search[ed] for signal described above....

An RB-47 similar to the one commanded by Major Lewis Chase in 1967.

The Condon Committee report noted that the pilot had seen a white light that crossed in front of the plane, "moving to the right, at a velocity far higher than airplane speeds." The pilot, according to this report, said the light was as large as a barn. The copilot also saw the light.

In what might be a confusion of the events, given that Craig was gathering the information some ten years later, he reported that after the light disappeared, McClure switched his monitoring equipment back to the original frequency and picked up something at the two o'clock position. At this point, Chase requested permission to switch radio frequencies to a "ground interceptor control radar and check out the unidentified companion." The ground radar showed the object on their radar and that it was holding about ten miles from the RB-47.

After the UFO had held the two o'clock position and the ten-mile range and as Chase had varied speed, heading, and altitude, the number-two monitoring officer, McClure, reported the object was beginning to move up scope to a position in front of the aircraft. According to Craig:

It moved to a position ahead of the plane, holding the ten-mile range, and again became visible. The pilot went to maximum speed. The target appeared to stop, and as the plane got close to it and flew over it, the target disappeared from visual observation, from monitor number two, and from ground radar. (The operator of monitor number two [McClure] also recalled the B-47 navigator having this target on his radarscope at the same time.) The pilot began to turn back. About halfway around the turn, the target reappeared on both the monitor and the ground radarscopes and visually at an estimated altitude of 15,000 ft. The pilot received permission from Ground Control to change altitude, and dove the plane at the target, which appeared stationary. As the plane approached to an estimated distance of five miles, the target vanished again from both visual observation and radar. Limited fuel caused the pilot to abandon the chase at this point and head for his base. As the pilot leveled off at 20,000 ft. a target again appeared on number-two monitor, this time behind the B-47. The officer operating the number-two monitoring unit, however, believes he may have been picking up the ground radar signal at this point. The signal faded out as the B-47 continued flight.

In summary, if the information is accurate, the UFO was seen by a ground-based radar, by the aircraft-based radar, was seen visually by the flight crew, and was detected by monitoring equipment on the aircraft, emitting an electromagnetic signal at about 3,000 mHz. More precisely, there are three chains of evidence, from the visual sighting to the radar returns and to the detection of the electromagnetic signal. That makes this a very strong case.

To add to the impressive array of evidence, according to Craig, both the copilot, McCoid, and the number-two monitoring officer, McClure, said that they were impressed with the way the UFO disappeared and then reappeared. They said that during some of the encounter, the object could be tracked on the navigator's radar. McClure said that he remembered the navigator, Thomas Hanley, was receiving a return on his radar and that the bearings to the object matched exactly what McClure was receiving on his scope.

Craig, during his investigation, developed a series of questions about the sighting. He wondered if the monitoring station might have picked up a ground-based radar or a reflected signal. He wondered if the visual sightings could be airplane lights, afterburners, or meteors. He wondered if the visual sightings were actually the same as the objects on the radars. In other words, he was wondering if the sightings were separated into individual events if they might be explainable. Craig could see that the overall event was mysterious but that elements of it might have conventional explanations.

Craig could see that the overall event was mysterious but that elements of it might have conventional explanations.

Craig also noted that there was a sharp divergence on the report of the sighting and the data that might have been gathered. Chase seemed to believe that records in the form of scope photographs and wire recordings (which was standard on all flights, including training flights) had been made, but others disagreed. They thought that this was a "shakedown" prior to deployment of the aircraft overseas and that such records were not made. In his search, Craig was unable to find any such records.

Assuming that these sorts of records were not made and therefore did not exist, Craig decided on another course. He wrote:

> Since it appeared that the filmed and recorded data we were seeking had never existed, we renewed the effort to locate any special intelligence reports of the incident that might have failed to reach Project Blue Book. A report form of the type described by the pilot could not be identified or located. The Public Information Officer at ADC [Air Defense Command] Headquarters checked intelligence files and operations records but found no record of this incident. The Deputy Commander for Operations of the particular SAC [Strategic Air Command] Air Wing in which the B-47 crew served in 1957 informed us that a thorough review of the Wing history failed to disclose any references to an UFO incident in Fall 1957.

Later, others would discover some documents, including the form that Chase said that he had filled out. Their problem was that they had the date of the event wrong, believing that it happened in September 1957 rather than July 1957.

With no documentation, with only the testimony of the half the members of the crew taken a decade after the event, there wasn't much else that could be done. In the conclusion, Craig wrote:

> If a report of this incident, written either by the B-47 crew or by Wing Intelligence personnel, was submitted in 1957, it apparently is no longer in existence. Moving pictures of radarscope displays and other data said to have been recorded during the incident apparently never existed. Evaluation of the experience must, therefore, rest entirely on the recollection of the crew members ten years after the event. These descriptions are not adequate to allow identification of the phenomenon encountered.

And that was the end of it. This was an intriguing case that contained some interesting evidence that could have led to some important conclusions. Visual sightings of the UFO, radar contacts on the ground and in the air, and electromagnetic radiation from the UFO, all possibly documented with wire recordings, scope photographs, and with written reports by crew members and ground radar stations.

Details of the case as they were known then were lost when two members of the Condon Committee quit in a dispute over the ultimate purpose of the study; it was Dr. James McDonald who straightened out the mistakes in the case. David R. Saunders and R. Roger Harkin published *UFOs! Yes!* in 1968, before the final report from the Condon Committee was issued.

The RB-47 case should have resulted in more conclusive results, since it included radar contacts, visual sightings, and evidence of electromagnetic radiation. But these details were lost (artist's conception of UFO).

McDonald determined that the date of the sighting was July 19, 1957, rather than September, which was why they couldn't find the case file. When it was located, many of the things that the Condon Committee reported were found to be untrue. In fact, part of the massive report included an appendix Q, which were weather records for Mineral Wells, Texas, on September 19, 1957, but are wholly irrelevant to understanding the case.

There are four long analyses of this case. As mentioned, McDonald and Klass wrote opposing views. Later, Brad Sparks and Tim Printy did the same thing. Sparks endorses the extraterrestrial, believing this is one of the best cases for that. Printy's analysis points out the problems with the case but in the end, he isn't sure what it proves.

Taking a page from Klass, which was to deal with each element of the sighting alone rather than as a whole, some of the flaws in the case can be seen. What we know was that the aircraft had flown from Forbes Air Force Base in Kansas south out into the Gulf of Mexico for a gunnery exercise and as a problem in celestial navigation. When that was finished, they turned north heading toward Meridian, Mississippi. As they approached the coast, the Number Two Raven, McClure, saw a radar signal that was confusing to him.

According to McClure, the detected signal started at the rear of his scope and began to move upward, in what is now thought of as the "Up Scope Incident." This sort of thing was, according to nearly everyone, impossible. The purpose of the monitoring system in the aircraft was to detect the signal emitted from enemy ground-based radars and therefore, they would always be moving down scope. The system is passive, which means they don't emit a signal but search for other radar signals. The only way for them to move up scope was if the radar was airborne and the craft carrying it was approaching the RB-47 and then passing it.

McClure, interviewed by the Condon Committee in 1967, said:

I had … a radar receiver.… It had a DF [Direction Finding] capability, which can tell you the bearings from you to the object.… Any ground radar that you intercept has to go down your scope because the airplane is moving forward.… This particular signal … it was behind me and it moved forward, which indicates it was either in the air or the aircraft was in a turn.… So I called the front because I asked them, were they turning? He said, "No." They were flying straight and level. So I just ignored the thing because I figured that's something that can't happen, and I'll just forget about it.…

Chase would tell investigators that at this point McClure changed frequencies that he was searching. He was thinking that his equipment had malfunctioned in some fashion. McClure didn't think much about it at the time it happened. Only after the other events of the evening did McClure and the others attach significance to this sighting.

Philip Klass, in studying this aspect of the sighting, believed that the problems were a malfunction in the equipment and a signal received from a station near Biloxi, Mississippi.

Sparks, in his analysis, said that the aircraft crossed the coast closer to Gulfport, which meant there were no ground-based radars to account for the signal. He based this on the information that Chase had supplied to the Condon Committee. He also said that the radar site, at Keesler Air Force Base, was not in operation at the time. It was a training site, and this was summer and long after midnight.

While the source of the signal has not been identified, according to Printy, the site at Keesler could well have been in operation on July 17, early in the morning. It is true that the site was a training facility, but they did hold late-night classes, and they did work on the radars in the hours when it would necessarily conflict with nighttime training.

Keesler Air Force Base in Mississippi, shown here in 1992, became a base for the Radio Operations School in 1949. Air craft controllers, radar mechanics, and traffic service technicians were all trained here.

In the end, there is no evidence that the signal came from a ground source, but it does mimic one of the types of radars being used at the time. It was radiating on the proper frequency. In other words, there is no positive solution for this part of the case.

Raven Two, McClure, didn't mention this problem to the pilot at the time, other than request information about the attitude of the aircraft. If it was in a turn, then the strange movement of the return could be explained. If they were in straight and level flight, then there was some sort of a problem.

Once the flight reached the area of Meridian, Mississippi, they turned to the west, heading toward the Dallas–Fort Worth area, or to a point somewhat south of there, north of Waco. According to the Wing Intelligence report, quoted above, the bright light startled Chase. He thought it was another aircraft heading directly at him, at the same altitude, and that he would have to take evasive action. Chase warned the crew to prepare, but then the light flashed by from left to right. Chase said, according to the documentation in the Condon files:

> I didn't have any time to react at all—that's how fast it was, and it went out to about the 2 o'clock position and all the lights go out on.... I asked him [McCoid], "Jim," I said, "Did you see that?" He gave me some remark like, "Well, I did if you did." He wasn't going to admit to anything.... Then one of us made the remark, "Well, it must be a flying saucer...." We were laughing about it in the interphone.

According to the Air Defense Command sighting questionnaire, filled out by Chase some three months after the event, the object, or light, was an intense "blue-white light." He thought it was about two miles away, but then it was a light seen in the sky without a point of reference. He told the Condon investigators that it was impossible to estimate the distance to an unknown light in the sky. Or, in other words, it could have been much farther away if it was a very bright object.

Interestingly, nearly everyone who has studied the case agreed with the idea that this was a meteor. It matches descriptions of other such fireballs seen under a variety of conditions. Sparks, in fact, wrote, "This meteor fireball sighting is the only part of the RB-47 incident having a mundane explanation, in this case, as a natural phenomenon."

It was during the next phase of the flight, as the RB-47 approached the next turn, that the sighting changed in nature. According to what Chase told Klass:

> We actually turned over Meridian, but by the time we got over Jackson we have to be very accurately on course, straight and level for the work to be done. So Meridian would have been the actual turning point with the ECM [Electronic Counter Measure] mission

starting at Jackson, in other words the Navigator would have to have a precise fix and you're on course with no turns so he [would] chart the points along the line.

After the visual sighting and the discussion of "flying saucers," McClure began to search for some sort of signal. At about 4:30 (CST), McClure found a signal that mimicked the characteristics of the CPS-6B radars, like the signal he had detected when they had crossed the coast into Mississippi earlier. The signal was scanning at the same rate as that of the radar, meaning there would be a signal, and it would disappear as the radar antenna spun and reappear when the antenna was pointed at the aircraft.

McClure wondered if the UFO that had been seen earlier was the source of the signal that he was now watching. If it was, then it would suggest that the UFO had changed course and was pacing the aircraft, clearly something that no ground station could do. McClure told Chase about what he was seeing on his scope and wondered if he had visual contact with anything out there. He continued to make his observations.

> ... McClure found a signal that mimicked the characteristics of the CPS-6B radars, like the signal he had detected when they had crossed the coast into Mississippi earlier.

The wing intelligence report, which was created within hours of the aircraft landing, said:

A/C [aircraft commander Chase] notified crew and ECM nr 4 [McClure] for signal described above, found same approximately 1030Z [4:30 CST], at a relative bearing of 070 degrees; 1035Z, relative bearing of 068 degrees; 1038Z, relative bearing 040 degrees. At 1039Z, A/C sighted huge light, which he estimated to be 5000 feet below aircraft at about 2 o'clock. Aircraft altitude was 34,500 feet; weather perfectly clear. Although A/C could not determine shape or size of object, he had a definite impression [sic] light emanated from top of object. At 1040Z, ECM operator nr 2 reported he then had two signals at relative bearings of 040 and 070 degrees. A/C and copilot saw these two objects at the same time with the same red color. A/C received permission to ignore flight plan and pursue object. He notified ADC site UTAH [the radar at Duncanville, TX] and requested all assistance possible. At 1042Z, ECM nr 2 had one object at 020 degrees, relative bearing. A/C increased speed to Mach 0.83, turned to pursue, and the object pulled ahead. At 1042.5Z, ECM nr 2 again had two signals at relative bearings of 040 and 070 degrees. At 1044Z, he had a single signal at 050 degrees, relative bearing. At 1048Z, ECM nr 3 was recording interphone and command-position conversations. ADC site requested aircraft to go to IFF [Identification, Friend or Foe] mode III for positive identification, then requested position of object. Crew reported position of the object as 10NM (nautical miles) north west [sic] of Ft. Worth, Texas, and ADC site UTAH immediately confirmed presence of object on their scopes. At approximately 1050Z, object appeared to stop, and aircraft overshot. UTAH reported they lost object from scopes at this time, and ECM nr 2 also lost signal. Aircraft began turning, ECM nr 2 picked up signal at 160 degrees, relative bearing, UTAH regained scope contact, and A/C regained visual contact. At 1052Z, ECM n2 had signal at 200 degrees, relative bearing, moving up his D/F scope. Aircraft began closing on object until the estimated range was 5NM. At this time, object appeared to drop approximately 15,000 feet altitude, and A/C lost visual contact. UTAH also lost object from scopes. At 1055Z, in the area of Mineral Wells, Texas, crew notified UTAH they must depart for home station because of fuel supply. Crew queried UTAH whether a CIRVIS [Communications Instructions for Reporting Vital Intelligence Sightings] report had been submitted, and UTAH replied the report had been transmitted. At 1057, ECM nr 2 had signal at 300 degrees, relative bearing, but UTAH had no scope contact. At 1058Z, A/C regained visual contact of object approximately 10NM northwest of Ft. Worth, Texas, estimated altitude 20,000 feet, at 2 o'clock from aircraft. At 1102Z, aircraft took up, heading for home station. This placed area of object off the tail of the aircraft. ECM nr 2 continued to D/F [direction finding] signal of object between 180 and 190 degrees, relative bearing, until 1140Z, when aircraft was approximately abeam Oklahoma City, Oklahoma. At this time, signal faded rather abruptly. 55SRW DOI has no doubt the electronic D/F coincided exactly with visual observations by A/C numerous times, thus indicating positively the object being the signal source.

> The memories of the crew would be fresh and suggest that these are the best of the interviews conducted.

The report was taken by Captain Elwin T. Piwetz within hours of the aircrew landing in Kansas. The memories of the crew would be fresh and suggest that these are the best of the interviews conducted. Those held some ten years after the fact don't agree precisely with these statements, but the discrepancies are all minor and relatively unimportant.

This interview, conducted by the Wing intelligence officer, would seem to provide a good case. Observations were backed up by both airborne radars and ground-based radars, but the Blue Book file has some contradictory information in it. There is a Telex alerting those at ATIC [Air Technical Intelligence Center] and Blue Book that a sighting had been made. Most of the information in that Telex reflects what the Wing intelligence report said, but there is one line that is troublesome. Although partially hidden by a piece of paper obviously put there to hide some of the information, the line says, "UTAH had negative contact with object."

On the Telex, someone had identified UTAH as the ground radar and had also written, "Note," with an exclamation point. This document was created within hours of sighting as well, and is in direct contradiction of what was reported by Chase and his crew. They also reported that all the documentation they had created had been removed by someone, and none of that appeared in the Blue Book file.

This demonstrates that the Blue Book file is no help in resolving the questions raised by the sighting. It seems inconceivable that the aircrew would believe that the ground radar station reported they had tracked the object and that those at that station would deny it.

The same can be said for the CIRVIS report. The aircrew said the report had been filed, but if there was no radar contact on the ground, then the report might not have been filed. Or, the ground station filed the report based on what the aircrew said. The search for the CIRVIS report is ongoing.

It also seems odd that the Condon Committee investigators could not find the Blue Book file on the case. True, in 1967, as they were investigating UFOs, some of them had access to the Blue Book files. Ironically, as they investigated a series of sightings at Malmstrom Air Force Base, they were dealing with the base UFO officer, Lieutenant Colonel Lewis Chase. In the course of that investigation, or rather the documents surrounding it, it became clear that some members of the Condon Committee had been granted security clearances so that they could pursue specific sightings.

> Their conclusion that the information is no longer available is inaccurate.

What that means, simply, is if they wanted to follow up on what Chase had told them about his sighting in 1957, they would have had access to the files. Granted, the information supplied by Chase gave the sighting date as September 1957 instead of July, but even a limited search of the records should have turned it up. After Condon finished his work and after Blue Book was closed, James McDonald did find the case file. It wasn't as if it would have been in another file cabinet or that the Project Card didn't contain sufficient information to suggest that it might be the case. Their conclusion that the information was no longer available was inaccurate.

Brad Sparks, in his report published in Jerome Clark's massive *UFO Encyclopedia*, second edition, wrote:

> The RB-47 incident is the first conclusive scientific proof for the existence of UFOs. Calibrations of the RB-47's electronic measurements provide an irrefutable case. By comparing the measures of the airborne UFO microwave emissions against a known microwave

source (the Duncanville, Texas, air defense radar [known in the documentation as UTAH]), with both signals compared simultaneously, the accuracy of the UFO measurements becomes scientifically unassailable. Since both signals were measured at the same time as 30 degrees apart, this proves that it was impossible for the UFO signal to have been a misidentification of the Duncanville radar signal. The UFO signal was the dominant signal since the Duncanville signal was not detected until the RB-47 flew into the strongest part of the Duncanville radar beam.

Even if this statement is considered to be hyperbole, it does suggest that the case was mishandled by the both the Air Force and the Condon Committee. It screamed for a follow-up in 1957, when the aircrew was reporting radar contacts from the air, reporting electromagnetic radiation detected as emanating from the UFO and with visual sightings of the UFO. As noted, the Blue Book file contains contradictions that should have been resolved in 1957. Did Duncanville track the object or not? And if they didn't, why did the flight crew believe they did? Those simple questions should have been answered in 1957.

> **Even if this statement is considered to be hyperbole, it does suggest that the case was mishandled by the both the Air Force and the Condon Committee.**

Tim Printy, at his skeptical website, wasn't quite as enthusiastic about the case as was Sparks. Printy wrote, "Is the case solved? I would *never* suggest so, unless there was much more evidence as to aerial activities that morning. As a result, the case is still unidentified."

Which, of course, seems to be a proper solution here, because there are so many aspects that were not explored when various individuals and entities had the opportunity. In 1957, with the Air Force charged with the investigation of UFOs and with a case that seemed to have so many independent chains of evidence, it would be expected that the Air Force would investigate. That investigation was apparently reduced to having Chase fill out their questionnaire and paying attention only to the visual sighting that took place near Fort Worth. According to the Project Card, the case file referred only to the "1ˢᵗ sighting," which, of course, it was not. They claimed that it was solved as an aircraft, specifically American Airlines flight number 655. Unfortunately for the Air Force, that flight was on the ground in El Paso, Texas, at the time of the sighting. What this demonstrates was that they simply didn't care to continue to investigate.

Klass concluded that the sightings were a combination of things and taken separately, they were all explainable in the conventional. The first radar sighting was a simple electronic error that flipped the image on the radar screen so that it appeared traveling up scope rather than down. The first visual sighting was of a meteor, with which Brad Sparks agrees. The other radar sightings from the ground were misidentifications of the ground radar beams since the frequencies of those beams matched, to a degree, the pattern emitted by the UFO. The second of the visual sightings was American Airlines flight number 966, which according to Klass, "If American Airlines flight #966 was on time, it would have been approaching the Dallas airport at the time that the Duncanville radar operators noted an unidentified target in the same location.... On final approach, the airliner's landing lights would have been turned on, and this could explain the RB-47 crew's observation that it had overflown a bright light northwest of Dallas."

Unfortunately for Klass, American Airlines flight number 966 was involved in a near-miss situation in West Texas and was nowhere near Dallas at the time. There is no explanation for the sighting, which doesn't mean that it was alien, only that it is unidentified.

It is interesting, however, that Klass acknowledges the Duncanville (Utah) radar tracking an object when the Blue Book file suggests otherwise. Again, this is one of the unresolved points in the case.

> **Unfortunately for Klass, American Airlines flight number 966 was involved in a near-miss situation in West Texas and was nowhere near Dallas at the time.**

In the end, the consensus seems to be that this case is unidentified. The explanations offered for it, or rather the radar displays on the airborne detectors, might be explained, in part, by ground stations. As noted, there is no evidence that the radar at Biloxi was in operation at the time, and if that is the case, then the explanation fails at that point.

It should also be noted that the flight crew, while unsure of how much was recorded or when the recording started, all agree that there were some recordings made and photographs of the scopes taken. Those have all disappeared, and there is no evidence that they were ever part of the Blue Book file.

Given what has been documented, there should be other evidence somewhere. The Condon Committee had the best opportunity to find it in the late 1960s. Members of the team had the clearance to see the files, unless there was something there that would be considered a threat to national security and classified at a level that would not have allowed review by the civilians of the Condon Committee. Chase told one of the committee members who was attempting to learn about the Belt, Montana, sightings in 1967 (because of allegations that missile launch capability had been compromised) that he couldn't get into that because of the classified nature of the reports.

However, given the instructions the Air Force had given Condon, it is not surprising that nothing came from that information. To probe too deeply could have exposed a significant case. Today, we have the remnants of the case and nothing else. Condon did his job, but here it was not in the public interest.

September 18, 1976: Tehran, Iran

A Defense Intelligence Agency (DIA) document would later say, "A remarkable report. This case is a classic that meets all the necessary conditions for a legitimate study of the UFO phenomenon."

The series of sightings began with a routine telephone call made to the control tower at the Mehrabad Airport in Tehran. The night supervisor, Hossain Pirouzi, would later say that the first telephone call came in at about 10:30 P.M., from the Shemiran area of Tehran. The woman said that the object was about 3,000 feet above her, that its color changed from orange to red to yellow. It had a shape that she described as a fan with four blades. She wasn't sure if it was a single object or two because it seemed to sometimes separate into two distinct pieces. Pirouzi told her not to worry about it because he would check it out.

But he didn't bother to check it out. His radar systems were down because they were undergoing repair. At 10:45 P.M., he received a second call from a woman who had been on the roof of her house when she saw an object seeming to dart around. Like the first, she wasn't sure if there was one object or two. She said that they seemed to divide into two and then joined up again. Just as he had handled the first call, Pirouzi told her not to worry about it.

On September 18, 1976, UFOs were sighted near Mehrabad International Airport in Tehran, Iran.

By 11:15 he had received four telephone calls about the object, and although the trainees with him had been outside to search for the object without results, he was now curious. Taking a pair of binoculars with him, he walked out onto the balcony that surrounded the tower. Although he didn't see it at first, he finally did spot it and as he would tell investigators, "I was amazed, flabbergasted."

He said that the object looked like a bright star to the unaided eye, but through the binoculars he saw a rectangular shape that was about 6,000 feet overhead. Both the right ends and left ends were blue, and there was a red light in the center that, while not flashing, seemed to be rotating. The object also seemed to be oscillating.

> "The object and the pursuing F-4 continued on a course to the south of Tehran when another brightly lit object ... came out of the original object."

Interestingly, four aircraft that transited the area reported that they had received an emergency radio beacon signal. They called the tower to ask if there had been some sort of aircraft accident or a crash, but of course there was none. With this new information, Pirouzi began to worry and decided that it was time to alert the Iranian Air Force. At 12:30, now on September 19, Pirouzi called the duty officer and told him what he had seen. There still was no radar contact and other facilities that were alerted had nothing showing on their screens, but the distances and mountains might account for that.

The Duty Officer also alerted General Parviz Youssefi, who stepped out on his porch and saw the object. It was Youssefi who contacted the other radar facilities asking what they had on their scopes. Even without the radar confirmations, Youssefi ordered an F-4D Phantom into the air to investigate.

The Phantom launched at 1:30 A.M., and the pilot spotted the UFO almost immediately. Using Pirouzi as a relay, Youssefi ordered the aircraft to get as close as possible to the UFO to get a good look at it but to do nothing else. The pilot approached above the speed of sound and said that the object was about half the size of the moon and that it had violet, orange, and white lights that were much brighter than moonlight.

He chased the object until he thought he was over the border and into Afghanistan. At that point, he turned to head back to Tehran and saw that the object was still in front of him but closer to Tehran. He was ordered to close on the UFO, and when he was about thirty miles away, his avionics, radios, and electronics failed. When he maneuvered away from the UFO, the electronics came back online, but he was now running low on fuel. He had to end the chase.

According to Lawrence Fawcett and Barry Greenwood in *Clear Intent*, Charles Huffer, using the Freedom of Information Act, received a report from the Defense Intelligence Agency that covered the details of the attempted intercepts. According to that document, the description of the second attempted intercept began:

At 0140 hrs a second F-4 was launched. The backseater [the radar officer who sits behind the pilot in the F-4 cockpit] acquired a radar lock on at 27 NM [nautical miles], 12 o'clock position with the VC [rate of closure between the fighter and the object] at 150 NMPH [nautical miles per hour]. As the range decreased to 25 NM, the object moved away at a speed that was visible on the radarscope and stayed at 25 NM.

The size of the radar return was comparable to that of a 707 tanker. The visual size of the object was difficult to discern because of its intense brilliance. The light that it gave off was that of flashing strobe lights arranged in a rectangular pattern and alternating blue, green, red, and orange in color. The sequence of the lights was so fast that all the colors could be seen at once. The object and the pursuing F-4 continued on a course to the south of Tehran when another brightly lit object, which was estimated to be one-half to one-third the apparent size of the moon, came out of the original object. This second object headed straight toward the F-4 at a very fast rate of speed. The pilot attempted to fire an AIM-9 [sidewinder] missile at the object, but at that instant his weapons control panel went off and he lost all communications (UHF and interphone). At this point, the pilot initiated a turn and negative G dive to get away. As he turned, the object fell in trail at what appeared to be about 3–4 NM. As he continued in his turn away from the primary object, the second object went to the inside of his turn, then returned to the primary object for a perfect rejoin.

Shortly after the second object joined up with the primary object, another object appeared to come out of the other side of the primary object, going straight down at a great rate of speed. The F-4 crew had regained communications and the weapons control panel and watched the object approach the ground, anticipating a large explosion. This object appeared to come to rest gently on the earth and cast a very bright light over an area of about 2–3 kilometers. The crew descended from their altitude of 25,000 to 15,000 and continued to observe and mark the object's position. They had some difficulty in adjusting their night visibility for landing, so after orbiting Mehrabad [Airport] a few times, they went out for a straight in landing. There was a lot of interference on the UHF, and each time they passed through a mag. [magnetic] bearing of 150 degrees from Mehrabad they lost their communications (UHF and interphone) and the INS [inertial navigation system] fluctuated from 30 degrees to 50 degrees. The one civil airliner that was approaching Mehrabad during the same time experienced communications failure in the same vicinity (Kilo Zulu) but did not report seeing anything. While the F-4 was on a long, final approach, the crew noticed another cylinder-shaped object (about the size of a T-bird at 10M) with bright, steady lights on each end and a flasher in the middle. When queried, the tower stated there was no other known traffic in the area. During the time that the object passed over the F-4, the tower did not have a visual on it but picked it up after the pilot told them to look between the mountains and the refinery.

"The attempt by Klass to trivialize this case shows how solid it is."

During daylight, the F-4 crew was taken out to the area in a helicopter where the object apparently had landed. Nothing was noticed at the spot where they thought the object landed (a dry lake bed), but as they circled off to the west of the area they picked up a very noticeable beeper signal. At the point where the return was the loudest was a small house with a garden. They landed and asked the people within if they had noticed anything strange last night. The people talked about a loud noise and a very bright light, like lightning. The aircraft and area where the object is believed to have landed are being checked for possible radiation.

Attached to the report was an internal form that was titled, "Defense Information Report Evaluation." This was an assessment of the quality of the Iranian sighting information that indicated the information was "confirmed by other sources" and that the information value was "High (Unique, Timely, and of Major Significance)," and the information was "Potentially Useful."

In the remarks section of the report, and as noted by the COMETA officials, this case was considered:

A remarkable report. This case is a classic that meets all the necessary conditions for a legitimate study of UFO phenomenon:

a. the object was seen by multiple witnesses in different locations (i.e., Shemiran, Mehrabad, and the dry lake bed) and viewpoints (both airborne and from the ground).

b. The credibility of many witnesses was strong (an Air Force general, qualified aircrews, and experienced tower operators).

c. Visual sightings confirmed by radar.

d. Similar electromagnetic effects (EME) were reported by three separate aircraft.

e. There were physiological effects on some crew members (i.e., loss of night vision due to the brightness of the object).

f. An inordinate amount of maneuverability was displayed by the UFOs.

The final comment about this in the COMETA report is, "The attempt by Klass to trivialize this case shows how solid it is." This refers to Klass' book, *UFOs: The Public Deceived*, in which he claimed that the first witnesses saw Jupiter, and pilot incompetence and equipment malfunctions accounted for the remainder.

But one of those ground witnesses was General Youssefi, who eventually ordered the interceptors into the air. When the launching airfield is taken into consideration, which was west-southwest of Tehran, and the distance the first fighter traveled, Jupiter was about 90 degrees off where the UFO was reported.

Klass also claimed that the Westinghouse technician who was stationed at the Shahrokhi Air Base said that only the first of the F-4s reported equipment failure, and that particular aircraft was known for equipment failures and had a history of electrical outages. This same man also suggested that the F-4 radar could have been in manual track, causing a wrong interpretation of the radar lock. Or, in other words, the radar officer in the rear seat of the F-4 made an error that caused him to believe he had radar contact.

And keeping with his belief that meteors cause many UFO sightings, Klass pointed out that the Gamma Percids and the Eta Draconids meteor showers were at their height. He believed that it was likely that witnesses had been fooled by bright meteors.

He also suggested that where the falling light supposedly crashed, they found a beeping transmitter that came from a C–141 aircraft, according to a report filed by Lieutenant Colonel Mooy. But that isn't exactly accurate. According to Mooy's report, "… but as they circled off to the west, they picked up a very noticeable beeper signal. At the point where the return was the loudest was a small house with a garden. They landed and asked the people within if they had noticed anything strange last night. The people talked about a loud noise and a very bright light, like lightning.…" So there was no mention of a C–141 in that report.

Jerome Clark, in his *UFO Encyclopedia*, probably put it best. He wrote of Klass' attempted explanations:

No satisfactory explanation for the incident has ever been proposed, though Philip J. Klass, author of several debunking books on UFOs, would attempt one. In Klass' view, the witnesses initially saw

Klass claimed that one of the F-4s was experiencing equipment failure and that there actually wasn't radar contact.

an astronomical body, probably Jupiter, and pilot incompetence and equipment malfunction accounted for the rest.... Klass' theory presumes, without clear or compelling evidence, a remarkable lack of even rudimentary observing and technical skills on the parts of the Iranian participants. In some ways it would be easier to credit the notion, for which no evidence exists either, that the witnesses consciously fabricated the sighting.

Or, in other words, the skeptical argument against the reality of the sighting fails because of the assumptions made about evidence that does not exist. Klass is forced to invent explanations rather than look at the evidence that is gathered. And this does not address his dismissal of the aircrews as incompetent, based, it seems, on their nationality rather than their actual abilities.

March 21, 1990: Moscow, Russia

Although mentioned in the COMETA report, few details of this attempted intercept on March 21, 1990, are available. The story moved into the public arena when Aviation General Igor Maltsev, Air Defense Forces commander, told of more than one hundred sightings made that night. Fighters were scrambled, including one flown by Lieutenant Colonel A. A. Semenchenko, who was sent up at 21:30 hours (9:30 P.M.).

According to what he told the newspaper, "I was following a true course of 220 degrees, and it was ahead and to the right, at an angle of ten degrees.... With the permission of the command post, I locked my eyesights [gun sights] onto the radiation [UFO] after checking to be sure that the weaponry was switched off The target did not respond to the 'identify, friend or foe' request [which is transponder interrogation of the unidentified aircraft to identify itself]."

There was an order issued to the pilots that told them not to fire on the UFO. According to the General of the Army Ivan Tretyak, the order was issued because "such an object may possess formidable capabilities for retaliation."

That suggests that there had been a history of Soviet fighters attempting to engage UFOs and that, at some point, there had been retaliation. Had such a circumstance not happened, then there would have been no reason to issue such an order. To this point, no one has found anything in the documents from the former Soviet Union to explain this.

Semenchenko said, "I approached the target to within a range of 500 to 600 meters. I passed above the target, trying to define its character. I observed only two bright, flashing, white lights. I briefly saw the silhouette of the target against the background of the illuminated city. It was difficult to determine its nature and classification due to limited lighting."

There were indications that, based on the pilot's reports, they were able to estimate the speed of the UFO. The object flew from a distance of about twenty kilometers to a distance of one hundred kilometers from the fighter in about one minute. They estimated the speed at five thousand kilometers per hour, or about three thousand miles per hour.

One of the most important aspects of the case is that it was reported that the UFO had been detected by both optical and thermo (heat) sensors on the fighter but was not seen by the onboard radar. It was also suggested that photographs had been taken.

In this case, then, there were reports of eyewitness testimony, detection of the UFO on various sensors, and there were photographs. Given all this, the Chairman of the Science and Technical Committee of the Commonwealth of Independent States, General Yevgeniy Tarosev, said, "The reality of UFOs" is beyond doubt, but the physical nature of the phenomenon is unknown.

In the COMETA report, they complete their rather short section dealing with this sighting by noting that General Maltsev said:

> I am not a specialist in UFOs, and therefore I can only link the data together and express my own hypothesis. Based on the data collected by these witnesses, the UFO was a disk 100 to 200 meters in diameter. Two lights were flashing on its sides.... In addition, the object turned around its axis and performed an S-shaped maneuver in both the vertical and the horizontal planes. Next the UFO continued to hover about the ground, then flew at a speed two to three times greater than that of modern combat aircraft.... The objects flew at altitudes ranging from 100 to 7000 meters. The movement of the UFOs was not accompanied by any type of noise and was characterized by an astounding maneuverability. The UFOs appeared to completely lack inertia. In other words, in one fashion or another they had overcome gravity. At present, terrestrial machines can scarcely exhibit such characteristics.

If the information reported to the media by the Russian military is accurate, then this case does provide a basis for additional research. Not only were there the witness testimonies available, but there were other chains of evidence that add credibility to the sighting. The detection of the object by the fighter's instrumentality and the claims that photographs have been taken, makes this a very strong case.

July 31, 1995: San Carlos de Bariloche

The final case for the aviation section of the COMETA report was reported from South America. An Aerolineas Agentinas Airline (flight AR 674) Boeing 727 was flying from Buenos Aires to a resort in the central Andes. According to COMETA:

> … it was preparing to land. At that precise instant, a power outage plunged the town into darkness, and the pilot received the order to stay on standby for a few minutes before making his final approach. When he began his approach, the pilot noticed a strange star. At the same time, the control center put a second airplane that had arrived in the sector on standby. Flight AR 674 continued its approach, but when it had completed its turn and was in the axis of the runway, an object resembling a large aircraft appeared on its right side and flew parallel to it! This object had three lights, one of which was red, in the middle of it. The airport lights failed again, and the runway and the approach ramp lights also went out. The airplane on standby observed the same phenomenon from its position.

Since the pilot could not land, he pulled up and turned again in order to reposition himself in the axis of the runway. At that moment, the object, which had become luminous, moved behind the airplane, stopped, ascended vertically, and once again stopped. It moved back in front of the airplane before finally disappearing in the direction of the Andes Cordillera. The crew and passengers of flight AR 674, those on the other airplane, the airport controllers, and some of the inhabitants of San Carlos watched the unusual aerial ballet dumbfounded.

This case is interesting in more than one aspect:

- the sighting was corroborated by multiple independent observers both in flight and on the ground,
- the phenomenon lasted several minutes,
- there were different trajectories, some of which closely followed those of the airplane,
- there was an observation of an electromagnetic phenomenon (the lights of the town and the airport when out) directly related to the presence of the object.

That was the last of the sightings cited in the report that were made by pilots in the air.

The Andes Cordillera, where the UFO was last seen before it disappeared, according to the pilot of an Argentine passenger plane.

The remainder of the chapter dealt with sightings made on the ground, going back to the wave of sightings from the European Wave of 1954.

August 16, 1954:
Antananarivo, Madagascar

At 5:00 P.M., the people at the Air France office in Antananarivo were waiting for the mail to arrive when someone spotted what was later described as a large green ball moving through the sky at high speed. Among the witnesses was Edmond Campagnac, who had been a military officer and at one time was the chief of technical services for Air France. He was interviewed by the COMETA members. According to them:

> The first thought of the witnesses was that it was a meteorite. The phenomenon disappeared behind a hill, and they thought that the green ball was going to crash into the ground and that they were going to feel the impact.

The large, green ball moved through the sky over Antananarivo, Madagascar, according to staff at the Air France office in 1954 (artist rendering).

However, it reappeared after a minute. In passing directly over the observers, it revealed itself to be a "sort of metal rugby ball, preceded by a clearly detached green lens [-shaped portion] with sparks issuing from the rear." In the estimation of the witnesses, the "ball" was the length of a DC4 [i.e., a four-engine] airplane, or some forty meters long. The green lens separated itself [and remained] a little less than 40 m out in front, with fairly long sparks [coming out] in the rear. The craft flew over Antananarivo at an estimated height of 50 to 100 meters, an estimation that was made possible by comparison with the height of a nearby hill. When the craft was moving, shop lights went out, and animals exhibited a real anxiety.

After having flown over Antananarivo, the craft departed in a westerly direction. When it flew over the zebu park in the town, the craft caused a violent fright reaction among them. This is a surprising detail, since normally these animals do not show any agitation when Air France planes pass by. Two or three minutes later, an identical craft was observed 150 km from there above a farm school. There, too, herds were overcome with panic. If the craft was the same one as the one in Antananarivo, its speed would have had to be on the order of 3000 km/h [about 1800 mph]. According to Campagnac's [report], General Fleurquin, Commander-in-Chief in Madagascar, assembled a "*scientific commission*" [emphasis in original] to conduct an investigation into these phenomena. No trace of this investigation could be found in the Air Force archives; however, GEPA [Aerospace Phenomena Study Group] bulletin no. 6 of the 2nd half of 1964 described this sighting.

Campagnac appeared on French television in 2001, again telling of the sighting. The sighting didn't affect his life, and because of his science background, it inspired an interest in UFOs. He was granted access to the military records of the French Gendarmerie. He found no reference to this sighting but did find there were many other significant sightings.

Of particular interest in this case was the mention of the electromagnetic effects. The shop lights went out until the UFO was gone and there was a reaction by the animals. Both are frequently reported in conjunction with UFO sightings, and this does provide a clue about the nature of the phenomenon.

December 9, 1979: France

Those on the COMETA investigation were impressed by witnesses of sightings who were pilots, especially those who were military pilots. They seemed to select the best cases based on the quality of the witnesses and how long those

> According to Fartek, the object looked like two saucers that were taped together and had no portholes or lights.

witnesses were able to observe the craft or object. Such is the case of French Air Force Lieutenant Colonel Jean-Pierre Fartek, who at the time of the sighting was a pilot of a Mirage III fighter. He made his observation, along with his wife, while at home.

His house was located on the outskirts of a village near Dijon, which has a view of open fields. At about 9:15 in the morning, he and his wife saw what was described as an "unusual object" in the field near his house. The craft was about 20 meters [65 feet] in diameter and about 7 meters [nearly 23 feet] thick and was hovering just over 9 feet above the ground in front of a grove of trees that were just over eight hundred feet away.

According to Fartek, the object looked like two saucers that were taped together and had no portholes or lights. It was a metallic gray on the upper saucer and a bluish color on the bottom, with a line separating the two halves. Fartek thought the difference in the color might have been caused by the sunlight highlighting the upper portion.

The object seemed to be in constant motion and seemed to be oscillating slowly, like a saucer spinning on a pole to maintain balance. There was no noise associated with it and it didn't seem to be disturbing the ground underneath it as it hovered or later, when it flew away. There were no traces left on the ground.

As they watched, the craft seemed to "oscillate faster," and Fartek had the impression that it tilted forward slightly in the same way that a helicopter's rotor will tip as it begins to take off. It flew off in horizontal flight without making noise or leaving any sort of trail, finally flashing off at high speed to disappear over the horizon in a matter of seconds. Fartek reported the sighting to the police and he was sure that some of his neighbors had seen the same thing, but they failed to report it.

The COMETA officials were impressed with the sighting and wrote, "This sighting by a pilot professionally well informed of aeronautical phenomena was never explained."

January 28–29, 1989: Kaputin Yar, Astrakhan Region, USSR

When the Soviet Union collapsed, western UFO researchers had the opportunity to look through the files of the KGB. George Knapp was one of the first to study them and published some of his results in "What the Russians Know about UFOs" in the *MUFON 1994 International UFO Proceedings*. This research was also covered by Don Berliner in his *Unidentified Flying Objects*

Briefing Document published by the Center for UFO Studies, the Fund for UFO Research, and the Mutual UFO Network in 1995. And, of course, it was one of the cases cited in the COMETA study.

> ... Colonel Boris Sokolov ... learned that on the night of July 28–29, 1989, witnesses at a Soviet Army missile base saw an object maneuvering overhead.

According to Knapp, who was working with Colonel Boris Sokolov, the colonel learned that on the night of July 28–29, 1989, witnesses at a Soviet Army missile base saw an object maneuvering overhead. Statements from seven of the witnesses, two officers and five enlisted soldiers, were gathered. While the witness in one of the statements is not identified, it said:

> Military personnel of the signal center observed UFOs in the period from 22:12 hrs. [10:12 P.M.] to 23:55 hrs. [11:55 P.M.] on 28 July, 1989. According to the witnesses' reports, they observed three objects simultaneously, at a distance of 3–5 km [2 to 3 miles].

There was another report from a nearby base. This sighting lasted from 11:30 P.M. until about 1:30 A.M. on July 29. The KGB report said:

> After questioning the witnesses, it was determined that the reported characteristics of the observed UFOs are: disc 4–5 m. [13–17 ft.] diameter, with a half sphere on top, which is lit brightly. It moved sometimes abruptly, but noiselessly, at times coming down and hovering over the ground at an altitude of 20–60 m. [65–200 ft.]. The command of [censored] called for a fighter ... but it was not able to see it in detail, because the UFO did not let the aircraft come near it, evading it. Atmospheric conditions were suitable for visual observations.

Although it is clear from the report that a fighter had been scrambled, there is nothing in the report about it. There is no mention of radar observations, which would make the case even stronger. But one of the officers involved is mentioned. The best of the written reports was made by Ensign Valery N. Voloshin, who was the officer on duty. He wrote that a captain from the telegraph center told him at 11:20 P.M. that an unidentified flying object, which he called a flying saucer, was hovering over the military unit for over an hour.

After confirming the sighting with the operation signal officer, Voloshin and Private Tishchayev climbed up the first part of an antenna tower. This was described this way:

> One could clearly see a powerful, blinking signal, which resembled a camera flash in the night sky. The object flew over the unit's logistics yard and moved in the direction of the rocket weapons depot, 300 meters [1,000 ft.] away. It hovered over the depot at a height of 20 meters [65 ft.]. The UFO's hull shone with a dim green light, which looked like phosphorous. It was a disc, 4 or 5 m. [13–17 ft.] in diameter, with a semispherical top.

While the object was hovering over the depot, a bright beam appeared from the bottom of the disc, where the flash had been before, and made two or three circles, lighting the corner of one of the buildings.... The movement of the beam lasted for several seconds, then the beam disappeared and the object, still flashing, moved in the direction of the railway station. After that, I observed the object hovering over the logistics yard, railway station, and cement factory. Then it returned to the rocket weapons depot and hovered over it at an altitude of 60–70 m [200–240 ft.]. The object was observed from that time on by the first guard-shift and its commander. At 1:30 hrs., the object flew in the direction of the city of Akhtubinsk and disappeared from sight. The flashes on the object were not periodical; I observed all this for exactly two hours: from 23:30 to 1:30 [11:30 P.M. to 1:30 A.M.]

The others, Private Tishchayev, Corporal Levin, and Privates Bashev, Kulik, and Litvinov, all tell essentially the same story about the UFO. What they saw and reported was:

Suddenly, it flew in our direction. It approached fast and increased in size. It then divided itself in three shining points and took the shape of a triangle. Then it changed course and went on flying in the same sector.

"While the object was hovering over the depot, a bright beam appeared from the bottom of the disc, where the flash had been before...."

After veering, it began to approach us, and its speed could be felt physically. (It swelled in front of our eyes.) Its flight was strange: no aircraft could fly in this manner. It could instantly stop in the air (and there was an impression that it wobbled slightly up and down); it could float (exactly that: float, because the word "fly" would not be adequate; it was as if the air was holding it, preventing it from falling). At all times that I observed it, it was blinking, blinking without any order and constantly changing colors (red, blue, green, yellow). The point itself was not blinking but something above it.

Here is what I observed: there was a flying object, resembling an egg, but flatter. It shone brightly, alternating green and red lights. This object gathered a great speed. It accelerated abruptly and also stopped abruptly, all the while doing large jumps up or down. Then appeared a second and then a third object. One object rose to low altitude and stopped. It stayed there in one place and was gone. Later a second object disappeared, and only one stayed. It moved constantly along the horizon. At times, it seemed it landed on the ground, then it rose again and moved.

As mentioned, there is no written record of the attempted intercept, but there were those on the ground who witnessed it. According to Lieutenant Klimenko's statement, "the airplane, which could be identified by its noise, approached the object, but the object disengaged so fast that it seemed the plane stayed in one place."

> "Here is what I observed: there was a flying object, resembling an egg, but flatter. It shone brightly, alternating green and red lights."

The COMETA report covered the sighting in less detail, noting that "five testimonies from the first center were provided by Lieutenant Klimenko, two corporals, and two soldiers.... Two other testimonies from a center near the first one concern the sighting of a UFO.... In a report that was consistent with the report of his superior soldier, Tichaev stressed the lack of noise made by the object, even when a short distance away, which prevented him from confusing it with a helicopter."

Like so many other cases, here was one with multiple witnesses, one group separated from another, telling of seeing the same thing. It is clear that there was an attempted intercept, but no official documents of that attempt were available. There probably was radar data as well, which would provide additional evidence, but this was not located. If all the possibilities were available, the case would be even stronger.

July 1, 1965: Valensole, Alpes-de-Haute-Provence, France

This was described as an "in-depth investigation by the *Gendarmerie Nationale*," which suggests that it was conducted by those who had no real interest in proving that some sightings are of alien craft but in finding out what had been seen.

This is only the first of the two cases in the COMETA report that contain a mention of alien creatures, and it seems that those who investigated it found no reason to reject the report and do not believe it to be it a hoax.

In an article that was published in the *Flying Saucer Review* in the November/December issue, GEPA provided more details of the case. According to them, and other documents, including those found in the Project Blue Book files, Maurice Masse was in his lavender field at about 5:30 A.M. As he was lighting a cigarette, he heard a whistling noise, but he couldn't see where it was coming from. He moved away from a mound of debris and out into the open. About eighty meters away … he saw some sort of a machine that had landed in his field. He was familiar with military aircraft, but he didn't know what he was seeing. He said that it was shaped like a rugby ball with a dome or cupola on top. It was standing on six legs, or rather, six legs were visible.

Because there had been problems in his fields from what he believed to be vandals, he started walking toward the craft. Near the craft, he saw two small beings that he described as being about the size of an eight-year-old boy. When he was about twenty feet away, they seemed to straighten and pointed some sort of tube at him. Masse said that he felt as if he had been glued to the ground and was unable to move.

He told investigators, including a member of the gendarmerie, that the creatures had enormous heads. The face looked human except for the mouth,

Lavender farmer Maurice Masse comes face to face with aliens near Valensole, France, in this painting by Michael Buhler.

which had no lips and resembled a hole. There was no hair. The skin was very smooth and white. The beings wore coveralls.

After a few minutes, they entered the craft with surprising agility. He thought he saw one of the creatures through a porthole or clear area on the dome. The machine began to emit the whistling sound, and with incredible speed took off at a forty-five degree angle. It vanished in seconds and left no trail behind it.

Masse had thought that his paralysis would disappear when the craft was gone, but it didn't. For another fifteen minutes he stood there, unable to move, but then, slowly, he regained control of his body.

That evening, with his eighteen-year-old daughter, he returned to the landing site. There were markings left behind. There were four holes where four of the legs had touched the ground, and the ground was hard-packed, as if made of concrete.

When the gendarmes investigated, they found the four marks from the landing gear and a center hole that was twenty centimeters in the center. According to them, the ground around what they had called the central pivot was baked and hard, almost like concrete. The surrounding soil was normal.

The COMETA report on this sighting concludes with, "Despite a few contradictory elements in Maurice Masse's account, the data collected by the two gendarme brigades confirmed the plausibility of the facts, particularly the effect on the environment and on the witness himself, who slept twelve to fifteen hours a night, followed by the paralysis of which he had been a victim, for several months. The investigation into the witness' character did not turn up any specific information that would permit one to suspect him of mythomaniac behavior or of staging a hoax."

August 29, 1967: Cussac, Cantal, France

The second case that involved a sighting of alien creatures was made by thirteen-year-old François and his sister, nine-year-old Anne-Marie. They were in a field watching a small herd of cattle at about 10:30 A.M. When the cattle attempted to enter a nearby field, François got up to stop them and noticed four children he didn't recognize in the field about 250 feet from him. He called to his sister and then saw a bright sphere behind the figures.

As he attempted to get closer, he realized that they weren't children but small, black beings without any distinctive clothes. He thought that they were normally proportioned, although they did seem to have light beards. Two of them were standing near the sphere, another was kneeling in front of it, and the last was standing with a mirror of some kind that flashed, blinding François and Anne-Marie.

When François yelled at them, the creatures dashed for the sphere. They seemed to rise from the ground and enter the top of the sphere, diving into it headfirst. Once they were all inside, the sphere lifted off with a hissing sound, rising in a continual spiraling motion. The hissing faded and the sphere disappeared, heading to the northwest. A strong odor of sulfur filled the air. The sighting lasted about thirty seconds.

The children headed home and told their father, who in turn called the local police. They arrived about 4:00 P.M. but still could detect the odor of sulfur. They also found a circle of yellowed grass about fifteen feet in diameter. It faded from sight after a few days.

The children, however, weren't the only witnesses to the event, though these witnesses hadn't seen the sphere. According to the COMETA report:

> The highlights of this counterinvestigation did not have to do with the facts or the account but with new elements, such as secondary witnesses found at the site who provided supplemental information and strengthened the credibility of the case. In particular, a gendarme who arrived on the scene immediately following the incident found tracks on the ground at the place indicated by the children and noted the very strong odor of sulfur. Likewise, another witness also came forward who admitted being in a granary close to the site and clearly remembered a hissing sound very different from a helicopter of the time.
>
> The reconstructions at the site in the presence of the two main witnesses confirmed both the descriptive accounts and the circumstances that followed the sighting. At the time the children gave off a strong odor of sulfur, but above all, they suffered from physiological disorders, and their eyes ran for several days. These facts were certified by the family doctor and confirmed by their father, who was mayor of the village at the time. In the conclusion of this counterinvestigation, the judge gave his opinion on the witnesses and their testimony: "There is no flaw or inconsistency in these various elements that permit us to doubt the sincerity of the witnesses or to reasonably suspect an invention, hoax, or hallucination. *Under these circumstances, despite the young age of the principal witnesses, and as extraordinary as the facts that they have related seem to be, I think that they actually observed them.*" [Emphasis in the original.]

They seemed to rise from the ground and enter the top of the sphere, diving into it headfirst.

Given the nature of the case and the age of the witnesses, it seems extraordinary that those investigating for the COMETA report would suggest this as one of the strongest cases. However, as noted, there was some supporting evidence as well as additional witnesses. That certainly helped.

January 8, 1981:
Trans-en-Provence, Var, France

At about five in the afternoon, Renato Niccolai, originally identified with the last name of Collini to protect his identity, said he was working outside when he heard a whistling sound in the east. He then spotted an object that he described as "a somewhat bulging disc, like two plates glued to each other at the rim," descending. It passed over two trees and then seemed to land some fifty-five yards away. Given the lay of the land, he lost sight of the UFO, but walked to an elevated place where he could again see the object. It was sitting on the ground in an alfalfa field. He would tell investigators, "I clearly saw the device resting on the ground."

> ... when they walked into the field where the UFO landed, they found some odd traces. These seemed to indicate that a large vehicle had been sitting on the ground.

He watched for only a few seconds before it began to whistle again and then it lifted off, heading back the way that it had come. He said that "underneath the brace I saw, as it took off, two kinds of round pieces with what could have been landing gear or feet. There were also two circles, which looked kind of like trap doors. The two feet or landing gear extended about 20 centimeters beneath the body of the whole ship."

As the UFO took off, it kicked up a small cloud of dust. It flew between two trees as it gathered speed and disappeared into the distance. The whole sighting took about forty seconds, but because of the terrain, the object was not in sight the whole time.

When Niccolai told his wife what he had seen, she didn't believe it, but the next day, when they walked into the field where the UFO landed, they found some odd traces. These seemed to indicate that a large vehicle had been sitting on the ground. It was something that was relatively heavy.

A neighbor alerted the gendarmerie, and the next day they were at the site to collect samples. They mentioned, in their official report, "We observed the presence of two concentric circles, one 2.2 meters in diameter and the other 2.4 meters in diameter. The two circles form a sort of corona 10 centimeters thick ... one within the other. There are two parts clearly visible, and they also show black striations."

They also took plant and soil samples from within the circles, outside, and several from a distance away as controls. They returned fifteen days later to gather additional samples, and GEPAN arrived forty days later to collect even more samples. Skeptics would later criticize the gathering of the samples, suggesting that amateurs couldn't have done any worse.

Skeptics also complain that GEPAN didn't arrive for forty days and found that the site was still visible. They interviewed Niccolai again and con-

> "The evidence indicates a strong, mechanical pressure on the ground surface, probably due to a heavy weight of about 4 to 5 tons."

cluded that he was telling the truth. Skeptics suggested that the tale was an invention by Niccolai as a joke. He was reported to have told his wife, "Your cat is back. Extraterrestrials brought him home." It is only in the skeptical accounts that this statement is contained. He apparently said nothing like it to either the gendarmerie or the GEPAN investigators.

According to the reports, the soil and plant samples were taken to botanist Michel Bounias of the National Institute of Agronomy Research. Over the next two years, Bounias conducted extensive research, which was sometimes aided by Toulouse University and the University of Metz. The results were published in GEPAN's *Technical Note 16* in 1983. It said, in part:

> The chlorophyll content of the wild alfalfa leaves in the immediate vicinity of the ground traces was reduced 30 percent to 50 percent, inversely proportional to distance.

> Young alfalfa leaves experienced the highest loss of chlorophyll and, moreover, exhibited signs of premature senescence.

> Biochemical analysis showed numerous differences between vegetation samples obtained close to the site and those more distant.

But that wasn't all that had been found. In the analysis of the ground traces, that is, the marks left when the craft landed, it was noted:

> The evidence indicates a strong, mechanical pressure on the ground surface, probably due to a heavy weight of about 4 to 5 tons.

> At the same time or immediately after this pressure, the soil was heated up to between 300 and 600 degrees Celsius.

In a report titled "Scientific Approach and Results of Studies into Unidentified Aerospace Phenomena in France," published in the *MUFON 1987 MUFON International UFO Symposium Proceedings*, Jean-Jacques wrote:

> The effects on plants in the area can be compared with that produced on the leaves of other plant species after exposing seeds to gamma radiation. Data show that a considerable amount of gamma radiation (10 to the sixth power rads) must be applied to produce a disturbance equivalent to that observed at the site. Should we consider the presence of ionizing (nuclear) radiation? Almost certainly not, since no measurable residual radioactivity is present in the plants. However, could the trauma be caused by an electromagnetic field? Probably.

The COMETA section on the Trans-en-Provence sighting concluded with a positive statement:

According to Professor Bounias … who performed the analyses, the cause of the profound disturbances suffered by the vegetation present in that ecosystem could likely be a powerful, pulsed electromagnetic field in the high frequency (microwave) range. Studies and research are still being conducted in regard to this case, and numerous leads have been explored. None of these leads has been able to satisfy all of the conditions that would enable the object that landed in Trans-en-Provence on January 8, 1981, to be identified with certainty, and this is all the more true with respect to determination of its origin.

But the findings weren't without some controversy. Skeptics in France suggested that the case wasn't that impressive to the scientists working for France's space agency or in the report from GEPAN. In fact, French ufologist Éric Maillot claimed that he had found many flaws in the GEPAN investigation, which he believed to be a practical joke that had simply gotten out of hand. He said that no GEPAN investigators were dispatched until some forty days after the sighting and then they ignored "significant discrepancies in Niccolai's accounts" of the event.

> The skeptics note that Niccolai said the object hovered three meters above the ground, but the markings found suggested that it had been on the ground.

But most of what is used as an example could be claimed as observational errors. The skeptics note that Niccolai said the object hovered three meters above the ground, but the markings found suggested that it had been on the ground. This overlooks the fact that Niccolai said that he lost sight of the object for a short period as he moved to a higher location. It is possible that the craft touched down and then rose again to a hover.

The skeptical arguments did not impress those who created the COMETA report. They wrote:

> The expert's appraisals of the ground—the taking of soil and plant samples followed by analyses—showed unequivocally that it really was a case of an unidentified heavy metal object that had actually landed on the platform of earth. The analyses of the plant samples taken at the site indicated that they were not dealing with any type of [known] aircraft, or even a helicopter or military drone, which were the hypotheses that were considered and analyzed. The vegetation at the landing site—a sort of wild alfalfa—had been profoundly marked and affected by an external agent that considerably altered the photosynthesis apparatus. In fact, the chlorophylls, as well as certain amino acids of plants, exhibited significant variations in concentration, variations which decreased with the distance [of the plants] from the center of the mechanical track.…

They ended the section on this sighting by saying, "Studies and research are still being conducted in regard to this case, and numerous leads have been explored. None of these leads has been able to satisfy all of the conditions that would enable the object that landed in Trans-en-Provence on January 8, 1981, to be identified with certainty, and this is all the more true with respect to the determination of its origin."

October 21, 1982: Nancy, Meurthe-et-Moselle (the So-Called "Amaranth" Case)

The last of the unidentified ground cases cited in the COMETA report is a sighting made by a cellular biology researcher, who saw an object hovering over his garden for twenty minutes. According to COMETA:

> The witness was in his garden in front of his house at around 12:35 P.M. after work on October 21, 1982; he saw a flying craft, which he first took for an airplane, coming from the southeast. He saw a shiny craft. He indicated that there were no clouds, that the sun was not in his eyes, and that visibility was excellent. The craft's speed of descent was not very great, and he thought that it was going to pass over his house. Once he realized that the trajectory of the craft was bringing it toward him, he backed up 3 to 4 meters. This craft, which was oval in shape, stopped approximately one meter from the ground and remained hovering at this height for about 20 minutes.

> The witness stated that since he had looked at his watch, he was absolutely certain about the length of time the craft hovered. He described the craft as follows: ovoid in shape, approximately 1 m in diameter, 80 cm thick, the bottom half metallic in appearance like polished beryllium and the upper half the blue-green color of the inner depths of a lagoon. The craft did not emit any noise, nor did it seem to emit any heat, cold, radiation, magnetism, or electromagnetism. After 20 minutes, the craft suddenly rose straight up, a trajectory which it maintained until it was out of sight. The craft's departure was very fast, as if it were under the effect of strong suction. The witness indicated, finally, that there were no tracks or marks on the ground and the grass was not charred or flattened, but he did remark that when the craft departed, the grass stood straight up, then returned to its normal position.

> The interest of this sighting, apart from its strangeness, lies in the visible traces left on the vegetation and namely, on an amaranth

bush, the tips of whose leaves, which had completely dried up, led one to think that they had been subjected to intense electrical fields. However, despite short time delays before intervention, the sampling conditions and then the storage of the sample did not permit this hypothesis to be verified definitively. Based on an earlier study on the behavior of plants subjected to electrical fields, it emerged that:

- the electrical field, which was what probably caused the blades of grass to lift up, had to have exceeded 30 kV/m,

- the effects of the amaranth that were observed were probably due to an electrical field that had to have far exceeded 200 kV/m at the level of the plant.

The amaranth plants on the field had leaves that were dried up, and a biologist believed this showed evidence of a strong electrical field.

With this case, the last of the testimonial evidence was finished. There were two additional cases reviewed, but both them were examples of "Phenomena That Have Been Explained."

Counterexamples of Phenomena That Have Been Explained

The first of these reports concerned an auto mechanic who was driving along a freeway and saw a large, red ball cross the road and roll away. It was reflecting light and was enveloped in a dense smoke. It came to rest in the field. This bothered him, and he reported it to the "highway gendarmes," who then sealed off the highway. They were concerned that there might be some radioactivity involved, because the Cosmos 1900 Soviet satellite was predicted to re-enter and it was equipped with a nuclear power plant. They learned, however, that at the time of the sighting, the satellite was flying above the Indian Ocean.

Eventually they did learn the source of the red ball. It was supposed to be part of the decorations at a concert, but had fallen from a truck. Small mirrors stuck to it to reflect the light of the show created part of the effects seen by the auto mechanic.

The second case study is equally mundane. On March 31, 1979, the local police were told that a UFO had flown over the town two days earlier. While investigating the sighting, they found three others, who had seen what was

> Eventually they did learn the source of the red ball. It was supposed to be part of the decorations at a concert, but had fallen from a truck.

described as a bluish and purplish, luminous mass that might be about fifty feet in length. The light was so bright that the photoelectric cells that controlled the street lights were tripped, and those lights went out.

Another strange occurrence was when a fish farmer said that he had been awakened by a dull noise and a bright blue light. The next day, he found that all the fish in one of the tanks were dead. There was a power line over the tank, which suggested that the glow might have been caused by intense electric current.

The investigation by SEPRA was conducted a few days later. They found that the power line had melted. The French electric company found that the line was thirty years old and badly corroded. This could have caused an arcing, which would explain the glow and the noise heard by the fish farmer. This would also explain the power failure experience in the village street lights. Explanations were found for all the various phenomena reported, and the case was closed.

The Rest of the COMETA Report

From that point, the report moves into Part II, labeled as "The Extent of Our Knowledge." This looked at the various organizations in France that would need to participate in the investigation. These included both military and civilian aviation, the French Air Force, the *Gendarmerie Nationale*, and academic research facilities. It also discusses the uses of various kinds of evidence and the evaluation of it.

Later, in a section that focuses on GEPAN and the department that replaced it, SEPAN, called "Methods and Results of GEPAN/SEPRA," there is a discussion of a "method for studying rare, randomly occurring phenomena." They mention that this method was developed by GEPAN and approved by its scientific council. They write:

It basically consists of identifying initially unknown phenomena and performing a joint analysis of four types of data concerning:

- witnesses: physiology, psychology, etc.
- testimonies: accounts, reactions to questions, general behavior, etc.
- the physical environment: weather, air traffic, photographs, radar data, traces left on the environment, etc.
- the psychosociological environment: readings and beliefs of the witnesses, possible influence of the media and various groups on these witnesses, etc.

They go on to say that the initial reports provided by the gendarmerie often contain the detail to explain the sightings, but an in-depth study could take as long as two years. The landing traces, for example, could require the use of specialized laboratories for analysis.

And finally, in this section, they noted that the term UAP, for unidentified Aerospace Phenomena, was preferred to UFO. They thought UFO was more well-known but was also more restrictive.

They came up with a classification system that included Category A, which were sightings that were completely identified; Category B, which were sightings that could probably be identified but lacked the evidence to do so; Category C, which were sightings that were not identified because of a lack of data; and, finally, Category D, which were phenomena that could not be identified despite having the proper data available.

Like nearly every other investigation into UFOs, or UAPs, COMETA noted that only four to five percent of the cases were called "UAP Ds," or those with all the necessary data but no identification.

They also supplied some theories on various types of reports. For example, in tackling the vehicle interference reports, they speculated about what sort of radiation might be used to stop the engines. They didn't solve the riddle, but did suggest ways that it might be done, such as with microwave emissions.

And they examined the theories about what might cause a UAP sighting. These range from some sort of group or organization or even alien creatures that are manipulating us, to secret weapons and disinformation, and finally on to the extraterrestrial, which includes highly advanced, hidden civilizations on Earth. They conclude that "both these hypotheses have, to their credit, the fact that they place the UFO problem outside the realm of the paranormal and promote thought about the future of our planet."

Part Two ends with a discussion about some of the worldwide aspects of the UFO research. Surprisingly, they spent some time on the stories told by Lieutenant Colonel Philip Corso. This is somewhat troubling, but in fairness, when the COMETA research was being

COMETA classified sightings into four categories: "A" for completely identified, "B" for sightings that could have been identified if there had been enough evidence, "C" unidentified for lack of data, and "D" for unidentified despite having data.

done, Corso's tales hadn't been examined carefully. They do note the problem with the foreword to Corso's book and how it had to be pulled from later editions. Then they seem to mitigate this by suggesting that Strom Thurman, the late U.S. senator from South Carolina, who had written the foreword, had asked that it be removed. It was a request that was granted. They then write, "But it is difficult to believe that the foreword writer, the third in line in the U.S. government to succeed to the president, and the publisher, Simon & Schuster, were not acting with full knowledge of the facts at the time of the first printing."

The truth here is that Thurman had provided a foreword for a book entitled *I Walked with Giants* that had nothing to do with UFOs. When Corso changed the book into one that dealt with UFOs, Roswell, and the seeding of alien technology into American industry, he took the foreword and slipped it into his UFO book. None of the other participants knew this had been done until after the book was printed. Simon & Schuster had no choice but to pull the foreword.

They conclude with a look at UFO organizations in other countries, which provides a glimpse into the worldwide nature of the phenomenon, but also suggests that it is something more than delusions in the United States or just in Europe. Everyone is having trouble with the sightings.

Part Three is about "UFOs and Defense." It begins with a general statement that suggests that "credible, confirmed UFO sightings began in 1944. Certainly, this subject still sometimes elicits amused skepticism, if not a certain mistrust with regard to those who mention it seriously, but in the absence of explanations for the phenomena sighted, the hypothesis of an extraterrestrial origin can no longer be ruled out...."

But the focus of the section is a theory that there has been some sort of contact between humans and alien creatures. They provide a brief description of the types of craft most often seen, that is, a saucer, luminous sphere, or cylinder that can accelerate at high speed. But much of anything else is labeled as mysterious.

Once these theories are mentioned, the report then delves into an interesting area that had once been covered by the Brookings Institution, and that concerns what would happen after contact, or in the world of today, after disclosure. They do note that after a brief suggestion that something real is happening, "It emerges from this that these objects truly do exist. But since then, the United States has followed a policy of increasing secrecy ... and constant disinformation. The strange conclusions of the Condon report are just one case in point."

They also explain that in the United States disclosure of UFO-related information, if the sighting has not been identified, was illegal. They wrote,

The COMETA report also speculates and makes recommendations as to what should happen should contact be made with an alien race.

"... and the second [Joint Army Navy Air Force Publication, that is, JANAP 146], making the unauthorized disclosure of a UFO sighting by the witness an infraction punishable by ten years in prison and a $10,000.00 fine. The JANAP regulation applies to military personnel, but also to commercial airline pilots and captains in the merchant marine."

The interesting part of this is under the section labeled "Political and Religious Implications." This is "an assessment of the impact that the formal confirmation of the existence of UFOs and extraterrestrial civilizations would have on the political and religious situation of the countries on earth, which could be a bit of a challenge." But rather than speculate on contact by alien creatures, the section was set up as if people from Earth had found another world that held sentient beings.

While that section could have been the most interesting, it fails simply because it postulates that alien creatures would develop civilization in the same fashion as it developed on Earth. It assumes that any other sentient race would develop various competitive states scattered over the planet rather than a single cooperative civilization. What they describe is the UFO phenomenon as it has been represented on Earth.

First they mention Phase One, which would be observation from a distance. This does not include any sort of physical contact, but could be done from deep space without detection by the local inhabitants, depending on their level of civilization. Of course, given our capabilities today, such surveillance would be detectable at great distances. But the detection of our surveillance could be kept from the general populace by a ruling establishment.

> The problem here is that these assumptions are based on human history and an alien civilization might bear no real relation to something developed on Earth.,...

In the second phase, there would be sampling done in secret. This would be to analyze the various elements of the planet, including plants, animals, and mineral deposits. They suggest that even if this was selected, our technology wouldn't be sufficient to go undetected. Or, in other words, our craft would be seen by the locals, who might not be able to do anything about the violation of their airspace.

Assuming that the craft were seen, and assuming that the humans from inside were seen, or their robotic analogs were seen, they discuss the impact of those sightings on a preindustrial civilization and on industrial civilizations, including religious and political effects. The problem here is that these assumptions are based on human history and an alien civilization might bear no real relation to something developed on Earth, which means these speculations are nothing more than theory without a basis in fact.

They suggest, for example, that their religions might incorporate elements of the sightings into their religious structures. But, of course, they might have no religious structure; their observations of the natural world around them might not allow for a religion to develop. They could see the ship and the human occupants for what they are and not develop a mythology about them.

The same can be said for their political structures. While the writers seem to believe that the inhabitants of the planet would react in the same way as we have, that might not be true. They might have a single ruling faction that is sure of its place in the world and believe there is no need to hide the information. The COMETA writers cite examples from human history, but those examples might be irrelevant. And one thing they don't address is the possibility of some sort of telepathy that would render secrecy impossible.

COMETA continues in this vein, finally arriving at direct contact. Direct contact must be carefully considered, and it must be carefully accomplished. But the intriguing aspect is that a "serious, technical accident affecting one of our spacecraft could be the start of an unofficial contact, a necessary settlement, or colonization, or even, if necessary, an information–disinformation campaign."

They continue, suggesting, "Bear in mind that direct or prolonged contacts would inevitably lead the indigenous populations to believe, *in fine*, that we are not so different from them. It would be prudent, however, to send remote-controlled androids in advance in order to assess the reactions that such an intrusion would arouse or to acclimate the population to the idea through furtive, episodic appearances."

Again they explain what such a contact would mean to both preindustrial and industrial civilizations. They seem to avoid mentioning, other than in passing, that on Earth, when a technologically superior civilization contacts a technologically inferior civilization, that technologically inferior civilization ceases to exist. It might be nothing more than the introduction of new technologies, but the civilization is radically altered at the point of contact and forever after.

Lost in all this, in the middle of discussing direct contact with industrial-age civilizations, they wrote, "Before or after the implementation of an influencing program, why not imagine having bionic robots that look like humans or resemble the living beings there appear in order not to risk the lives of members of our expeditions?"

This raises an interesting point, which is the skeptical argument that aliens reported by witnesses around the world speak of humanoids. A race that has conquered the technological problems of interstellar travel might have a way of creating entities that resemble those on the worlds they visit. In other words, we're not seeing the aliens as they are, but as they believe we wish they are or the aliens think we wish to see them.

But most of this is theory and not very interesting theory. Such things have been discussed throughout the UFO community for decades. What is interesting are the "Conclusions and Recommendations." Here, the authors of COMETA wrote:

The UFO problem cannot be eliminated by mere caustic and offhand witticisms. Since the publication of the first report by

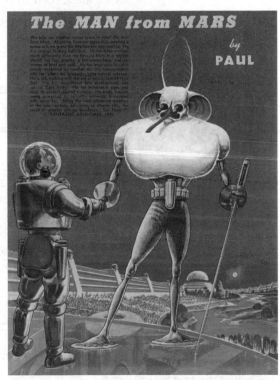

What would an alien race look like? How would it behave? Would its culture be similar to ours or very different? Even in this 1939 issue of *Fantastic Adventures* we imagined them as being very exotic.

the Association des Anciens Autideurs of IHEDN 20 years ago, CNES has conducted serious studies in close collaboration with the *Gendarmerie Nationale* and the Air Force primarily, as well as other State agencies (Civil Aviation, Weather Service, etc.). These studies tally with other research conducted more or less discretely abroad, mainly in the United States.

They demonstrate the almost-certain, physical reality of completely unknown flying objects with remarkable flight performances and noiseless, apparently operated by intelligent [beings]. With their maneuvers, these flying objects considerably impress civilian and military pilots, who hesitate to speak [about them]. The fear of appearing ridiculous, alienated, or simply gullible is the principal reason for this reserve. Secret craft definitely of earthly origin (drones, stealth aircraft, etc.) can only explain a minority of cases. If we go back far enough in time, we clearly perceive the limits of this explanation.

Thus we are forced to resort to other hypotheses. Some can neither be confirmed nor invalidated. They are therefore not scientific, and, certainly, it is very difficult to scientifically study rare, elusive, and chance phenomena when science is based on experiments and their reproducibility. However, the example of meteorites shows that this type of phenomenon can nevertheless end up being accepted by the scientific community after centuries of doubt and rejection.

A single hypothesis sufficiently takes into account the facts and, for the most part, only calls for present-day science. It is the hypothesis of extraterrestrial visitors. Advanced as of 1947 by certain U.S. military personnel, today it is popular worldwide. It is discredited by a certain elite, but is plausible. Scientists (astronomers, physicists, engineers, futurologists, etc.) have elaborated on it enough for it to be receivable—as a hypothesis—by their peers. Different, plausible variants concerning the voyage of one or more civilizations from a remote solar system to ours have been developed. A model of magnetohydrodynamic technology, which could be employed to propel the UFOs in the atmosphere, has been well developed. Other manifestations of these objects have begun to receive physical explanation (automobile breakdowns, truncated beams [of light], etc.).

> "The purposes of these possible visitors remain unknown, but they must be [the] subject of indispensable speculations and the development of prospective scenarios."

The purposes of these possible visitors remain unknown, but they must be [the] subject of indispensable speculations and the development of prospective scenarios.

The extraterrestrial hypothesis is far from the best scientific hypothesis. It certainly has not been categorically proven, but strong presumptions exist in its favor and if it is correct, it is loaded with consequences.

These conclusions were drawn, not by the members of a UFO organization, but by men who had risen high in their fields, who were well educated, and who had studied the evidence. Though this was not an "official" research project, it was provided to the president of France.

This is an example of a proper study that reached the conclusion that the extraterrestrial hypothesis, while not proven, is strongly presumed to be correct. Unlike the Condon Committee that had its conclusions presented to it prior to the investigation and then ignored the evidence it developed, this study attempted to investigate a phenomenon without prior conclusions. When we look at the world, we see that this is another investigation completed by top-level researchers that tells us that UFOs deserve a proper investigation.

UFOs in the Twenty-first Century

In the middle of the 1990s, Karl Pflock and I wondered why the UFO sightings being reported were not as robust as those that had come much earlier. The Lubbock Lights, for example, had dozens of witnesses, photographs, and an in-depth investigation by the Air Force at a time when they cared about the research. The Levelland sightings had dozens of witnesses spread all around the Levelland area, which isn't all that far from Lubbock, but this time there were law-enforcement officers, a fire marshal, and electromagnetic effects reported. The next night there were more sightings in New Mexico, some of them mimicking those in Levelland.

There were sightings with photographs, sightings with landing traces, sightings by dozens of people, aircraft chases, and car pacings, and finally abductions. Case files were hundreds of pages and investigations lasted weeks and months, and a few spanned years. A catalog of landing-trace cases was compiled, as were catalogs for radar cases and photographs.

Sometime after 1973, when a wave of sightings swept through the United States, there were many sightings of the UFOs on the ground, and in some cases the occupants were outside and it seemed as if they were taking samples. But then, in late November or early December, the number of sightings dropped off dramatically.

January 31, 2009: Morristown, New Jersey

We noted that, moving into the twenty-first century, there were still many reports of UFOs, but many of them were of objects seen in the distance or objects that, when research was conducted, turned out to be nothing more than

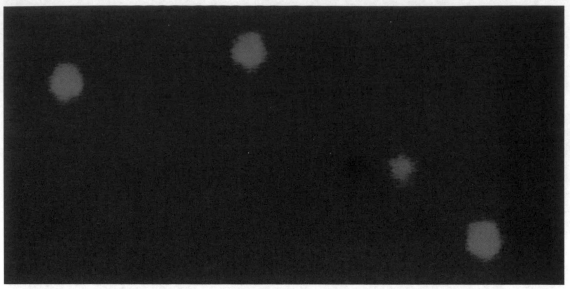

The UFOs photographed over New Jersey. They were explained as balloons with railroad flares.

some sort of hoax or alleged experiment to prove that UFOs were hyped by UFO researchers who were inclined to believe everything and reject nothing.

Chris Russo and Joe Rudy, two geniuses from Morristown, New Jersey, thought that they would confirm their belief that UFO research wasn't very good.

They, after pointing out that the first UFO reports were made in the 1940s, wrote this: "… 60 years later, despite the fact that there still is no evidence, the UFO myth is as strong today as ever, fed by cable channel shows that prop up UFO 'experts,' who claim to be authorities on the subject that's on a par with astrology and palm reading. These charlatans make a career by perpetuating the E.T. fairy tale and exploiting credulous people, who want nothing more than a good conspiracy theory to believe in."

Their self-described mission? According to them, "It is in this context that we set out on a mission to help people think rationally and question the credibility of so-called UFO 'professionals.' We brainstormed the idea of producing a spaceship hoax to fool people, bring the charlatans out of the woodwork to drum up the controversy, and then expose it was nothing more than a prank to show everyone how unreliable eyewitness accounts are, along with the investigators of UFOs."

How well did they do? The first persons to be interviewed after the first "light" show were the Hurley family, who had taken videotape of the drifting, red lights. The father, Paul, worked at the airport and had a pilot's license; he said he had about five hundred hours of flight time. He was not a commercial pilot, meaning an airline pilot, nor was he a military pilot. He said the lights were not aircraft, and he was right about that.

He said that there were "five red lights," in what he said was a "strange pattern." There was no real reason for him to conclude it was a strange pattern, but that really doesn't mean much. He would later say, under questioning by others, that he had seen no smoke and that one light seemed to drop out (burn out?), and two others seemed to take off to the south at a fast pace.

The second witness, who was presented by the news media by way of his 911 call to the police, said, "I walked out of my house, it's like these parachutes with these, uh, or balloons with these five lights flying over right now."

This witness hit the nail right on the head. There were no media types there to attempt to create the mystery for their broadcasts later that night. Just a single witness saying that he saw the five lights in the sky and that he suggested they were balloons.

The local police, who offered a statement to television station KDTV, said that the best guess was a prank with roadside flares attached to helium balloons. That showed that the police had nailed the explanation as well.

On the compilation of video clips made by the perpetrators to prove their point, the second was of a breathless reporter who was all set to believe in alien visitation and flying saucers and who seemed to know very little about the overall topic. Unfortunately, she worked for a FOX affiliate, so the interviews she conducted were used by the national FOX News cable channel on several of their reports. It was the reporter, in talking to witnesses, who often introduced the idea of UFOs, meaning alien craft rather than lights in the night sky.

But what she didn't seem to get—nor did either Russo or Rudy—was that the descriptions offered by the witnesses were often very accurate. It was the interpretation put on those observations by the media and others, most of whom had no experience in investigating UFO sightings and knew nothing about UFOs, who took these reports from what would normally be labeled as viewings of nocturnal lights into the realm of alien spacecraft.

This reporter talked to a witness who said the lights didn't seem to be moving at all, and another who suggested they had a purpose but added they could have been anything … and then said, "A UFO? Why not?", suggesting here that it was the reporter who asked if it was a UFO and not a spontaneous utterance by the witness.

That reporter then interviewed a little girl with a sucker who said, "Aliens?" in obvious response to a question. But it was never established if she had seen anything or if she just happened to be standing around with her lollipop in hand and the reporter thought it would be a cute segment. It, of course, did little to explain the mystery or provide any important facts.

There was another witness who said that he thought the lights had streaked down toward New York, but it's not clear if this was the result of the balloons and flares drifting in that direction and giving the impression they were getting lower or if he actually thought he saw something like that. He did say that one winked out. He said, "It just sort of went blip and disappeared," which, of course, is the description of a flare burning out.

It seemed that everything pointed to balloons, but there were two witnesses who had a much closer encounter. The first said the lights "zipped over the car." He said, "They literally flew over the car." When it was suggested these were flares he said, "No way. They zipped over our car."

He also said he wanted "… someone to tell me what it was, because I cannot tell you what it was."

His friend, in the car with him as they had gone out to find something to eat, said, "They seemed to ascend and descend almost in a sequence—they'd rise up and dip down."

Here is the first time that there was a description of something other than lights drifting in the sky. They were zipping over a car, which would suggest that the lights were close to the ground and powered by something other than the wind. The witnesses were identified as Chris Russo and Joe Rudy, the same two who had thought up the experiment, but who had now contaminated it, making it useless.

Even with those two attempting to change the narrative, one of the news reports quotes from a police report that identified the objects, the lights, as flares and helium balloons. Once again, that explanation is right on target, even though there is no testimony suggesting something more than just lights in the sky.

FOX News went back to the Hurleys and interviewed them again. They repeated that they saw five lights slowly drifting across the sky. They said the lights were not aircraft, which is true. Paul Hurley did say that the lights drifted out of sight but also said that "a couple of them appeared to take off" and that one of them "appeared to drop out of the sky." He did qualify his statements by suggesting that from his perspective, and at night, it was hard to tell but that "one of the two … seemed to take off to the south at a very fast pace." That, of course, was incorrect.

> It seemed that everything pointed to balloons, but there were two witnesses who had a much closer encounter.

One of those interviewed said that if it was a hoax, it was a very good one. He also said that it seemed as if the lights were communicating, whatever that means.

Russo and Rudy found an ad in the local newspaper in which a Ford dealer was exploiting the UFOs for some kind of sale. They headed to the dealership and apparently were unable to convince any of the people there to go on camera, but they left it running, pointing at the ground (or floor) to record the thoughts of the sales force, although it is not clear, and it doesn't seem that anyone bothered to check if this sort of recording is legal in New Jersey. Remember, they just left the camera running, recording the "witnesses" after they were not allowed to film. They were surreptitiously recording the interviews without telling those being interviewed that the tape was running.

> They believed the lights were moving against the wind, but there is no evidence to support this claim.

As the camera runs, Russo and Rudy ask their questions in a showroom filled with alien mock-ups, an ad campaign designed to take advantage of the publicity generated by the news media, who believed that UFO means alien spacecraft, and by the two guys who launched the balloons and flares in an experiment to prove that UFO investigators are not very good and are actually a bunch of charlatans. Those unidentified witnesses in the showroom seemed to believe that the lights couldn't be flares, because they were in a tight pattern, and that flares could fall into someone's backyard, causing fires. They believed the lights were moving against the wind, but there is no evidence to support this claim. Winds aloft are often radically different than the winds at ground level so such a comment, without benefit of the proper weather data, means very little.

The perpetrators of this hoax seem to believe they proved their point because the news media talked of UFOs and some of them made the leap from UFOs to alien spacecraft, but the witnesses were reluctant to do that. Instead, they were fairly accurate with their descriptions of what they had seen. Cindy Hurley talked of lights in the sky and even explained the twinkling on the videotape as they were filming of the lights through the trees, so it looked as if the lights were twinkling. Her descriptions were accurate and correct.

Of the UFO "experts" consulted, Peter Davenport, from his reporting center in Washington, after watching the tape, said that the lights were definitely not aircraft, and, of course, he was correct. On the tape, he offered no speculation of what the lights might be and therefore hadn't made the leap from UFO to alien spacecraft.

Another investigator was Marc D'Antonio, who was alerted by Richard Lang of the Mutual UFO Network (MUFON), who works with one of MUFON's STAR (Strike Team Area Research) teams. These teams are set up to respond quickly to a UFO sighting that might provide some form of physical evidence. D'Antonio reported that he noticed, immediately, that the lights seemed to operate independently and that there was a "flame-based light source.... By flame-based, I mean a flying light created by a Chinese lantern or a flare."

D'Antonio also said, "Whether this event was due to Chinese lanterns, as I thought they could be, or flares, didn't matter actually.... It was clear to me after viewing the video that this is not a UFO but was a man-made hoax."

And, of course, he was dead-bang-on. It was flares, and it was a man-made hoax.

It should be noted that the MUFON STAR team did exactly what it was designed to do. It got investigators into the area who did their science by looking at all the data and in the end, they came to the correct conclusion. The media didn't have much to say about this.

Bill Birnes, of *UFO Hunters* and *UFO* magazine, talked to the witnesses and got some of the same responses. He didn't believe that these lights were flares, as identified almost immediately by the police, and offered that his experts and their experimentation had proven the flare explanation as implausible. He was, of course, wrong on that.

> The majority of the witnesses were accurate in reporting what they saw, and one of them who called 911 even said that it was balloons.

The majority of the witnesses were accurate in reporting what they saw, and one of them who called 911 even said that it was balloons. The only ones to really take this and run with it were Russo and Rudy, who said that their car had been buzzed. And don't forget the people in the showroom, who had some interesting observations but who, in the end, basically reported the lights accurately while misinterpreting what they saw when they were questioned by the two "experimenters."

When those conducting the "experiment" interject themselves into the experiment, they taint it, especially when they add information that is inaccurate and untrue. This is why many experiments are conducted in a double-blind situation, meaning that those gathering the data are not part of the scientific team that will review it. That way they can't influence the outcome and invalidate the research.

In the end, this experiment didn't prove anything about the gullibility of the witnesses or even of the news media. The witnesses explained what they had seen, which was an accurate representation, and the news media, for the most part, didn't go too far overboard. It was reported early on and often that one solution was flares on a balloon, and flares on a balloon is the final answer.

In the end, the solution was suggested early, and if Bill Birnes got it wrong, that is no reason to smear the rest of the UFO research community. Everyone makes mistakes, and if Birnes interviewed these two guys, or more likely, reviewed what they had told the media in what can only be called a bald-faced lie, then anything they said about him is irrelevant. After all, if the objects buzzed a car, then they probably weren't flares and balloons.

This then, is one part of the world of the UFO in the 21st century. Two young men set out to prove something about the reliability of those who see and report UFOs, but ironically, in the end, fail to do so. Instead, this is a case that was solved by UFO researchers and investigators, but there were others that weren't so easily resolved.

March 5, 2004: Mexico

One of the most interesting UFO sightings in the 21st century was made by members of the Mexican military as they performed their routine duties searching for drug smugglers. Major Magdaleno Castanon was the pilot in command and was flying with radar operator Lieutenant German Marin and infrared equipment operator Lieutenant Mario Adrian Vazquez. They were flying a Mexican Air Force Merlin C26A twin-engine aircraft.

At about 5:00 P.M., they detected an unknown aircraft at 10,500 feet over the Cuidad del Carmen. They moved closer to the unknown to record it on their equipment and reported that they had spotted something to their base. Since the mission was to find drug smugglers, it seems that their first impression was that they had found them.

The radar had the objects on the scope, and the infrared cameras were recording it. They wanted visual confirmation but before they could do so, the object, or objects, flew away at high speed. But then, moments later, the object reappeared and seemed to be following the aircraft.

The radar displayed two objects, but none of the crew could see anything. They became alarmed when they seemed to be unable to maneuver in such a way as to get a visual on the UFOs.

According to a press release made by Mexico's Defense Department, the radar operator, Marin, said, "Was I afraid? Yes. A little afraid because we were facing something that had never happened before."

Not long after the two objects appeared on the radar, only a minute or two later, nine more objects were spotted. They seemed to be circling the aircraft, at least according to some of the reports. Even with this, they had no visuals on the UFOs.

Vazquez didn't let that worry him. He said, "I couldn't say what it was ... but I think they were completely real." He also said that there was no way to have altered the images.

This means, simply, that while the flight crew could not see the objects, the infrared equipment could. That equipment was used to find drug smugglers at night. While the crew of the aircraft engaged in finding smugglers might not be able to see them at night, the infrared could. Now it was showing the UFOs at a distance.

Though they were close enough that they should have been able to acquire the targets visually, they still couldn't see them. They

The crew of the Mexican Air Force Merlin C26A.

watched them on the radar, and suddenly, the objects were all gone. At that point, the Merlin returned to base.

The case remained in the hands of the Mexican military until April 20, 2004, when they issued a press release. Because there were multiple chains of evidence from sources that were believed to be credible, there was an explosion of interest in the case. There were the radar images and the lights seen on the infrared film. These could be analyzed and examined for some sort of a solution.

Skeptics offered a number of solutions, but in some cases these solutions were proposed without inside knowledge or special information, or even a glance at the evidence. A Mexican astronomer said that the UFOs were probably meteors. Another said that it was returning space junk, and still another suggested ball lightning, apparently not knowing that ball lightning is quite rare, seen on or near the ground, and doesn't last very long.

On CNN, Michael Shermer suggested that the story kept changing. He said, "Initial reports indicated that the UFOs were only discovered upon later review of the footage after the flight. Subsequent reports stated that the pilots saw the UFOs during the flight, but nothing much was made of it until the infrared footage was later reviewed. Still later reports claimed that the pilots not only saw the UFOs during the flight, but that they chased them, were surrounded by them, but were unable to continue the chase. It was like a fisherman's tale, growing with each retelling."

Just as happened in the twentieth century, the skeptics were blaming the witnesses for changes in the story that were born of the mistakes made by the journalists. Too often, it is assumed that the journalists have the information correct and have reported it accurately, but frequently the journalists have made the errors and then blamed them on the witnesses.

But there is another aspect of this that is new for the twenty-first century, and that is the in-depth investigation that takes place in a search for the answers. James C. Smith, an aerospace engineer in Fairfax, Virginia, wrote a report published to the Internet entitled *The Mexican Air Force UFO Affair: Aliens, Ball Lightning, or Flares*. He wrote, "I would like to suggest something else entirely as the cause. I believe that the UFO lights were no more than oil platform burn-off flares. This idea comes from Captain Alejandro Franz (www.alcione.org)."

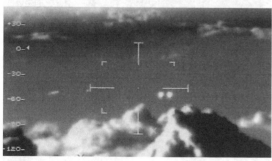

The images were invisible to the unaided eye but were visible to the infrared.

Smith began an examination of all the data that was available to researchers in this century. He wrote at http://www.skeptic.com/eskeptic/04–07–24/:

Starting with Franz' hypothesis, I attempted to confirm its feasibility. To see if the Campeche oil flares were significant light sources, I examined the Defense Meteorological Satellite Program (DMSP) data for the area. DMSP satellites provide daily coverage of the Earth's surface in the infrared and visible light spectrum. I then looked at the publicly accessible averaged year 2000 nighttime light sources database. Camera viewpoint data stored on the video showed that there was a very good correlation with the bright platforms. Unfortunately, the DMSP data did not resolve independent oil flares, so individual UFOs could not be matched.

To see if the UFO images matched existing oil flares, all of the oil platform flares had to be geolocated. Transponder coordinates for some oil platforms were found, but this data source was of limited use, since a transponder was not likely located near the flares themselves. A platform could have multiple flares but only one transponder, or the transponder might be located some distance away on a nonflare part of the platform.

An Internet search revealed a freely available public archive of Landsat satellite datasets for the Campeche area. Datasets at a variety of wavelengths, in particular the short and long infrared, and at very good resolution (15–30 meters), were available. Detailed examination of these datasets allowed each oil platform flare (which clearly saturated the sensor elements) to be located. The data was several years old, so no new flares were included, and it was possible that some flares were inactive during the imaging. Using the flare coordinates, a 3D model of the camera field of view and flares was created, and a very good match with the UFO images was demonstrated.

The best match of existing flares to UFO images occurred with the most complicated light grouping referred to as the "ten UFO" segment. These lights match the flares on three oil platforms (Akal-C with 4 flares, Akal-J with 4 flares, and Nohoch-A with 2 flares)....

(Data used to generate the data is available from U.S. Geological Survey, EROS Data Center, Sioux Falls, SD. Source for this dataset was the Global Land Cover Facility, http://glcf.umiacs.umd.edu.)

When the exact locations of the flares were known, it was possible to determine their distance to the aircraft. The distance to the horizon as viewed from the given 11,500-foot altitude for this video segment is about 130 miles. The distance to the oil platforms ranges from 110 to 120 miles. Thus, the flares were probably viewed directly rather than being mirage images from below the horizon. Of interest is that the 3D model demonstrated that the separation or

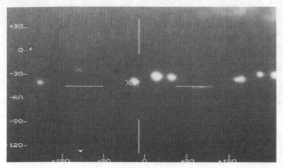

Close up of the infrared images.

splitting of "UFOs" during this segment is a result of one more distant flare seeming to move from behind a closer one due to the motion of the aircraft.

This analysis was created using a great deal of data that was available on the Internet that wouldn't have been available to everyone not all that long ago. Without it, Smith couldn't have made the analysis he did. Facts, figures, and information that would have taken months, if not years, to assemble could be found quickly, improving UFO research and eliminating cases from the UFO listings that had been solved.

But it wasn't just the skeptics who were able to put together a proper analysis of a complicated case. The *International UFO Reporter* for the summer 2004, in a short analysis, agreed with what Smith had learned. According to that source:

> During a visit to Mexico City in May 2004, National Aviation Reporting Center on Anomalous Phenomena [www.narcap.org] Chief Scientist Richard Haines, Executive Director Ted Rowe, and Spanish Language Coordinator Ruben Uriarte were advised of an impending announcement regarding an alleged aviation-related UAP [unidentified aerial phenomenon] case that occurred near Campeche, Mexico, in March 2004....
>
> It is the opinion of NARCAP, based on the evidence available, that the most likely source of this alleged UAP observation was the oil flares from the Cantrell oil fields in the Gulf of Campeche. While we have not posted our findings yet [2004], we are in general agreement with the findings of Captain Alejandro Franz Navarrete, whose documentation can be found at www.alcione.org/FAM/FLIR _CONCLUSION.html.
>
> NARCAP applauds Captain Franz for his attention to detail as well as his objectivity.... It is reasonable to remind all of those who are interested in unidentified aerial phenomena that NARCAP has taken the position that UAP do indeed exist and seem to represent a threat to safe aviation. However, there is nothing to be gained by declaring a case to be anomalous when it clearly is not. Premature comments and declarations, unfound speculations, a lack of understanding of the basics of investigation and inquiry, and a failure to maintain an object image and position have created an untenable position from many of the more vocal elements of the UFO com-

munity, who publicly invested their opinions without a thorough analysis of the material and the conditions surrounding its release.

In other words, the *International UFO Reporter* agreed with skeptical analysis, such as that offered by Smith, because that was where the evidence led them in their research. They weren't going to take a position about the sighting that they could not support, even when that position offered a mundane solution. This case, to their satisfaction, had been solved by the hard and unbiased work of the Mexican officer, Franz, assigned to investigate it.

That, too, is a point in the twenty-first century. Those who accept the idea that some UFO reports are of something that is not easily explained are not going to endorse a case simply because it originally appears to be exciting. Instead, they are going where the evidence leads and reporting those findings as they make them.

July 27, 2009: Minnesota

The incident took place on July 27, 2009, in the Forest Lake area of Minnesota. According to the original reports, an eyewitness said that something fell out of the sky and hit the surface of Lake Sylvan, causing a thirty foot wave as it disappeared.

Several local agencies, including the Forest Lake Fire and Rescue and the Washington County Dive Team, responded. They searched the lake about 165 yards from the shore to a depth of twenty-six feet, but could see little in the murky water.

The county team used side-scanning radar and, according to the sheriff's office, something about the size of a washer or dryer was located at the bottom of the lake. No one suggested that what had been found was either of those appliances, only that the size was similar.

Rich Webb, who was described as a MUFON field investigator and a member of the MUFON STAR Team, left Omaha, Nebraska, and made the trip to Minnesota after someone had left a tip about the crash on the MUFON website. Webb made it clear, though, that no one actually saw something fall; they had just seen the rippling of the water, and it was assumed that something had fallen into the lake. There had been a report to the Forest Lake Police Department that there had been a large swirl of water, the waves rippling outward and the water churning.

Reports indicated that the disturbance lasted from five to seven minutes and that the waves had gone out from the center for about thirty to forty feet, but they were not that high. No debris suggesting any sort of aircraft accident had been found. Only the Washington County Sheriff's Office report of the object found by sonar on the bottom of the lake gave any hint that something had happened. Webb did say that there were two unusual things: there was a centrally circular wave moving outward and a twenty-foot diameter of air bubbles coming from the bottom of the lake.

Richard Lang, another of the MUFON investigators who made the trip to Minnesota, said that based on their findings, they didn't believe a UFO had fallen into the lake.

By October, things had settled down, but there still had been no answers about what caused the disturbance. On September 10, divers found a boulder that weighed about forty pounds; it had a hole drilled in it and a bit of nylon rope attached to it. Clearly this was nothing from a UFO or of extraterrestrial manufacture, but sounds suspiciously like an old-fashioned, homemade boat anchor.

Sheriff Bill Hutton said that they didn't know what had fallen into the lake, though dozens of rescue workers had responded in July. He just said he didn't think it was a meteor or anything from an airplane.

In contrast, Steve McComas, who appeared on Joe Soucheray's KSTP-AM radio's *Garage Logic*, thought it might have been something that fell from an aircraft. He thought it might be "blue ice," which is a mixture of human waste and blue liquid disinfectant that sometimes leaks from the lavatories of commercial airliners.

But then, no one saw anything fall.

Frank Kvidera said that he might have a solution for the rock that had been found. He said that something like forty years earlier, he had been out in a rowboat with a friend who had a rock with a hole drilled through it. They lost their makeshift anchor when the rope broke. Odd as it might seem, this sounds like a plausible answer for that one small part of the mystery.

In the end, there is no explanation for the swirling mass of water. It could have been some sort of natural release of gases trapped at the bottom of the lake, which Webb had sort of suggested earlier. Such things have been reported in the past.

While interesting, there is little reason to suspect any sort of alien or extraterrestrial explanation here. But this is also an example of some of the UFO sightings reported in the 21st century. There are many more reports of things falling from the sky, and there are those who equate that with alien visitation. In very few of the cases is that the final result, but sometimes things are found that suggest an extraterrestrial origin.

November 7, 2012: Samalayuca, Mexico

UFO research in the twenty-first century can be quite different than it was in the last century. Before the Internet, before easy access to newspaper files, it was often necessary to actually visit their morgues, which were the clipping files of the material that appeared in the newspaper, look through the huge, bound books that some newspapers retained, or use microfilm records at the newspaper office or in libraries' files. Sometimes a telephone call would result in someone at the newspaper searching out the material, if a date was known, and sometimes, it just resulted in a nasty comment from the newspaper reporter, who would then hang up.

A case in point is the October 11, 1947, report of a crash into the Samalayuca area of Mexico. A newspaper clipping said:

FLAMING MYSTERY STARTLES TEXANS, CROSSES BORDER

El Paso, Tex., Oct. 12—(AP) An unidentified flaming object soared over the Texas-Mexico border today, apparently smashing into the Samalayuca mountains of Mexico with a loud explosion and billows of smoke.

The approximate impact area was estimated to be less than 10 miles from the point where a V-2 rocket off its track crashed south of Juarez May 20.

The public relations officer at the White Sands proving grounds where the V-2 rockets have been launched, said none of the missiles had been fired since Oct. 9.

Maj. Gen. John L. Homer, Fort Bliss [near El Paso] commander and military official at air fields and other installations in the southwest, said that no guided missiles had been fired today, and no rocket planes were missing from the fields in the area.

At least four persons saw the fiery object darting through the skies "with the speed of a falling star" at approximately 9:30 A.M.

This case is number 93 in the Project Blue Book files and provides very little information about it. The index and the project card list it as multiple witnesses and calls the case "solved" as an "astro," meaning a meteor.

Yes, it sounds like a meteor. The witness's descriptions of it moving "with the speed of a falling star," the loud explosions, and the billows of smoke are all characteristics of a bolide, that is, a very bright meteor.

However, there is a teletype message in the file that came from "Helmick CO AAFLD

A fireball that some thought was a meteor shot over Texas and into Mexico, apparently crashing into the desert region of Samalayuca.

[commanding officer, army airfield] Alamogordo on Oct. 15" and was sent to the Commanding General, AMC [air mobility command] at Wright Field in Dayton that suggests otherwise. It said that the Mexican government in Mexico City had reported the "unidentified flaming object that landed about 35 miles from Juarez, Mexico [across the border from El Paso], was definitely a rocket to have been launched from some Texas base."

There is also a report from an officer in charge of the Juarez military garrison, who claimed the false report of a rocket crash came from the Mexican Department of War. He said they were continuing their search for whatever had hit, but that implies they had not found any wreckage.

The file contains another newspaper clipping that provides additional information, an official letter dated October 13, 1947, to "D/I Army Intelligence," a letter from the Military Attaché in Mexico City dated October 16, an unclassified teletype dated October 21 and signed by Colonel Millard Lewis, another signed by Lt. Col. Douglass Eiseman dated October 24, and a diary page for General Hoyt S. Vandenberg. These documents are on the Internet at the Project 1947 historical group website.

The Internet, then, provided additional information. When a report on the case was posted to a blog (www.kevinrandle.blogspot.com), several others became interested in the case. They were able to find additional information, much of it by accessing other parts of the Internet. For example:

Zanesville, Ohio

Monday, 13 October, 1947

page 1

Mexicans Report Bomb Explosion Near Border

EL PASO, Tex., Oct. 12—(AP) An unidentified flaming object soared over the Texas-Mexico border today, apparently smashing into the Samalayuca mountains of Mexico with a loud explosion and billows of smoke.

The approximate impact area was estimated to be less than 10 miles from the point where a V-2 rocket, off its track, crashed south of Juarez on May 29.

The public relations officer at the White Sands proving ground, where the V-2 rockets have been launched, said none of the missiles had been fired since Oct. 9.

Maj. Gen. John L. Homer, Fort Bliss commander and military official at air fields and other installations in the southwest, said that no guided missiles had been fired today, and no rocket planes were missing from fields in the area.

At least four persons saw the fiery object darting through the skies "with the speed of a falling star" at approximately 9:30 A.M. Mexican time (8:30 A.M. MST [Mountain Standard Time])) and many people in the Fabens, Tex., area, 28 miles east of El Paso on the Mexican border, heard the explosion of the body when it struck.

Two persons on the highway between El Paso and Fabens reported seeing an unaccounted-for billow of smoke in the Zamalayuca [sic] mountains about the time that the explosion was heard.

Sabas Aranda, a reserve captain in the Mexican army, was the first to report the incident. Captain Aranda, unable to reach the Juarez military garrison by telephone, went to the U.S. Customs house, four miles southeast of Fabens, and reported the incident to J. C. Bunnell, U.S. Customs inspector.

A posting on the blog from another newspaper of the time shows that the story had gone over a news wire and someone had added notes or details to the story.

This V-2 Rocket is on display at the Smithsonian National Air and Space Museum. One like it reportedly went down in the Samalayuca mountains in 1947.

Mystery U.S. missile strikes in the Mexican hills

El Paso, Texas, Oct. 12 (AP) An unidentified object in flames rose over the Texas-Mexico border today, apparently impacting Zamaleyuca Mountains (sic) in Mexico, with a loud explosion and column smoke.

The impact area is estimated to be approximately less than 10 miles from the point where a V-2 rocket, out of its path, crashed south of Juarez on May 29.

The public relations officer at the White Sands Proving Ground, where the rockets were launched, said none of the missiles had been fired from October 9.

No rocket planes lost.

Major General John L. Homer, commander of Fort Bliss and military official in the fields of air and other facilities in the Southwest, said no guided missile had been launched today....

At least four persons saw the fiery object darting through the skies "with the speed of a falling star" at approximately 9:30 o'clock this morning and many people in the Fabens area, 28 miles east of El Paso on the Mexican border heard the explosion of the body with [sic] it struck.

Two people on the road between El Paso and Fabens reported seeing smoke in the mountains of Samalayuca while the explosion was heard.

There was a terrible noise.

Sabas Aranda, a reserve captain in the Mexican Army, was the first to report the incident. Captain Aranda, unable to telephone the military garrison of Ciudad Juarez, went to the office of the U.S., four miles southeast of Fabens, and reported the incident to J. C. Bunnell, U.S. Customs inspector.

J. W. Hooten, editor of the El Paso Times, said he telephoned Sheriff Alan Bunnell Falby here and that the mayor and other officials of Guadalupe, Mexico, across the border from Fabens, had reported seeing the object, about five meters long and three meters in diameter, coming to town traveling about 30 feet above the ground and exploding with a terrible noise, and heavy smoke was still in the impact zone three hours later.

Hooten said Guadalupe officials stated that the bomb came from the direction of the United States.

Captain Aranda said the object moved from east to west, indicating that it came from the direction of the United States.

Harold Wilkins, who wrote about UFOs in the early 1950s, including the book *Flying Saucers on the Attack*, said:

Some witnesses compared the importance of the UFO event to seeing Halley's Comet in 1910.

Down south, in the territory of Mexico, southeast of El Paso, on October 10, 1947, a mysterious flaming object exploded in the sky and left behind him what he described as a "vast cloud of smoke." Whether this was a fireball meteor of unusual size cannot be said, but it is very remarkable that seven hours before this mysterious explosion in the sky over Mexico, five west-coast residents reported to the *San Diego Tribune–Sun* that they had seen the biggest celestial thing from Halley's comet....

This referred to a report of some sort of a Saturn-shaped object that was claimed to be as large as a four-motor aircraft. This sighting had no relevance to that in Mexico, other than that it happened just hours prior to the crash in Mexico.

Chris Perridas, again writing on Kevin Randle's blog, provided additional information from a variety of other newspapers:

El Paso Herald Post, October 14, 1947

Biggs Field Planes Join Hunt for Trace of "Flaming Object"

Two Biggs Field planes today joined the search for a "flaming object" that reportedly fell to Mexico south of Fabens Sunday.

Permission for the search was obtained from 12th Air Force headquarters at March Field, Calif.

Brig. Gen. Enrique Diaz Gonzales, commander of the Juarez military garrison, last night asked that U.S. Army planes aid in the search.

The Air Rescue Services plane pilots were prepared to drop smoke bombs to direct Mexican cavalrymen to likely spots.

Six horsemen were searching the area today.

A jeep-borne party abandoned a search for the object yesterday when the jeep balked at climbing sandhills southwest of Cazeta, a tiny Mexican village opposite Fabens.

One Man Saw Missile

The party, headed by General Diaz Gonzalez, followed a trail for nearly a mile into the desert, but found no trace of the mystery missile.

General Gonzalez' party could find only one man who said he actually saw a strange object flash across the sky Sunday at 8:30 A.M. He is Sabas Aranda, farmer, of Cazeta.

Four others told the general they heard explosions about that time in the general direction of Arroyo Cotilloze, between Cazeta and Samalayuca. They said the explosions must have occurred about 10 miles south of the border.

The horsemen, at General Diaz Gonzalez' direction, will search the Arroyo Cotilloze area.

Seen at Caballo Dam

Farmer Aranda's report to U.S. Customs officers at Fabens, that he saw a strange blue object go over his farm, also caused Ft. Bliss officials to investigate.

A Las Cruces man, who declined to permit use of his name, reported today that he and a friend were hunting at Caballo Dam between Las Cruces and Hot Springs Sunday, and he glanced to the southeast about 8:30 in time to see a fiery ball "about the shape and color of an orange" streak across the lower part of the sky, moving from east to west.

It had a tail of black smoke and disappeared in a moment below the crest of mountains between the dam and El Paso.

So there was a great deal of information about the case out in various newspapers of the time, though they didn't have a solution for what had fallen. Perridas provided one more bit of information:

> The Chicago meeting of the section on astronomy of the A.A.A.S. [American Association for the Advancement of Science]
> Author: Wylie, C. C.
> *Popular Astronomy*, Vol. 56, p.217
> "Contributions of the Meteoritical Society"
> (Known formerly as The Society for Research on Meteorites)
> Edited by Frederick C. Leonard, Department of Astronomy, University of California, Los Angeles
>
> *A Proposed Sky Patrol by the Meteoritical Society*
> C. C. Wylie, Director of the Meteor Section
> State University of Iowa, Iowa City
>
> On page 218 it said, "… The flaming object which crashed near the Texas-Mexico border on October 12th of this year (1947) was reported by Mexicans as a V-2 bomb, but investigation by a member of the Meteoritical Society showed that it was a meteor."

What is worth noting is that this event, though happening in 1947, was researched today through resources that were unavailable at the time it happened. The Project Blue Book files have been available in the public arena since 1976, but were not available online until recently. Now practically everything about Project Blue Book is available for scrutiny, and researchers can find the answers in minutes rather than days, weeks, or, sometimes, months.

Sightings from the Twenty-first Century

The following list of raw sighting information is compiled from a variety of sources, including Peter Davenport's National UFO Reporting Center at http://www.nuforc.org/pdbio.html, Fran Ridge's National Investigations Committee on Aerial Phenomena (NICAP) site at http://www.nicap.org/, the Center for UFO Studies and the *International UFO Reporter*, the Mutual UFO Network and the *MUFON UFO Journal*, Albert Rosales at his website http://www

.ufoinfo.com/humanoid/, and a variety of newspapers, magazines, websites, and other sources of information.

While many of these cases were reported in short sentences, these are the best of the cases to have been reported to these organizations and databases. The following provides a glimpse into how the data are collected today, and it provides enough information that if someone in one of the locations mentioned wished to do a follow-up investigation, it is possible. Not all of these will result in a case that is unidentified, and I suspect that many, upon additional work, will be solved, and this information might be of assistance to some.

Sightings: 2003

Jan. 2, 2003—At 5:20 P.M. PST, two black, triangular craft flew above San Jose, California, at an altitude estimated to be above 30,000 feet. They hovered, then moved very slowly toward the east, then reversed direction moving slowly toward the west. Two hours later a huge, cigar-shaped flying object with three to five blindingly bright, horizontal lights flew low overhead in Los Angeles, California.

Jan. 4, 2003—In Fulton, Missouri, Bob Simon, age twenty-five, awoke at 3:00 A.M. while he was being dragged toward the bedroom window by an unknown intruder. He looked up to see a very tall, thin humanoid with red eyes, no mouth, and a gray body. It had huge hands with very long fingers. Recovering his senses, Simon struggled with the alien and managed to grab a small knife next to his bed and stab at the alien. The alien seemed to have been hurt and relaxed his grip on Simon. There was a sudden blast of bright light, and the creature vanished. Simon claimed to have scratch marks on his body.

Jan. 5, 2003—At 1:13 A.M., a witness in Plain Dealing, Louisiana, reported several multicolored lights maneuvering in the sky under the cloud cover. They made no sound and were red, blue, and green in color. They moved up, down, and side to side and stopped to hover at times but made no fast movements. The sighting lasted 54 minutes.

Jan. 6, 2003—The witness' car headlights and engine died when an ovoid UFO approached the car in Moundville, Alabama, at 4:00 A.M. Two egg-shaped objects were later seen moving in a Z pattern in the sky.

Jan. 8, 2003—At 3:30 P.M., a reflective, metallic craft was sighted high in the sky over the mountains in Santa Barbara, California, and at 10:00 P.M. in Union City, California, a UFO was seen entering a triangular-shaped light. The light then pinched shut and vanished.

Jan. 16, 2003—Several interesting cases occurred on this day. At 1:34 A.M. EST in Westchester County, New York, a witness in Portchester sighted a large, dark object in the night sky with a watery reflection. It looked to be cylindrical in shape. At 4:30 P.M. in Wildrose, North Dakota, a man called to report that he saw a gray, triangular UFO in the sky that was making a buzzing or humming noise. He reported that he got to within an eighth of a mile of the object before it flew away.

Jan. 22, 2003—The witness had just left work and was driving home when he reached a place by a small lake in Prospect, Connecticut, at 10:03 P.M. He noticed someone walking along the road, so he flashed on his high beams. He then saw the figure walk out from the side of the road, stop in the center for a second, then continue across. The figure was grayish in color and it was walking on two legs, but it ambulated like an ape walks, swaying as it walked erect. The feet were small, with brownish-black areas on the side. When it reached the other side it stopped and looked at the witness, waving its skinny arms. Lights appeared behind it. The man described the creature as around six feet tall, with large, foot-long pointy ears. The face had dark black eyes and no apparent nose. Although the weather was cold, the witness did not see any condensed breath come from its small mouth. The mouth had a red-silver strip on top. As the witness drove by, he looked back to see the creature still standing by the road, and the woods behind the creature suddenly lit up like day.

> "I was almost abducted, along with my friends; I think we all feared for our [lives]."

Jan. 24, 2003—At 6:13 P.M., a black, equilateral triangle with three glowing, white dome lights on the tips of its apexes, plus a small, red blinking light and a small, constant red light, was sighted over Kingston, Ontario, by a woman. It flew just above the tree line and passed silently, directly over her car.

Feb. 11, 2003—A failed alien abduction attempt was alleged in a report filed with the National UFO Reporting Center: "I was almost abducted, along with my friends; I think we all feared for our [lives]." The experience reportedly occurred at 12:13 A.M. in Merrillville, Indiana.

Feb. 13, 2003—A police crime scene technician in Seattle, Washington, was driving home from a crime scene at 2:30 A.M. when it started to rain. His car suddenly began making weird noises and the car radio turned on automatically, scanning through numerous stations at a rate of one a second. Lights inside and outside the car were also flashing. When he looked up he saw a huge, triangular-shaped object above the car. In a few seconds, blinding, blue lights distracted the witness. The next thing he remembered, all action suddenly stopped, and his car was parked on the side of the road with everything switched off. When he looked at his watch, it was 3:03 A.M. He had lost track of 33 minutes of time. He turned his car engine on and drove back to his office.

Feb. 16, 2003—At 11:00 P.M., a huge, "jet-black," triangular UFO with lights came slowly toward a witness driving on 109th Avenue NE in suburban

Juanita, Washington. He pulled his truck to the side of highway and watched the craft for thirty seconds. It made no sound, and it had a yellow searchlight on the front apex that moved its beam of light and then went out.

Mar. 8, 2003—A silent "flying wing" was seen by a couple leaving their home in Greenbelt, Maryland, at 8:15 P.M. It flew below the clouds at an estimated 600 to 1,200 feet altitude. It had "pure white," circular lights on the wingtips and small, red lights in the middle that brightened and dimmed.

Mar. 14, 2003—While pulling his car into the parking lot of the Behavioral Health Services Building in Winfield, Illinois, the witness noticed three flashing objects coming down in the sky in front of the car. He next noticed more dropping out of the sky until there were several. Most had red and white, flashing lights, with no visible wings, and did not make a sound. Some had blue and aqua lights. Some were triangular, some cigar-shaped, and some were like a small box with four perpendicular lights. The main witness brought several people out from the building, and they all watched the spectacle together. Also during the sighting, a bona fide helicopter with multicolored lights flew over. A few of these objects left a contrail. The witness spent seven years in the Air Force and is confident that these were not conventional aircraft. He called 911, and a Winfield police officer responded and watched them with him. The lit objects also discharged balls of light every once in a while that also flew around.

Apr. 4, 2003—At 11:38 P.M. in Coral Springs, Florida, a man saw a dark figure outside his window and at first thought it was a man. It slightly resembled a naked man standing in the middle of the road, but after about thirty seconds the figure walked away. As it went behind some trees the witness thought he would go out to see who it was, but then a triangular UFO appeared, encased in an eerie glow with three lights, one in each corner. The craft then zoomed up into the sky, leaving a trail of white fog behind.

Apr. 21, 2003—An employee of a local manufacturing plant in Concord, North Carolina, had just finished his shift at 8:00 P.M. and had stepped out onto a dock behind a large stack of pallets to have a smoke. He then had the feeling of being watched, and he whirled around expecting to see a coworker. Instead he saw a large, purple light emanating from a teardrop-shaped craft with a round bottom, hovering nearby. The craft had a concave windshield, and behind the windshield he could see two glowing lights or eyes. They moved independently from one another. Terrified, the witness ran but was unable to scream, so he pointed out the object to a forklift operator. Next, a beam of white light shot out of the UFO and struck the forklift. Immediately, the electrical system of the vehicle shut down, and the operator began screaming. The witness's next memory was of sitting in the plant manager's office. Someone was giving him oxygen and wiping his forehead with a cool cloth.

May 1, 2003—A married couple driving in West Seattle, Washington, sighted a silent, triangular object moving across the sky at 10:00 P.M. It had a dim, orange light at each apex, and the lights seemed striped rather than solid. It flew off to the northwest. When the couple got home, they noticed that their dog was trembling and acting very lethargic.

May 2, 2003—Three young women were returning from a bonfire in the Illinois countryside and had just finished putting away equipment and chairs. As they got back into their van, at around 3:30 A.M., one of them saw a figure standing a short distance off the driveway by a house. She pointed it out to the other two. Somewhat spooked, they drove back toward town. They described the figure as manlike, wearing light-colored or white clothing. They headed over to the site of the bonfire, the embers of which were still glowing. Suddenly, in the glare of their van's headlights, they all saw two separate rows of creatures, with perhaps fifteen figures in each row. They were about three or four feet tall and were standing only fifteen feet away from them, directly in front of the van. One of the women wrote that they had "Christmas light heads" that were connected to their body, but she couldn't see how. Their arms were up in the air, but she couldn't see any hands. They appeared to be sticklike and dark gray or brown in color. They did not move but stood perfectly still. The two girls riding as passengers began to scream for the driver to leave the area immediately. Terrified, they drove away and continued to drive around for the next two hours before they had enough courage to return to their homes.

> Their arms were up in the air, but she couldn't see any hands. They appeared to be sticklike and dark gray or brown in color.

May 3, 2003—At 3:30 A.M., a man was sitting on his back porch in North Richland Hills, Texas, looking out at the horse pasture behind his home. The pasture held several horses, but he could not see them because they were at the other end of the field. He heard what sounded like the horses kicking a metal sheet and squealing loudly. He also heard dogs barking in the distance. Just as he strained to look over to the horse shed, everything became completely quiet. The witness started to feel scared by the eerie silence, and as he stepped off his porch, he started to hear a low, whirring sound. He next saw a light beam flash on the ground in the middle of the pasture. The source was a black craft, hovering about one hundred feet above the ground. It was shooting flashes of light at the ground from a pod on the right end of the craft. The craft had a multicolored mist or hot-looking gas on the bottom of it, and on the left side was what looked like a red, rectangular window. Inside he could see movement, but at that moment he began to feel sick. The craft appeared to be about 50 feet long, with a dull, blue light on the top. After five minutes, the whirring sound faded and the craft hovered silently for another two seconds before it zipped straight up and out of sight without a sound. He then noticed that the electrical power seemed to be off in the neighborhood.

A Texas man saw a UFO flying above pasture land near Richland Hills.

May 8, 2003—A female hospital worker, driving home from work at 12:45 A.M., saw a low-hovering, metallic-looking UFO that was as big as a house along Highway 13, south of Highway 2 in Clinton, Missouri. Its bottom perimeter looked octagonal, and it had four small, yellow lights, with a large, red light in the middle. It directed a beam of light down to ground; the UFO swayed, and then blinked out. It made no sound.

May 11, 2003—A California Highway Patrol officer saw a metallic disc in the morning sky over the freeway in Goleta, California, at 9:20 A.M. It was circular in appearance and tumbling "end over end." At about the same time a shiny, thin, metallic disc was seen moving over the beach at Laguna Niguel, California, toward the southwest. It soared, drifted slowly, then swooped down like a bird in a thermal air current. It had "turbine blades" on the underside. It moved off to the northwest in the general direction of Vandenberg AFB.

May 27, 2003—A cigar-shaped UFO hovered low near a mountain near Phoenix, Arizona, at 10:10 P.M. It had pinpoint lights along its side that flickered sometimes. It had a large, red light at each end and was soundless. It suddenly took off so fast vertically that it seemed like it almost disappeared.

May 28, 2003—A fast-moving, "shimmering shadow," with orange, triangular leading edges, moved through the sky over Boise, Idaho, at 11:00 P.M.

It shimmered as if emitting a great deal of heat. It flew in a straight line and crossed the sky in eight to ten seconds without making a sound.

May 29, 2003—An early-morning jogger saw a cross-shaped object with three big lights that was hovering at a low altitude over Watertown Square in Watertown, Massachusetts. It was estimated to be no more than 30 stories above the ground when it was seen at 4:45 A.M. It emitted beams of light that filtered through the fog and mist. It changed direction and then silently lifted away.

Jun. 2, 2003—At three o'clock in the morning, the witness awoke in West Chester, Ohio, to a beeping sound coming from a UPS (universal power supply) because the power had gone out. There was a smell of ozone and no sound at all. The witness then saw an oval-shaped craft with two oval-shaped lights. The bottom of the craft was a deep blue color.

Jun. 30, 2003—At around 9:00 P.M. in New Brighton, Pennsylvania, a black. triangular-shaped object surrounded by silver spheres was sighted moving to the south toward Pittsburgh.

Jul. 12, 2003—The witness and her mother were driving home down a road in Ashland, Kentucky, at around 10:00 P.M. when they saw a moving light in the sky. They first assumed it was a plane, but then it started moving faster. It sped up to an unbelievable speed and shot back and forth between two stars, then stopped as if it had spotted them. At this point, their car stopped running. The UFO had disappeared, but they had a feeling it was still present, watching them. It reappeared, this time closer. They next saw twenty to thirty lights zooming across the sky. These all stopped at the same star in the sky as the first one, and they all vanished in a bright flash. The witnesses heard no sound during any of this. The daughter reports that she then fainted, but her mother continued to watch. The mother reported the light got bigger and brighter, and in the midst of the light, she claims to have seen dark figures carrying strange instruments. When the daughter woke up, the car was on the side of the road about twenty feet from where it had been. About half an hour had passed, but it seemed to have been much longer. Her mother was now passed out and outside of the car. She appeared unharmed, but she did have a scar on the back of her neck. The mother convinced herself that the mark was from the back of the car door when she "fell" out of the car. For subsequent nights, the pair has seen strange lights in the sky at night, dashing across the sky.

> They next saw twenty to thirty lights zooming across the sky. These all stopped at the same star in the sky as the first one, and they all vanished in a bright flash.

Jul. 18, 2003—In Vancouver, Washington, a businessman and a retired Navy man observed three rectangular objects, the size of small planes, that appeared overhead as shadows in the sky at 10:40 P.M. They were slightly illuminated but not bright. The objects zigzagged and crisscrossed into the distance.

Aug. 13, 2003—A black, boomerang-shaped object passed low and fast over Napoleonville in southern Louisiana at 7:25 P.M. It made no sound as it flew. The sighting was brief, lasting about six seconds.

Aug. 17, 2003—Witnesses in Federal Way, Washington, reported seeing six green, glowing, egg-shaped objects overhead at 12:30 A.M., flying to the east, followed by a flashing, blue, saucer-shaped object.

Aug. 31, 2003—At 10:30 P.M., a white, flying ball of light, too large to be a plane or satellite, flew in a zigzag pattern, disappeared, and reappeared in the sky over Ryan, Iowa. It made no sound and was visible for about five to ten seconds.

Oct. 25, 2003—At two o'clock in the morning, a witness reported seeing two disc-shaped objects flying overhead in Springfield, Illinois. The objects seemed to be "chasing each other and just playing around."

Dec. 16, 2003—A married couple saw a "flying saucer" or disc-shaped object over their backyard in Valencia, Kern County, California, at about 10:00 P.M. It was low, hovering above the ground no higher than 75 feet, and was above them for about 35 seconds.

Dec. 30, 2003—A hovering object with a circle of lights was seen in a field in Tatum, New Mexico, at around 9:30 P.M. It shot straight up and stopped twice in the sky, then the lights went out and the object vanished. The sighting lasted 45 seconds.

Sightings: 2004

Feb. 8, 2004—At 6:25 P.M. EST, a silent UFO with one light, no running lights or tail light, and no vapor trail passed over a home in Chester County, South Carolina. As it flew over, dogs in the neighborhood were barking loudly. At 5:45 P.M. CST or about twenty minutes later, a small, reddish, spherical object that flashed red at varying intensities and intervals was sighted over Houston, Texas. It seemed to wobble laterally as it flew.

Feb. 16, 2004—At 8:30 P.M., a large, silent, fast-moving, oval-shaped object with light moved back and forth in the sky over a residential neighborhood in Amityville, New York, on Long Island.

Mar. 12, 2004—At four A.M., Mr. M. N. was driving east on Wellington Street in Sault Sainte Marie, Ontario, at the southeastern end of Lake Superior, and as he came to the center city (known to locals as Soo, Canada), he noticed a vertical beam of light in the early morning sky from the top of a hill to the north. He stopped his vehicle at a cross street and looked all the way to the end of the street, about seven blocks away, where the street ends at the base of the hill and has a metal stairwell leading to McDonald Avenue. His eyes focused on a little, dark figure standing very still. This caught his curiosity, so he slowly drove toward it. It then started moving from side to side, using fluid movements as if it was floating in the air. It moved as if confused, or afraid, and Mr. M.N. didn't know what to do. As he got closer, the figure's appearance seemed to have metamorphosed into a transparent, shadowlike entity that very swiftly flew up the stairs. To his astonishment, the beam of light that he had seen in the distant sky a few minutes before was now at the top of the hill, only 100 feet away. With his heart racing, he drove as fast as he could eastward along the base of the hill until he came to the nearest street that climbed the hill and drove up McDonald Avenue to see what was happening. He arrived at the top of the hill, only to find three circle-shaped burn markings on the pavement of the street. About ten seconds later, he heard a weird kind of gunshot sound. When he looked up to the sky, he saw a bright light shooting up into the stars. As he watched the spectacle, a peaceful feeling came over him, and he felt as if every hair on his body was standing on end. The feeling of well-being felt like it lasted only a brief 30 seconds, but when he looked again at his watch, it was at least forty minutes later.

Mar. 21, 2004—Two young women in Kingfisher, Oklahoma, both college students, witnessed two very bright lights in the night sky at 7:26 P.M. The lights suddenly descended and an object, triangular in shape, appeared to land. It was brightly lit with what looked like halogen-type lights and was clear or hollow in the center. Other cars stopped to park along the highway to look at it.

Mar. 25, 2004—At around 7:00 P.M., the crew of a commercial airliner flying near Omaha, Nebraska, reported seeing four disc-shaped objects, which remained visible ahead of the aircraft for between ten and fifteen minutes. The objects did not appear on FAA radar at any time during the entire sighting. The objects had many lights and flew off to the west, where they were lost from view.

Apr. 5, 2004—At 11:00 A.M., a witness in Newport, Tennessee, spotted a bizarre flying creature resembling an arrowhead flying backward, with what looked like a head or knob on the front. It didn't look mechanical; it was more like some kind of animal. It did not have extended wings like a bird but seemed to have some stubby wings which may have been part of the body, like some type of bat. They protruded out near the end and tapered back to a point at the rear. The creature appeared to be around three feet long and a little over two feet wide. It was moving very fast in a straight line at an altitude of approximately 150 feet. The witness did not see any method of propulsion, such as wing movement. It just seemed to be gliding, but at a high speed. It maintained a level flight path moving westward, where the witness eventually lost sight of it. It was light brown in color along the sides of the wings, with a dark body color, possibly dark brown or black.

Apr. 15, 2004—A woman awoke at around 6:00 A.M. and walked to her screened bedroom window in Orlando, Florida. She saw a small, oval, slightly glowing object hovering just above the ground, low outside the window. The object was about twelve inches in diameter . A cat noticed the object and attempted to stalk it, whereupon it made a quick zigzag maneuver and suddenly streaked away in a nearly instantaneous acceleration.

May 14, 2004—A massive, triangular-shaped object crossed the sky from south to north at 2:30 A.M. in Scappoose, Oregon. It was dark without lights but blocked the backdrop of stars as it flew over.

May 17, 2004—A woman was cleaning house in Culloden, West Virginia, on this evening when she spotted a black figure run

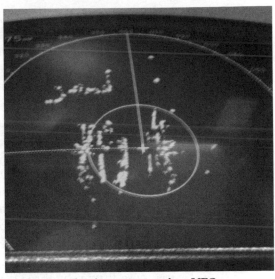

A commercial airline crew saw four UFOs near Omaha, but they didn't appear on FAA radar.

past her window. She looked outside and could not see anyone. She resumed her cleaning, but again saw another figure run by the window, this one not as dark as the first. Ten minutes later, she was in the kitchen when she was blinded by a bright flash of light that came in through both of her back windows. She then closed her curtains. The next day her dogs were acting strangely, and there was a local power outage in the area.

May 17, 2004—At 11:30 P.M. a saucer-shaped object, flickering green and blue lights and only about thirty feet in the air, was reported by a witness in Vicksburg, Michigan. There was a big, bright flash that blinded the witness for thirty seconds, and when his sight recovered, the UFO was gone.

Jun. 12, 2004—In Torrance, California, at 3:03 P.M., a high-altitude, metallic, disc-shaped object was watched for seven minutes. It reflected sunlight at times as it moved first west, then to the northwest.

Jul. 17, 2004—At 3:00 A.M., a triangular craft was seen hovering over I-70 in Lewisburg, Ohio. At 10:45 P.M., a white, circular object came out of nowhere in Portsmouth, Ohio, and dropped above a tree. It hovered at fifty feet altitude, emitting four light beams that were directed onto the street below. It made no sound. There were two witnesses, and the close encounter lasted an hour.

Jul. 26, 2004—During a power failure in Kerman, California, that occurred at 1:20 A.M., Ms. E. B. was looking for a flashlight when the power came back on. Earlier that night, around 12:30 A.M., she had seen an unusual light in the sky and now went out to look in the sky where she had seen it.

What she saw was a glowing, silvery, manlike figure that was flying above the neighborhood at a height of twenty to twenty-five meters. The figure flew at a reasonably fast pace. The moment she saw it, she screamed and ran back inside, locking the door behind her, but she continued to watch it through a window. The figure went behind some trees and when it emerged on the other side, it shot off toward the north at the speed of a rocket.

Jul. 27, 2004—A truck driver driving south on I-25 in New Mexico reported that the night sky was pitch black, with no moon nor even cloud cover visible. At 1:30 A.M., driving at 63 mph he noticed a bright blue light about a half mile ahead on the exit ramp for southbound Exit 138. It appeared to be like a blue laser, similar to the light some people use on the hoods of their cars. When he got closer to the ramp, he saw two figures approximately three to four feet tall. Each was either holding a blue light or was wearing a blue head lamp. He couldn't tell for sure. The figures appeared to be looking to the north and south, and they looked at his truck as he drove by. They appeared to be wearing loose-fitting, bright silver outfits, similar to HAZMAT suits. He couldn't tell if they were wearing helmets. The terrain was very flat, and he did not see any vehicles in the area. He was sure that he would have seen any vehicle that they could have come from. He slowed to turn around, but the nearest exit was another 30 miles down the highway, so he decided not to go back.

The witness in the 2004 New Mexico event said that the aliens appeared to be wearing something similar to this HAZMAT suit.

Jul. 27, 2004—While driving home from a dinner party at two o'clock in the morning, a married couple in Ashland, Massachusetts, observed a round, silver, disc-shaped object about thirty feet in diameter that had landed in an open field off of Chestnut Street. They both got out of their car and approached the disc, and when they got close enough they both touched the craft. It was very cold to the touch, and it was glowing red to blue. They were able to see inside the craft through a small window and saw three small beings. All appeared to be sleeping or meditating; they did not respond to the witnesses' voices. As the couple began to walk around the craft, it began to rise up into the air and eventually flew off without making any sound at all.

Aug. 10, 20 04—A lit object, circular in shape, was sighted at 2:26 A.M. in Pottstown, Pennsylvania. It shot straight up into the sky and made the TV "go haywire." The sighting lasted about ten seconds.

Aug. 11, 2004—At 9:30 P.M., a triangular-shaped object hovered over the road briefly in Guilderland, Albany County, New York. It had white lights at the points.

Aug. 20, 2004—Over Staten Island, New York, four hazy, white objects traveled in a circle at 10:00 P.M. and came together about a dozen times into a center point, "like they were playing a game."

> What she saw was a glowing, silvery, manlike figure that was flying above the neighborhood at a height of twenty to twenty-five meters.

Oct. 2, 2004—A man was driving home at 5:30 A.M. in rural Tennessee when he noticed what first appeared to be a fire on a nearby ridge. As he drove, he got closer and realized that it was not a fire at all but a series of three reddish-orange lights affixed to the bottom of a huge, triangular craft. He neared an intersection and got out of his car to watch this metallic craft as it approached from the north and moved directly toward him. He became fearful and started to run from his car, but realized that there was nowhere to run. As the giant object passed overhead, it blocked out all the stars, and he estimated its size to be some 300 feet in length. The bottom of the craft was illuminated from three flamelike, symmetrical appendages, and there was a ribbed structure running across the bottom of the object. As it passed directly overhead, he felt an energy that reverberated through his body. He stated that he felt many sensations all at once but could find no description for what he actually felt. The object also made a pulsating or drumming noise, which also passed throughout his body. After the object passed him, it suddenly turned west and moved behind some nearby hills. The witness reported a metallic taste in his mouth and a nosebleed. Later he found that his face and back were slightly sunburned and his hair was falling out, and he also felt lethargic. He realized later that he had experienced fifteen minutes of missing time.

Nov. 25, 2004—A triangular UFO with red and blue lights was sighted flying over Ottumwa, Iowa, at 5:00 A.M. The lights appeared to be rotating in a clockwise pattern. The object was completely silent as it flew.

Nov. 27, 2004—A huge, disc-shaped object accompanied by other smaller craft came over the witness' apartment building in Gardena, California, at around one o'clock in the morning. It seemed to be close and could change direction and speed in the blink of an eye. It had lights and was very quiet, making no noise at all. The sighting lasted 30 minutes.

Dec. 4, 2004—Orange flashes in the sky in Burlington, Indiana, were followed by the appearance of several objects at 8:30 P.M. One object that flew over the witness was triangular in shape, with three red, illuminated areas, like tips. The outer points were brightest, fading into black at the center. The color was like a piece of red-hot metal.

Dec. 5, 2004—Driving west on I-88 in Bainbridge, Chenango County, New York, a witness spotted a disc-shaped object hovering above a field at 9:35 P.M. It was silver-gray in color, with blinking, yellowish-orange lights evenly spaced all the way around it. It was estimated to be about eight stories above the ground.

Sightings: 2005

Jan. 31, 2005—At ten o'clock at night, a triangular object hovered over a frozen pond in Columbia City, Indiana, for three minutes and melted the ice. On the same night in Wood River, Nebraska, a bright, oval-shaped object allegedly picked up a cow.

Feb. 21, 2005—A man and his son spotted a huge, triangle-shaped UFO flying over Southfield, Michigan, at 6:30 P.M. It flew at a high rate of speed, suddenly stopped and made a quick turn, then shot off into the atmosphere.

Apr. 6, 2005—In Oakdale, California, a glowing, orange-colored, spherical object zigzagged across the sky at a high rate of speed at 8:40 P.M. It was completely silent.

Apr. 25, 2005—There were two reports on this date made from Lompoc, California to the National UFO Reporting Center. They both described a dia-

An oval-shaped UFO allegedly picked up a cow in Wood River, Nebraska, on January 31, 2005.

mond-shaped UFO with four main lights, together with a bunch of small, white lines on the underside. The sighting occurred at 2:50 A.M. The UFO made a horribly loud, high-pitched humming sound.

May 5, 2005—At nine o'clock in the evening, a triangular object appeared over a small lake in Louisville, Kentucky, with beams entering the water. After fifteen minutes, it then ascended into the sky.

May 14, 2005—A large, black, triangular UFO flew over Grand View, Idaho, at a slow speed at 10:38 P.M., flying at a high altitude and moving from the northwest to the southeast.

May 25, 2005—In Oriental, North Carolina, an eerie, purple and greenish glow came from a craft that was estimated to be about twenty-four feet in diameter. It hovered next to some tree limbs and was partly concealed by them.

Jun. 19, 2005—At 3:15 in the afternoon in Silverdale, Washington, a black, rectangular object was sighted flying from south to north in a straight line and at a constant speed, making no sound. The sighting lasted less than thirty seconds.

Jul. 8, 2005—A bright silver, cigar-shaped UFO was sighted coming out of a cloud near a military base in Killeen, Texas, at 12:35 P.M. Within ten seconds, it disappeared into another cloud but never reappeared.

Aug. 6, 2005—At 1:30 P.M., a spherical object was sighted one hundred feet over the ocean from a boat off Newport Beach, California. It came closer to the boat, stopped and hovered for ten minutes, then reversed and went back in the same direction and at the same speed it had come, disappearing from sight.

Aug. 11, 2005—At 8:40 P.M., a man and his son saw a large, triangular UFO with three lights fly over Edmonton, Kentucky, with the object flying with the broad part of the triangle facing forward.

Sep. 7, 2005—A boomerang-shaped object, white with multiple colors on the bottom, was seen over Williamsport, Pennsylvania, for about an hour beginning around two P.M. It took off sideways at blinding speed, while other objects were suspended in the air below it.

Sep. 7, 2005—In Big Sur, California, at 2:00 A.M., a large, bright, diamond-shaped object, initially stationary, moved quickly across a large area of the sky, dropping "balls of light," before accelerating into outer space.

Sep. 28, 2005—At 2:38 A.M., a huge, triangular-shaped object with lights glided smoothly to the southeast over Jacksonville Beach, Florida, without a sound.

Oct. 6, 2005—At 1:15 A.M., an object trailed by a military aircraft flew over Coon Rapids, Minnesota, at a high rate of speed, knocking out electrical power in homes.

In a flash they grew into a large, nearly blinding light source. He went outside and walked in the direction of the lights....

Oct. 6, 2005—A cigar-shaped object was seen leaning to the left as it moved through storm clouds over Huachuca City, Arizona, at 5:30 P.M. It moved to lean to the right, then became a dot and moved toward another large storm cloud.

Nov. 7, 2005—At 6:25 P.M., five bright amber lights were sighted over Navarre, Florida, in a diamond formation at forty-five degrees elevation. A fifth object was above the diamond at a ten o'clock position. There were two separate reports with multiple witnesses received by the National UFO Reporting Center, including one with Air Force personnel in rural Santa Rosa county. The sightings lasted ten minutes.

Nov. 7, 2005—In Denham Springs, Louisiana, a disc-shaped UFO was first sighted around 9:27 P.M., moving at a very fast constant rate of speed to the northwest. The object appeared to be disc-shaped, but standing on edge. It had lights around its periphery.

Nov. 25, 2005—A man was having a late dinner with his family in Wichita, Kansas, at 10:30 P.M. when he saw three lights on the horizon. In a flash they grew into a large, nearly blinding light source. He went outside and walked in the direction of the lights, and he could see a cigar-shaped object moving up and down in a vertical motion. He had two dogs, and one was barking uncontrollably, while the other—a normally more aggressive dog—was whimpering and hid under the back deck. As he stood watching the UFO, a man about five feet tall approached him. The man spoke to him in a foreign language, which he was certain was German. He could not remember anything after that point. The next morning, he woke up on his bed. His family had gone and his entire body felt sore, particularly below the waist.

Dec. 17, 2005—At 5:45 P.M., a slow-moving, silent, triangular object with red lights was seen in Hockinson, Washington State. It was flying low to the ground and was quite bright from a distance. It was in view for 90 seconds. At 9:30 P.M., a dark, triangle-shaped object with V-shaped lights flew over the St. Johns River in Jacksonville, Florida, for three minutes.

Sightings: 2006

Mar. 5, 2006—A slow-moving, chevron-shaped object with bright lights on the underside of the wings made no sounds as it passed over Pittsburgh, Pennsylvania, at 9:00 P.M.

Apr. 27, 2006—A large, rectangular object with red, blinking lights that formed an arch was reported over Santa Maria, California, at 4:30 P.M. It made erratic flight movements, flew low over the area for a minute, then suddenly disappeared.

Apr. 29, 2006—Three black, triangle-shaped objects were observed flying slowly east over Vancouver, Washington, at 1:55 P.M. At 7:30 P.M., a man and his brother saw three cylindrical objects flying over the 11203 zip code area of Brooklyn, New York, heading east out toward Long Island. Two of the objects were flying in tandem, and the third was following behind.

Aug. 5, 2006—At around 11:00 P.M., while night hunting for wild boar, three men in Bonaire, Georgia, came upon a stand of oak trees alongside a field, where they had just run their dogs, and saw some lights coming from the woods. They decided to investigate and walked into the woods approximately sixty yards before they heard a loud, whooshing sound. Their dogs then tucked their tails and began whining. When the men tried to get a closer look the lights dimmed, and another whooshing sound was heard. The men then saw two small, green "midgets" run from behind a tree toward what appeared to be a large "concrete mixer" with lights on it. Later on, after waiting a while and drinking a beer, the men ran back up the hill with their dogs. The light and the object had gone, and there was an eerie silence throughout the woods, so that even the insects were completely quiet. The next day, the men returned to the spot and found nothing out of the ordinary. Later that next evening, one of the men went to feed his dogs and found that "Judo," his best hunting dog, was sick and would not eat anything. He claims the dog died later that week without any apparent reason.

Aug. 6, 2006—A man was driving in a remote area of Tapiola, Michigan, at 11:30 P.M. when a square, metallic craft overtook and hovered above his vehicle. The witness sped up to 80 mph but his car kept slowing down. He came to a sharp curve and the craft was still over him, so he tried to drive faster after taking the turn, but the car continued to slow down until it finally came to a complete halt. He and his dog got out of the vehicle and ran into some bushes to hide. He next saw many lights shining through the brush that were maybe a thousand yards distant, and there were about fifty "figures" moving about among the lights. There was a "cocoon"-shaped object about twelve feet long, and there were body lights on this object. The activity reminded him of an ant colony. Apparently the creatures noticed him, because he saw three creatures coming toward him into the brush. These were somewhat humanlike, with normal-sized heads, but had very long legs and very long arms and large torsos. He did not see the eyes, for they were backlit by the light coming from behind them. The man and his dog ran further from the area and hid again. The beings appeared to search for him but gave up. From his new location, he saw two more cocoonlike craft, with numerous creatures moving around them.

> The men then saw two small, green "midgets" run from behind a tree toward what appeared to be a large "concrete mixer" with lights on it.

Aug. 26, 2006—A man was out for a midnight stroll in Winterset, Iowa, and on his way back home at around 12:30

The witness made several hand gestures at the UFOs, and they seemed to respond to him.

A.M., he looked up into the sky and saw what appeared to be a saucer-shaped object, about as large as anything he had ever seen. It was just hovering there silently. Next, two more similar-looking, silent objects appeared. All three craft had lights that changed color from red to white and then to green. The witness made several hand gestures at the UFOs, and they seemed to respond to him. He suddenly felt that there was someone behind him, so he turned around and saw a small, Gray being, about 3½ to 4 ft. tall, with a pear-shaped head, huge eyes, and no visible mouth. It communicated with the witness via telepathy. The creature and the witness exchanged messages back and forth for about five minutes. The creature communicated that they were not here to harm us but were here just to view and observe us. The witness then asked about the "Roswell" crash, and the creature supposedly confirmed that the event had indeed taken place and added that they "had been trying to get their ship back." After this, the small creature turned around and entered one of the hovering craft, then all three took off, emitting a final light show before disappearing from sight.

Dec. 4, 2006—A multicolored object was sighted over Hicksville, New York, in Nassau County at 12:25 P.M. It made security alarms go off and left behind a cloud of bluish fog.

Sightings: 2007

March 5, 2007—A hovering, saucer-shaped object with yellow lights was reported in the sky over Washington, D.C., at 7:00 P.M. It was approached by a bronze-colored object, triangular- or flying wing-shaped, which hovered nearby.

March 31, 2007—A witness saw a silver object that was moving at a high rate of speed before stopping to hover near Redondo Beach, California. While it hovered, the witness took a single photograph. Seconds later, the UFO accelerated to the south and disappeared.

Jul. 18, 2007—A triangular-shaped object with solid, white lights and a solid, amber light in the center was seen in Columbia, Missouri, on this night at 11:00 P.M.

Aug. 6, 2007—Fifteen to twenty cigar-shaped objects with red and blue lights were sighted over Texarkana, Arkansas, at 10:20 P.M. There were also numerous bright white lights appearing and disappearing. A second independent report was filed at 10:45 P.M. from ten miles south of the city, reporting inexplicable bright lights and moving objects.

Aug. 16, 2007—A single light was witnessed making ninety-degree turns, starting and stopping instantly without acceleration, over Reading, California, at 11:08 P.M.

Aug. 29, 2007—At 11:34 P.M., a man had just let his dogs out into his backyard in Stafford, Virginia, when they starting acting very aggressively. The older female dog got out the door and immediately ran down a hill as if to attack something. When the witness walked out and followed behind the dog, he illuminated the area with his handheld spotlight and saw what appeared to be two small beings, about four feet tall. They looked to be made out of light that was faint but only illuminated their heads and hands, as if their bodies were cloaked by clothing. Next these two figures retreated quickly about ten feet down the hill, and, incredibly, seemed to crawl up into an unseen opening or portal. It looked like they were going up into a completely darkened craft. The witness could only describe it as a portal or windowlike opening, which didn't emanate any light. He could still see that there must have been some sort of craft present, because when it started to move away it caused an air turbulence and a moving shadow two feet off the ground. He tried to shine his light on it, but it seemed to absorb all light. As it moved away, it rose up into the sky and then he could begin to make out a shape. Before the small figures entered the craft, they looked back at the witness and their eyes glowed softly with a pale blue light, but he could not see any other facial features. His dog stopped barking when the object left. The witness described the object as arrow shaped, about 20 feet long, with the pointed and narrow end in front and wider end at the rear.

Sep. 20, 2007—At 5:30 P.M. (EDT), two University of Michigan at Flint, Michigan, college students observed 11 discs making formations in the early evening sky for 15 minutes. At 8:30 P.M. (EDT), a cylindrical object with a purple underglow was spotted moving very fast across the sky in Palm Harbor, Florida.

Sep. 20, 2007—At 8:00 P.M. (PDT), a cigar-shaped object, possibly hundreds of feet long, was viewed for 12 minutes from Coos Bay, Oregon, as it flew slowly along the Pacific Ocean coastline. At the same time (9:00 P.M. MDT), three black, triangular craft maneuvered across the sky from the horizon and then hovered over the witnesses' location for two minutes in Kingston, New Mexico.

Sep. 20, 2007—At 11:30 P.M., a circular object with white lights on the underside was seen from Trabuco Canyon in Mission Viejo, California, flying over Orange County toward Riverside County.

Sep. 21, 2007—A 37-year-old service technician in Spencerville, Ohio, stepped outside for a cigarette before going to bed at 1:50 A.M. and sighted a pair of lights just over the horizon. There was a dark, cigar-shaped object with two lights at both ends, larger than a normal aircraft, and it made no sound as it moved west-northwest overhead.

> ... these two figures retreated quickly about ten feet down the hill, and, incredibly, seemed to crawl up into an unseen opening or portal.

Sep. 21, 2007—An undisclosed witness had an apparent abduction experience with missing time beginning in the predawn morning hours in Lexington, Kentucky. He reported to the National UFO Reporting Center that while out walking the dog at 4:30 A.M., the small dog "who never barks," began to growl and spasm uncontrollably. Then a white light appeared and a sensation of warmth came over the witness, and he was knocked to the ground. When he awoke it was early afternoon, he was in a different location, his clothes were tattered, and he had several sore spots on his body, including his anus. At first he thought he must have been the victim of an automobile hit and run, but to his dismay, his arms and legs had various burn marks of unknown cause, and he suspects the cause may be UFO related. The report form lists the shape of the UFO as a disc.

Sep. 21, 2007—At 4:13 P.M., a father and son in Bastrop, Texas, were playing catch with a baseball when a silver, cigar-shaped object appeared out of nowhere and hovered one thousand feet in the sky. It had two wings in the front and two wings in the back. It backed up, came forward, then went up and down in a controlled pattern, then quickly disappeared into thin air. The sighting lasted 45 seconds.

Sep. 21, 2007—Three reports of triangular craft were made from Ohio between 8:00 P.M. and 9:00 P.M. At 8:00 P.M. in West Chester, Ohio, a triangular craft with an array of bright lights glided silently near the tree line. At 8:25 P.M. in Deer Park, Ohio, an observer witnessed a triangular object with hundreds of bright yellow lights near Cincinnati. At 9:00 P.M., a "really big" craft was seen in Evendale, Ohio, that came close but remained silent the whole time.

A bright-white, cigar-shaped UFO was seen flying over the Bisti Badlands in San Juan County, New Mexico, in 2007.

Sep. 21, 2007—A couple was traveling north on Highway 371 near the Bisti Badlands in San Juan County, New Mexico, at 10:34 P.M. when they saw a bright-white, cigar-shaped craft near the ground about one hundred yards off the east side of the road. They slowed their vehicle down, and the craft took off very quickly. It shot up very vertically and left behind no traces.

Oct. 15, 2007—A spherical, metallic object was seen in broad daylight above University Hospital for twenty-two minutes in Aurora, Colorado.

Nov. 7, 2007—At 5:20 P.M., two discs or saucer-shaped objects were seen gliding side by side before doing some acrobatic maneuvers in the sky over San Jose, California.

Nov. 13, 2007—At 6:50 P.M. and again at 7:10 P.M., there were two reports of a huge, low-flying, triangular craft that was seen in San Diego, California. It was reported to be larger than a stealth bomber.

Nov. 22, 2007—A black, chevron- or boomerang-shaped object with circling lights, estimated to be about 100 yards long, flew over Wellington, Florida, at 12:45 P.M.

Dec. 23, 2007—At 1:30 P.M. CST, a dark, disc-shaped object was spotted among the clouds over Chicago, Illinois. It stayed still long enough for the witness to make a three-minute-long video recording of it. At 6:45 P.M. EST, a disc-shaped, blue and white light flew low and fast over Bowie, Maryland.

Sightings: 2008

January 13, 2008—The witness, who worked offshore in the Gulf of Mexico, was riding the crew boat back to shore when he saw what he thought was a high-flying bird. He pointed it out to one of the others in the boat, who said, "That's no bird." The object, which was described as white, curved at the top and flat on the bottom, was stationary for five minutes, but then it vanished.

January 19, 2008—The witness, who was outside late in the morning,. saw two triangular-shaped objects hovering over some pine trees in the distance. The objects made no sound as they took off rapidly.

June 7, 2008; Antioch, South Carolina—A married couple with many years of aviation experience was returning from a visit with friends. They were discussing one of the movies they had just seen when the wife said, "Look at that; what in the world is that?" They saw a black, triangular craft in the air with lights and several windows. There was a purple beacon in the center of the bottom, but no position lights or anticollision lights anywhere on the object. They thought for a moment that it might be a B-2 bomber, but it made no noise at all, and after "zooming" up to them, it stopped right over their vehicle. About this time, they turned onto their private road and made it up to their

A B-2 bomber looks quite similar to the triangle-shaped UFOs some people have reported seeing.

house. This was around 11:20 P.M. The next thing that either of them remembers was being in the car at 2:24 A.M. The car was running, but the wife was in the driver's seat and the husband in the passenger's. Since he is 6'5" and she is 5'7", this meant that his knees were forced into the dashboard. Neither remembered anything whatsoever after parking the car. They do not remember what happened during the lost time, why they were in different positions in the car, or why they were still sitting outside their house with all of the car windows still down and the moonroof open. The husband woke up with a headache the next morning, and his wife felt ill enough to stay in bed for most of the next day. There were other good reports of flying triangles that same night in Brooklyn, Michigan, and Mountain View, California.

Jun. 19, 2008; Roanoke County, Virginia—At around 11:35 P.M., a police officer responded to a call about a strange, unidentified object in the sky over the Catawba area, ten miles west-northwest of the Roanoke Regional Airport. The officer reported seeing the object in the air slowly moving parallel to Interstate 81. The object was semicircular in appearance and had approximately half a dozen red and orange, flashing lights around it. It made no sound as it moved. The police department received a second call at 12:15 A.M. looking for answers about the object reported over Catawba. Police said at least two additional witnesses besides the officer saw the object.

Jun. 30, 2008, between Cardiff and Atlantic City, New Jersey, 10:25 P.M.—A close encounter occurred on the Atlantic City Expressway. A twenty-five-foot-wide, triangular craft was seen hovering or moving very slowly, just forty feet directly above the expressway, very close to and in front of the witnesses. Its speed appeared to be quite slow, moving at an estimated ten miles per hour, and it passed directly over their vehicle. They saw it again twice in the next five minutes.

Jul. 18, 2008; Columbia, Missouri—Exactly one year after a similar sighting at the same hour, a black, triangular object hung motionless in the sky in St. Charles, Missouri, over the south side of Missouri Highway 370, just off of Discovery Bridge. It had three white and one red, nonblinking lights.

Aug. 8, 2008; Wrentham, Massachusetts—A missing time experience during a humanoid encounter occurred early this night in. A man and his sister were hiking through the Joe's Rock area and were taken aback by a very

The UFO flew parallel to Interstate 81, making no sound as it moved.

strange being they saw lurking behind a tree. Curious, both witnesses approached the creature as it shyly walked out from behind the tree. It was incredibly thin, and its color looked pale and much washed out. Its skin was also very wrinkly and looked like old, soft leather. The creature then began making strange clicking and moaning sounds. Both witnesses were stunned and could not react to what they were seeing. The main witness does not remember much of the experience; he found himself back at the car and it was then that he realized, when checking his cell phone, that the time was already 1:46 A.M. The creature was described as being about 4.5 feet tall with dark black eyes.

Humanoid Reports in the Twenty-first Century

While sightings of the objects in the sky or close to the ground are important, those that are more exciting are those in which the creatures or aliens are seen. Albert Rosales, who runs a website that details these sightings, has been collecting them for years. He provides a wide variety of information on a diverse set of UFO reports. His site can be found at: http://www.ufoinfo.com/humanoid/.

He generously gave his permission to report on many of the cases that have been included in his huge databases. The following are some of the more interesting of his reports.

Humanoid Reports: 2011

March 1, 2011: Seal Beach, California. Time: 2:00 A.M.–3:00 A.M.

Joseph Stillwell had awakened to use the bathroom and had returned to his room. He had a habit of going to the window (facing west) and looking at the night sky before getting back in bed. At that time of year the moon and Orion constellation are up to the left, looking out. The night was crystal clear, calm, and the moonlight remarkably bright. Wanting to locate Orion, he looked to the left. Immediately, he sensed movement in the sky to his right. He turned and saw a structure moving slowly overhead, brightly lit, and unlike anything he had ever seen or heard described. It could not have been more than three hundred feet away. It was shaped like a brick and was, by volume, the largest thing he had ever seen in flight. It had four sides, each rectangular, and ends that were about one-third the area of the sides, also rectangular. The sides were approximately ninety to one hundred feet long, with the ends forty feet wide and thirty feet tall. It was moving toward and parallel to the rear of his house. At a point directly behind his house, it would have been around twenty-five feet (horizontally) from the building. It moved very slow, maybe ten miles an hour, and was alarmingly low, less than two hundred feet from the ground.

> He was unable to move, though he must have been breathing normally, and possessed clear thought.

The color was dull black, solid, seamless, with no windows or doors. The two sides and end that he could see were perfectly flat and nonreflective. The perimeter of the lower face (bottom) of the object was encircled with large, red and green lights the size and shape of footballs. The colors alternated, with every other one being red or green. The lights switched on and off in sequence running clockwise around the perimeter with at least four equally spaced points turning off simultaneously, giving the impression of rotation (as a theater marquee). These lights easily numbered more than one hundred. There was no sound. The movement of this thing was straight ahead, with no deviation in altitude nor laterally. Its flight was completely independent. There was nothing above or below the object, and nothing pulling or pushing it through the sky. He watched, never looking away, until it disappeared behind his house. He turned from the window with the intent of walking across the hall to the bedroom on the other side to watch the object pass. He managed just one step and stopped, at the foot of his bed, in the center of his room.

He had not wanted to stop; he just stopped. He was unable to move, though he must have been breathing normally, and possessed clear thought. He was completely paralyzed, standing. He was thinking that he just needed to walk a few steps to the other room, but no part of him would move. He had lost all feeling and sensation. He does not know how long he was incapacitated, but at some point he moved forward without intention to do so. However, instead of walking to where he originally intended, he turned and sat on the edge of the bed. He did not want to be there and thought that he should just get up and go see the object in the sky fly away, but again he could not move. His mind seemed completely disconnected with his body, but he felt no concern.

He was sitting at the edge of the bed, suddenly exhausted, when the room lit up brightly. A light shone through the window to his left (about two feet away), facing the backyard. No part of him could move and he quickly lost all strength, slumping forward, but could only think about, and be awestruck by, the "whiteness" of the light. Although exceptionally bright, its absolute clarity was the focus of his thought. Other than awe, he felt no emotion, and to this point he had experienced no fear. He could not move, and his strength was depleted. He was seated about halfway up the right side of the bed, sitting well back. He had slumped so far forward that his face was almost touching his hands. He felt as though he was about to crumple to the floor and remembered thinking, "They are at the window, don't look." At that instant, he fell over onto his left side onto the bed. His legs were still over the side of the bed, with both of his feet still on the floor. His eyes closed, and he was confused as to why his feet were "stuck" to the floor. He wondered why he couldn't open his eyes, why he couldn't lift his arms, and why his feet were so heavy. He had no thought of the craft in the sky or the light in his room. His concern was his feet and how he could retrieve them. Both of his hands had been on his lap when he fell over and were now lying at the edge of the bed, over which his legs were hanging. He managed to move the fingers of his right hand, grab his right knee, and pull. He could not move it. He was barely able to move the fingers of his left hand and grip his right wrist. He pulled as hard as he could, and his foot slowly lifted off the floor. He could not open his eyes, and he heard no sound. It took quite a while, but eventually he dragged his right leg up onto the bed. The same process for the left leg was successful, and at that point he believes he lost consciousness. He has no further memory of that night. He opened his eyes, and it was morning. For additional information, see: Joellstone@hotmail.com.

March 18, 2011: Between Chicora and East Brady, Butler County, Pennsylvania

Stan Gordon, a well known UFO investigator, reported that a local businessman was driving down the road when from about a quarter of a mile away, he observed something on the right side in a grassy area. He first thought that it was a deer. The driver stepped on the gas to move closer to get a better view. From about fifty yards away, he observed something that appeared to be hunched down. A moment later, it stood up and the driver observed a very tall, muscular creature. At this point, the driver had his high beams on and watched as the creature walked in front of a yellow, reflective road sign, then crossed the two-lane road in three long steps and continued into a wooded area. What the driver described was a humanoid figure that stood at least eight feet tall that appeared to have smooth leatherlike skin that was of either a darker tan or light brown color.

The creature never looked at the witness and was only observed from its side. The head appeared to be flat in the front section and then rounded out. "At the top back of its skull, it was like one of those aerodynamic helmets. The top was not quite a point, but it looked like a ridge on top of the head." The face was flat, and the eyes were not clearly defined, but the man thought that they might have been pointed in the corner. The ear that was observed on the left side was long and flat, and it came up and back and was pointed backward, like a flap. The arms were muscular and a little longer than that of a human. The hands looked more like a claw, but the number of fingers was unclear. One physical trait that stood out was the extremely muscular legs. The witness stated that it was hard to explain, but the legs did not move like that of a human and "looked like they bent backward." The witness also saw what appeared to be wings on its back which were tucked into its body, with the wingtips extending toward the side of its head. No unusual sounds or smells were noticed during the observation, which was estimated to have been about seven to eight seconds. As the motorist approached the location where the creature entered the woods, it could no longer be seen.

> The witness stated that it was hard to explain, but the legs did not move like that of a human and "looked like they bent backward."

The next day, the witness decided to drive back to the location of the encounter to look for any evidence. The ground conditions were not suitable for tracks, and nothing was found. The witness did, however, measure the road sign that the creature had walked in front of. The sign was just over eight feet high, and the head of the creature was estimated to have reached about four inches above the sign.

May 9, 2011: Westminster, Maryland

The witness M. told Rosales directly that he was in bed getting ready to sleep and was lying there when a "voice" popped into his head that simply said, "Something to think about." This took him by surprise, and he started to look around his bedroom. It was very dark, but he saw what he thought to be a dark figure about three feet in height with long spindly arms and legs standing in the doorway. He could not tell if its color was black or if it just looked black because of the darkness. He observed this for several minutes, trying to engage in communication by asking questions "telepathically," but never got a response. This was also accompanied by strange lights that seemed to be emanating from the floor of the witness' bedroom. As he went to get up from bed, a sudden wave of tiredness swept over him, and he at once fell asleep.

June 4, 2011: Kailua-Kona, Hawaii

A family of five reported seeing a man floating in the air wearing a black, aviator-type suit. First the two-year-old yelled out, "A balloon, a balloon!" The rest of them looked up and saw a thin man wearing a black suit. He appeared to be floating in the air. He was stationary. There were no wires attached to him, nor was he wearing any wings. They contacted their local newspaper (*West Hawaii Today*) to see if anyone else reported seeing the floating man, but there was no response.

June 17, 2011: Naples, Florida

The witness had gone to sleep around 10 P.M. in a room with another person sleeping in a bed next to his bed, similar to sharing a hotel room. When he went to sleep, everything seemed normal. He regained consciousness in what seemed like a hospital room. The first thing he noticed was that he was lying flat on his back on what appeared to be a hospital bed. He immediately assumed he was in a hospital, but then he realized that there was no way possible that he could be in a hospital, so he began to look around. He noticed that the walls of the room seemed to be a metallic color. This "freaked" him out because he knew that hospital rooms have bright colors and do not have metal walls. At this point, he went on a "defense mode." He began trying to understand the surrounding environment, and the more details he noticed, the more confused and scared he became. He made a quick glance to his right and saw two people and near his feet another two. Then to his left, there was a person sitting in a chair perpendicular to his "hospital bed." His attention was struck by the person on his left in the chair.

This person looked to be a human female. He was so frightened that he remembered the woman telling him that it was OK, that it would all be over soon. The witness then watched as the woman stuck a needle into his left arm. It was similar to an IV needle, but their technique of placing the needle required no tape or gauze to hold it in place. The needle itself was metal but its luster was odd; he couldn't remember if it was too dull or too shiny. It was nothing he had seen before, possibly an unknown metal. When he heard the woman telling him that there was nothing to be worried about, he went from defense mode to "panic mode." The last thing he remembered seeing at that point was

A man testified being abducted in 2011. Strange tests were peformed on him, though he was returned home unharmed.

the person in front of him (one of the people at his feet). They had what seemed to be a wire connected to something resembling an LED flashlight; it was all white, and he could see "LED bulbs" in the "flashlight." It was explained to him through a mental communication that this was a way to decipher or something. The flashlight implement was designed so the placement of each bulb could be measured through its complex variations and measurements so that it could be calculated to individually differentiate people.

He woke up in the same room. He had no idea how much time had passed by. No one else was in the metal room; he was alone. Near where his feet were, there was a door, the same color as the walls. Apparently, he was now able to move and he walked out that door, entering a diagonal hallway. Opposite the door, there was a solid metal, flat wall, maybe one hundred feet long, from what he could see. He went ten feet to the right and then saw a door and opened it. He passed maybe ten rooms identical to the one he just came out of. When he got to what seemed to be a pivot point in the ship (he imagined the ship he was in as V-shaped) there was a giant window, maybe thirty feet tall and seventy-five feet wide. When he looked out the window he saw what appeared to him as Earth. It made him realize that he was not on his own planet. Needless to say, he panicked and then saw beings walk by him that were not human. The one he focused on had an olive-colored skin, looked wet but dry, maybe like a lizard or snake. The facial features looked like a mixture of Hispanic-African-Asian combined. The strangest thing about these beings was that they had what resembled fish gills on the side of their face, where the human cheeks are located. The figures must have been 6.5 to 7 feet tall. He asked the being "if this was real," and it grabbed his hand. Next thing he knew, he regained

> He asked the being "if this was real," and it grabbed his hand. Next thing he knew, he regained consciousness inside his own bathroom.

consciousness inside his own bathroom. He was staring at the mirror in his bathroom. When he snapped into reality, he realized that he was in shock. He looked at where the needle was inserted into his arm, and there was a blood spot or scab. He was feeling very groggy and had the strange feeling that he had been in an ocean the whole day or skiing on a mountain all day. At this point he also realized that it was 6:45–7:00 A.M. Almost nine hours had passed. He felt as if he hadn't slept the whole night. A week later, a spot identical to the shape of the "LED" lights that had been placed on his foot appeared. According to the witness, he still has the strange mark.

July 5, 2011: Phoenix, Arizona

The witness was in his backyard, and his dog was barking wildly; he was trying to get her to be quiet, but she kept running back and forth in the yard, jumping the fence as if chasing a cat. She kept barking and sat in the middle of the yard. The witness then went out one last time to bring her inside but as soon as he got next to her, she stopped barking. It was very silent and pitch black outside. He looked up and could not see the stars but thought he saw a sort of black ellipse; suddenly, his cell phone shattered for no reason at all, and the battery was dripping. He couldn't recall what happened next, and he woke up in his room later.

His next encounter occurred when he was in the living room in the morning; the sun was barely rising. It was around four or five. He looked out the window and there was a being. Its face was very thin and "bony," very skeletal. It had no eyes or nose, but had holes on the sides of its head that the witness thought looked like a reptile's ears. It looked human, but its flesh was pale with the slightest green tint to it, and in some spots a blue hue, and it was easy to see through the flesh. It was tall but hunched over, with four arms, very small legs, and a large, prominent spine. Where the ribs would have been, it had something that looked like gills, bright pink in color. Stunned, the witness dropped his glass of milk, and the creature turned to look at him. It stared at the witness for what felt like hours. He blacked out and woke up later at around 12.

November 20, 2011: Near Troy, Pennsylvania

Stan Gordon reported that a man and his girlfriend were driving onto Mud Creek Road traveling west toward Highway 14 near Troy. As they continued down the dark road, their attention was drawn to the left side of the roadway. The man, who was the driver, saw some movement and mentioned it to his girlfriend. The woman initially thought that a naked man was crawling on the side of the road. The driver decreased his speed, swerved his truck in the middle of the road, and directed the high beams of his headlights toward the subject. The driver stopped about thirty to forty feet away. They soon realized that this was not a person but instead a creature that was crawling very low to the ground. As they watched, the creature moved into a squatting position with its back completely straight, somewhat like the stance of a kangaroo.

> The head of the beast appeared to be oversized and shaped like that of a wolf. At the top of its head were two pointed, batlike ears that looked to be about four to six inches long.

The arms of the creature were held tightly to its body. Long claws that resembled the talons of an eagle were clearly visible. The claws were estimated to be about eight to ten inches in length. One claw was shorter than the other three. The creature had a muscular body. The head of the beast appeared to be oversized and shaped like that of a wolf. At the top of its head were two pointed, batlike ears that looked to be about four to six inches long. The entire creature, according to the man, was covered with "dull, wrinkly, dark black skin." The man described seeing large, caninelike teeth in its mouth. The eyes of the creature were about the size of a silver dollar and were shiny black. The man said that even though he had his high beams directed at the creature, its eyes did not reflect at all. The man said he looked over the body during the twelve-second encounter, and for some reason he thought the creature should have wings, but none were apparent. In the squatted position, the creature seemed to be about five feet tall. At this point, the creature was in the left lane of the road and about one to two feet onto the pavement.

As the couple watched in amazement, the creature began to stretch its body. The man said that at this point, the animal started to stand up on its back legs while also falling over onto its front feet. The driver said that in this position, the creature seemed to be about six to seven feet tall. The animal then fell over on all four legs. The witnesses observed that the front claws of the creature were now two feet across the center line of the highway, while the back feet remained one to two feet from the edge of the road. The creature then turned its head to the right and looked toward the vehicle. The driver said that it looked directly at them, with a horrific expression, "like it was panicked." The witness saw it take a deep breath. Once the creature realized it was being observed, it leaned back slightly and then reached forward with its claws. The creature then took one tremendous leap and cleared a seven-foot embankment and moved out of sight into a wooded area. The man estimated the leap was about forty feet long. As it was in the process of leaping, it was perfectly straight and held its front claws forward. The legs, as it was leaping, "were only slightly larger than broomsticks, or about the size of a walking crane, and were very long." Then, just a second after the creature was gone from sight, something else odd occurred. A large bird, possibly an owl, suddenly rushed at the passenger-side window, almost hitting the glass, then took off and did not return. It happened so fast, they were unsure if it was an owl or not. The witnesses indicated that this creature appeared to be changing form. The driver said, "Its shape was nothing like when it was squatted." The woman stated that it "shaped into another form." She thought it was a dark brown color and looked like a werewolf with little back hair. She estimated that when it was leaping into the woods, she thought it stood about nine feet tall. The woman reluctantly said, "I think it was a man changing into a werewolf." The man, after the experience, went onto the Internet to try to figure out what he saw, and he told the investigator that the closest way he could describe the creature would be a gargoyle with no wings. The man commented, "I will never forget what we saw that night."

> The legs, as it was leaping, "were only slightly larger than broomsticks, or about the size of a walking crane, and were very long."

Humanoid Reports: 2012

March 2012: Kendall, Miami-Dade, Florida

In a handwritten letter to Albert Rosales, the main witness, Reinerio (Ray) Hernandez reported that on a Sunday morning, he and his wife saw two different "objects" inside their home, in their living room, located on the first floor of the house. At approximately seven A.M. on that day, their sixteen-year-old Jack Russell terrier, Nena, barked at his wife in her bedroom, notifying her that she wanted to go outside for a bathroom call. Nena had had a stroke the previous day and was partially paralyzed on half her body. They were supposed to take her to their veterinarian the next day to put her to sleep. His wife then carried Nena downstairs. Once downstairs, she saw a glowing, "3/4 orb," shaped like an upside-down letter U. It was approximately 2 feet in width and 1.5 feet in height. The object was light gray/silver in color, and it had two small, vertical, round lights on "the front," which blinked a green, pulsating, laserlike light, and were pointed directly at his wife. The light stream was not wide. From the object's bottom left side, bursts of a very bright, fluorescent white light began to flare out—some long and some short. Being very religious, his wife began to pray. The object was located near the corner of a wall and appeared to be floating about four to five feet off the floor.

His wife thought that the object must have been some type of religious signal, perhaps even a "heavenly angel." She knelt down and began an attempt to communicate telepathically with the "angel." The object seemed to respond by emitting more bursts of light from its sides and more blinking of the green, laserlike lights, this after each of her questions or inquiries. The whole time, she was holding the dog, Nena, and begged at whatever the light or entity was that their dog, Nena, not suffer in her illness. Both green lights on the object then began to blink rapidly, and the white bursts of light from the object's side then began to travel at a greater distance. She believed that this indeed was a "positive" response to her prayers.

After about fifteen minutes of communicating with the "entity," she began screaming at Reinerio to come immediately downstairs. However, he ignored her, since he had not slept well the night before, and after five minutes of no response, she went upstairs and pulled him from the bed and told him what she had seen. Being of a rationalist mind, he was very skeptical. However, he finally decided to go downstairs. Once there, he did not see the U-shaped object but saw a small "plasma cylinder," which did not appear to have edges but seemed like a fluid object which displayed constant movement inside and on the edges of the object. Inside he could see translucent, multi-colored lights, which blended together like "colored water" and appeared to be constantly mixing together. This object appeared to be about one to two feet in length and six to twelve inches in height. It hovered about four to five feet from the floor in the same corner where his wife had seen the other object. In a strange reaction, the witness stared at this strange object for no more than fifteen seconds, and with a wave of his hand he dismissed it. He went upstairs and attempted to get more sleep, but fifteen minutes later suddenly awoke with a start, apparently realizing what he had just seen, and ran downstairs. However, the object was now gone. At this point, he was stunned to see his stricken dog walking and running around like she was perfectly fine. His wife told him that the "angel" had cured their dog.

> At this point, he was stunned to see his stricken dog walking and running around like she was perfectly fine. His wife told him that the "angel" had cured their dog.

On July 8, 2012, at around 3:30 A.M., his wife had seen a huge craft the size of a football field, perhaps about a quarter mile from their home. It was illuminated with dozens of bright, multicolored lights. Also, in August, the main witness, along with four other witnesses, including his daughter, saw a very large craft with thousands of circular- and oblong-shaped, thin, white lights.

April 23, 2012: Washington County, Pennsylvania

A man heard an odd animal sound coming from outside. The sound was a level growl or screeching sound that he listened to for about five minutes. The sound seemed as though it was just outside the window. The witness, intrigued by the odd noise, awakened his wife to see if she could recognize what type of animal it might originate from. When his wife got up and they both heard the sound, she looked out the window across the road to a creek about fifteen to twenty feet away. She then noticed what she thought was a deer standing up in the middle of the creek. Her husband questioned why there would be a deer standing in the creek and why it would be making such a strange noise. He then looked out the window and saw an undetermined creature, dark brown in color and about the size of a deer. It could have actually been larger than a deer, since it was peering over the retaining wall. The man said when it turned its head, it appeared to have an elongated face, almost deer shaped, but not as stubby in the snout. It appeared to be more pointed in shape.

> The witness commented that the freaky part was that it was staring right at their house toward them.

What could be easily seen were two big, round, amber-colored eyes that seemed to be glowing. The man estimated that they looked to be the size of a golf ball. He didn't think the glow was from reflection because the street lights were some distance away. The witness commented that the freaky part was that it was staring right at their house toward them. The couple noticed that whatever it was, the glowing eyes were staring directly in their direction. The man told his wife that he was going to check out what it was. Just then, something very strange occurred. Suddenly, the creature took one step and took off into the sky at a forty-five-degree angle and was gone. The witness stated, "The speed was insane; I never saw anything move that fast." He also stated that he never saw a bird that big and that he saw no signs of wings flapping.

May 21, 2012: Superior, Wisconsin

Two men had just finished eating dinner and playing a round of golf and were driving on a two-lane road that led back to the east side of the city. As they turned right at a corner that leads back into the main road, they drove another hundred feet until on the right side of the road they saw an eight- to nine-foot tall figure that was walking back into the edge of the forest located alongside the street. The driver immediately hit the brakes, unsure of what he saw; the passenger looked shocked, and the driver yelled, "I think that was an alien!" The car came to a stop, and the passenger yelled, "Go, go, go!" They sped away from the area and drove to their nearby apartment. They picked up some friends and returned to the scene of the incident but did not see the figure again.

The figure stood eight to nine feet tall, had a tall, rounded, crown-shaped head as big as a human abdomen, and it was somewhat muscular. It had big eyes—but not stereotypically alien-like eyes—and long legs, and it did not startle whatsoever.

May 24, 2012: Avery, Iowa

Three neighbors were outside their homes discussing a "previous encounter with an orb," and as they talked about what they had seen, one of them saw a light on the railroad tracks about 75 feet away. As he looked closer, he noticed that it was humanlike and about seven to nine feet tall with an inner light emanating from the chest area. It had also long, white hair. He yelled at his friends and pointed at the being, which turned abruptly and seemed to vanish, speeding across the tracks. After this incident, the main witness had a constant feeling of something watching him. Another neighbor reported seeing the same thing.

June 8, 2012: Lawrenceville, Georgia

A man and his girlfriend were in the backyard in the middle of an argument, when suddenly she got his full attention as she questioned a strange source of light approaching in their direction. As it got closer, it appeared to be in the shape of a green orb, traveling on the ground with a small, bright light following, about five feet above the green orb. There was a strip of land behind the fence of the backyard, which ran parallel to the house; this was where the "orb" was moving. Even stranger, the man's dog was sitting next to the fence and did not seem to sense what was behind it. At that time of night, there were no other loud noises outside to distract the dog or conceal the movement of the object behind the dog.

Behind the fence was a couple of bushes, then a perfectly clear spot where the man could see the object when it passed by. When the object finally reached that point, he could see clearly that it wasn't an orb but a tall, lanky, humanoid body that was glowing green from head to toe. The object was so bright that it could only be identified as a blob of light. The glowing figure then continued down the strip of land (following underneath power lines) until it reached the elementary school playground. There the witnesses saw an array of lights moving frantically in an oval movement and then the array of lights formed back into the original green, fluorescent light, and it zipped off into a nearby trail at an astounding rate of speed. A period of approximately five minutes went by until the man and his girlfriend spotted the bright light that was initially trailing behind the orb above the tall brush (about thirteen to fifteen feet high). It was approaching their line of vision again, just the opposite way this time; however, now it was making a strange, vibrating sound.

Once it got about thirty to fifty yards from both witnesses, they both headed to the front of the house because the approaching object "sounded unpleasant."

June 18, 2012: Belcourt, North Dakota

The witness was out in the woods collecting firewood when he saw what he described as an S-shaped object floating about six feet in the air. It had no lights, but he could see what appeared to be "weird-looking words" along the side, almost like "old Cree writing." The witness thought that it was not a drone and could see what appeared to be orbs of "energy" gathering something from the ground; one of them flew toward the witness and was emitting a strange, humming sound when it suddenly flashed a deep purple light at the witness, and that was the last thing he remembered of the encounter. He found himself lying on the ground, as if nothing had happened. He later recalled hearing a strange language around the object and estimated that he had seen the object for about 25 minutes.

August 2012: North Port, Florida

The witness, Kathy Rotundo, provided Albert Rosales with the following report. She said that back in the early '70s, while driving back to Cleveland from Chicago during daylight hours, she saw five intensely bright orbs the size of moons flashing and bouncing all over the sky and reported that while on the beach in southwest Florida, she encountered two quite unusual beings that she "knew" were from "off world." Standing only about six or eight feet from her were a man and woman, looking about seventy years in age, who were in full body suits. This was not something you would normally see on the beaches due to hot temperatures and warm waters. Their heads were covered also, and they were quite thin. All that was exposed were their faces and hands. What were so notable were their highly unusual-looking faces. They looked like cats without the fur. When she saw them, "she knew immediately" that they were from another planet. There was eye contact between them with telepathic communication; when she pointed out that she noticed they were nonhuman, they confirmed this. They then proceeded to go out into the Gulf waters without tanks and swim much farther out than you would normally see anyone dare to go. Kathy watched them for what seemed like maybe a half hour and then they just disappeared in the waters.

August 15, 2012: Panorama City, California

A man was outside smoking a cigarette when he called his son to come outside to see that the object (apparently seen before) was there again. The man came out with his binoculars to view the object. The mother also came

The object in the clouds looked strange. First he thought it looked like a face, then an ordinary plane, but he wasn't sure.

out to look. Through the binoculars, he saw what looked like a yellow light with a red, blinking light. It stood stationary. Then some clouds began to come in and block the object. A few minutes later, he saw a white object with a red, blinking light move in a south-to-northeast trajectory. As he looked through his binoculars, it began to speed away and the red light turned off, then the white light dimmed out. About thirty minutes later, he went outside again and took his binoculars with him in case he saw something else. He noticed while smoking a cigarette that the clouds were still there, and there was the shape of an alien face in the clouds, and he saw a white flash, like a strobelight, behind the cloud where the face shape was. It then looked like the object was about to move out of the cloud cover. When it did, he noticed that it looked like an ordinary plane, but just to make sure, he looked through his binoculars, and to his surprise, the object looked pretty strange.

At first view through his binoculars, it looked like a blimp, but blimps don't fly that high or that fast. He noticed it had a blinking strobe on the underbelly and a red light on what looked like a tail. It also had three rows of white lights that were windows. They looked like windows on a cruise ship. In one of the windows he could see a head looking out, and it looked humanoid. As he looked, the object began to rush away. Without binoculars, all he could see was a white and red light. The object was on a northern trajectory. Then about fifteen minutes later, he went outside again to see if it came back, and he saw another light, so he looked through his binoculars and saw a triangular-shaped object with red and green lights and a yellow light blinking on and off. There was an appearance underneath like a circuit board. This flying object went from south to north and then turned west. After that, the witness went out of the apartment building and noticed two military helicopters that were going north in the direction where the big object had gone.

August 31, 2012: Kihei, Maui, Hawaii

The witness awoke with a black mass hovering over her entire body. She felt a slight burning sensation on her arms and legs. The reason she knew the time was 7:40 P.M. was because she could see the cable box next to her TV on a shelf across the room from the bed. She knew for a fact that she was not in a dream because she could see and feel the black mass, everything in the bedroom, and her husband, who was sound asleep. Within a short time, she was in some type of "pod" with a dark blue/gray, metallic-like material, but she could see some light through a very small, foggy window. She felt like she was lying on some slimy, gelatinous substance underneath her, and it covered her entire body like a blanket. She was screaming at the top of her lungs, but she could not move the rest of her body. She felt the presence of someone or something around her, but could not see anything in clear sight, except the pod she was in. She eventually lost consciousness.

On September 1, 2012, around 5:45 A.M., the witness awoke in a complete state of hysteria on the opposite side of the bed. Her hair was soaking wet, with a sticky, gel-like residue throughout. Her husband awoke to help her. He said he had awakened earlier at 2:30 A.M. to use the toilet, and she had not been on the bed. He thought that she had awakened and was painting in her studio. The first thing he noticed was her hair. He went to touch or pull the gelatin residue from her hair. It generated some sort of electrical spark and dissipated immediately. Her hair was still soaking wet, as if she had just stepped out of the shower. The next thing they noticed was that she had a red rash on her left arm, approximately the size of a silver dollar. He immediately placed a cold compress on it. Over the next three weeks the rash/burn healed, but a visible scar/discoloration remained.

> He went to touch or pull the gelatin residue from her hair. It generated some sort of electrical spark and dissipated immediately.

On October 28, 2012, around 11:38 P.M., she got up to use the bathroom when she saw two strange, "wriggly wire"-shaped light forms just bouncing around in the hall. She went to step closer toward them, and they vanished. She also remembered that night having a weird dream in full color that she was waving to other people in a bubble that was floating or flying in the sky. The sky was a vivid, bright blue. There was a big, boomlike sound, then no sound at all. She looked down from the sky and saw clear water that had no current, with dark gray/black slates on the bottom. The entire area seemed very familiar to her, and she was not afraid. She turned to someone in the "dream" and asked them when she would be going back home. She does not remember a face, but they had a long, metallic, shimmering, hooded robe on. She awoke the next morning with a round, red/purple burn or rash on her right cheek. Just when it seemed to heal, it got inflamed and red all over again.

September 12, 2012: Rumney, New Hampshire

A man and his girlfriend were heading toward Plymouth from Warren, New Hampshire, when he noticed some oddly placed, red lights up in the sky, too high for mountaintops but too low for any aircraft. The lights were moving alongside the couple as they drove along. They finally stopped near an RV campground and got out. There were lots of night clouds hovering low. They then noticed that the lights were part of one giant ship, as big as a football field, slowly moving. It was very low, hovering over the campground, but had no sound. They shot some cell phone pictures, which came out poorly, but it looked like it had a few windows with humanlike shapes in them. Then it disappeared without any notice or sound or movement. No one else in the campground seemed to have seen it.

November 2012: Between Ethete and Ft. Washakie, Wyoming

During a local elk hunting contest sponsored by the Wind River Indian Casino, a hunter, Ben, found himself standing with his rifle aimed at a huge elk, which he shot at and hit nearly a half mile away. The elk got up and staggered into the Shoshone National Forest. Ben set out on foot, leaving his cousin Al to head back on the ATV four-wheeler to retrieve their truck to load the elk once it dropped.

Entering the forest, Ben was immediately struck by a blinding flash of light. He heard no sound. He was surprised, but thinking the flash might have originated from Al, he continued on. He located the blood trail from the elk and followed it approximately a mile up the mountain. Climbing over a few boulders, he came upon the point where the blood trail had clearly stopped, but there was no elk. He immediately backtracked the animal's trail twenty meters and then circled the entire area around to see if he was following another animal's blood trail and tracks, but he saw no other. It was as if the animal had simply ceased to exist. Suddenly, he was filled with a sense of alertness and fear at the same time. It didn't feel "right" or normal. Ben, a tall Native American who wasn't easily alarmed, turned around, shifted his shouldered rifle into the ready position, and made his way back to the tree line, running. Just as he emerged back onto the open fields, another blinding flash of light hit him again. This time, his cousin was hit by the flash as well; he was sitting in the truck waiting for Ben. Jumping into the truck, Ben ordered Al, "Let's go now!"

Ben was hunting elk near Shoshone National Forest when he saw a blinding flash of light, and the bull elk he shot disappeared.

As they came onto Highway 287 from the dirt road, they found that two Wyoming sheriffs' deputy patrol trucks had closed off the roadway in both directions. Then they saw an entire convoy of fast-moving highway patrol vehicles and dark-colored SUVs were racing toward the direction Ben and Al had come from. Ben never heard anything on the news as to what might have occurred on that day.

December 18, 2012: Los Angeles, California

The witness, who communicated directly with Albert Rosales, was sleeping alone in her room; however, there were other family members in the house at the time. She suddenly had the urge to get up but as she attempted to, she realized that she was unable to move. She then saw a human-shaped figure of average height (1.65 meters) in her room, which approached her and touched her head. When the strange figure touched her head, she felt an intense "electrical discharge" go through her body. She was able to describe the intruder as manlike with "steely, gray eyes" and wearing some sort of hooded outfit. She also heard what appeared to be "others" walking around in the house. In the spot around her neck where the entity had touched her, there remained a "sticky spot," and according to the witness, the hand of the intruder felt "soft or gelatinous." Soon the intruder and the others left, and after five minutes the witness was able to move again. She immediately washed the spot where she had been touched by the stranger.

> When the strange figure touched her head, she felt an intense "electrical discharge" go through her body.

Late December 2012: Brooksville, Florida

The main witness and a friend drove to an isolated spot and jumped a fence to get into an isolated field to have a beer and talk about politics, religion, and which one of the many genres of music their band could play. Time passed, and they found themselves very far from where they had parked. They had wandered at least two miles into the woods. While in the forest, they began to notice a slight illumination. The light kept getting brighter without being bright; it was more like moonlight filling an area than a sunrise. With the slight glow came a lot of condensation in the air. It was cold that night. If it was a natural fog, it wouldn't have set in so fast and capriciously. They then heard voices, coupled with more light and fog. The voices were ethereal in nature, almost like singing without melody. Curious, the witness felt he had to find the voices, and the source of the fog. He then saw his friend collapse, and not long after, he blacked out.

They awoke in what he thought of as a "ship." They were shackled in a bath of light—no bindings, yet they were still unable to move amid the glow. Before them stood three large humanoids. They had pale, grayish-pink skin, almost like the alien Thor in *Stargate*. Six eyes, lined in two columns of three long slits that opened and closed randomly and out of sync with one another. The humanoids were thin and unclothed, but wore odd pendants and jewelry with obvious technological purposes, because the creatures pressed the jewels to open doors and to exchange what he assumed was data about him and his friend.

They had no outlines of muscle, perfectly smooth skin, no definition, no nipples, no navel. They stood at least seven feet tall or more. They had long,

> ... the humanoids tried to communicate in a language primarily with h's and long ah's, kind of like Arabic or any other variant of Middle Eastern languages.

strung-back tubes for hair, fashioned and worn like dreadlocks, but made out of organic tubes. They had more or less normal mouths, but no lips. He never saw them open their mouths, so he had no idea if they had teeth or not. The "ship" they were in seemed "organic." The rest of the witnesses' time aboard was uneventful; the humanoids tried to communicate in a language with "h" sounds and long "ah"s, much like Arabic or other Middle Eastern languages. The only word the witness kept hearing was "Eheb." After a long, failed communication attempt, the witnesses blacked out again. They found themselves back in the wooded field with no other recollections.

Humanoid Sightings: 2013

January 1, 2013: South Greensburg, Pennsylvania

Stan Gordon reported that two women and a young boy decided to take a walk through a wooded area near South Greensburg to enjoy the beautiful scenery. It was about thirty-two degrees and clear in the area. The area had a cover of snow from a previous storm. Around three P.M., the three people advanced into the woods and were looking at a tree that still had leaves on it. When they were about twenty to twenty-five feet from the tree, the two women saw something that startled them. The boy was apparently looking elsewhere. They both said, at the same time, "Did you see the size of that bird?" What they saw was what appeared to be a bird unfolding huge wings. A witness described the wingspan as being approximately six to seven feet wide and described how the creature unfolded its wings and almost rolled them out, flapped them once, and folded them back up as it moved along the ground behind the tree.

The witnesses immediately moved toward the area where the creature had been seen. They were only twenty to twenty-five feet away, yet when they got to the spot, the creature was nowhere to be seen. There weren't that many trees at that location, and the area was quite open. There were no bird tracks at the location, just deer hoof prints. They heard no sounds of flapping or other sounds when the sighting occurred. The two women were mystified as they could not explain how the winged creature seemed to suddenly disappear. As one of the women commented, "We would have seen it fly away, but it didn't." The wings were described as black and gray in color. One woman said she thought she saw a blue tinge within the wings as well. The source asked one of the local bird experts for his thoughts. The women thought that the most likely candidate for what was observed was a great blue heron, which are seen around the area. The coloring would fit as well. He also speculated that if there

The winged creature resembled, in some ways, a great blue heron.

was a crust on the snow cover, possibly the bird did not break through and leave any tracks. Another possibility is a sandhill crane. The bird expert said that the wingspan and coloring is quite similar to the great blue heron. But he thought it was quite odd that at a twenty-five-foot distance, the witnesses could not identify the bird, if it was a heron. He also indicated that the great blue heron does not fly fast as it lifts off to become airborne and thought it was unusual that the women could not see it fly away from that nearby location.

January 9, 2013

Greg Posada and Eugene Pointer called the paranormal hotline with their report of two werewolves seen near Grass Lake in Wisconsin. They claim that these two creatures that appeared to be werewolves were definitely bipedal. One of the creatures had grayish hair, while the other had brownish hair. Both creatures had snouts. When the creatures were observed, they both seemed to be bent down drinking water from the lake. Eugene and Greg both claim that the creatures sniffed the air and then turned and looked at them. They let off a howl that sounded like a regular wolf and ran off into the near-by thickets. The encounter occurred around two in the afternoon, and Eugene and Greg were both shaken from this encounter. Greg said that the brown-coated creature was at least seven feet tall, while the gray-coated creature was perhaps six feet tall. Eugene said that this is not the end of the story. After their encounter with the "werewolves," it was no more than ten minutes later that they spied a silver disc in the surrounding forest. The silver disc hovered, tilted, then shot up into the sky. The sighting of the disc lasted only about three minutes, but during the time of the sighting everything felt *surreal*. Everything moved in slow motion. Eugene and Greg felt relaxed and at ease while they watched the disc in the sky. Eugene does not understand how they could have two paranormal encounters in one day.

January 7, 2013: Springfield, Massachusetts

A young man and a woman were awakened by a loud, humming sound and were pressed down in their beds. The sound appeared to emanate directly over their residence. They looked out the window of their bedroom and were shocked by how bright it was in their yard. They were both unable to move. They gave no other information.

January 9, 2013: Burbank, California

The witness was watering plants in the backyard when suddenly she noticed a shimmering, silver disc in the sky with flashing lights. It was a bit larger than the size of the sun, perhaps about the size of a football field in length, facing west. There seemed to be an auburn-colored, smoky haze around the object, and it was moving quite slowly. She watched for about ten seconds, too shocked to react. And then it vanished, it seemed to fade away, almost as if it was camouflaging with the evening sky. Strangely, right after the ship disappeared, she found herself in the kitchen, but didn't recall walking all the way across her yard and up the steps to unlock the door.

January 27, 2013: Kelso, Washington

The forty-year-old witness told Albert Rosales that he was out taking his usual walk. During his walks he is very observant, always looking around, in the lookout for anyone possibly trying to rob him. He did not see anyone around, but all of a sudden he looked to his left, and there was a girl. It was like she had appeared out of nowhere. He did not hear her approaching. She was about four feet from him. Normally, if someone was walking nearby, he could hear them. The girl appeared to be in her early twenties; she was about five feet tall and small framed. He could tell that she was an adult and not a child. She had shoulder-length, bright blonde hair that looked almost white. Her eyes were black with no white showing. She was wearing sweatpants and a hoodie, but the hood was not covering her head. When he saw her, he said, "Hi, how you doing this evening?" She mumbled something, but he could not hear what she said. She moved her head back and forth as she stood there checking him out curiously. He felt there was something not quite right about her and felt a definite chill. Though it was cold outside, the chill was not due to the weather. He cautiously took a few steps toward her, and she backed up. In a moment she took off running, but not like any human or animal he had ever seen. She ran with a fluid movement, and there was no sound as her feet hit the ground. She quickly disappeared out of sight.

> He felt there was something not quite right about her and felt a definite chill.

February 11, 2013: Near Falls Village, Connecticut

The witness was driving home from work and was only two miles from her residence, located in a very rural area south of Falls Village. The roads were still slippery from the heavy snow they had received, so she was driving very deliberately. All at once, a deer jumped from behind a snowbank and bolted in front of her car. She slammed on the brakes but still skidded into the back of the deer. She didn't see where the deer went, but she was now stuck in the snowbank. She got out and noticed that her driver's-side headlight was smashed as well. She tried to push the car out of the snowbank, but it was not budging, She had no choice but to call for a tow truck.

About fifteen minutes after she called for help, one of her neighbors was on his way home and stopped to ask if he could help. She told him that she had called for a tow truck, but she didn't know how long it would be before it showed up. He said he would go home, get some chains, and return with his four-wheel-drive pickup in order to pull her out. She thanked him, and he left. Not long after her neighbor left, she noticed lights coming toward her on the road. The lights were large and very bright, so she figured that it was the tow truck. As the lights slowly proceeded toward her, several more lights illuminated above and below the others. The vehicle, or whatever it was, stopped about fifty yards from her and remained there for several minutes. Then, she saw a brightly lit "being" floating through the woods across from her. It reminded her of those bright white aliens from the film *Cocoon*, though she didn't see any facial features. This being quickly floated through the trees, then out onto the road. It started to come toward her, but she was petrified and could not move. It didn't have arms or legs, but there was definitely a head and something on the end that resembled a fishtail. It stopped directly in front of her and hovered no more than ten feet away. There were no eyes or mouth, but she did feel warmth coming from it. It was very calming and comforting. Then, it suddenly whisked toward the lights. After a few minutes, the bright lights started to fade until they were completely gone. Her neighbor soon returned, as well as the tow truck operator. She asked them both if they had noticed any vehicle with intensely bright lights, but they both looked at her like "she was crazy." After they pulled her from the snowbank she drove home, quickly took a bath, and headed for bed. She was still feeling the calm sensation and desperately wanted to go to sleep.

April 13, 2013: Cannon Beach, Oregon

The main witness and her sons were staying at the Schooner Inn and were on the beach enjoying a bonfire. At around 10:30 P.M., her oldest son (thirteen years old) noticed, and pointed out to her, that there was a figure illuminated and glowing that was traveling either along the shoreline in front of their hotel or out in the water. She caught sight of it as it traveled past them and continued on down the beach. It made a sharp, right-angle turn onto the beach and continued on until it disappeared in the line of houses. It appeared human in form, and what was remarkable was that it was glowing from head to what appeared to be the end of a torso. None of them saw any arms or legs. Also remarkable was that it was traveling at a very high rate of speed, perhaps twenty-five miles per hour, and it was not bobbing up and down as you would expect a runner to be. There were others in their hotel standing on their decks and pointing. Another couple came out and said they had seen it as well. They saw no indication that it was a beam of light, nor was there any indication that it was a human form. It was going too fast and too steady. The whole form emitted a whitish light.

May 23, 2013: Canon City, Colorado

While hiking, the witness came into a clearing on a mountain trail; the weather was cool with some cloud cover. Ahead of him, about one hundred yards, a chevron-shaped craft was hovering approximately five feet above the ground. It had no windows or lights on it, but had an indentation all the way around "resembling a hamburger bun." About fifteen feet from the craft were two aliens dressed in shiny, silver uniforms. One had on red boots, but the other had on boots the same color as the uniform. They were carrying what appeared to be a third unresponsive alien to the craft. They had dark gray skin, appeared to have trouble moving, and were somewhat uncoordinated. A beam of blue light was coming from out of the bottom of the craft. The aliens carried the apparently lifeless body of the third alien into the beam, and the beam appeared to take on a rippled appearance, like water. Then the light went off, and the aliens were gone. Next, the craft began to slowly rise until it was very high and then it began to move quickly until the witness could not see it anymore. According to the witness, he is a retired military man and is currently employed at the department of corrections in Florence.

July 30, 2013: North East Pennsylvania

The witness was sitting in his driveway looking up at the stars when he heard something come out of the woods at the end of his street. There was a creek at the end of his street, so the witness wondered how the figure came out of there. The thing or figure started walking up the street; it was walking very strangely and was wearing black robes and a weird hat with a point and a curve "and had feathers on it." The witness hid behind his car waiting until it walked near his house. It walked at the same pace the whole time. The witness yelled out, "Hey, what are you doing?" but received no response as the strange figure kept walking at the same pace up the street. The witness then started following it toward the other end of the street and more woods. He was right behind it. The figure came up to someone's yard; the witness was five feet behind it, and it started walking toward the woods. Without stopping, the witness turned on the "flashlight" on his cell phone. However, when he looked up, the figure was gone; it had apparently vanished into thin air. The witness looked around with his cell phone, but found nothing. He remembers hearing every dog in the neighborhood barking.

The aliens carried the apparently lifeless body of the third alien into the beam, and it appeared to take on a rippled appearance, like water.

December 16, 2013: Eden Mills, Vermont

The witness had just left his aunt's Christmas party and had gone outside to get some fresh air. He then saw a light in the sky; it was shining down a cone-shaped beam of light, like some sort of "giant flashlight pointed to the ground." He knew it was not a common aircraft, and he saw no blinking lights. The beam moved around like it was looking for something. Suddenly, he saw a black, human-shaped figure floating up toward the object within the beam of light. This was in the middle of a forested area. His mother and aunt came out and saw this also.

December 26, 2013: Cowan's Gap State Park, Fulton County, Pennsylvania

The day after Christmas, a couple had decided to get out of the house and take a walk. They enjoyed walking the trails at Cowan's Gap State Park, and it was not too cold, so they took the short drive to the park. The park is empty during the winter, unless there's snow for skiers and ice skating on the lake. They were alone, or at least they thought. They were walking a trail that passed by several of the rental cabins and after a while took a short break and sat down at a picnic table located in a cabin pavilion. They were discussing how quiet it was when the husband noticed four "children" walking toward them. As they approached he noticed that their eyes, especially the taller and older boy's, were very dark with large irises. There was, he believed, two males and two females of various ages. All four wore light jackets. When they reached the couple one of them who appeared to be an older male asked, "Do you live here?" The husband answered, "No, this is a rental cabin." There was no reaction. One of the females, who was very pale, reached down into her pocket and pulled out a pack of cigarettes. She looked no older than ten years of age. The husband then asked, "Aren't you too young to smoke?" She looked at him and, and her eyes seemed to get darker and larger. She gave him a scowl that both will remember for the remainder of their lives. It was so vile and foreboding—the wife felt afraid immediately. Then they turned on a dime together and started to walk away. The wife was left speechless and shaking—her husband then said, "Let's go." They briskly walked in the opposite direction toward the car. The wife was very frightened and wanted to go home. They pulled out onto Aughwick Road and headed east toward their home, which is only half a mile or so from the park.

A few days later, they were driving to Chambersburg to do some shopping and first needed to stop and post some mail in Fort Loudon. The husband walked into the post office while she sat in the car. After a few minutes, she noticed the same four "kids" walking through the post office parking lot. She felt chills going down her spine. When her husband returned to the car, she told him what happened and said she wanted to go home immediately. Since that time, the wife has suffered numerous episodes of anxiety and fear.

Notes to Chapter One

[i]Nathan F. Twining to Brig. General George Schulgen, 23 September, 1947, Project Blue Book files. See also Randle, Kevin D. and Donald R. Schmitt. *The Truth About the UFO Crash at Roswell*, New York: M. Evans and Company, 1994: 87–89; Swords, Michael, Robert Powell, et al. *UFOs and Government*. San Antonio, TX: 2012: 476–478.

[ii]Gillmor, Daniel S., Ed. *Scientific Study of Unidentified Flying Objects*. New York: Bantam Books, 1969: 502–525.

[iii]Clark, Jerome. *The UFO Encyclopedia, Second Edition*. Detroit: Omnigraphics, 1998: 747–748; Hynek, J. Allen. *The Hynek UFO Report*. New York: Dell, 1977; Ruppelt, Edward J. *The Report on Unidentified Flying Objects*. New York: Ace Books, Inc., 1956.

[iv]Chester, Keith. *Strange Company*. San Antonio, TX: Anomalist Books, 2007; Wilkins, Harold T. "The Strange Mystery of the Foo Fighters." *Fate*, 4,6 (August/September 1951): 98–106.

[v]Berliner, Don. "The Ghost Rockets of Sweden." *Official UFO*, 1,11 (October 1976): 30–31, 60–64; Farish, Lou and Jerome Clark. "The 'Ghost Rockets' of 1946." *Saga's UFO Report*, 2,1 (Fall 1974) : 24–27, 62–64; Svahn, Clas. "The 1946 Ghost Rocket Photo." *International UFO Investigator*, 27,3 (Fall 2002): 12–14, 23; Svahn, Clas and Liljegren, Anders. "Close Encounters with Unknown Missiles." *International UFO Reporter*, 19,4 (July/August 1994): 11–15.

[vi]Hall, Michael and Connors, Wendy. "Alfred Loedding: New Insight on the Man Behind Project Sign." *International UFO Reporter*, 23,4 (Winter 1999): 3–8, 24–28; personal correspondence with Wendy Connors, 2013.

[vii]Project Blue Book Files, Administration files, Final Report on Project Grudge.

viii In communication with Wendy Connors, she said that the documentation for this unofficial investigation was now buried under the Wright-Patterson Air Force Base golf course. It is also clear from the documentation that the investigation of the Ghost Rockets, which should have been transferred to the official project, disappeared from the files, though hints of those sightings can be found in what is left.

ix Memo from D. M. Ladd for E. G. Fitch, endorsed by Clyde Tolson and J. Edgar Hoover, dated July 10, 1947.

x Ruppelt. *Report on UFOs.*

xi Ibid., 58.

xii In 1947 and 1948, when they discussed extraterrestrial visitation, they were thinking in terms of interplanetary as opposed to interstellar flight. Mars was thought of as the most likely source of those interplanetary craft, though Venus was also mentioned.

xiii At first, this seems to make no sense. If the document was declassified, then there was no reason to have it burned, other than to keep it out of the hands of civilians, which the classification would do. With the report declassified, then it could be given to anyone, regardless of who they were, because the report was declassified. It should have been left as classified and then destroyed. That, of course, would produce a record, because the destruction of classified material required that it be documented. That means that a record would exist, proving that the report had existed. This way, no record of destruction was required, which, of course, explains why it was ordered declassified and then burned.

xiv Hall, Michael D., and Wendy Connors. *Alfred Loedding and the Great Flying Saucer Debate.*

xv In fact, the Air Force announced that Project Sign had been closed. They did not mention that it had been renamed Project Grudge but retained the same mission as Sign.

xvi Ruppelt. *Report on UFOs.* pp. 126–127.

xvii Ruppelt. *Report on UFOs.* 1956. For a transcript of the press conference, see Randle, Kevin D. *Invasion Washington: UFOs over the Capitol.* New York: Avon Books, 2001: 77–126; Project Blue Book Administration files.

xviii Project Blue Book Sighting Index; Peebles, Curtis. *Watch the Skies!* New York: Berkley Books, 1995, 77–80; Menzel, Donald H., and Ernest H. Taves. *The UFO Enigma: The Definitive Explanation of the UFO Phenomenon.* Garden City, New York: Doubleday & Company, Inc., 1977: 121–124.

xixDurant, F. C. *Report of Meetings of Scientific Advisory Panel on Unidentified Flying Objects Convened by Office of Scientific Intelligence, CIA: January 14–18, 1953.* Washington, DC: Central Intelligence Agency, 1953. See also Randle, Kevin D. *Conspiracy of Silence.* New York: Avon Books, 1997: 107–126; Clark, *UFO Encyclopedia*, 802–804; Ruppelt, *Report on UFOs*, 1956; Gillmor, *Scientific Study*, 1969; Swords, *UFOs and Government*, 2012.

xxSee both Durant, *Report of Meetings* and Randle, *Conspiracy.*

xxiAir Force Regulation 200–2, 1953, revised 5 February, 1958.

xxiiHynek, J. Allen, and Jacques Vallee. *The Edge of Reality: A Progress Report on Unidentified Flying Objects.* Chicago: Henry Regnery Co., 1975.

xxiiiAir Force Regulation 200–2, revised February 5, 1958; see also Clark, *UFO Encyclopedia*, pp. 731–732.

xxivProject Blue Book Administration files accessed at Maxwell Air Force Base, January 1975; Randle, Kevin D. and Robert Charles Cornett. "The Project Blue Book Cover-Up: How the Air Force Hid UFO Evidence from the Public." *UFO Report* 2,5 (Fall 1975): 18–21, 53–54, 56–57.

xxvProject Blue Book Administration files.

xxviFor a complete discussion of the Socorro case, see Clark, *UFO Encyclopedia*, 856–867; Randle, Kevin D., *Scientific Ufology.* New York: Avon Books, 1999: 128–133; Klass, Philip. *UFOs Explained.* New York: Random House, 1974: 105–114, 131; Peebles, *Watch the Skies!* 180–183; Lorenzen, Coral and Jim Lorenzen. *Encounters with UFO Occupants.* New York: Berkley Medallion Books, 1976: 8–11; Steiger, Brad. *Project Blue Book: Top Secret UFO Findings Revealed.* New York: Ballantine Books, 1976.

xxviiHynek, J. Allen. Report of his findings in Socorro, available in the Project Blue Book files.

xxviiiKlass, *UFOs Explained*, 112.

xxixIbid., 113.

xxxMosley, Jim. "Saucer Smear." Volume 41, No. 8, November 1, 1994.

xxxiHarden, Paul. "The 1964 Socorro UFO Incident." *El Defensor Chieftain*, August 2, 2008; See also Clark, *UFO Encyclopedia*, 856–866; Klass, *UFO Explained*, 113.

xxxii*Swords, UFOs and Government*, pp. 306–307.

xxxiiiIbid.

xxxivHall, Richard. *Uninvited Guests.* Santa Fe, NM: Aurora Press, 1988: 257.

xxxvProject Blue Book files, case 10252. See also Peebles, *Watch the Skies!*, pp. 203–205; Edwards, Frank. *Flying Saucers—Here and Now.* New York: Bantam Books, 1967.

xxxvi Project Blue Book files. Department of the Air Force letter, dated March 23, 1966, p. 5.

xxxvii Teletype report, Project Blue Book files.

xxxviii Project Blue Book files; Peebles, *Watch the Skies!*, p. 204.

xxxix "AF Report On UFOs' 'Mockery.'" *The News and Observer* (Raleigh, NC): March 27, 1966: p. 1; Edwards, *Here and Now*: 12–18; Gillmor, *Scientific Study*, 538–539.

xl Project Blue Book files, case 10252. Various newspaper articles contained in those files, though few have identifying information on them, including "Swamp Gases Blamed for Michigan Sightings"; "UFOs Very Likely Swamp Gas: Hynek."

xli Ibid.

xlii Dolan, Richard M. *UFOs and the National Security State*. Charlottesville, VA: Hampton Roads Publishing Company, Inc., 2002: pp. 300–301.

xliii Originally, the grant was for $313,000.00, but the budget was increased later, bringing the total to better than a half million dollars.

xliv Swords, *UFOs and Government*, 306–309.

xlv Story, Ronald D. *The Encyclopedia of UFOs*. Garden City, NY: Doubleday & Co., 1980: 80–81.

xlvi Various letters contained in the Project Blue Book Administration files, including those by Edward Trapnell, Robert Friend, and Edward H. Wynn. See also Randle, Kevin D., and Robert Charles Cornett. "How the Air Force Hid UFO Evidence from the Public." *UFO Report* 2,5 (Fall 1975): 19–21, 53–54, 56–57.

xlvii Swords, *UFOs and Government*, 306–310.

xlviii Craig, Roy. *UFOs: An Insider's View of the Official Quest for Evidence*. Denton, TX: University of North Texas Press, 1995; Robert Hippler, letter to Edward Condon, dated January 16, 1967, copy at American Philosophical Society; Randle, *Conspiracy*, p. 208.

xlix Robert Low, letter to Hippler, dated January 27, 1967, copy available at the American Philosophical Society.

l Olive, Dick. "Most UFOs Explainable, Says Scientist." *Elmira* [New York] *Star-Gazette*. January 26, 1967.

li Vallee, Jacques. *Dimensions: A Case Book of Alien Contact*. New York: Ballantine Books, 1988: p. 211.

lii Personal interview with Dr. Michael Swords, August 7, 1995.

liii In Gillmor, *Scientific Study*, p. 5.

livThis was a variation on a theme that played out in the meetings for the staff. Condon was outraged that some writers were making money off the exploitation of UFOs and that children were at risk. For a complete analysis, see Swords, *UFOs and Government*, pp. 307–327.

lvIn Gillmor, *Scientific Study*, p. 5.

lviGillmor, Daniel S., Ed. *Scientific Study of Unidentified Flying Objects*, New York: Bantam Books, 1969: 481–502; Vallee, Jacques. *Anatomy of a Phenomenon*, New York: Ace Books, 1965: 15–35; Randle, Kevin D. *Alien Mysteries, Conspiracies and Cover-Ups*, Detroit: Visible Ink Books, 2013: 1–34.

lviiTorres, Noe and Mark Murphy. Dublin, 1891. http://roswellbooks.com/mus eum/?page_id–143 (accessed November 24, 2014. See also Randle, Kevin D. *Crash: When UFOs Fall from the Sky*, Franklin Lakes, NJ: New Page Books, 2010: 18–19.

lviiiBaxter, John and Thomas Atkins. *The Fire Came By*. Garden City, NY: Doubleday, 1976; Zabawski, Walter. "On the Track of a Crashed UFO— Part II," *Official UFO* 2,3 (May 1977): 31–33, 59–62; Matthews, Mark. "Armageddon at Tunguska." *Official UFO* (Oct 79): 28–30, 58, 60; Davies, John K. *Cosmic Impact*. New York: St. Martin's Press, 1986: 14–21; Huneeus, J. Antonio. "Soviet Scientist Bares Evidence of 2 Objects at Tunguska Blast," *New York City Tribune*, November 30, 1989: 11. "New Explanation for 1908 Siberian Blast," *Cedar Rapids Gazette*, January 25, 1993; McCall, G. J. H., *Meteorites and Their Origins*. New York: John Wiley & Sons, 1973: 247–249; Chaikin, Andrew. "Target: Tunguska." *Sky & Telescope*, January, 1984: 18–21; Brown, J. C., and D. W. Hughes. "Tunguska and the Making of Pseudo-Scientific Myths." *New Scientist*, March 6, 1980: 50–51; Plekhsnov, G. F., Kavalevski, A. F., Zhuravlev, V. K. and Vasil'yev, N. V. *Geology and Geophysics*, No. 6, 1961: 94–96; Zigel, F. Yu. "Nuclear Explosion over the Taiga." U.S. Department of Commerence, April 17, 1962; Olbison, Vivienne. "Did a UFO Blast a Hole in Russia?" *UFO Magazine* (UK version) 13,4 (Nov/Dec 1994): 8, 46–49; Randle, "Crash," 28–30.

BIBLIOGRAPHY

"AF General Warns UFOs Serious, Will Increase," *UFO Investigator* 1,9 (March 1960): 3

Air Defense Command Briefing, January 1953, Project Blue Book Files.

Aldrich, Jan. "Investigating the Ghost Rockets," *International UFO Reporter* 23,4 (Winter 1998): 9–14.

———. "Project 1947: An Inquiry into the Beginning of the UFO Era," *International UFO Reporter* 21,2 (Summer 1996): 18–20.

Alexander, John B. *UFOs: Myths, Conspiracies, and Realities*. New York: St. Martin's Press, 2011.

Allan, Christopher D. "Dubious Truth about the Roswell Crash," *International UFO Reporter* 19, 3 (May/June 1994), 12–14.

Anderson, Dennis K. "The Arthur Kill Sightings, July 14–15, 2001," *International UFO Reporter* 28, no. 2 (Summer 2003): 3–6, 26–27.

Anderson, Michele. "BIOSPEX: Biological Space Experiments," *NASA Technical Memorandum 5821* 7, NASA, Washington, DC, 1979.

Andrus, Walt. "Air Intelligence Report No. 100-203-79," *MUFON UFO Journal 207* (July 1985): 3–19.

Asimov, Isaac. *Is Anyone There?* New York: Ace Books, 1967

ATIC UFO Briefing, April 1952, Project Blue Book Files.

"The Aurora, Texas Case," *The APRO Bulletin* (May/June 1973): 1, 3–4.

Barker, Gray. "America's Captured Flying Saucers—The Cover-up of the Century," *UFO Report* 4, no. 1 (May 1977): 32–35, 64, 66–73.

———. "Archives Reveal More Crashed Saucers," *Gray Barker's Newsletter* (14 March 1982): 5–6.

———. "Chasing Flying Saucers," *Gray Barker's Newsletter* 17 (December 1960): 22–28.

———. "Von Poppen Update," *Gray Barker's Newsletter* (December 1982): 8.

Basterfield, Keith. "Angel Hair: An Australian Perspective," *International UFO Reporter* 27, no. 1 (Spring 2002): 6–9, 32.

Baxter, John, and Atkins Thomas. *The Fire Came By*. Garden City, NY: Doubleday, 1976.

Berliner, Don. "The Ghost Rockets of Sweden," *Official UFO*, 1, no. 11 (October 1976): 30–31, 60–64.

———, with Marie Galbraith and Antonio Huneeus. *Unidentified Flying Objects Briefing Document: The Best Evidence Available*. Washington, DC, 1995. 33–35.

Berlitz, Charles, and William L.Moore. *The Roswell Incident*. New York: Berkley, 1988.

"Big Fire in the Sky: A Burning Meteor," *New York Herald Tribune*, December 10, 1965.

Binder, Otto. *Flying Saucers Are Watching Us*. New York: Tower, 1968.

———. "The Secret Warehouse of UFO Proof," *UFO Report* 2, no. 2 (Winter 1974): 16–19, 50, 52.

———. *What We Really Know about Flying Saucers*. Greenwich, CT: Fawcett Gold Medal, 1967.

Bloecher, Ted. *Report on the UFO Wave of 1947*. Washington, DC: privately printed, 1967.

———, and Paul Cerny. "The Cisco Grove Bow and Arrow Case of 1964," *International UFO Reporter* 20, no. 5 (Winter 1995): 16–22, 32.

Blum, Howard. *Out There: The Government's Secret Quest for Extraterrestials*. New York: Simon and Schuster, 1991.

Blum, Ralph, with Judy Blum. *Beyond Earth: Man's Contact with UFOs*. New York: Bantam Books, 1974.

Bontempto, Pat. *The Helgoland Crash: A Dissection of a Hoax*. privately printed, 1994.

———. "Incident at Heligoland," *UFO Universe* 5 (Spring 1989): 18–22.

Bourdais, Gildas. "From GEPAN to SEPRA: Official UFO Studies in France," *International UFO Reporter* 25, no. 4 (Winter 2000–2001): 10–13.

———. *Roswell*. Agnieres, France: JMG Editions, 2004.

Bowen, Charles, editor. *The Humanoids*. Chicago: Henry Regency, 1969.

Braenne, Ole Jonny. "Legend of the Spitzbergen Saucer," *International UFO Reporter* 17, no. 6 (November/December 1992): 14–20.

Brew, John Otis, and Edward B. Danson. "The 1947 Reconnaissance and the Proposed Upper Gila Expedition of the Peabody Museum of Harvard University," *El Palacio* (July 1948): 211–222.

Briefing Document: Operation Majestic, 12, November 18, 1952.

"Brilliant Red Explosion Flares in Las Vegas Sky," *Las Vegas Sun* (19 April, 1962): 1.

Britton, Jack, and George Washington, Jr. *Military Shoulder Patches of the United States Armed Forces.* Tulsa, OK: MCN Press, 1985.

Brown, Eunice H. *White Sands History.* White Sands, NM: Public Affairs Office, 1959.

Bullard, Thomas E. *The Myth and Mystery of UFOs.* Lawrence, KS: University of Kansas Press, 2010.

Burleson, Donald R. "Deciphering the Ramey Memo," *International UFO Reporter* 25, no. 2 (Summer 2000): 3–6, 32.

———. "Levelland, Texas, 1957: Case Reopened," *International UFO Reporter* 28, no. 1 (Spring 2003): 3–6, 25.

Cahn, J.P. "The Flying Saucers and the Mysterious Little Men," *True* (September 1952): 17–19, 102–112.

———. "Flying Saucer Swindlers," *True* (August 1956): 36–37, 69–72.

"California Man Beseiged [sic] by 'Occupants,'" *The A.P.R.O. Bulletin* (July/August 1966): 5

Candeo, Anne. *UFO's The Fact or Fiction Files.* New York: Walker 1990.

Cannon, Martin. "The Amazing Story of John Lear," *UFO Universe* (March 1990): 8.

Carey, Thomas J., and Donald R. Schmitt. *Witness to Roswell Revised and Expanded.* Pompton Plains NJ: New Page Books, 2009.

Carpenter, Joel. "The Ghost Rockets." Project 1947. http://www.project1947.com/gr/grchron1.htm.

———. "The Lockheed UFO Case, 1953," *International UFO Reporter* 26, no. 3 (Fall 2001): 3–9.

———. "The Senator, The Saucer, and Special Report 14," *International UFO Reporter* 25, no. 1 (Spring 2000): 3–11, 30.

Catoe, Lynn E. *UFOs and Related Subjects: An Annotated Bibliography.* Washington, DC: Government Printing Office, 1969.

Cerny, Paul, and Robert Neville. "U.S. Navy 1942 Sighting," *MUFON UFO Journal* 185 (July 1983): 14–15.

Chaikin, Andrew. "Target: Tunguska," *Sky & Telescope* (January 1984): 18–21.

Chamberlain, Von Del, and David J. Krause. "The Fireball of December 9 1965—Part I," *Royal Astronomical Society of Canada Journal* 61, no. 4.

Chariton, Wallace O. *The Great Texas Airship Mystery*. Plano, TX: Wordware, 1991.

Chavarria, Hector. "El Caso Puebla," *OVNI*: 10–14.

Chester, Keith. *Strange Company: Military Encounters with UFOs in WW II*. San Antonio, TX: Anomalist Books, 2007.

Clark, Jerome. "Airships: Part I," *International UFO Reporter* (January/February 1991): 4–23.

———. "Airships: Part II," *International UFO Reporter* (March/April 1991): 20–23.

———. "A Catalog of Early Crash Claims," *International UFO Reporter* (July/August 1993): 7–14.

———. "Crashed Saucers—Another View," *Saga's UFO Annual 1981* (1981): 44–47, 66.

———. "Crash Landings," *Omni* (December 1990): 91–92.

———. "The Great Crashed Saucer Debate," *UFO Report* (October 1980): 16–9, 74, 76.

———. "The Great Unidentified Airship Scare," *Official UFO* (November, 1976).

———. *Hidden Realms, Lost Civilizations and Beings from Other Worlds*. Detroit: Visible Ink Press, 2010.

———. "UFO Reporters. (MJ-12)," *Fate* (December 1990).

———. *UFO's in the 1980s*. Detroit: Apogee, 1990.

Committee on Science and Astronautics, report, 1961.

Cohen, Daniel. *Encyclopedia of the Strange*. New York: Avon, 1987.

———. *The Great Airship Mystery: A UFO of the 1890s*. New York: Dodd, Mead, 1981.

———. *UFOs—The Third Wave*. New York: Evans, 1988.

Cooper, Milton William. *Behold a Pale Horse*. Sedona, AZ: Light Technology, 1991.

"Could the Scully Story Be True?" *The Saucerian Bulletin* 1, no. 2 (May 1956): 1.

Creighton, Gordon. "Close Encounters of an Unthinkable and Inadmissible Kind," *Flying Saucer Review* (July/August 1979).

———. "Continuing Evidence of Retrievals of the Third Kind," *Flying Saucer Review* (January/February 1982).

———. "Further Evidence of 'Retrievals," *Flying Saucer Review* (January 1980).

———. "Top U.S. Scientist Admits Crashed UFOs," *Flying Saucer Review* (October 1985).

Davison, Leon, editor. *Flying Saucers: An Analysis of Air Force Project Blue Book Special Report No. 14.* Clarksburg, VA: Saucerian Press, 1971.

Davies, John K. *Cosmic Impact.* New York: St. Martin's, 1986.

Davis, Richard. *Results of a Search for Records Concerning the 1947 Crash Near Roswell, New Mexico.* Washington, DC: GAO, 1995

DeGraw, Ralph C. "Did Two Iowans Witness the Famous Socorro Landing?" *The UFO Examiner* 3, no. 6 (1982): 18–20.

Dennett, Preston. "Project Redlight: Are We Flying The Saucers Too?" *UFO Universe* (May 1990): 39.

"Did A UFO Blast a Hole in Russia?" *The New UFO Magazine* 13, no. 4 (November/December 1994): 8–9, 46–49.

Dobbs, D.L. "Crashed Saucers—The Mystery Continues," *UFO Report* (September 1979): 28–31, 60–61.

"DoD News Releases and Fact Sheets," 1952–1968.

Dolan, Richard M. *UFOs and the National Security State: The Cover-Up Exposed, 1973–1991.* Rochester, NY: Keyhole Publishing, 2009.

Douglas, J.V., and Henry Lee. "The Fireball of December 9, 1965—Part II," *Royal Astronomical Society of Canada Journal* 62, no. 41.

Earley, George W. "Crashed Saucers and Pickled Aliens, Part I," *Fate* 34, no. 3 (March 1981): 42–48.

———. "Crashed Saucers and Pickled Aliens, Part II," *Fate* 34, 4 (April 1981): 84–89.

———. "The Maury Island Hoax, Part Four and Conclusion," *UFO*, 24, no. 4 (October 2011): 38—52.

———. "The Scam that Failed: Fred Crisman and the Maury Island Incident," *UFO* 24, no. 1 (October 1, 2010): 12–13, 65.

———. "The Scam that Failed: Fred Crisman and the Maury Island Incident, Part Two," *UFO*, 24, no. 2 (January 2011): 12–13.

Eberhart, George. *The Roswell Report: A Historical Perspective.* Chicago: CUFOS, 1991.

Edwards, Frank. *Flying Saucers—Here and Now!* New York: Bantam, 1968.

———. *Flying Saucers—Serious Business.* New York: Bantam, 1966.

———. *Strange World.* New York: Bantam, 1964.

"Effect of the Tunguska Meteorite Explosion on the Geomagnetic Field," Office of Technical Services U.S. Department of Commerce (December 21, 1961).

Eighth Air Force Staff Directory, Texas: June 1947.

"Evidence of UFO Landing Here Observed," *El Defensor Chieftain* [Socorro, New Mexico] (April 28, 1964).

"Experts Say a Meteor Caused Flash of Fire," *Deseret News*, April 19, 1962, p. 1.

Fact Sheet, "Office of Naval Research 1952 Greenland Cosmic Ray Scientific Expedition," October 16, 1952.

"Facts about UFOs," Library of Congress Legislative Reference Service, May 1966.

Farish, Lucius, and Jerome Clark. "The 'Ghost Rockets' of 1946," *Saga's UFO Report* 2, no. 1 (Fall 1974): 24–27, 62–64.

———. "The Mysterious 'Foo Fighters' of World War II," *Saga's UFO Report* 2, no. 3 (Spring 1974): 44–47, 64–66.

Fawcett, Lawrence, and Barry J. Greenwood. *Clear Intent: The Government Cover-up of the UFO Experience*. Englewood Cliffs, NJ: Prentice-Hall, 1984.

Final Report, "Project Twinkle," Project Blue Book Files, November 1951.

Finney, Ben R., and Eric M. Jones. *Interstellar Migration and the Human Experience*. CA: University of California Press, 1985.

"Fireball Explodes in Utah," *Nevada State Journal*, April 19, 1962, p. 1.

First Status Report, Project STORK (Preliminary to Special Report No. 14), April 1952.

"Flying Saucers Are Real," *Flying Saucer Review* (January/February 1956): 2–5.

Foster, Tad. Unpublished articles for Condon Committee Casebook. 1969.

Fowler, Raymond E. *Casebook of a UFO Investigator*. Englewood Cliffs, NJ: Prentice-Hall, 1981.

Gevaerd, A. J. "Flying Saucer or Distillation Machine?" *Brazilian UFO Magazine* (November 2006).

Gillmor, Daniel S., editor. *Scientific Study of Unidentified Flying Objects*. New York: Bantam Books, 1969.

Good, Timothy. *Above Top Secret*. New York: Morrow, 1988.

———. *Alien Contact*. New York: Morrow, 1993.

———. *The UFO Report*. New York: Avon Books, 1989.

Gordon, Stan. "After 25 Years, New Facts on the Kecksburg, Pa. UFO Retrieval Are Revealed." *PASU Data Exchange* 15 (December 1990): 1.

———. "Kecksburg Crash Update," *MUFON UFO Journal* (September 1989).

———. "Kecksburg Crash Update," *MUFON UFO Journal* (October 1989): 3–5, 9.

———. "The Military UFO Retrieval at Kecksburg, Pennsylvania," *Pursuit* 20, no. 4 (1987): 174–179.

———, and Vicki Cooper. "The Kecksburg Incident," *UFO* 6, no. 1 (1991): 16–19.

Graeber, Matt. "The Reality, the Hoaxes and the Legend." Privately printed, 2009.

Greenwell, J. Richard. "UFO Crash/Retrievals: A Critque," *MUFON UFO Journal* 153 (November 1980): 16–19.

Gribben, John. "Cosmic Disaster Shock," *New Scientist* (Mar 6, 1980): 750–752.

"Guidance for Dealing with Space Objects Which Have Returned to Earth," Department of State Airgram, July 26, 1973.

Hall, Michael. "Was There a Second Estimate of the Situation?," *International UFO Reporter* 27, no. 1 (Spring 2002): 10–14, 32.

———, and Wendy Connors. "Alfred Loedding: New Insight on the Man Behind Project Sign," *International UFO Reporter* 23, no. 4 (Winter 1999): 3–8, 24–28.

Hall, Richard. *Contributions of Balloon Operations to Research and Development at the Air Force Missile Development Center 1947–1958*. Alamogordo, NM: Office of Information Services, 1959.

———. "Crashed Discs—Maybe," *International UFO Reporter* 10, no. 4 (July/August 1985).

———. "NICAP: The Bitter Truth," *MUFON UFO Journal* 145 (March 1980): 11–12.

———. "Pentagon Pantry: Is the Cupboard Bare?" *MUFON UFO Journal* 108 (November 1976): 15–18.

———. *Uninvited Guests*. Santa Fe, NM: Aurora Press, 1988.

———, editor. *The UFO Evidence*. Washington, DC: NICAP, 1964.

Hastings, Robert. *UFOs and Nukes*. Bloomington, IN: Author House, 2008.

Haugland, Vern. "AF Denies Recovering Portions of 'Saucers," *Albuquerque New Mexican* 23 (March 1954).

Hazard, Catherine. "Did the Air Force Hush Up a Flying Saucer Crash?" *Woman's World* (February 27, 1990): 10.

Hegt, William H. Noordhoek. "News of Spitzbergen UFO Revealed," *APRG Reporter* (February 1957): 6.

Henry, James P., and John D. Mosely. "Results of the Project Mercury Ballistic and Orbital Chimpanzee Flights," *NASA SP-39*, 1963.

Hessmann, Michael, and Philip Mantle. *Beyond Roswell: The Alien Autopsy Film, Area 51 and the U.S. Government Cover-up of UFOs*. New York: Marlowe % Company, 1991.

Hippler, Robert H. "Letter to Edward U. Condon," January 16, 1967.

"History of the Eighth Air Force, Fort Worth, Texas" (Microfilm), Air Force Archives, Maxwell Air Force Base, AL.

"History of the 509th Bomb Group, Roswell, New Mexico" (Microfilm), Air Force Archives, Maxwell Air Force Base, AL.

Hogg, Ivan U., and J. B. King. *German and Allied Secret Weapons of World War II*. London: Chartwell, 1974.

Houran, James, and Kevin Randle. "Interpreting the Ramey Memo," *International UFO Reporter* 27, no. 2 (Summer 2002): 10–14, 26–27.

Hughes, Jim. "Light, Boom a Mystery". *Denver Post*, January 12, 1998.

Humble, Ronald D. "The German Secret Weapon/UFO Connection." *UFO* 10, no. 4 (July/August 1995): 21–25.

Huneeus, J. Antonio. "A Full Report on the 1978 UFO Crash in Bolivia," *UFO Universe* (Winter 1993).

———. "Great Soviet UFO Flap of 1989 Centers on Dalnegorsk Crash," *New York City Tribune*, June 14, 1990.

———. "Roswell UFO Crash Update," *UFO Universe* (Winter 1991): 8–13, 52, 57.

———. "Soviet Scientist Bares Evidence of 2 Objects at Tunguska Blast," *New York City Tribune*, November 30, 1989, p. 11.

———. "Spacecraft Shot Out of South African Sky—Alien Survives," *UFO Universe* (July 1990): 38–45, 64–66.

"Hunting Old and New UFOs in New Mexico," *International UFO Reporter* 7, no. 2 (March 1982): 12–14.

Hurt, Wesley R., and Daniel McKnight. "Archaeology of the San Augustine Plains: A Preliminary Report," *American Antiquity* (January 1949): 172–194.

Hynek, J. Allen. *The Hynek UFO Report*. New York: Dell, 1977.

————. *The UFO Experience: A Scientific Inquiry*. Chicago: Henry Regency, 1975.

————, and Jacques Vallee. *The Edge of Reality*. Chicago: Henry Regency, 1972.

"Ike and Aliens? A Few Facts about a Persistent Rumor," *Focus* 1, no. 2 (April 30, 1985): 1, 3–4.

"International Reports: Tale of Captured UFO," *UFO* 8, no. 3 (1993): 10–11.

"It Whizzed through the Air; Livonia Boys Find Fireball Clues," *Livonian Observer & City Post*, December 16, 1965.

Jacobs, David M. *The UFO Controversy in America*. New York: Signet, 1975.

Johnson, J. Bond. "'Disk-overy' Near Roswell Identified as Weather Balloon by FWAAF Officer," *Fort Worth Star-Telegram*, July 9, 1947.

Jones, William E., and Rebecca D. Minshall. "Aztec, New Mexico—A Crash Story Reexamined," *International UFO Reporter* 16, no. 5 (September/October 1991): 11.

Jung, Carl G. *Flying Saucers: A Modern Myth of Things Seen in the Sky*. New York: Harcourt, Brace, 1959.

Kean, Leslie. "Forty Years of Secrecy: NASA, the Military, and the 1965 Kecksburg Crash." *International UFO Reporter* 30, no. 1: 3–9, 28–31.

Keel, John. "Now It's No Secret: The Japanese 'Fugo Balloon,'" *UFO* (January/February 1991): 33—35.

————. *Strange Creatures from Space and Time*. New York: Fawcett, 1970.

————. *UFOs: Operation Trojan Horse*. New York: G.P. Putnam's Sons, 1970.

Kennedy, George P. "Mercury Primates," *American Institute of Aeronautics and Astronautics*, 1989.

Keyhoe, Donald E. *Aliens From Space*. New York: Signet, 1974.

————. *Flying Saucers from Outer Space*. New York: Henry Holt & Company, 1953.

Klass, Philip J. "Crash of the Crashed Saucer Claim," *Skeptical Inquirer* 10, no. 3 (1986).

————. *UFOs Explained*. New York: Random House, 1974.

————. *The Public Deceived*. Buffalo, NY: Prometheus Books, 1983.

Knaack, Marcelle. *Encyclopedia of U.S. Air Force Aircraft and Missile Systems*. Washington, DC: Office of Air Force History, 1988.

LaPaz, Lincoln, and Albert Rosenfeld. "Japan's Balloon Invasion of America," *Collier's*, January 17, 1953, p. 9.

Lasco, Jack. "Has the US Air Force Captured a Flying Saucer?" *Saga* (April 1967): 18–19, 67–68, 70–74.

Lester, Dave. "Kecksburg's UFO Mystery Unsolved," *Greenburg Tribune-Review*, December 8, 1985, p. A10.

"Little Frozen Aliens," *The APRO Bulletin* (January/February 1975), 5–6.

Lore, Gordon, and Harold H. Deneault. *Mysteries of the Skies: UFOs in Perspective*. Englewood Cliffs, NJ: Prentice-Hall, 1968.

Lorenzen, Coral, and Jim Lorenzen. *Encounters with UFO Occupants*. New York: Berkley Medallion Books, 1976.

———. *Flying Saucer Occupants*. New York: Signet, 1967.

———. *Flying Saucers: The Startling Evidence of the Invasion from Outer Space*. New York: Signet, 1966.

Low, Robert J. "Letter to Lt. Col. Robert Hippler," January 27, 1967.

Maccabee, Bruce. "Hiding the Hardware," *International UFO Reporter* (September/October 1991): 4.

———. "What the Admiral Knew," *International UFO Reporter* (November/December 1986).

"The Magical Meteor," *Nebraska State Journal*, June 10, 1884.

"Man Burned in Canada Landing," *The A.P.R.O Bulletin*, May–June 1967, pp. 1–2.

Mantle, Phillip. "Alien Autopsy Film, R.I.P.," *International UFO Reporter* 32, no. 1 (August 2008): 15–19.

———. *Roswell Alien Autopsy*. Edinburg, TX: RoswellBooks, 2012.

Marcel, Jesse, and Linda Marcel. *The Roswell Legacy*. Franklin Lakes, NJ: New Page Books, 2009.

Matthews, Mark. "Armageddon at Tunguska!" *Official UFO* (May 1979): 28–30, 58, 60.

McAndrews, James. *The Roswell Report: Case Closed*. Washington, DC: Government Printing Office, 1997.

McCall, G. J. H. *Meteorites and Their Origins*. New York: Wiley & Sons, 1973.

McClellan, Mike. "The Flying Saucer Crash of 1948 is a Hoax," *Official UFO* 1, no. 3 (October 1975): 36–37, 60, 62–64.

"McClellan Sub-Committee Hearings," March 1958.

"McCormack Sub-Committee Briefing," August 1958.

McDonald, Bill. "Comparing Descriptions: An Illustrated Roswell," *UFO* 8, no. 3 (1993): 31–36.

McDonough, Thomas R. *The Search for Extraterrestrial Intelligence*. New York: Wiley & Sons, 1987.

Menzel, Donald H., and Lyle G. Boyd. *The World of Flying Saucers.* Garden City, NY: Doubleday, 1963.

———, and Ernest Taves. *The UFO Enigma.* Garden City, NY: Doubleday, 1977.

Michael, Donald N., et. al. "Proposed Studies on the Implications of Peaceful Space Activities for Human Affairs." The Brookings Institution. (December 1960): 182–184.

Michel, Aime. *The Truth about Flying Saucers.* New York: Pyramid 1967.

Moore, Charles B. "The New York University Balloon Flights During Early June, 1947," privately printed, 1995.

———, Benson Saler, and Charles A. Ziegler. *UFO Crash at Roswell: Genesis of a Modern Myth.* Washington, DC: Smithsonian Institute Press, 1997.

Moseley, James W., and Karl T. Pflock. *Shockingly Close to the Truth.* Amherst, NY: Prometheus Books, 2002.

Mueller, Robert. *Air Force Bases,* Volume 1: *Active Air Force Bases within the United States of American on 17 September 1982.* Washington, DC: Office of Air Force History, 1989.

Murphy, John, "Object in the Woods," WHJB Radio, radio broadcast (December 1965).

National Security Agency. Presidential Documents. Washington, DC: Executive Order 12356, 1982.

Neilson, James. "Secret U.S./UFO Structure," *UFO* 4, no. 1 (1989): 4–6.

"New Explanation for 1908 Siberian Blast," *Cedar Rapids Gazette,* January 25, 1993.

NICAP, *The UFO Evidence.* Washington, DC: NICAP, 1964.

Nickell, Joe. "The Hangar 18 Tales," *Common Ground* (June 1984).

"No Reputable Dope on Disks," *Midland [Texas] Reporter Telegram,* July 1, 1947.

Northrup, Stuart A. *Minerals of New Mexico.* Albuquerque: University of New Mexico, 1959.

"No Sign of 'UFO'–NSRI." *News 24,* May 5, 2006.

Oberg, James. "UFO Update: UFO Buffs May Be Unwitting Pawns in an Elaborate Government Charade," *Omni* 15, no. 11 (September 1993): 75.

Oldham, Chuck, and Vicky Oldham. *The Report on the Crash at Farmington.* Lansdowne, PA: privately printed, 1991.

Olive, Dick. "Most UFO's Explainable, Says Scientist." *Elmira [NY] Star-Gazette* January 26, 1967, p. 19.

Packard, Pat, and Terry Endres. "Riding the Roswell-Go-Round." *A.S.K. UFO Report* 2 (1992): 1, 1–8.

Papagiannis, Michael D., editor. *The Search for Extraterrestrial Life: Recent Developments.* Boston: 1985.

Peebles, Curtis. "In Defense of Roswell Reality." *MUFON Report* (February 1995): 5–7.

———. *The Moby Dick Project.* Washington, DC: Smithsonian Institution Press, 1991.

———. "Roswell, A Cautionary Tale: Facts and Fantasies, Lessons and Legacies." In Walter H. Andrus, Jr., ed. *MUFON 1995 International UFO Symposium Proceedings.* Seguin, TX: MUFON, 1990: 154–168.

———. *Roswell: Inconvenient Facts and the Will to Believe.* Amherst: NY: Prometheus Books. 2001.

———. "Roswell, The Air Force, and Us," *International UFO Reporter* (November/December 1994): 3–5, 24.

———. *Watch the Skies!* New York: Berkley Books, 1995.

Pflock, Karl. *Roswell in Perspective.* Mt. Rainier, MD: FUFOR, 1994.

"Physical Evidence: Landing Reports," *The U.F.O. Investigator* 2, no. 11 (July/August 1964): 4–6.

Press Conference—General Samford, Project Blue Book Files, 1952.

"Press Release—Monkeynaut Baker is Memorialized," Space and Rocket Center, Huntsville, AL (December 4, 1984).

"Project Blue Book" (microfilm). RG [Record Group] 341, T-1206 National Archives, Washington, DC.

Prytz, John M. "UFO Crashes," *Flying Saucers* (October 1969): 24–25.

Randle, Kevin D. *Conspiracy of Silence.* New York: Avon, 1997.

———. *Crash: When UFOs Fall from the Sky.* Franklin Lakes, NJ, 2010.

———. "The Flight of the Great Airship," *True's Flying Saucers and UFOs Quarterly* (Spring 1977).

———. *A History of UFO Crashes.* New York: Avon, 1995.

———. "MJ-12's Fatal Flaw and Robert Willingham," *International UFO Reporter,* 33, no. 4 (May 2011): 3–7.

———. "Mysterious Clues Left Behind by UFOs," *Saga's UFO Annual* (Summer 1972).

———. *The October Scenario.* Iowa City, Iowa: Middle Coast Publishing, 1988.

———. "The Pentagon's Secret Air War against UFOs," *Saga* (March 1976).

———. *Project Moon Dust.* New York: Avon, 1998.

———. *Reflections of a UFO Investigator.* San Antonio, TX: Anomalist Books, 2012.

———. *Roswell Encyclopedia.* New York: Avon, 2000.

———. *Roswell Revisited.* Lakeville, Minn: Galde Press, 2007.

———. *Roswell, UFOs and the Unusual.* Kindle eBooks, 2012.

———. *Scientific Ufology.* New York: Avon, 1999.

———. *The UFO Casebook.* New York: Warner, 1989.

———, and Robert Charles Cornett. "Project Blue Book Cover-up: Pentagon Suppressed UFO Data," *UFO Report* 2, no. 5 (Fall 1975).

———. "Siberian Explosion, Comet or Spacecraft?" *Quest UFO* 1, no. 1 (1977): 10–15.

Randle, Kevin D., and Russ Estes. *Spaceships of the Visitors.* New York: Fireside Books, 2000.

Randle, Kevin D., and Donald R. Schmitt. *UFO Crash at Roswell.* New York: Avon, 1991.

———. *The Truth about the UFO Crash at Roswell.* New York: M. Evans, 1994.

Randles, Jenny. *The UFO Conspiracy.* New York: Javelin, 1987.

Ramsey, Scott, and Suzanne Ramsey. *The Aztec Incident: Recovery at Hart Canyon.* Mooresville, NC: Aztec 48 Productions, 2012.

Redfern, Nick. *On the Trial of the Saucer Spies.* San Antonio, TX: Anomalist Books, 2006.

———. *The Real Men in Black.* Pompton Plains, NJ: New Page Books, 2011.

———. "Tunguska: 100 Years Latter [sic]." In *6th Annual UFO Crash Retrieval Conference.* Broomfield, CO: Wood and Wood Enterprises, 2008.

Reichmuth, Richard. "The Cisco Grove Bow and Arrow Alien Encounter." *MUFON UFO Journal* 468 (April 2007): 3–6.

"Report of Air Force Research Regarding the 'Roswell Incident,'" July 1994.

"Rocket and Missile Firings," White Sands Proving Grounds, January–July 1947.

"Rocket Craft Encounter Revealed by World War 2 Pilot." *The UFO Investigator* 1, no. 2 (August/September 1957): 15.

Rodeghier, Mark. "Roswell, 1989," *International UFO Reporter.* (September/October 1989): 4.

———, and Mark Chesney. "The Air Force Report on Roswell: An Absence of Evidence," *International UFO Reporter* (September/October 1994).

Rosignoli, Guido. *The Illustrated Encyclopedia of Military Insignia of the 20th Century*. Secaucus, NJ: Chartwell, 1986.

Ruppelt, Edward J. *The Report on Unidentified Flying Objects*. New York: Ace, 1956.

———. "What Our Air Force Found Out about Flying Saucers," *True* (May 1954): 19–20, 22, 24, 26, 30.

Russell, Eric. "Phantom Balloons Over North America," *Modern Aviation* (February 1953).

Rutkowski, Chris. "Burned by a UFO? The Story of a Bungled Investigations," *International UFO Reporter* 12, no. 6 (November/December 1987): 21–24.

———. "The Cold, Hard Facts about UFOs in Canada," *International UFO Reporter* 34, no. 1 (September 2011): 7–10, 22–23.

Rux, Bruce. *Hollywood vs. the Aliens*. Berkley: Frog, Ltd., 1997.

Sagan, Carl, and Thornton Page, editors. *UFO's: Scientific Debate*. New York: Norton, 1974.

Sanderson, Ivan T. "Meteorite-like Object Made a Turn in Cleveland, O. Area," *Omaha World-Herald*, December 15, 1965.

———. *Invisible Residents*. New York: World Publishing, 1970.

———. *Uninvited Visitors*. New York: Cowles, 1967.

———, and R. Roger Harkins. *UFOs? Yes!* New York: New American Library, 1968.

Schmitt, Donald R. "New Revelations from Roswell." In Walter H. Andrus, Jr., editor. *MUFON 1990 International UFO Symposium Proceedings*. Seguin, TX: MUFON, 1990: 154–168.

———, and Kevin D. Randle. "Second Thoughts on the Barney Barnett Story," *International UFO Reporter* (May/June 1992): 4–5, 22.

Scully, Frank. *Behind the Flying Saucers*. New York: Henry Holt, 1950.

———. "Scully's Scrapbook." Variety (October 12, 1949): 61.

"The Search for Hidden Reports," *The U.F.O. Investigator* 4, no. 5 (March 1968) 7–8.

Sheaffer, Robert. *The UFO Verdict*. Buffalo, NY: Prometheus, 1981.

Simmons, H.M. "Once upon a Time in the West," *Magonia* (August 1985).

Skow, Brian, and Terry Endres. "The 4602d Air Intelligence Service Squadron," *International UFO Reporter* 20, no. 5 (Winter 1995): 9–10.

Slate, B. Ann "The Case of the Crippled Flying Saucer," *Saga* (April 1972): 22–25, 64, 66–68, 71, 72.

Smith, Scott. "Q & A: Len Stringfield," *UFO* 6, no. 1, (1991): 20–24.

Smith, Willy. "The Curious Case of the Argentine Crashed Saucer," *International UFO Reporter* 11, no. 1 (January/February 1986): 18–19.

Special Report No. 14, (Project Blue Book) 1955.

Spencer, John. *The UFO Encyclopedia.* New York: Avon, 1993.

———, and Hilary Evans. *Phenomenon.* New York: Avon, 1988.

Stanyukovich, K. P., and V. A. Bronshten. "Velocity and Energy of the Tungusk Meteorite," National Aeronautics and Space Administration (December 1962).

Status Reports, "Grudge—Blue Book," Nos. 1–12.

Steiger, Brad. *The Fellowship.* New York: Dolphin Books, 1988.

———. *Project Blue Book.* New York: Ballantine, 1976.

———. *Strangers from the Skies.* New York: Award, 1966.

———. *UFO Missionaries Extraordinary.* New York: Pocket Books, 1976.

———, and Sherry Hansen Steiger. *Conspiracies and Secret Societies.* Canton, MI: Visible Ink Press, 2006.

———. *The Rainbow Conspiracy.* New York: Pinnacle, 1994.

———. *Real Aliens, Space Beings, and Creatures from Other Worlds.* Canton, MI: Visible Ink Press, 2011.

Stone, Clifford E. *UFO's: Let the Evidence Speak for Itself.* CA: printed, 1991.

———. "The U.S. Air Force's Real, Official Investigation of UFO's." private report, 1993.

Stonehill, Paul. "Former Pilot Tells of Captured UFO," *UFO* 8, no. 2 (March/April 1993): 10–11.

Story, Ronald D. *The Encyclopedia of Extraterrestrial Encounters.* New York: New American Library, 2001.

———. *The Encyclopedia of UFOs.* Garden City, NY: Doubleday, 1980.

Stringfield, Leonard H. *Inside Saucer Post ... 3-0 Blue.* Cincinnati, OH: Civilian Research, Interplanetary Flying Objects, 1975.

———. *Situation Red: The UFO Siege!* Garden City, NY: Doubleday, 1977.

———. "Retrievals of the Third Kind." In *MUFON Symposium Proceedings* (1978): 77–105.

———. "Roswell & the X-15: UFO Basics," *MUFON UFO Journal* 259 (November 1989): 3–7.

———. *UFO Crash/Retrieval: Amassing the Evidence: Status Report III* Cincinnati, OH: privately printed, 1982.

———. *UFO Crash/Retrievals: The Inner Sanctum Status Report VI*. Cincinnati, OH: privately printed, 1991.

———. *UFO Crash/Retrieval Syndrome: Status Report II*. Seguin, TX: MUFON, 1980.

Sturrock, P.A. "UFOs—A Scientific Debate," *Science* 180 (1973): 593.

Sullivan, Walter. *We Are Not Alone*. New York: Signet, 1966.

Summer, Donald A. "Skyhook Churchill 1966," *Naval Reserve Reviews* (January 1967): 29.

Svahn, Clas. "The 1946 Ghost Rocket Photo," *International UFO Investigator* 27, no. 3 (Fall 2002): 12–14, 23.

———, and Anders Liljegren. "Close Encounters with Unknown Missiles," *International UFO Reporter* 19, no. 4 (July/August 1994): 11–15.

Swords, Michael, and others. *UFOS and the Government: A Historical Inquiry*. San Antonio, TX: Anomalist Books, 2012.

———. "Too Close for Condon: Close Encounters of the 4th Kind," *International UFO Reporter* 28, no. 3 (Fall 2003) 3–6.

———. "Can UFOs Cause Physiological Effects? Part 2," *International UFO Reporter* 34, no. 1 (September 2011): 3–6.

Tafur, Max. "UFO Crashes in Argentina," *INFO Journal* 75 (Summer 1996): 35–36.

Tech Bulletin. "Army Ordnance Department Guided Missile Program," January 1948.

Technical Report. "Unidentified Aerial Objects, Project SIGN," February 1949.

Technical Report. "Unidentified Flying Objects, Project GRUDGE," August 1949.

Templeton, David. "The Uninvited," Pittsburgh Press (May 19, 1991): 10–15.

Thomas, Dick. "'Flying Saucers' in New Mexico," *Denver Post*, May 3, 1964.

Thompson, Tina D., editor. *TRW Space Log*. Redondo Beach, CA: TRW 1991.

Torres, Noe, and Ruben Uriarte. *The Other Roswell*. Edinburg, TX: Roswell Books, 2008.

———. *Aliens in the Forest*. Edinburg, TX: RoswellBooks.com, 2011.

"Tunguska and the Making of Pseudo-scientific Myths," *New Scientist*, March 6, 1980, pp. 750–751.

"Two Dubuquers Spot Flying Saucer," *Dubuque* [Iowa] *Telegraph Herald*, April 29, 1964, p. 1

"UAO Landing in New Mexico," *The A.P.R.O. Bulletin* (May 1964): 1, 3–10.

"UFOs and Lights: 12 Aliens on Ice in Ohio?" *The News* 10 (June 1975): 14–15.

U.S. Congress Committee on Science and Astronautics. Symposium on Unidentified Flying Objects. July 29, 1968, Hearings, Washington, DC: U.S. Government Printing Office, 1968.

U.S. Congress, House Committee on Armed Forces. Unidentified Flying Objects. Hearings, 89th Congress, 2nd Session, April 5, 1966. Washington DC: U.S. Government Printing Office, 1968.

Vallee, Jacques. *Anatomy of a Phenomenon.* New York: Ace, 1966.

———. *Challenge to Science.* New York: Ace, 1966.

———. *Dimensions.* New York: Ballantine, 1989.

———. *Revelations.* New York: Ballantine, 1991.

War Department. *Meteorological Balloons* (army technical manual). Washington, DC: Government Printing Office, 1944.

Weaver, Richard L., and James McAndrew. *The Roswell Report: Fact vs. Fiction in the New Mexico Desert.* Washington, DC: Government Printing Office, 1995.

Webber, Bert. *Retaliation: Japanese Attacks and Allied Countermeasures on the Pacific Coast in World War II.* Corvallis: Oregon State University Press, 1975.

Wilkins, Harold T. *Flying Saucers on the Attack.* New York: Citadel, 1954.

———. *Flying Saucers Uncensored.* New York: Pyramid, 1967.

——— "The Strange Mystery of the Foo Fighters," *Fate* 4, no. 6 (August/September 1951): 98–106.

Wise, David, and Thomas B. Ross. *The Invisible Government.* New York: 1964.

Wood, Robert M. "Forensic Linguistics and the Majestic Documents." In *6th Annual UFO Crash Retrieval Conference.* Broomfield, CO: Wood and Wood Enterprises, 2008, pp. 98–116.

———. "Validating the New Majestic Documents." In MUFON *Symposium Proceedings* (2000): 163–192.

Wood, Ryan. *Majic Eyes Only.* Broomfield, CO: Wood Enterprises, 2005.

"World Round-up: South Africa: Search for Crashed UFO," *Flying Saucer Review* 8, no. 2 (March/April 1962): 24.

Zabawski, Walter. "UFO: The Tungus Riddle," *Official UFO* (May 1977), 31–33, 59–62.

Zeidman, Jennie. "I Remember Blue Book," *International UFO Reporter* (March/April 1991): 7.

INDEX

Note: (ill.) indicates photos and illustrations.

ALSO FROM VISIBLE INK PRESS